W9-BUF-422

A
**Study of Postmodern
Antirealistic American
Fiction**

ALTERNATE

WORLDS

JOHN KUEHL

**With an Introduction and Interview by
James W. Tuttleton**

The publication of this work has been supported in part by a grant from the Abraham and Rebecca Stein Faculty Publications Fund of New York University, Department of English.

Manufactured in the United States of America

Library of Congress Cataloging-in-Publication Data

Kuehl, John Richard, 1928–
Alternate worlds: a study of postmodern antirealistic American fiction/by John Kuehl; with an introduction and interview by James W. Tuttleton.
p.   cm.——(The Gotham library of the New York University Press)
Bibliography: p.
Includes index.
ISBN 0-8147-4598-9 (alk. paper)
1. American fiction——20th century——History and criticism.
2. Postmodern (Literature)——United States. 3. Realism in literature. I. Tuttleton, James W. II. Title.
PS374.P64K8
813'.54'09——dc19   89-30409
                                              CIP

New York University Press books are printed on acid-free paper, and their binding materials are chosen for strength and durability.

Book design by Ken Venezio

Alternate Worlds

A Study of Postmodern
Antirealistic American Fiction

by John Kuehl

*with an Introduction and Interview
by James W. Tuttleton*

New York University Press
NEW YORK AND LONDON

The Gotham Library
of the New York University Press

The Gotham Library is a series of original works and critical studies.
Devoted to significant works and major authors and to literary topics
of enduring importance, Gotham Library texts offer the best in literature and criticism.

JAMES W. TUTTLETON, EDITOR

In Memoriam
COLEMAN DOWELL
MARY LOU GLICK

Contents

Preface   ix

JAMES W. TUTTLETON
Introduction: The American Roots of
Contemporary Antirealism   1

PART I   THE AUTHOR AS GOD   59

CHAPTER 1
Reflexivity   61

CHAPTER 2
The Ludic Impulse   83

CHAPTER 3
Maximalism versus Minimalism   104

PART II   THE UNIVERSE AS MADHOUSE   119

CHAPTER 4
Fragmentation/Decentralization   122

CHAPTER 5
The Grotesque and the Devil   144

CHAPTER 6
Imaginary Landscapes   158

CHAPTER 7
Absurd Quests   180

PART III   THE FUTURE AS DEATH   205

CHAPTER 8
Fictitious History   208

CHAPTER 9
Conspiracy and Paranoia   232

CHAPTER 10
Entropy   251

CHAPTER 11
Nightmare and Apocalypse   268

INTERVIEW
James W. Tuttleton and John Kuehl   285

Notes   313

Select Bibliography   343

Index   353

Preface

When a business executive friend inquired about my last sabbatical leave, I mentioned finishing *Alternate Worlds* and gave him its subtitle. He commented, "Isn't that redundant? Isn't *all* fiction necessarily nonrealistic?" Almost every writer represented here would commend this insight, since, if we can trust the dictionary, which calls fiction "the act of feigning, inventing, or imagining," stories must, at the very least, be fabricated. With the advent of literary realism during the nineteenth century, however, novelists, playwrights, and even poets would pretend otherwise by projecting verisimilar worlds based on mimetic theory. John Hawkes—perhaps the first post–World War II American antirealist—had already eschewed the techniques that sustain this illusionist position before he argued that "plot, character, setting, and theme" constitute "the true enemies of the novel."[1] Hawkes attributed the term antirealist to Albert Guerard, his former creative writing teacher, who substituted it for surrealism and wrote an article in 1960 discussing the Cambridge antirealists.[2]

Nineteenth-century realism became so entrenched, until recently, that antirealism—a countertradition older than the novel—was considered secondary. Even now, after twenty-odd years of dominance, American antirealists, descending from native as well as foreign models, are overshadowed by realists like Bellow, Mailer, Roth, Styron, Updike, and Vidal, some of whom, ironically, show signs of their influence. To be sure, certain antirealistic fictions have achieved prominence, but often for the wrong reasons: for example, *Naked Lunch, Invisible Man, Catch -22, One Flew Over the Cuckoo's Nest,* and *Lolita.* So too have certain authors, probably because they published stories or novellas: for example, Barth, Barthelme, O'Connor, Vonnegut. Meanwhile, few people outside the academy recognize the names of Chandler Brossard, Robert Coover, Coleman Dowell, Raymond Federman, William Gaddis, William Gass, John Hawkes, Joseph McElroy, Thomas Pynchon, Ishmael Reed, Susan Sontag, Gilbert Sorrentino, Ronald Sukenick, Alexander Theroux, Marguerite Young. Therefore, one can hardly expect such massive achievements as *Letters, The Recognitions, J R, Women and Men, Ada, Gravity's Rainbow, Mulligan Stew, Darconville's Cat,* and *Miss MacIntosh, My Darling* to receive much currency.

Antony Lamont, the chief protagonist of *Mulligan Stew,* tells a female correspondent, "[T]his book will establish me as the most interesting spokesman for the American avant-garde, and for Surfiction, as well as Ur-fiction, and Post-Modern fiction to boot."[3] Through the deranged, pretentious hack Lamont, Sorrentino is here satirizing the proliferation of designations associated with current innovative prose, which has also been labeled supramodern, postcontemporary, and transfiction. These categories tend to obscure rather than to illuminate, so for that and other reasons I rely on the term antirealism, with occasional references to metafiction. In *Alternate Worlds,* antirealism implies both the whole body of nonimitative writing, including earlier domestic instances, and an adversarial stance toward what many besides F. R. Leavis consider the great realistic tradition. I have affixed the word postmodern, or contemporary, as a chronological term to circumscribe its latest flowering since about 1945. Although my subject remains American literature, the reader should note the international scope of this insurgence.

Individuals familiar with past antirealistic texts will be prepared for several patterns explored during my investigation, since reflexivity, the ludic impulse, maximalism (if not minimalism), imaginary landscapes, and the grotesque and the devil have often characterized established countertraditional works. Less precedented are the patterns proliferating in the twentieth century: fragmentation/decentralization, absurd quests, fictitious history, conspiracy and paranoia, entropy, and nightmare and apocalypse. All eleven patterns emerged during my research and evolved naturally under the rubrics "The Author as God," "The Universe as Madhouse," and "The Future as Death." If there is a major split among the included writers, it would be in the area of metafiction, as several practice autoreferential craft and several do not. However, even those who avoid authorial self-consciousness, represented by Barth, may invoke narratorial self-consciousness, represented by Hawkes.

Because whole books have explicated subjects like reflexivity or metafiction, no effort was made to analyze such phenomena in depth. Rather, my task has been threefold: to detect the presence of a given pattern; to describe its salient features; and to show how this pattern functions in certain antirealistic novels and/or stories. During the coda that concludes "Nightmare and Apocalypse," I postulate one text that would contain everything previously discussed. No such all-inclusive text exists, though many incorporate much from the eleven interrelated patterns cited. These were illustrated by works I considered important; some recur while other worthy texts remain totally absent or were published too late for discussion. To their authors I apologize, reminding them how imperfect alternate worlds are. Finally, whenever possible, I have retained the typographical idiosyncrasies of the various texts because they are germane to authorial intentions.

Two individuals have aided me in this study. My wife not only made cogent overall suggestions, but expertly edited the manuscript prior to submission. Besides assessing what I had written, my friend and colleague, James W. Tuttleton, contributed the lengthy introduction that provides the historical and intellectual background for *Postmodern Antirealistic American Fiction*. He suggested that we cap the manuscript, which is largely *explication de texte*, with an interview intended to evaluate the literature already interpreted. This was appealing on various grounds, one being the balanced view that could be achieved through a duologue between an Americanist associated with realism and an Americanist associated with antirealism. Always our aim has been to help the uninitiated reader understand and appreciate the impressive contemporary antirealistic canon, which is still rather obscure partly because its central achievements are so huge.

I would also like to thank *The Review of Contemporary Fiction* and *The Journal of Narrative Technique* for permission to reprint the brief excerpts from *Alternate Worlds* they originally published.

JOHN KUEHL

Notes

1. John Enck, "John Hawkes: An Interview," *Wisconsin Studies in Contemporary Literature* 6: 149. In *In Form: Digressions on the Act of Fiction* (Carbondale, Ill.: Southern Illinois Univ. Press, 1985), p. 237, Ronald Sukenick succinctly distinguishes between realistic and antirealistic fiction: "Mimetic fiction depends on the suspension of disbelief, nonmimetic fiction does not."

2. See Albert J. Guerard, "Introduction To The CAMBRIDGE ANTIREALISTS," *Audience* 7 (Spring 1960): 57–59. Among other things, Guerard said:

The Cambridge writers share the French refusal to say *why* certain things happen. Beyond this, they belong rather in the modern tradition that finds positive pleasure and value in frank grotesque distortion, in black humor and fantasy, in a personal recreation of the visible and the inner world. They belong, that is, with Lautréamont (whose sadistic reveries involved recompositions of time and space), with Raymond Roussel, with Ernst Junger, with at least one of the Kafkas, with Samuel Beckett and Djuna Barnes and the fiction-writing Dylan Thomas. They touch "pure poetry" in their occasional decadent willingness to let language overwhelm life, but touch life as well as traditional fiction in their love of the picaresque.

3. Gilbert Sorrentino, *Mulligan Stew* (New York: Grove 1979), 358.

JAMES W. TUTTLETON

Introduction: The American Roots of Contemporary Antirealism

As will be plain to any reader of *Alternate Worlds*, John Kuehl has provided here a remarkably incisive, full, and coherent analysis of the themes and techniques of contemporary American antirealistic fiction. His analysis of the self-reflexive character of this art and its ludic spirit; its deployment of techniques like fragmentation and decentralization; its parodic treatment of established genres like the quest, the detective story, and the fairy tale; and the preoccupation of contemporary antirealism with entropy, conspiracy, the nightmare, and the apocalypse—all this richness may leave the reader with a sense of contemporary fictive materials and methods of a wholly original character. And indeed the remarkable inventive genius at play in much of the fiction he has studied marks this work as surprisingly exceptional. When we examine the wild innovations of William Burroughs, Raymond Federman, Ronald Sukenick, and John Hawkes (for example), one may wonder whether they have sprung full-blown from their authors' imaginations or are quite independent of any historical tradition.

Certainly postmodern antirealism in fiction is an international phenomenon, of which the fiction of John Barth, Donald Barthelme, Vladimir Nabokov, Coleman Dowell, William Gaddis, Thomas Pynchon (and the other writers analyzed here by Kuehl) is but the North American manifestation. In my view, cultural and literary influences are always complex and difficult to trace; and modern writers, avid to win a reputation for originality, have a way of concealing those who have most influenced them. But so voluble are the much-interviewed writers whom Kuehl presents here that we can be sure of the affinity they feel with the great European and South American antirealist masters of the twentieth century—Joyce, Kafka, Beckett, Borges, Cortázar, Pirandello, and Márquez, for example.

The readiness of our American antirealists to acclaim the merits of their international contemporaries reflects the extent to which they reject the idea of their own work as merely the expression of the American national culture. No one, of course, can object to their wish for universality; and, on a certain plane, masterworks of literature know no national boundaries. But to celebrate one's contemporaries is implicitly to deny one's fathers, especially the older American writers who have shaped the realist literary tradition which it is the task of postmodern antirealists to discredit and surpass. Another set of influences, perhaps not sufficiently acknowledged by them, is constituted of the older European antirealists who are predecessors of the present generation—for example, Cervantes, Sterne, Diderot, and Walpole, not to speak of the author(s) of *A Thousand and One Nights*, whose anonymity has allowed John Barth to indulge a rather extravagant admiration for this never-ending collection.[1]

But the purpose of this introduction is not to identify the European (or Arabian) sources of postmodern antirealism but, rather perversely, to insist that *the roots of contemporary American antirealist fiction lie embedded in the nourishing soil of the native American literary tradition*. Without discounting the older European antirealist tradition from Cervantes onward or twentieth-century masters like Joyce and Kafka, the task for the present is to bring to light some of the elements of antirealism that form a native American tradition available to Barth, Coover, Burroughs, Pynchon, Sorrentino, and our other contemporaries.

The reader should not expect contemporary antirealists to give many signs of the influence of James, Howells, Wharton, Fitzgerald, and other such masters of American realism. The contemporary American antirealists pay virtually no positive attention to realistic fiction—the tacit assumption being that, fortunately, its historical period is over. An instance of this view is Alexander Theroux's remark that "The 'realistic' novel and the way one reports to it is to me a *locus molesti*. The threats of the realistic novel, for which I believe I have a constitutional disinclination, force me into an anti-world with a fantasy and bedevilment all its own which refuses (ready?) to 'hold a mirror up to nature.' "[2] Nevertheless, contemporary American antirealistic fiction cannot be fully understood except as a reaction to the tradition of American realism, and as a continuation of the American romance tradition reflected in the work of Hawthorne, Melville, Poe, and others.

What is at ontological issue, quite simply, is what William Gass has called a war between "the empirical realist, for whom the novel is in one way or another a report upon the world, and that of the rationalist, for whom the novel is an intense interior, formed like a flower from within, and opening out only into absence." In this contest, many contemporary antirealists appear to assume, as Gerald Graff has remarked in "'The Politics of Antirealism," that

The imagination's independence from reality exemplifies the human spirit's break with political oppression and psychic repression, with all preestablished ideas of reality. As Frank Kermode writes, echoing [Roland] Barthes, "the whole movement towards 'secretarial' realism" represents "an anachronistic myth of common understanding and shared universes of meaning." By refusing to hold a mirror up to nature and by exploding the very idea of a stable "nature," art undermines the psychological and epistemological bases of the ruling order. The revolt against realism and representation is closely tied to the revolt against a unitary psychology of the self. As Leo Bersani argues in *A Future for Astyanax*, "the literary myth of a rigidly ordered self," a myth perpetuated by realism, "contributes to a pervasive cultural ideology of the self which serves the established social order."[3]

Furthermore, the idea—espoused by Gass and others—that the new antirealism opens out "only into absence" tacitly assumes the truth of the deconstructionist claim of Derrida and others that language does not, because it cannot, refer to a real world. As Jacques Lacan has remarked in *Ecrits*, "we cannot cling to the illusion that the signifier answers to the function of representing the signified, or better, that the signifier has to answer for its existence in the name of any signification whatever."[4] Likewise, Paul de Man in *Allegories of Reading* finds language to be essentially rhetorical "rather than representational or expressive of a referential, proper meaning."[5] Hence, a form of cognitive atheism underlies the antiworlds of some contemporary antirealists. To illustrate features of earlier American romance that reappear in current antirealistic fiction is not to claim that earlier romancers share this deconstructionist ideology, although it is clear that for Poe, Melville, and Hawthorne the representational function is sometimes at best secondary. Nor is it to claim in every case a direct influence between the authors invoked in the introduction and those studied in Kuehl's wonderfully comprehensive analysis. Rather it is to link contemporary antirealists to a complex American literary tradition available to whichever of them has wished to make use of it—in however sublimated, disguised, or transformed a way.

We begin with the premise that contemporary antirealism is the current mode of the romance form. Richard Chase's *The American Novel and Its Tradition* perhaps best discriminates the romance from the novel by emphasizing the differences in "the way in which they view reality." For Chase

the romance, following distantly the medieval example, feels freer to render reality in less volume and detail. It tends to prefer action to character, and action will be freer in a romance than in a novel, encountering, as it were, less resistance from reality. . . . The romance can flourish without providing much intricacy of relation. The characters, probably rather two-dimensional types, will not be complexly related to each other or to society or to the past. Human beings will on the whole be shown in ideal relation—that is, they will share emotions only after these have become abstract or symbolic. To be sure, characters may become profoundly involved in some way, as in Hawthorne or Melville, but it will be a deep and narrow, an obsessive involvement. In American romances it will not matter much what class people come from, and where the novelist would arouse our interest in a character by exploring his origin, the romancer will probably do so by enveloping it in mystery. Character itself becomes, then, somewhat abstract and ideal, so much so in some romances that it seems to be merely a function of plot. The plot we may expect to be highly colored. Astonishing events may occur, and these are likely to have a symbolic or ideological, rather than a realistic, plausibility. Being less committed to the immediate rendition of reality than the novel, the romance will more freely veer toward mythic, allegorical, and symbolic forms.[6]

To this serviceable definition we need add only two observations. First, as Joel Porte has noted in *The Romance in America*, there are stylistic implications to practicing the romance form. For one thing the earlier romancer was likely to agree with William Gilmore Simms, in the Preface to *The Yemassee: A Romance of Carolina* (1835), that the romance approximates the poem. This disposition toward the poetic —whether it results in the epic dimensions of maximalist fiction, as in *Moby-Dick* (1851), or in the imagist minimalism of a novel like *The Red Badge of Courage* (1895)—frees the romancer to soar upward, in language, toward the wonderful and rhapsodic, or to refine language into the spare, the lyrical, or the lapidary, in ways that prosaic fictional representation does not ordinarily permit. At the same time, as Michael Davitt Bell has observed in *The Development of American Romance*, if "a good deal of modern and 'postmodern' literature" turns in on itself "to explore such matters as the nature and validity of linguistic statement and fictional representation," the same might be said of the nineteenth-century romance, at least in the case of Hawthorne and Melville, who above all others question the capacity of language itself to represent any external reality.[7]

The romance as a literary mode in America has been continuous with at least the impulse, however colored by didacticism and sentimentality, to produce realistic prose fiction, which is the norm against which contemporary antirealism reacts. The evolution of the realistic novel in America into anything like a distinguished art was a lengthy process, for there were few realistic novelists of literary distinction until after the Civil War. Still, however subliterary in its origins, the realistic novel was immensely more popular with the American people than the rhapsodies of the romancers, who almost invariably sold poorly and were ill-read by comparison. We can easily observe in the popular forms of fiction—the narrative of Indian captivity, the fiction of the American Revolution, the early satires of Imlay, Brackenridge, and Tyler, temperance novels, domestic sentimental novels, Civil War novels, and the local color writing up to the end of the nineteenth century—the will and intention to tell a truth about American experience through mimetic representations, however imperfect, rather than through the invention of improbabilities in the manner of the romancers. The literary method of realism which Howells and his followers finally formulated was merely a crystallization of the earlier but inchoate theory and practice of late eighteenth- and nineteenth-century novelists. And it has persisted, as a fiction practice, right down into our own time. Well before Howells, that is, the realistic novel vied with the romance. It does so even today, as the oppositional methods of Bellow and Auchincloss versus Coover and Burroughs will suggest.

Generally speaking, we may describe narrative realism as a commitment to verisimilitude that requires the deployment of fictional techniques that will achieve what is widely agreed to be fidelity to "the common, the average, the everyday" experience of ordinary people. As Howells remarked in "Novel-Writing and Novel-Reading," the "business of the novelist is to make you understand the real world through his faithful effigy of it."[8] Concentrating on middle-class life and manners, understood as a reflection of an interrelationship of diverse social elements, the realistic novel takes the revelation of character as its principal aim.

Now, character in fiction may be presented in several ways. Realists generally *compose* a character; antirealists, as Kuehl demonstrates, tend to *fragment* this composition of the self. To understand the difference, some attention to realistic character-creation is warranted here. Ordinarily, the realist's focus is on a single character—like James's Isabel Archer or Howells's Silas Lapham. Usually this character is understood to have a more or less stable core of identity and is immersed in relations of a social and familial complexity. This character—whose passions, feelings, and ideas are presented within the limited range of "normal" human experience—may be susceptible to change under the pressure of changing experience. But the representation of character-in-the-process-of-change is generally understood to manifest the freedom of the will actualizing the potentialities of that core of stable identity. Realists generally assume the stable core of identity as a given fact, a part of the mystery of human life, that uniqueness possessed by each soul.[9] Certainly realists are unlikely, on unarticulated metaphysical grounds, to see identity as fragmented, dissociated, or expressive of a mere cluster of roles. Frequently enough, in earlier American fiction, real people (or their names) are introduced into the fiction essentially to establish the existence of a nonlinguistic world anterior and exterior to authorial consciousness—as when both Royall Tyler and Isaac Mitchell bring Benjamin Franklin into *The Algerine Captive* (1797) and *Alonzo and Melissa* (1811), respectively; when Cooper reveals "Mr. Harper" to be George Washington in *The Spy* (1821); when Hawthorne creates the witch Mistress Hibbins, who had studied with the real magician Simon Forman, in *The Scarlet Letter* (1850); when James brings the Pope into *Roderick Hudson* (1875); when Twain resurrects Henry VIII in *The Prince and the Pauper* (1881); or when Edith Wharton has Teddy Roosevelt inspire Newland Archer's political career in *The Age of Innocence* (1920). Except in the stray instance like Twain's burlesque, real historical personae are respectfully treated: their conduct and speech are generally faithful to what can be documented of their lives, and anachronisms are eschewed. For earlier writers history was a material and conceptual reality and not, in the case of Coover and other current antirealists, "nothing but words." In any case, the general intent of earlier realistic fiction is to reveal a coherent personality under the process of changing experience and, in the demonstration, thus to say something about normative human nature in the real world.

This, in general, I take to be the intention of the element of "biography," which, however it may dip into melodrama or sentimentality, animates Cooper's *The Pioneers* (1823), and *Home as Found* (1838), Catherine Maria Sedgwick's *Hope Leslie* (1827) and *The Linwoods* (1835), Caroline Kirkland's *A New Home . . . ; or, Glimpses of Western Life* (1839), Maria Cummins's *The Lamplighter* (1854), Marion Harland's *Alone* (1854), De Forest's *Miss Ravenel's Conversion* (1867), J. G. Holland's *Arthur Bonnicastle* (1873), Howells's *The Rise of Silas Lapham* (1885), James's *The Portrait of a Lady* (1881), Wharton's *The House of Mirth* (1905), Willa Cather's *My Ántonia* (1918), Lewis's *Babbitt* (1922), Ellen Glasgow's *Vein of Iron* (1935), Marquand's *The Late George Apley* (1937), Auchincloss's *Sybil* (1952), Bellow's *Augie March* (1953), Updike's *Rabbit, Run* (1960), O'Hara's *Elizabeth Appleton* (1967), and others. Of course, to cite these novels is to be brought face to face with the historic continuum of *the novel of character* which posits the ordinary individual as the center of all significant experience. Such works by and large project that sense of unified character, that paradigm of character stability, that some early American romancers began to rebel against, thus initiating the alternative paradigm of fragmented character in our postmodern contemporaries.

Since there is a core of identity or stability to character, realistic novelists saw no reason why an interesting character could not be revived from novel to novel, in the manner of the *roman à fleuve*, a device latched onto by the early romancers as well. Cooper carries Natty Bumppo through the whole five-novel sequence of The Leatherstocking Tales, and characters occur and recur in *Homeward Bound* (1838) and *Home As Found* (1838). Henry James revives the 1876 *Roderick Hudson*'s Christina Light and Gloriani in *The Princess Casamassima* (1886) and *The Ambassadors* (1903), respectively. Basil and

Isabel March appear in some eight of Howells's novels and stories, from *Their Wedding Journey* (1872) through *A Hazard of New Fortunes* (1890). Twain's Huck and Tom appear in *The Adventures of Tom Sawyer* (1876), *Adventures of Huckleberry Finn* (1885), *Tom Sawyer Abroad* (1894), and *Tom Sawyer, Detective, and Other Stories* (1896). (This last, like a good many contemporary antirealistic novels, parodies the detective story form, even as Crane's "The Bride Comes to Yellow Sky" parodies the Western.) And more recently, Thomas Wolfe repeated Eugene Gant in *Look Homeward, Angel* (1929) and *Of Time and the River* (1935), and George Webber in *The Web and the Rock* (1939) and *You Can't Go Home Again* (1940). Faulkner never did finish with the Compson family and the Snopes clan, an ongoing preoccupation adumbrating the character revivals of Barth and Burroughs.

Since the revelation of ordinary, normative but interesting human nature, through characterization, was a general intention of the realistic novel, the kind of action presented therein constitutes a norm against which romance and antirealistic fiction must react. Howells speaks for all realists in commending narratives about observed action, action common to our experience, and not narratives about extraordinary events, as in the romance of Barthelme, Coover, and Hawkes. James in "The Art of Fiction" even doubted whether there is any distinction to be drawn between character and action: "What is character but the determination of incident? What is incident but the illustration of character?"[10] This point of view was not original with James but underlay the realists' general project throughout the nineteenth century. The realistic novel generally makes no separation of character from action or plot—but tends, as James remarked of Trollope, toward "a complete appreciation of the usual."[11] But in the romance bizarre action and unusual incident must be instigated, often in the form of quests leading nowhere or possibly even to destruction. Furthermore, if the realistic novel tends to have a beginning, middle, and end, a moderate degree of suspense, and an appreciation of the relation between cause and effect, particularly in the moral sphere, these features are rebelled against by romancers, particularly in the postmodern phase. Perhaps the simplest way to understand what antirealism reacts against is to note John Hawkes's observation that plot, character, setting, and theme are "the true enemies of the novel."[12] These are not, in fact, enemies of *the novel as such* but rather enemies of antirealistic fiction; hence they are readily dispensed with in Hawkes, Burroughs, Sukenick, and Federman.

The task of antirrealism, then, is to destroy those elements of fiction that have historically constituted the realistic novel, if only because, as Wallace Stevens remarked in *The Necessary Angel*, "modern reality is a reality of decreation."[13] This kind of modernity, however, began some time ago, for it was the early American romancers who first turned away from the longueurs of stable character in favor of decreating the self or fragmenting identity. In America, Charles Brockden Brown staked an early claim to the irrational psychology that disintegrates stable character—thus producing extraordinary incident and action. In *Wieland; or The Transformation* (1798), the madman Wieland murders his wife and children at the command of imaginary voices (perhaps projected by the sinister ventriloquist Carwin) and, in a fit of remorse, then undergoes a spontaneous combustion. But of the early antirealistic romancers fascinated with aberrational psychology and character fragmentation, it is of course Poe who is most important. It was Poe's brilliance in representing the spectacle of mental disintegration that led Allen Tate rightly to remark that "Poe is the transitional figure in modern literature because he discovered our great subject, the disintegration of personality, but kept it in a language that had developed in a tradition of unity and order."[14] In "The Fall of the House of Usher" (1839), the fissured house images the collapsing mind in the tale's own allegorical poem, "The Haunted Palace." The preoccupation of Brown and Poe with abnormal states of consciousness may be said to lay the groundwork for the deranged protagonists of Burroughs, the paranoid characters of Pynchon, the schizoid thought disorder we find in Barthelme's stories, and Nabokov's madmen.

Not only does Poe introduce the fragmentation of character in a *doppelgänger* tale like "William Wilson" (1839), he transforms "the terror of Germany" (the clanking contrivances of the Gothic novel) into the terror of the soul as it is expressed in the gradations of abnormal or altered states of consciousness ranging from inebriation ("The Black Cat" [1845]), hypnosis, ("The Facts in the Case of M. Valdemar" [1845]), nightmares and cataleptic trances ("The Fall of the House of Usher"), to drug-induced hallucinations ("Ligeia" [1838]) and the free-association madness of obsessional paranoia and schizophrenia ("The Cask of Amontillado" [1846], "The Tell-Tale Heart" [1843]). But if, as Daniel Hoffman has observed, Poe's "entire enterprise is a desperate effort to *unify* our existence on this suffering globe of shards," he himself sees that

all of our passions, intuitions, thoughts, are susceptible of inversion, may become their opposites. . . . Identity itself, the very vessel of perception, may be fatally flawed, fatally broken in twain. One of Poe's themes is the fate of the man haunted by his own double, his anima, his weird. Which is the real consciousness, the "I" who speaks or the doppelgänger who pursues him?[15]

Nabokov's *Lolita* (1955) is so centrally influenced by Poe's preoccupation with character doubling and disintegration in tales like "William Wilson" that he is obliged to parody his own narrator, Humbert Humbert, in order to render his indebtedness to Poe a form of self-mockery intended to disarm source hunters.

Although he thought Poe to be puerile, Henry James in "The Jolly Corner" (1908) also deviated into this kind of Poe-esque romance by fragmenting the character of Spencer Brydon into himself and an alter ego, the latter representing the deformed and mutilated man he might have been had he stayed in America and pursued a business career. In most early *doppelgänger* tales, the better self wins out over the monstrous self. But postmodern antihumanism begins to be apparent in Samuel L. Clemens, whose "The Facts Concerning a Recent Carnival of Crime in Connecticut" (1876) is a black comedy worthy of any current antirealist. Venting his rage at the Moral Sense because the tortures of his conscience were unbearable, Clemens created a *doppelgänger* for his narrator Mark Twain. The moral Twain, the self with a conscience, is presented as an ugly little dwarf, covered with green mold, who is finally strangled by the alter ego. The "Twain" who is thereby liberated from the Moral Sense then runs amok— committing arson, defrauding widows and orphans, and murdering thirty-eight people in two weeks. In a grotesque finale suggesting that the amoral "Twain" is no longer conscience-stricken by his former treatment of tramps who begged at the door, he observes:

In conclusion I wish to state, by way of advertisement, that medical colleges desiring assorted tramps for scientific purposes, either by the gross, by cord measurement, or per ton, will do well to examine the lot in my cellar before purchasing elsewhere, as these were all selected and prepared by myself, and can be had at a low rate, because I wish to clear out my stock and get ready for the spring trade.[16]

The contemporary antirealists' notion of the fragmentation of personality was anticipated by other early writers as well. In Edward Bellamy's *Looking Backward* (1888), Julian West, hypnotized in 1887, lies in his underground vault in suspended animation until the year 2000. Upon waking, he is naturally confused because the identically beautiful woman Edith standing before him is the great-granddaughter of his nineteenth-century betrothed. Past and present, confused and intermingled, vie for supremacy in his consciousness and he experiences what Bellamy calls the "obscuration of the sense of one's identity." As Julian remarks, he has the feeling "that I was two persons, that my identity was double"[17] — as indeed it is.

Aside from the hypnosis device or the dream vision, earlier American antirealists found other ways to disintegrate stable character. In Frank Norris's *McTeague* (1899), for example, the suggestion is very strong that McTeague's character merely represents a biological organism's adaptation to its environment. When his comfortable world on Polk Street is shattered, McTeague's character and even his human identity vanish, and he devolves into an animal surviving by its cunning instincts. If, in the age of Darwin, human character could evolve upward, toward greater spirituality, why not devolve downward, toward one's animal origins? The reduction of character into a cluster of animal instincts has been a popular fictive technique at least since Hawthorne's dancing Merry-Mount orgiasts stooped over, in a devolving atavism, to cavort with the bear. Such treatments of the theme of the fragility of ethical character, even of our humanity, lead directly to works like *The Floating Opera* (1956), where John Barth's protagonist Todd (death) excogitates pointlessly about suicide while remembering his hand-to-hand animal combat with a German soldier in a foxhole. For Barth, like Twain and Norris, the transcendent capacity for ethical thought, typical of human consciousness, seems an impediment in the struggle for survival.

As Kuehl vividly demonstrates, postmodern antirealism makes much of character as merely a cluster of disguises. But it was always thought that, because of our unstable social structure (especially on the frontier), identity in America, if it was not truly protean, could at least be disguised at will, especially if there was profit in it. We see this assumption everywhere in the stories of American confidence men. Coover's *The Public Burning* (1977), with its "Sam Slick Show," could not, in fact, have been composed as it was without Thomas C. Haliburton's prior example of the frontier conman Sam Slick. Like Sam, J. J. Hooper's Simon Suggs also thinks that "It's good to be shifty in a new country."[18] Furthermore, the modern notion, advanced by modern social psychologists like Erving Goffman, that identity is merely a function of the several roles that one must play in the social drama, is anticipated by the Duke and the King, in *Adventures of Huckleberry Finn*, whose multiple identities lie behind Ralph Ellison's conman Reinhart in *Invisible Man* (1952). These frauds appear successively as the Dauphin and the Duke of Bridgewater, the Wilks Brothers, the actors Edmund Kean and David Garrick, Hugh Capet (King of France), the phrenologist Dr. Armand de Montalban and a Reformed Pirate turned preacher. But who are they? It is useless to ask this question since Twain gives us no ground for believing that there is any stable character beneath the changing disguises of these frauds. Nor is there much more point in asking "Who is Huck?" For this transparent satirical device is variously himself was well as George Jaxon, Tom Sawyer, and even a girl, Sarah Mary Williams—suggesting Clemens's interest in gender metamorphosis. That Clemens was obsessed with the metamorphosis of identity is suggested by his taking on the pen names of Thomas Jefferson Snodgrass, Quintus Curtius Snodgrass, W. Epamonidas Adrastus Blab, and John Snooks before finally settling on "Mark Twain," the pseudonymous double identity that, according to his biographer Justin Kaplan, Clemens in fact "became" in his final years. Such confusions of identity, and even of sex, underlie much postmodern antirealistic practice.

Susan Kuhlmann, Gary Lindberg, and Warwick Wadlington have so ably and extensively analyzed the theme of metamorphic or protean identity, in early confidence-man fiction,[19] that perhaps only a couple of instances are needed here to establish the American sources of what Kuehl has called the fragmented character in contemporary antirealism. Melville's masked, deceptive, and fraudulent characters in *The Confidence Man* (1857) lead him to anticipate readerly objections to character fragmentation in his own work: "[I]f the acutest sage be often at his wits' ends to understand a living character, shall those who are not sages expect to run and read character in those mere phantoms which flit along a page, like shadows along a wall?" Metamorphic character transformation, fragmented instability, as a literary device, he claims to ground on the actualities of life: "[N]o writer has produced such inconsistent characters as nature herself." In fact, "in real life, a consistent character is a *rara avis*." Melville's narrator thus paradoxically claims a higher realism for characterological incoherence in fiction: "[T]hat author who draws a character, even though to common view incongruous in its parts, as the flying-squirrel, and, at different periods, as much at variance with itself as the caterpillar is with the butterfly into which it changes, may yet, in so doing, be not false but faithful to facts."[20] Melville thus anticipates the modern antirealist's view that—in the words of Peter J. Bellis— "the self exists only in a state of constant metamorphosis, that it continually *differs from itself*, and thus that identity can never be fixed or stabilized."[21]

Likewise, in *The Guardian Angel* (1867), O. W. Holmes gives us a heroine, Myrtle Hazard, who is so fragmented a collection of the identities of the many ancestresses who constitute her biological inheritance that she serves to illustrate a new theory of identity:

It is by no means certain that our individual personality is the single inhabitant of these our corporeal frames. . . . [S]ome, at least, who have long been dead, may enjoy a kind of secondary and imperfect, yet self-conscious life in these bodily tenements which we are in the habit of considering exclusively our own. . . . Perhaps we have cotenants in this house we live in. No less than eight distinct personalities are said to have coexisted in a single female mentioned by an ancient physician of unimpeachable authority. In this light we may perhaps see the meaning of a sentence, from a work which will be repeatedly referred to in this narrative, viz.: *"This body in which we journey across the isthmus between the two oceans is not a private carriage, but an omnibus."*[22]

Myrtle is to be understood as an unintegrated composite of conflicting personalities, each with a life of its own. If Holmes's view seems rather radical, however, it is nothing compared to character fragmentation in the contemporary American novel. In general, though, American forms of character transformation usually involve a character's attempting to change his name and identity into another single coherent self—Bellow's Velvel Adler into Tommy Wilhelm, for example, or Dreiser's Carrie Meeber into Carrie Madenda. As in *The Great Gatsby*, where James Gatz self-creates Jay Gatsby, the new identity reflects a Platonic or Ideal conception of what one wants to be. Of course, it never works.

Poe was ahead of his time in recognizing that antirealism would always have a following amongst certain American readers, justifying his grotesque "Berenice" (1835) and other antirealistic tales on the popularity of "the ludicrous heightened into the grotesque: the fearful coloured into the horrible: the witty exaggerated into the burlesque: the singular wrought out into the strange and mystical."[23] Mental grotesquerie, in any case, is so pervasive in early American fiction, if not in life, that we may conclude the subject of character fragmentation merely by pointing to Sherwood Anderson's *Winesburg, Ohio* (1919), a story-sequence about a town so overpopulated with the mentally aberrant that Anderson's narrative alter ego George Willard, as the Old Writer, composes "The Book of the Grotesque" out of the procession of the twisted creatures who parade before him in dreams. That the artist is the portraitist of misshapen psyches leads quite naturally to the consideration of early American antirealistic distortions of the human body, which postmodern writers appear uniformly to loathe.

Parallel to the theme of psychic deformation—such as we get in Poe's many mental grotesques in *Tales of the Grotesque and Arabesque* (1840) —is the extensive use of physical deformity in contemporary American antirealism. If, as Kuehl has remarked below, the use of mutes, dwarves, hunchbacks, the crippled, and the blind expresses modern disgust at humanity (or, more rarely, sympathy with its afflictions), a like array physical deformities may be found in the earlier writers— the hunchback Chillingworth in *The Scarlet Letter*, the lightning-scarred and one-legged Captain Ahab, the pock-marked Eleanor and the birth-marked Georgiana in Hawthorne's tales, Poe's exophthalmic Ligeia, the old man with the cataract eye in "The Tell-Tale Heart," Poe's Berenice with her sentient and obtrusive teeth, Melville's stutterer Billy Budd, the harelipped Joanna in *Huck Finn*, the hideously painted and scarified Indians in Cooper, the beer-fat Bartley Hubbard in *A Modern Instance* (1882), the obese lecher in Crane's *Maggie*

(1892), the cadaverous Ichabod Crane of Washington Irving, the stone-hearted Ethan Brand, the serpentine-necked Elsie Venner, Hawthorne's Donatello with his pointed and furry ears, the one-armed Lindau in *A Hazard of New Fortunes* (1890), the stump-fingered Spencer Brydon, and the cross-eyed Mrs. Wix, in *What Maisie Knew* (1897), whose "obliquity of vision" requires "straighteners." (In the native tradition of grotesque physical deformity, moreover, we have a good many tall-tale freaks who represent themselves as half-horse, half-alligator, eye-gouging, mule-kicking, foot-stomping, hard-drinking ring-tailed roarers and gamecocks of the wilderness.)

As Professor Kuehl elaborates below, grotesque physical deformity in the fiction of the postmodern antirealists is frequently linked with the demonic. This linkage has deep historical roots in the demonology of the Puritans. Cotton, Edwards, and the Mathers offer early confirmations of the universally known truth that the Devil and his disciples are known by physical abnormalities involving protean shape-shifting, horns and hooves, blackness of visage, teats, moles, and wens, and grotesque deformity of the back, shoulders, legs, and feet. Of course, we have no *fictional* images of the Devil in Puritan writing, because we have no Puritan novels—fiction itself being a forbidden genre inspired by the Father of Lies.

As Puritanism gave way to the era of the Enlightenment, literary images of the Devil generally went out the window as reflections of a backward superstition, as in Irving's simple comedy in "The Devil and Tom Walker" (1824). But in the post-Enlightenment symbolism of a writer like Hawthorne, the power of darkness is *reintroduced* into our writing, and in "Young Goodman Brown" (1835) all the elements of the satanic are conjured up for us. The seemingly reverend old gentleman who encounters Brown on the forest path is in fact the shape-shifter Satan. He has preternatural cognizance of Brown's inner thoughts, has known Brown's family for generations, can create a stupefying spectral illusion by transforming his staff into a snake, and in his satanic form presides over the Black Mass at which he welcomes Brown's wife Faith into "the communion of your race." And, as the Father of Lies, he announces that "Evil is the nature of mankind," a point of view seemingly congenial to so many of the postmodern authors studied by Kuehl. The consequence of Brown's belief that there can be no virtue in a world where even Faith is corrupt is that he returns to town "stern," "sad," "meditative," "distrustful," a man "whose dying hour was gloom."[24]

The rational optimism of the Enlightenment balloons into the utterly optative mood of Transcendentalism, in the first half of the nineteenth century, Emerson dismissing evil as the "mere privation" of good.[25] But in "Never Bet the Devil Your Head" (1841), Poe parodies Emersonian optimism. In this tale, the narrator's friend Toby Dammit is so inexplicably gay-hearted that the narrator is inclined to believe Dammit "affected with the transcendentals." But he feels "not well enough versed . . . in the diagnosis of this disease to speak with decision upon the point; and unhappily there were none of my friends of the 'Dial' present." Dammit self-reliantly wagers to "bet the devil his head" that he can jump over a certain fence-stile. Mysteriously, of course, there appears "the figure of a little lame old gentleman of venerable aspect," clad in black, who calls the bet. Dammit tries the jump, misses, and loses his head to the vanishing devil. Stuck with the expenses of the funeral, the narrator "sent in my very moderate bill to the transcendentalists. The scoundrels refused to pay it, so I had Mr. Dammit dug up at once, and sold him for dog's meat." If, as Nabokov once remarked, "satire is a lesson" but "parody is a game," "Never Bet the Devil Your Head" parodies not only the transcendental denial of evil as an active agency in human affairs but also contemporary New England complaints that Poe's fiction was without redeeming ethical import. Subtitled "A Tale With a Moral," Poe's story is prefaced by two pages of self-reflexive complaint on "the charge brought against me by certain ignoramuses —that I have never written a moral tale. . . ."[26] Poe's story thus illustrates the dangers of denying the demonic powers of the universe and of "misrepresenting" a Southerner's's fiction.

The persistence of belief in evil as an active supernatural agency and in a Manichean universe, continues, then, to be invoked in earlier black-comic American writing as an explanation of catastrophes in life; thus the devil recurs. His voice is also heard in the cynicism of Ambrose Bierce's *The Devil's Dictionary* (1911), and his image appears and reappears in Twain's late work. In *What Is Man?* (1906), *The Mysterious Stranger* (1916), and *Letters from the Earth* (1963), Twain constructed a cosmos populated by "the damned human race," that is afflicted by a God who is in fact Satan, for He creates human life only to destroy it (inadvertently or for His pleasure), rationalizing His brutality by saying that He can always create anew. In *Letters from the Earth*, Little Satan describes God as possessed of "a wild nightmare of vengefulness," for He has "bankrupted his native ingenuities in inventing pains and miseries and humiliations and heartbreaks wherewith to embitter the brief lives of Adam's descendants." Humanity is contemptible to Little Satan, for man "equips the Creator with every trait that goes to the making of a fiend, and then arrives at the conclusion that a fiend and a father are the same thing. . . . What do you think of the human mind? I mean, in case you think there is a human mind?"[27] In the image of the Devil in John Updike's *The Witches of Eastwick* (1984) and William Gaddis's *The Recognitions* (1955), we see a reaction against the heresy of inverting Satan and God, but there seems little doubt that Twain's brooding affected both novels. In fact, Gaddis has said of postmodern antirealistic black humor that "we all came out of Mark Twain's vest pocket. No one has ever beaten 'The Mysterious Stranger.' "[28]

Wallace Stevens mused in "Esthetique du Mal" that "The death of Satan was a tragedy / For the imagination. A capital / Negation destroyed him in his tenement / And, with him, many blue phenomena."[29] But long ago, in an act of displacement, early American romancers shifted the demonic from Satan to mankind itself, so that we have a whole host of human devils in fiction, many of them Faustian fiends, all associated with physical and spiritual deformities, including Hawthorne's Rappaccini and Ethan Brand; Melville's Ahab and Fedallah; Twain's Injun Joe; James's Peter Quint; Faulkner's Popeye and Flem Snopes, and others.

But not all distortions of the human body in early American writing represent instances of satanic humanity. Perhaps the most grotesque adumbration of postmodern antirealistic uses of deformity, expressing utter disgust with the human body, occurs in Poe's "The Man That Was Used Up" (1839). This tale confirms Allen Tate's observation that "No other writer in England or the United States, or, so far as I know, in France, went so far as Poe in his vision of dehumanized man."[30] Here the mysteriously handsome General John A. B. C. Smith arouses the narrator's curiosity owing to reports of his having endured some unmentionable atrocity in the Indian campaigns. At length the narrator barges into the handsome general's dressing room only to observe the disintegrated form of a creature he cannot recognize—a monster with a cork leg, an arm that screws on, a wig, dentures, a false eye, and a "singular-looking machine" that functions as a larynx and tongue. When fully assembled ("Now, . . . slip on my shoulders and bosom"), the "bionic" General Smith is a handsome figure of a man but is utterly prosthetic, his body itself having been "used up."[31]

That the body is a source of utter disgust is also suggested by "The Facts in the Case of M. Valdemar," an odd tale in which Poe's narrator "P—" mesmerizes the dying Valdemar in order to see whether hypnosis can arrest death itself. For seven months "P—" keeps the body of Valdemar in a state of suspended animation. Throughout this time Valdemar's voice, pleading with "P—" that his body is dead, begs for deliverance. Finally "P—" relents and accedes to the request:

As I rapidly made the mesmeric passes, amid ejaculations of 'dead! dead!' absolutely *bursting* from the tongue and not from the lips of the sufferer, his whole frame at once—within the space of a single minute, or even less, shrunk—crumbled—absolutely *rotted* away beneath my hands. Upon the bed, before that whole company, there lay a nearly liquid mass of loathsome —of detestable putridity.[32]

It is difficult to disagree with Daniel Hoffman's astute critical comment: "Ugh. Yyecch!"[33] Not even Burroughs is this repulsive. In Poe's case, however, disgust with the body arises from a conception of the superior ideality of the soul, on which the flesh is a drag. In the case of the postmodern antirealists, no such concomitant belief in the soul is evident, often leaving the bodies of men and women utterly loathsome.

A like representation of human deformity, but more comically handled, occurs in Mark Twain's *Pudd'nhead Wilson* (1894), or rather in its appendage *Those Extraordinary Twins*. There Counts Luigi and Angelo Capello appear as a single creature with two heads, four arms, and but one pair of legs—which the two alternately take command of. Grotesque self-division is carried to a grimly hilarious extent, since one is a Democrat, the other Whig; one a Methodist, the other a freethinker; one a drinker, the other a teetotaler, and so forth. In the end, Luigi is hanged for a political crime—Angelo taking the rap too. This piece of grotesquerie leads straight to the Siamese twins of John Barth's "Petition" in *Lost in the Funhouse* (1968).

By 1884, Twain's antihumanist rage at life was so intense that he opined that "we are only the microscopic trichina concealed in the blood of some vast creature's veins, and it is that vast creature whom God concerns Himself about and not us."[34] By 1897, in *Following the Equator,* he was writing of a dream in which "the visible universe is the physical person of God" and that "we and the other creatures are the microbes that charge with multitudinous life the corpuscles." This conception of the human animalcule's infectious corruptions appeared full blown in the story "Three Thousand Years Among the Microbes" (1905). There we have "the autobiography of a microbe that has been once a man, and through a failure in a biological experiment transformed into a cholera germ when the experimenter was trying to turn him into a bird. His habitat was the person of a disreputable tramp named Blitzowski, a human continent of vast areas, with seething microbic nations."[35] But if the evolution of this tale suggests that man is the virulent disease-carrier of the universe, or that God is a cosmic drunkard, Twain's even more pessimistic ruminations—in the Great Dark Manuscripts—suggest that the Drunken Deity is, in fact, a Cosmic Devil.

Physical deformities in our older fiction are at times used for comic purposes but just as often symbolize moral imperfections, based on the Platonic notion—advanced in Emerson and symbolized by Hawthorne—that the body is the objectification of the soul, that the outer form reflects the inner spirit. In "The Poet" (1842) Emerson is sure that "the soul makes the body, as the wise Spenser teaches,"[36] and in *Nature* (1836) he remarks, "Every spirit builds itself a house," but since man heeds not the monitions of the oversoul, he is "the dwarf of himself."[37] Physical deformities in idealist thought, then, are always linked to sin and symbolize imperfections of the soul.

This notion was rejected by orthodox Christians like Cooper, who understood the mystery of man's physical affliction as a test of faith. And of course rationalists scoffed at the transcendental linkage of deformity to sin, for the physical ailment is scientifically diagnosed as the effect of natural causes. Dr. Holmes wrote what he called "medicated novels" intended to demolish the moral connection between sin and disease. This link, in his view, caused needless suffering that could be ameliorated through a proper understanding of how character is shaped by external physical forces over which the individual has no control. His heroine in *Elsie Venner: A Romance of Destiny* (1861) is a strange, sinister creature with lithe, serpentine movements, glittering diamond eyes, and a poisonous tongue. It would be easy to call her an "evil" woman; she is obviously a sister of Keats's Lamia and Coleridge's Christabel. About her one character remarks that something was "infused into her soul—it was cruel to call it malice—which was still and watchful and dangerous, which waited its opportunity, and then shot like an arrow from its bow out of the coil of brooding premeditation." If Elsie Venner's serpent-complex is bizarre, Holmes presents her character as the physiological result of her having been poisoned *in utero*, when her pregnant mother was bitten by the crotalus snake. Twenty years later, Holmes observed:

The real aim of the story was to test the doctrine of "original sin" and human responsibility for the disordered volition coming under that technical denomination. Was Elsie Venner, poisoned by the venom of a crotalus before she was born, responsible for the "volitional" aberrations, which translated into acts become what is known as sin and, it may be, what is punished as crime? If, on presentation of the evidence, she becomes by the verdict of the human conscience a proper object of divine pity and not of divine wrath, as a subject of moral poisoning, wherein lies the difference between her position at the bar of judgment, human or divine, and that of the unfortunate victim who received a moral poison from a remote ancestor before he drew his first breath?[38]

But the age-old association between disease and sin, between physical deformity and evil, with the accompanying self-righteousness, in society, of isolation and moral judgment, are not that easily dispensed with. Stephen Crane tries to decouple the two in "The Monster" (1899). There he presents us with a horribly mutilated Negro who has saved a white boy from a fire and been taken in by the family, only to have them ostracized by the bigoted townspeople for this act of charity to the town freak who "hasn't got any face."[39]

In *The Confidence Man*, Melville also tries to decouple the link between sin and deformity by introducing the character Black Guinea, described as "a grotesque negro cripple" who, "owing to something wrong about his legs, was, in effect, cut down to the stature of a Newfoundland dog."[40] Guinea dissociates himself from his affliction, jokes about his legs, even offers them for sale. Awash in the ambiguities, however, Melville makes the deformity serve the purposes of

incertitude by introducing a doubt as to whether the affliction is even
real, for the cripple may be one of the guises of the confidence man
himself. In any case, Melville seems to refute the Emersonian link
between deformity and evil (and thereby to anticipate postmodern
antirealism) when the character Cosmopolitan remarks, "You can
conclude nothing absolute from the human form."[41]

As John Kuehl has remarked below, the corollary of character fragmentation in contemporary antirealism is the decentralized novel.
This form is of course rare in the nineteenth century. For the focus
of both the realistic novel and (to some extent) the romance was likely
to be a prominently featured central character—Huck, Hester, Ahab,
Pym. But several works may be said to feature a decentralization of
character dictated by the method of composition. Of these James's
The Awkward Age (1899) is exemplary. It explores the problem of a
girl's adolescence in a series of chapters, each narrated from a different point of view, with the effect that no character is ever presented
as whole, but merely as a composite of various subjectivities. A like
technique emerges in *Absalom, Absalom!* (1936), where Faulkner presents Thomas Sutpen from the limited (even deranged) angles of
Rosa, Father, Quentin, and Shreve. If epistemological incertitude
about Sutpen invariably results from this method (which several postmodernists have found serviceable), Faulkner remains something of
a traditionalist in his view of character, for he once remarked that
"the truth, I would like to think, comes out, that when the reader has
read all these thirteen different ways of looking at the blackbird [that
is, Sutpen through the others' eyes], the reader has his own fourteenth image of that blackbird which I would like to think is the
truth."[42] Thus, it is the reader's task to unify partial perspectives so
as to produce a whole Sutpen, a task well-nigh impossible with many
contemporary antirealistic novels.

  The Whole Family, serialized anonymously in *Harper's Bazar* (1907–
1908), also created quite a guessing game for readers and is in some
ways as experimental as anything in contemporary antirealism.
Though superficially realistic, it was a novel of twelve chapters, sequentially written, each devoted to a different character, each chapter written by a different author—the twelve authors, when finally

identified, including (among others) Henry James, William Dean Howells, and Mary Wilkins Freeman. An attempt at ludic play with the reader, *The Whole Family* was likewise an experiment with multiple points of view, but had the unintended effect of fragmenting character and dispersing interest across the whole family. (Each chapter had a title like "The Father," "The Mother," "The Old-Maid Aunt," and so forth.) Since the twelve authors could not agree on any consistency of characterization or on the unity of plot development, instead setting traps for each other and ignoring the direction laid down by the preceding novelists, the book's incoherence inadvertently turned out to be postmodern. But this was not the first nor the last of such experiments before the era of current antirealism. In fact, in 1872, Harriet Beecher Stowe, Edward Everett Hale, and four others collaborated to produce *Six of One by Half a Dozen of the Other;* fourteen writers produced *The Sturdy Oak* in 1917; and Dorothy Parker, Alexander Woolcott, Louis Bromfield, Rube Goldberg, and G. P. Putnam produced *Bobbed Hair* in 1925. If such novelistic Rube Goldberg contraptions, which fail of the highest felicity, are indeed "stunts," as Alfred Bendixen has called them, what are we to say of similar effects in contemporary antirealistic fiction?[43]

Reflexivity, with the author as God presiding over his linguistic creation (and naturally finding it good), is, as Kuehl rightly remarks, a hallmark of the new fiction. But is this reflexive self-apotheosis genuinely original? *The Confidence Man*'s ruminations on the instability of character, fictional or otherwise, are reminiscent of Twain's admonition in *The Mysterious Stranger:* "Strange, indeed, that you should not have suspected that your universe and its contents were only dreams, visions, *fiction!*"[44] Poe likewise fictionalized the whole cosmos, remarking in *Eureka* that "The Universe is a plot of God," and that "the plots of God are perfect."[45] The view that life is a novel, that a human being is a fiction, and that a character in a novel is thus doubly fictive adumbrates the preoccupation in contemporary antirealism with authorial self-consciousness, the problems of writing fiction, the writer's insistence on his own fictionality, and allusions to himself or other real people in fiction. To call attention, in a novel, to fictional characters as "mere phantoms which flit along a page, like shadows along a wall," as Melville does, is essentially to subvert the illusion of reality that it is the conventional purpose of the realistic novel to create. Moreover, it inserts oneself, as author, into the text and calls attention to the fiction as fiction. Such a technique "defamiliarizes" the world of the fiction, as Viktor Shklovsky remarks, by self-consciously "baring the device" of characterization so as to call attention to its status as a device. In postmodern antirealism this technique "is fundamentally esteemed over its mere tacit and habitual functioning."[46]

But however modern this technique seems, American writers have always called attention to their fictions as fictions and made the story of writing at least an element of the writing of the story. As long ago as 1793, Susanna Rowson threw a "slight veil" over the facts of Charlotte Stanley's seduction in order to narrate *Charlotte* as a warning to her audience of female "flutterers in the fantastic round of dissipation." Justifying, *in propria persona*, a three-page digression on flibbertigibbet girls who were candidates for seduction, she remarked: "I confess I have rambled strangely from my story: but what of that? If I have been so lucky as to find the road to happiness, why should I be such a niggard as to omit so good an opportunity of pointing out the way to others?"[47] Likewise in *The Inquisitor* (1788), Mrs. Rowson interrupts the narrative for an ironical commentary, entitled "Sketch of the Modern Novel," in which the sentimental conventions of contemporary fiction are, like those in Barth's *Lost in the Funhouse*, mercilessly and reflexively parodied: "Be sure you contrive a duel; and, if convenient, a suicide might not be amiss—lead your heroine through wonderful trials—let her have the fortitude of an anchorite; the patience of an angel—but in the end, send her first husband to the other world, and unite her to the first possessor of her heart."[48]

But, as Kuehl remarks below, the reflexivity of postmodern antirealists is also marked by an authorial arrogation of the creative powers of God himself. Such hubris would have been irreligious to most eighteenth- and nineteenth-century American authors. But since Luciferian pride is antecedent to the world itself, it is not surprising to find Poe postulating himself, the author, as God, idolatrously creating alternate worlds through the power of his word, and expressing sublime confidence that even every other man would "at length attain that awfully triumphant epoch when he shall recognize his existence as that of Jehovah."[49] As Allen Tate has persuasively argued in "The Angelic Imagination: Poe as God," Poe believed himself to be supernaturally gifted and therefore arrogated God's powers to himself, believing in language as "a potential source of quasi-divine power."[50] For any Christian, this is heretical; consequently, Poe is, for Tate, not God but "a forlorn demon" (and therefore our cousin). Daniel Hoffman is likewise condemnatory of Poe for this aesthetic self-apotheosis:

The symbolist religion of art! The image of the artist as the autochthynous creator of his own universe—the perfect escape from the tyranny of time, from the baseness of the material life. The perfect substitute for that devotion to the spirit and *its* life which once was the business of the Christian Church to provide for the Western World, and which the world no longer takes as its business, having run away from its Father's business.[51]

It is a short step from conceiving oneself as God to ruminating in print about the problems of one's linguistic creation. Hence, the superminimalist Poe makes writing the subject of fiction in a pair of tales—"How to Write a Blackwood Article" and "A Predicament: The Scythe of Time" (1838). (In 1838, "article" served as a term for the tale or short story.) In the first tale, a ridiculous Philadelphia bluestocking calling herself Psyche Zenobia undertakes to master fiction writing by traveling to Edinburgh and soliciting from "Mr. Blackwood" the "exact method of composition" that makes the stories published there so internationally famous. Mr. B. advises her that "the secret, the soul, of intensity" is to compose an illegible manuscript along the lines of "The Dead Alive" (a record of "a gentleman's sensations when entombed before the breath was out of his body"): "Sensations are the great things after all. Should you ever be drowning or hung, be sure and make a note of your sensations—they will be worth to you ten guineas a sheet. If you wish to write forcibly, Miss Zenobia, pay minute attention to the sensations." In addition, he advises her to "get yourself into such a scrape as no one ever got into before"; next, "consider the tone, or manner, or your narration" (the tone didactic, the tone enthusiastic, the tone laconic, transcendental, and interjectional are recommended); make lists of and fill up the tale with *"Piquant Facts for the Manufacture of Similes"* and *"Piquant*

Expressions to be introduced as occasion may require"; and punctuate the tale with foreign expressions and literary allusions so as to parade an air of learning ("In a Blackwood article nothing makes so fine a show as your Greek").

"How to Write a Blackwood Article" thus fictionalizes the processes of writing fiction while satirizing the sensationalist fiction published in *Blackwood's*. We have here, then, fully thematized, a treatment of fiction writing—like that in Barth's "Lost in the Funhouse," where Ambrose Mensch ruminates on how to structure a tale to be called "Lost in the Funhouse," how to shape the style, how to effect the characterization of Ambrose, and work out the plot with Magda (for example, whether to use the "Freitag's Triangle" of exposition, conflict, rising action, complication, climax, and denouement). Poe ends his tale with Zenobia determined to write a tale following Blackwood's prescriptions. This story is then followed by the short story that Zenobia actually composes according to Mr. B.'s advice—"A Predicament: The Scythe of Time." In this sequel, set in "Edina" (Edinburgh disguised), a fictional "Zenobia" goes up into the windowless belfry of the town cathedral, feels that she must peer out through the only hole in the belfry wall, climbs up on the shoulders of her Negro servant Pompey (a bow-legged no-necked dwarf, aged eighty), and sticks her head out through the hole: "I observed that the aperture through which I had thrust my head was an opening in the dial-plate of a gigantic clock" in the steeple. Absorbed in the prospect below, Zenobia becomes conscious of a "something very cold which pressed with a gentle pressure upon the back of my neck. . . . Turning my head gently to one side, I perceived to my extreme horror, that the huge, glittering scimetar-like minute-hand of the clock, had, in the course of its hourly revolution, *descended on my neck.*" Unable to pull back, Zenobia (following Mr. B.'s advice) minutely registers her physical impressions, as well as the psychic effect produced by her situation. At precisely 5:25 P.M., "the ponderous and terrific *Scythe of Time*" ("I now discovered the literal import of that classical phrase") succeeds in decapitating her, and her head "rolled down the side of the steeple, then lodged, for a few seconds, in the gutter, and then made its way, with a plunge into the middle of the street." Like any self-consciously fragmented postmodernist character, Zenobia remarks that my feelings were now of the most singular—nay of the most mysterious, the most perplexing and incomprehensible character. My senses were here and there at one and the same moment. With my head I imagined, at one time, that I, the head, was the real Signora Psyche Zenobia—at another I felt convinced that myself, the body, was the proper identity.

The rest of the story, peppered with French, German, and Greek quotations, dissolves into postmodern chaos: "Dogless, niggerless, headless, what *now* remains for the unhappy Signora Psyche Zenobia? Alas—*Nothing!* I have done."[52] The comic nihilism of this ending, in which Zenobia (like Poe) is undone by time, will be evident to any reader.

These Poe tales thus ridicule the idea that good fiction can be written according to a formula. But, although these thematizations of the story of writing fiction do not involve an author named Edgar Allan Poe, Zenobia is in fact Poe's own psyche projected self-consciously. Both tales self-consciously parody Poe's own characteristic themes (premature burial and physical mutilation) as well as his techniques (the emphasis on physical sensations and psychic states, the creation of bizarre effects, the affectation of erudition, and the parody of learned wit in foreign allusions and quotations, together with colorful, highly charged phrasing and poetic similes).

Long before *The Canterbury Tales*—where the fictional Host complains that the "drasty rhyming" of the pilgrim "Geoffrey Chaucer's" tale of Sir Thopas "Is nat worth a toord!"[53]—writers have made fiction out of calling attention to their technical processes and fictionalizing their readers. Even the archrealist George Eliot, so influential on American fiction, inserts herself *and a fictive reader* into the imaginary world of *Adam Bede:*

"This Rector of Broxton is little better than a pagan!" I hear one of my readers exclaim. "How much more edifying it would have been if you had made him give Arthur some truly spiritual advice." Certainly, I could, if I held it the highest vocation of the novelist to represent things as they never have been and never will be. Then, of course, I might refashion life and character entirely after my own liking; I might select the most unexceptional type of clergyman, and put my own admirable opinions into his mouth on all occasions. But it happens, on the contrary, that my strongest effort is to avoid any such arbitrary picture, and to give a faithful account of men and things as they have mirrored themselves in my mind. The mirror is doubtless defective; the outlines will sometimes be disturbed, the reflection faint or confused; but I feel as much bound to tell you as precisely as I can what that reflection is, as if I were in the witness-box narrating my experience on oath.[54]

Most realistic American novelists affirmed Eliot's requirement of verisimilitude, but both James and Howells were vexed by the intrusion of the writer into her fiction, so as to comment on her characters, thus destroying the fictive illusion produced by dramatic and reportorial objectivity. Dramatize, dramatize, dramatize, is the note of James's fiction: sustain the reader's vision of a world and its inhabitants. And he criticized Trollope—in terms I find appropriate to a good many antirealists—for "taking a suicidal satisfaction in reminding the reader that the story he was telling was only, after all, a make-believe" and for admitting "that the events he narrates have not really happened, and that he can give his narrative any turn the reader may like best. Such a betrayal of a sacred office seems to me, I confess, a terrible crime."[55]

In their strictures forbidding the violation of the dramatic angle of vision, what James called "slaps at credulity," American realists were at war with a technique, authorial self-intrusion, common enough in the romance. Melville, for one, scrupled not to ejaculate in *Moby-Dick:* "If, then, to meanest mariners, and renegades and castaways, I shall hereafter ascribe high qualities, though dark; weave around them tragic graces; . . . Bear me out in it, thou great Democratic God!"[56] Likewise, in *The Confidence Man,* Melville violates the illusion of a world by devoting chapter 44 to a rambling essay on the problems of creating an original character in fiction, only to come to consciousness of himself as having "been led into a dissertation bordering upon the prosy, perhaps upon the smoky."[57] And so, retiring under the cover of the smoke, he returns to his story. And in case we missed *his* point, Hawthorne actually invades the world of *The Scarlet Letter* to define for us its significance: "Be true! be true!"[58]

The Scarlet Letter is of course reflexively paradigmatic in making the long "Custom House" chapter inextricable from the narrative. There "Hawthorne" introduces himself for the purposes of explaining "how large a portion of the following pages came into my possession, and as offering proofs of the authenticity of a narrative therein contained."[59] A good many readers have taken this Hawthorne to be the novelist himself. But this Hawthorne is substantially fictive and only partly the author speaking *in propria persona*. The fictive author is the putative editor of papers, said to have been "authorized" by the late Surveyor Jonathan Pue, found in the rubbish in the Custom House attic. This Hawthorne claims the privilege of going beyond the mere facts as Pue gives them: "I have allowed myself, as to such points, nearly or altogether as much license as if the facts had been entirely of my own invention." More interesting is how the personae of Pue's account are said to address Hawthorne with "all the rigidity of dead corpses," staring at him "with a fixed and ghastly grin of contemptuous defiance," demanding to know "What have you to do with us?" By this means they become "torpid creatures of my own fancy" who "twitted me with imbecility, and not without fair occasion," a sassiness to the author typical of the characters in Barth's *Letters*.[60]

Hawthorne also fictionalizes the writing process in "Wakefield," where the title character abandons his wife, only to spy on her from across the street for twenty years. Here Hawthorne encourages the reader to perform "his own meditation" about what Wakefield thought and did during those twenty years, for "we are free to shape out our own idea, and call it by his name."[61] In only one other case that I know of does Hawthorne fictionalize himself, here in response to a claim like Melville's that his fiction is too aetherial and needs "roast-beef done rare." Reinventing himself as M. de l'Aubépine in the 1854 preface to "Rappaccini's Daughter," Hawthorne remarks of M. Aubépine:

As a writer, he seems to occupy an unfortunate position between the Transcendentalists (who, under one name or another, have their share in all the current literature of the world) and the great body of pen-and-ink men who address the intellect and sympathies of the multitude. If not too refined, at all events too remote, too shadowy, and unsubstantial in his modes of development to suit the taste of the latter class, and yet too popular to satisfy the spiritual or metaphysical requisitions of the former, he must necessarily find himself without an audience,—except here and there an individual or possibly an isolated clique.[62]

The annoying reflexivity of *Aubépine*, which is of course the French word for "hawthorne," had already been sized up by Emerson well before Hawthorne had even written his first long romance. For Emerson remarks in his journals for May 1846 that "Hawthorne invites his readers too much into his study, opens the process before them. As if the confectioner should say to his customers Now let us make the cake."[63]

In fact, not even the realists successfully remain outside their fictions. James assumes the intrusive writer's prerogative, in *The Portrait of a Lady*, (1881), and orders us how *not* to react to Isabel Archer: "Smile not, however, I venture to repeat, at this simple young woman from Albany who debated whether she should accept an English peer."[64] And in *The Bostonians* (1886), he announces that he will not reproduce the Southern dialect of Basil Ransom: "It is not in my power to reproduce by any combination of characters this charming dialect; but the initiated reader will have no difficulty in evoking the sound, which is to be associated in the present instance with nothing vulgar or vain."[65] Though James is often acclaimed as the father of the single point of view, his violations of dramatic objectivity are so frequent as to have led John E. Tilford, Jr., to make a list of them in "James the Old Intruder."[66]

Howells also plays the postmodernist game of fictionalizing another author, in this case Henry James, by alluding to *Daisy Miller* (1879) in the opening chapter of *The Rise of Silas Lapham* (1885). And in *Indian Summer* (1886), Howells has a little fun at his *own* expense, when he has Mrs. Amsden remark that she, Colville, and Imogene form a dramatic grouping such as might appear in a play:

"Oh, call us a passage from a modern novel," suggested Colville, "if you're in a romantic mood. One of Mr. James's."

"Don't you think we ought to be rather more of the great world for that? I hardly feel up to Mr. James, I should have said Howells. Only nothing happens in that case."[67]

Furthermore, just two years before, Twain had announced *his own* fictive identity (in fact his mendacity), by opening *Adventures of Huckleberry Finn* with a reference to *The Adventures of Tom Sawyer*, of which Huck says: "That book was made by Mr. Mark Twain, and he told the truth, mainly. There was things which he stretched, but mainly he told the truth."[68] Here, however, "Twain" was indeed fictional, being the pen name of Clemens, who, as earlier remarked, disappeared into the identity of his fictive persona at the end. In any case, both the "nothing that happens" in a Howells novel and Twain's tall-tale stretchers are major features of their occasionally self-conscious art.

Twain is perhaps most forthright about fiction-writing processes in *Pudd'nhead Wilson* and *Those Extraordinary Twins*. There he complains that "A man who is born with the novel-writing gift has a troublesome time of it when he tries to build a novel." Recounting how his six-page tale has taken on a life of its own and swelled into a book against his authorial will (moreover, a book with a different theme), Twain narrates how the two stories—the tragic tale of Tom and Roxy and the farce of the Siamese twins, "this freak of nature for hero"—got "tangled together; and they obstructed and interrupted each other at every turn and created no end of confusion and annoyance." No such generic hash of styles would bother a postmodern antirealist, but Twain (still committed to Aristotelian unity) "pulled one of the stories out by the roots, and left the other one—a kind of literary Caesarean operation." In *Pudd'nhead Wilson*, he "took those twins apart and made two separate men of them." But, in the appended tale, they are left "composite," the tale of the twins having "no purpose but to exhibit that monstrous 'freak' in all sorts of grotesque lights." Twain concludes by remarking that there was no connection between the stories, "no interdependence, no kinship. It is not practicable or rational to try to tell two stories at the same time." Calling himself a "jackleg" novelist, he ends: "The reader already knew how the expert works; he knows now how the other kind do it."[69]

The chatty relationship between the jackleg author and his reader in postmodern antirealism is, in fact, only an extension of what had been going on in the American novel since virtually the beginning. In her description of a wild landscape of the Blue Ridge Mountains, the much-published Mrs. E. D. E. N. Southworth remarks in *Cruel as the Grave* (1871): "It was one of those fearful passes so frequently to be found in the Allegheny Mountains, and which I have described so often that I may be excused from describing this."[70] Indeed, why not? Her readers had seen it all before. And at the end of *The Family Doom* (1869), she advises the reader that "Whether . . . the lovers [will be] united in marriage, shall be told in the sequel to this story, to be published immediately, under the title of 'THE MAIDEN WIDOW.' "[71]

Well before the current antirealists Hemingway also got himself into the act in *The Torrents of Spring* (1926), thereby blurring the margins between fiction and autocriticism. Just after "The End," he appends an "Author's Final Note to the Reader": "Well reader, how did you like it? It took me ten days to write it. Has it been worth it? There is one place I would like to clear up. You remember back in the story where the elderly waitress, Diana . . ." Thus he continues the narrative past its "End."[72] Faulkner likewise sends himself up in *Mosquitoes* (1927), where this dialogue occurs between Jenny and Pat about an odd little man with no necktie or hat:

"He said he was a liar by profession, and he made good money at it, enough to own a Ford as soon as he got it paid out. I think he was crazy. Not dangerous: just crazy."

"What was his name? Did he tell you?" [Pat] asked suddenly.

". . . Yes. It was . . . I remembered it because he was such a funny kind of man. It was Walker or Foster or something. . . . It must be with an F, . . . Oh, yes: I remember—Faulkner, that was it."

"Faulkner?" the niece pondered in turn. "Never heard of him," she said at last, with finality.[73]

If such older reflexive practice suggests the long tradition that underlies the work of Barth, Burroughs, Gaddis, and others, it also represents, as Kuehl has demonstrated, a special form of the contemporary ludic spirit. This comic spirit—even in its blackest forms—is of course not absent from earlier American literature. Fictive play has had a long history in this country, although most novelists have presented themselves as sober didacticists given to representational truth-telling. The *roman à clef* was a perennially popular game for readers of older American fiction, Hawthorne stoutly denying that *The Blithedale Romance*'s Zenobia was Margaret Fuller, and Henry James complaining to William that, if anyone saw *The Bostonians*' Miss Birdseye as Elizabeth Peabody, it was the farthest thing from his mind. Emerson is parodied in Melville's *The Confidence Man* in the mystic Mark Winsome and, for all we know, Emerson (whom Henry James, Sr., called the "man without a handle") may be Melville's shape-shifting con man in *all* his disguises. Shelgrim in Frank Norris's *The Octopus* is clearly the railroad magnate Leland Stanford, and in case anybody missed the portrait of Jay Gould in Twain's *A Connecticut Yankee*, the novel's illustrator, Dan Beard, drew a perfect caricature of the robber baron as the slave-auctioneer. But these *roman à clef* games in the nineteenth century merely brought up to date an old practice. It took very little knowledge of Hartford society for eighteenth-century readers of Hannah Foster's *The Coquette* (1797) to see—in the sexual abandon of Eliza Wharton and her suitors—a veiled story of the beautiful but vain Elizabeth Whitman, daughter of a popular Hartford clergyman, who rejected two offers of marriage, allowed herself to be seduced, escaped to Danvers to hide her pregnancy, and died in childbirth in July 1788. Everyone knew that the two disappointed suitors were the Reverends Joseph Howe and Joseph Buckminster. But who was the seducer? Some said Pierrepont Edwards (the great theologian's son), others Aaron Burr. But, in this case, the playfulness of the *roman à clef* had a serious moral purpose—warning sentimental young girls about the wiles of the seducer.

Other literary games in older American fiction include cryptograms, anagrams, ciphers, and the text itself as an analogue for one or another type of game. Poe was fascinated by cryptograms and often inserted them into his tales (his detective Dupin is a great solver of puzzles). In his newspaper articles, Poe threw out verbal puzzles and even challenged his readers to send him theirs. So inundated was he by his readers that he was forced to call a halt to the whole business: "Will any body tell us how to get out of this dilemma? If we don't solve all the puzzles forwarded, their concocters will think it is because we cannot—when we can." And indeed he could. As Charles W. Alexander remarked in the Philadelphia *Daily Chronicle* for 13 July 1841: "The cyphers *now* solved by Mr. Poe, are far more abstruse than even those to which we allude. How it is *possible* to read them, is a mystery."[74] (Of course the claim that Bacon or some other had encoded his authorship in Shakespeare's plays started up a number of wild hares in the nineteenth century, the literary games culminating in Ignatius Donnelly's *The Great Cryptogram* [1888] and *The Cypher in the Plays and on the Tombstone* [1889], proving that Bacon wrote not only Shakespeare's plays but Montaigne's essays, Burton's *Anatomy of Melancholy,* and the plays of Marlowe as well.) Furthermore, Harold Frederic was in the spirit of the age in offering his readers anagramatic fun with the adulterous title character of *The Damnation of Theron Ware* (1896), which of course transposes into "Hawthorne."

In Poe's "Berenice," the narrator remarks that "To muse for long unwearied hours with my attention riveted to some frivolous device on the margin, or in the typography of a book" was one of the

"pernicious vagaries induced by a condition of the mental faculties
. . . bidding defiance to anything like analysis or explanation."[75] While
this preoccupation with the physical properties of discourse reflects
the narrator's madness, ludic lunacy of this sort, as John Kuehl
discloses, is standard fare in contemporary antirealism, which aspires
to unheard-of levels of transliteracy. As William Gass notes,

These days, the text is oozing out into the very shapes of the letters themselves . . . , out into the space of the print, into the nature of the page—in
placement, drawings, type size, binding, cover—into all the other items of
attribution and copyright and dedication which may have once been safely
'out of the book.' Nothing is now safely out of the book.[76]

But even earlier, a number of pre-McLuhan writers played with the
idea of the medium as the message.

Older typographical play was likeliest to be offered by a writer
familiar with the printing house. In "X-ing a Paragrab," Poe concocts
a tale in which all of the newspaper's o- fonts are stolen by a rival,
requiring the printer's devil to substitute an x for every o in all the
copy. The point of the tale is the comic illiteracy of a long paragraph
in which readers must decode such lines as: "Sx hx, Jxhn! hxw nxw!
Txld yxu sx, yxu knxw. Dxn't crxw, anxther time, befxre yxu're xut
xf the wxxds! . . ."[77] We no longer appreciate, as our grandfathers
did, the grotesquely illiterate spelling of the "phunny phellows" like
Petroleum V. Nasby (hence James's refusal of the dialect of Basil
Ransom). But they did help to initiate that comic play with orthography and typography which sometimes marks the highly inventive
artist. In *A Connecticut Yankee* (1889), Twain produces hilarity out of
illiterate errors in the Camelot *Weekly Hosannah and Literary Volcano*.
After Hank dynamites the blocked well, his feat is celebrated in
headlines where letters are reversed, printed upside down, and typos
proliferate: "HIGH TIMES IN THE VALLEY OF HOLINESS!"
reads one headline, "THE WATER-MORKS UNCORKED! . . . UN-
PARALLELED REJOIBINGS!"[78] These innocent printer's errors
only make more endearing one of the great democratic institutions
of American culture, print journalism, Twain believing that the news-
boy was one "greater than kings." Orthography and typography, thus
mangled, also prepare the way for the dadaist and surrealist nonsense in early modernism, which is replete with enigmas like Eliot's
DA syllables and "Co co rico" in *The Waste Land*. E. E. Cummings was

so taken with Picasso's disintegrated and rearranged images that he composed poems like "r-p-o-p-h-e-s-s-a-g-r" and praised the Spanish artist's beautiful, beyond wonder, murderings of reality—a fair description of what antirealism, in all its forms, undertakes to do.

The older full title page, containing a résumé of the novel itself (e.g., that of *Moll Flanders*) went out of fashion before fiction ever began to be written in America, but it does occasionally reappear. One such is Poe's *The Narrative of Arthur Gordon Pym of Nantucket. Comprising The Details of a Mutiny and Atrocious Butchery on Board of the American Brig Grampus, on Her Way to the South Seas—with an Account of the Recapture of the Vessel by the Survivors; Their Shipwreck, and Subsequent Horrible Sufferings, from Famine; Their Deliverance by Means of the British Schooner Jane Guy; The Brief Cruise of this Latter Vessel in the Antarctic Ocean; Her Capture, and of the Massacre of Her Crew; among a Group of Islands in the 84th Parallel of the Southern Latitude, together with the Incredible Adventures and Discoveries still further South, to which that Distressing Calamity gave Rise* (1838).

In addition, early American fiction offers a ludic repertory of anonymous and pseudonymous novels, many with playful titles, with and without dedications and prefaces (sometimes with two, three, and four of the latter), replete with prologues, epilogues, and epigraphs, illustrations, and even footnotes. Mostly these were seriously intended, but we may mention here, as instances of fictive play, the anonymous *Adventures of Jonathan Corncob, Loyal American Refugee* (1787) and the pseudonymous *A Journey to Philadelphia* (1804) by "Adelio." Game titles include James Butler's *Fortune's Foot-ball: or, the Adventures of Mercutio* (1798), the pseudonymous Frederick Augustus Fidaddy's *The Adventures of Uncle Sam, in Search after His Lost Honor* (1816), *A Pretty Story: Written in the Year of Our Lord 2774 by Peter Grievous, Esq., A.B.C.D.E.* (1774), and *The Life and Times of Father Quipes, otherwise Dominick O'Blarney. Written by Himself* (1820). The chapter epigraph was especially popular, Poe even inventing the epigraph quotation when the right one wasn't to hand. (No one will ever find the claim about the power of the will to overcome death, attributed to Glanville, prefixed to "Ligeia.") Mrs. E. D. E. N. Southworth loved to deal in improbabilities, made free with the asterisk, and footnoted anything bizarre by the simple declaration: "A Fact." I have already mentioned Dan Beard's illustration-likeness of Jay Gould, and perhaps it should be remarked that some illustrator-wag caused the first printing of *Adventures of Huckleberry Finn* to be stopped when Twain discovered that the figure of Silas Phelps, in the drawing, had an enormous erection. And of course many other kinds of games were played by, and on, authors in the nineteenth century.

More serious ludic play manifests itself in Poe's detective Dupin, who makes a game of reading the mind in "The Murders in the Rue Morgue" (1844). Dupin's wordless reconstruction of the thought processes of the narrator is advanced as the analytic means by which he solves his crimes. If Nabokov makes much of chess in *Lolita*, Poe regarded the game of whist as superior to the "elaborate frivolity" of chess."[79] Dupin, a whist player *par excellence*, is "the analyst in that moral activity which *disentangles*. He derives pleasure from even the most trivial occupations bringing his talents into play. He is fond of enigmas, of conundrums, of hieroglyphics; exhibiting in his solutions of each a degree of *acumen* which appears to the ordinary apprehension preternatural."[80] But in fact it is always the writer Poe who poses the enigmas, conundrums, and puzzles, especially in detective stories. The hermeneutic task of the analytic reader is to replicate the thought processes ascribed to Dupin and so deduce who done it before the crime is formally solved. In its way, then, the tale is for Poe a variety of literary clues encoded into the text, a game with the reader for the pleasure of his solving the crime.

James in "The Figure in the Carpet" (1896) also makes an interesting use of the idea of literature as a game. In that tale the author's concealed artistic intention—"the particular thing" Hugh Vereker has written his books "most *for*"—is figured not only as a design in the carpet of his complete works but as a Nabokovian chess game in which the narrator vies with Corvick and Miss Erme to solve the aesthetic puzzle posed by the author. The narrator remarks that the hours Corvick spent studying Vereker's works

were present to my fancy as those of a chess-player bent with a silent scowl, all the lamplit winter, over his board and his moves. As my imagination filled it out the picture held me fast. On the other side of the table was a ghostlier form, the faint figure of an antagonist [Vereker] good-humouredly but a little wearily secure—an antagonist who leaned back in his chair with his hands in his pockets and a smile on his fine clear face. Close to Corvick, behind him, was a girl who had begun to strike me as pale and wasted and even, on more familiar view, as rather handsome, and who rested on his shoulder and hung on his moves. He would take up a chessman and hold it poised a while over one of the little squares, and then would put it back in its place with a long sigh of disappointment.

The narrator never learns the secret key to Vereker's work. But, for James, writing—a gamble for immortality itself—was more than a game: "[L]iterature was a game of skill, and skill meant courage, and courage meant honour, and honour meant passion, meant life."[81] Whether the literary games played with (or on) the reader by the postmodern writer involve such high stakes or evoke such authorial virtues John Kuehl's readers will discover below.

One of the most popular early literary games was the hoax. Poe's *The Journal of Julius Rodman* (1840), with its fictitious account of "the first passage across the Rocky Mountains ever achieved by a civilized man," had them going for a while. In "The Unparalleled Adventures of One Hans Pfaall" (1835), the hero, to escape his creditors, takes off for the moon. The tale is remarkable for the verisimilitude of Poe's astronomical information, although astute readers will understand what is meant when Hans remarks that his balloon was inflated by "gas never yet generated by any other person than myself."[82] More convincing was "The Balloon-Hoax" (1844), Poe's fabricated news of a transatlantic crossing in a balloon in three days that had credulous New Yorkers agog.

Perhaps Poe's most elaborate hoax occurs in self-reflexive *Pym* (1838). There Pym narrates the tale of a fantastic voyage in which he and the dwarf Dirk Peters, a hybrid of mixed race and perhaps hermaphroditic too (thus adumbrating postmodern experiments with androgyny) survive a storm at sea that kills the crew; encounter another ship wholly manned by dead men; engage in cannibalism; and end up rushing in a small boat toward the chasmic vortex, a hole at the South Pole. This bizarre novel has a Preface by "Arthur Gordon Pym," the rhythm of whose name suggests Edgar Allan Poe, as well as "Imp" (of the Perverse). Nor can we fail to miss that the reflexive Pym's voyage set out from *Edgartown*. Pym notifies us that he was induced to compose the tale by several gentlemen of Richmond, among them "Mr. Poe, lately editor of the Southern Literary Messenger, a monthly magazine, published by Mr. Thomas W. White, in the city of Richmond." As Pym recounts it, Poe and White (a real publisher) were doubtful that the story would be received by the public as factual. And Poe proposed

that I should allow him to draw up, in his own words, a narrative of the earlier portion of my adventures, from facts afforded by myself, publishing it in the Southern Messenger *under the garb of fiction.* To this, perceiving no objection, I consented, stipulating only that my real name should be retained. Two numbers of the pretended fiction appeared, consequently, in the Messenger for January and February (1837), and, in order that it might certainly be regarded as fiction, the name of Mr. Poe was affixed to the articles in the table of contents of the magazine.[83]

Presenting the factual narrative as fiction was thus an inverted ruse initially perpetrated to secure a reading from a public too skeptical to receive the report as factual. But, according to Pym, "the public were still not at all disposed to receive it as fable, and several letters were sent to Mr. P.'s address, distinctly expressing a conviction to the contrary." At this Pym concludes that the facts of his narrative are such as "to carry with them sufficient evidence of their own authenticity," and he publicly acknowledges that *he* is the author and not Poe.

So fantastic is the narrative and so abrupt is its conclusion that Poe appended a "Note" to "Pym's" story. In this appendix, as putative editor, Poe laments that the now-deceased Pym never provided the final two or three chapters, questions the geographical description of the island of Tslal, and offers etymological analysis of several hieroglyphs with Ethiopian or Arabic verbal roots. Although the first two installments were published under his name, as fiction, editor Poe remarks that *he* is not going to complete the narrative, owing to "the general inaccuracy of the details afforded him, and his disbelief in the entire truth of the latter portions of the narration." His final remark is that unless the dwarf Dirk Peters, now missing in Illinois, can be induced to come forward and verify the facts, the whole narrative must be accounted a fraud on the public.[84]

But such ludic mixtures of fact and fancy merely bring up to date hoaxes like those contained in Irving's *A History of New York* (1809), which concocts a fictitious Diedrich Knickerbocker to narrate the events of Dutch New Amsterdam in a comic burlesque. In *The Sketch Book* (1819), Irving this time passes himself off as the fictitious Geoffrey Crayon, who merely prints the tale of "Rip Van Winkle," which was composed by the late Diedrich Knickerbocker, who then must be doubly fictitious, the whole suggesting the infinite regress of much postmodern writing.

If most novels feature a hero or heroine moving toward some rational denouement like marriage or manhood, *premodern* antirealism —like the postmodern novels analyzed in this book—often features an absurd quest where the ordeals faced by the protagonist eventuate in no achieved wisdom for either the protagonist or the reader. The viewpoint of existential absurdity is a more or less recent phenomenon, but that does not mean that previous American quest novels always had a purposeful goal. Possibly the best early pointless quest novel in America was Hugh Henry Brackenridge's *Modern Chivalry* (1792), a satire modeled on Cervantes's rambling romance (but filtered through *Tristram Shandy, Tom Jones,* Rabelais, Le Sage, and Swift). Brackenridge breezily offers us "a book without thought, or the smallest degree of sense" and therefore "useful to young minds, not fatiguing their understandings, and easily introducing a love of reading and study." The novel features a whimsical Captain Farrago and his bog-trotting sidekick, the rogue Teague O'Regan, "whose very name imports what he was." About the countryside they ride, often getting into scrapes, with the illiterate Teague improbably elected to learned societies, invited to presidential levees, and so forth. If this seems unreal, such was the ridiculous elevation of the incompetent, in the new egalitarian nation, that Brackenridge stoutly insists on the truth of Teague's successes. Narrative chapters alternate, as in *Tom Jones,* with chapters "Containing Reflections," and in these latter Farrago wildly attacks all the objects of Brackenridge's spleen—the leveling democratic mob, incompetent doctors, shyster lawyers, hypocritical men of the cloth, veterans, politicians, Indians, Negroes, and others. As the two ride about, tales are episodically strung together, and these tales are mixed in with other genres like sermons, orations, Hudibrastic poems, anecdotes with Latin tags, and (prefiguring Sorrentino's *Mulligan Stew*) even book reviews of earlier editions of *Modern Chivalry*—the whole constituting no plot whatsoever and the book heading for no conceivable ending. (Indeed, to the first four volumes of *Modern Chivalry* [1792–1797], Brackenridge added more material in 1804 and 1805, then appended even more episodes in 1815, and undertook additional revisions for the 1819 edition. Thus the tale might have gone on and on, like Pound's *Cantos*, had not Brackenridge died in 1816 a justice of the Pennsylvania Supreme Court.)

In the best postmodern fashion, Brackenridge claims that the one thing needful for his contemporaries was "some great master of style" who should "give an example of good language in his composition, which might serve as a model to future speakers and writers," and thus fix orthography, diction, idiom, syntax, and so forth. For that reason he undertook *Modern Chivalry*, observing "I shall consider language only, not in the least regarding the matter of the work." If he will "pay no regard to the idea," it is only because "it is not in the power of human ingenuity to attain two things perfectly at once" and "to expect good language and good sense, at the same time, is absurd, and not in the compass of common nature to produce." Since his book is intended "to speak nonsense," he feels out of the reach of carping critics. But by the end of Volume 3, Brackenridge is reflexively irked that his work has not made much noise and so bursts out:

Will nobody attack it, and prove that it is insipid, libelous, treasonable, immoral, or irreligious? If they will not do this, let them do something else, praise it, call it excellent, say it contains wit, erudition, genius, and the Lord knows what? Will nobody speak? What? Ho! are ye all asleep in the hold down there at Philadelphia? Will none of you abuse, praise, reprobate, or commend this performance? It is ill usage; that is all I can say; and I will take my revenge in a short time unless the matter mends.[85]

I have already touched upon the absurdity of the quest in Poe's *Pym* (1838), where the narrative abruptly concluded as Pym and Peters are drawn, with terrific velocity, toward a maelstrom at the South Pole guarded by "a shrouded human figure, very far larger in its proportions than any dweller among men. And the hue of the skin of the figure was of the perfect whiteness of snow."[86] The inexplicability of the ending, with that image, has given Freudian critics, from Marie Bonaparte on down, a provocation to sexual ingenuities. And the survival of the protagonist has been explained by reference to the nineteenth-century geological theory that the poles were hollow, permitting the oceans to flow into a South Pole vortex and reemerge at the North Pole—Pym's evident, if improbable, mode of escape from death and return to Virginia. Others have accounted for the abrupt ending by Poe's having been sacked at *The Southern Literary Messenger*, grown tired of the novel-writing, and returned to the poem and the tale, his natural métier. However suggestive may be these explanations, the text as given emphasizes the voyage of life as marked by natural disasters, bloody violence and murder, mutiny, cannibalism, and supernatural terror, ending in incomprehensibility. These phenomena are enough, in themselves, to establish the link with the many postmodern antirealistic quests, analyzed by Kuehl, that end in utter absurdity.

Melville's *Moby-Dick* also involves quests surd and absurd. For the owners and most of the mariners, the rational quest involves wealth through loading the holds with spermaceti oil. For Ishmael, the voyage is a quest for reintegration into human brotherhood as he tries to disburden himself of homicidal and suicidal impulses. Ahab, on the other hand, is voyaging on an absurd revenge-quest to destroy the creature that sheared off his leg. To the Manichean Ahab, this creature incarnates God as a cosmic demon mixing inscrutable malice with evil (or at the very least his agent). Whichever, Ahab has committed himself to a titanic struggle against the universe. That Ahab's quest reflects a deranged monomania all the thoughtful mariners realize, even though none is strong enough to withstand the indomitable power of his sultanic authority. But all of these quests lead to the same annihilating image of snow, the white whale. The end of the tale, narrating the utter destruction of the *Pequod* (named after an exterminated Indian tribe), and of all of the mariners save Ishmael, makes plain the absurdity of Ahab's war with Heaven. But such is the power of Melville's narrative of the irrational quest for self-destruction, with its demonic motto *Ego non baptizo te in nomine Patris sed in nomine diaboli,* and such is the formal inventiveness by which this extraordinary narrative is presented, that it has had a significant impact on virtually every postmodern maximalist novel. As Kuehl has remarked below, in straightforward quest novels the quester returns, not merely because the tale must be told but because the meaning of his experience must be set forth by the author. In the first English edition of *Moby-Dick*, however, the epilogue—with its "AND I ONLY AM ESCAPED ALONE TO TELL THEE"—was inadvertently left off by the printer, with the effect that readers thought that

Ishmael had perished too, could not tell who told the story, and were mystified by what the tale meant—an absurd quest indeed!

Postmodern antirealism, as John Kuehl demonstrates, oscillates between maximalism and minimalism. In our literary origins, the maximalist impulse was gratified by nationalistic imitation epics like Mather's *Magnalia Christi Americana* (1702), Dwight's *The Conquest of Canaan* (1785), the *Anarchiad* (1787) of Trumbull and others, and Barlow's *Columbiad* (1807). Shortly thereafter, it became plain that the Miltonic epic was a dead duck and the maximalist impulse would have to be served by fiction. Early American novels often swelled to the popular two- or three-decker length, and the necessities of serialization and printing often dictated the prolongation of episodes, events, and chapters. The popularity of *Don Quixote* in America made long episodic fictions well received, as we see in Tabitha Tenney's *Female Quixotism: Exhibited in the Romantic Opinions and Extravagant Adventures of Dorcasina Sheldon* (1801), Brackenridge's *Modern Chivalry* (1815), Twain's *Adventures of Huckleberry Finn* (1885), and Bellow's *Adventures of Augie March* (1953). In the episodic novel, there is theoretically no limit to the number of episode-beads strung on the narrative thread of the quixotic hero's adventures. Furthermore, nineteenth-century calls for "the great American novel" that would encompass the whole of American experience sanctioned the blockbuster form. Thus was inaugurated the century of maximalist novels that run from Stowe's *Uncle Tom's Cabin* (1852), De Forest's *Miss Ravenel's Conversion from Secession to Loyalty* (1867), and Cable's *The Grandissimes* (1880) to blockbusters like Carl Sandburg's *Remembrance Rock* (1948) and any of Michener's latest effusions.

The ludic spirit often animated the older fiction writer so as to produce the gigantism of the maximalist novel, sometimes festooning it with encyclopedic learning, or learned wit, and, like *Modern Chivalry*, featuring a medley of genres, styles, and modes. Epical *Moby-Dick* (1851) remains our most impressive "national" book—its enormous scale evident not only through the larger-than-life protagonist Captain Ahab, his antagonist the white whale, and their vast ocean battleground, but also through a text containing 700-odd pages and

135 chapters. Those that provide scientific data were researched in Thomas Beale's *Natural History of the Sperm Whale;* Frederick Debell Bennett's *Narrative of a Whaling Voyage Round the Globe* ... ; J. Ross Browne's *Etchings of a Whaling Cruise;* William Scoresby, Jr.'s *An Account of the Arctic Regions;* and Owen Chase's *The Narrative . . . of the Whaleship Essex.*

Moby-Dick's aesthetic (that is, literary) data seem even more comprehensive. After a dedication to Hawthorne, four prefatory sections follow, half entitled ETYMOLOGY and half EXTRACTS. ETYMOLOGY One invokes "old lexicons and grammars," while Two offers dictionary definitions of whale, then spells the word in several languages, some of which Melville apparently made up. (Perhaps this, as well as the Polynesian gobbledygook of the native-mariners' speech—anticipates the glossolalia or invented foreign languages of several postmodern antirealists.) During the first EXTRACTS passage, we are introduced to an anonymous SUB-SUB-LIBRARIAN, who, presumably supplied the eighty quotations drawn from various sources which fill the long second segment, likewise marked EXTRACTS, and which prefigure the countless epigraphs flooding later postmodern encyclopedic tomes. In addition, Melville's style is a mixture of genre-busting elements. While opening with a first-person narration, the novel then drops Ishmael for the third-person angle, then oscillates between the prosaic and the poetic ("The Sunset" chapter scans as verse), and offers scenic doses of maritime theater. (Asides are frequent; chapter 29 is entitled "Enter Ahab, to Him, Stubb"; chapter 40 is entirely in dialogue with named speeches; and the Epilogue concludes with Ishmael's saying "the drama's done.")

Charles Feidelson, Jr., has discussed the literature that helped to shape *Moby-Dick:*

In his childhood he had been thoroughly schooled in the Bible. Aside from his contemporaries, Scripture probably exercised the largest single influence on *Moby-Dick.* . . . Melville's awareness of Scripture was often colored by his reading of *Paradise Lost.* . . . As models of the epic in addition to *Paradise Lost,* he knew—or at least possessed copies of—the *Divine Comedy,* Homer (in Pope's translation), and the *Aeneid.* But next to the Bible, Shakespeare's plays were most in Melville's mind when he conceived his masterpiece.

Besides Shakespeare, Beaumont and Fletcher, and Marlowe and Jonson, Melville "had a taste for old, rambling, discursive books full of oddities," whose "encyclopedic and digressive" tendencies *Moby-Dick* shares as heir to the "Tradition of Learned Wit" and Menippean satire: *Gargantua and Pantagruel*, Montaigne's *Essays*, *Anatomy of Melancholy*, *Religio Medici*, and so forth. Also "he was building up a library of romanticism" both English and German, "at this time," a library that included influences like Byron, Carlyle, de Quincey, and Goethe.[87] Whereas early American readers rejected the obscene, scatological, and sexually explicit (so evident in decadent European writers such as Rabelais, Burton, Goethe, and Byron), Melville—adumbrating postmodernists like Pynchon—generates considerable sexual comedy out of the "homosexual wedding" of Ishmael and Queequeg, the sperm-squeezing scene, and the six-foot penis of the whale ("The Cassock").

Erudite allusions pepper the Melville text from chapter 1—which refers to Ishmael, Cato the Younger, Poseidon, Narcissus, the Stoics, I Timothy 6:10, Pythagoras, the three Fates—to the Epilogue, which mentions Ixion and bears the Biblical epigraph, "AND I ONLY AM ESCAPED ALONE TO TELL THEE" (Job 1:15). Complementing the occasional authorial footnotes are numerous annotations furnished by later editors. Thus in the Feidelson edition, ten-page chapter 99, "The Doubloon," receives thirty-seven commentaries!

The scope of maximalist novels like *Moby-Dick* is such that it could easily incorporate a minimalist novel, and indeed is authorized to do so by early romance collections, for example, the *Heptameron*. Both Cervantes and Fielding include novellas in their maximalist novels. And a good case can be made that Thomas Wolfe is best read in those *nouvelles* that C. Hugh Holman, in *The Short Novels of Thomas Wolfe* (1961), has surgically excised from the mass of verbiage constituting Wolfe's incoherent published novels. By the late eighteenth century, the total separation of the *novella, nouvelle,* short novel, or novelette from the form of the full-length novel was complete. Henry James characteristically refers to it as "the blest *nouvelle*," for it permitted him and others a fuller development of character and situation than the tale itself can offer. Hence, we have had a long succession of minimalist novels ordinarily discussed as *nouvelles*, works like *Billy Budd*, (1924), *The Turn of the Screw* (1898), Wharton's tetralogy *Old New York* (1924), Bellow's *Seize the Day* (1956), and so forth. *The Red Badge of Courage* is one of the most successful, Crane combining stripped-down characters, combat adventure, and a doubtful initiation into manhood with pictorial language, like the notorious image: "The red sun was pasted in the sky like a wafer." And Hemingway, elucidating an iceberg theory of fiction, according to which seven-eighths of the narrative matter can safely be submerged beneath the lines, won the Nobel Prize for *The Old Man and the Sea* (1952).

Since Kuehl has explored the extent to which postmodern antirealists blend historical fact with wild invention, it is worth remarking here that Irving treats the colonial past in burlesque terms, in *A History of New York* (1809), thereby offering postmodern writers an analogue, if not a source, for the parodic treatment of the genre of history writing. Although the madcap Irving did considerable research in order to recreate the factual basis of the Dutch colony, narrating the story of the old governors like Peter Stuyvesant in generally accurate fashion, his history is in fact as much fictitious as documented and, in its mixture of styles and genres, anticipates modern forms such as Barth's *The Sot-Weed Factor* (1960) and Mailer's *Armies of the Night* (1968). Likewise, the historical romance from Cooper onward blended historical fact and auctorial fancy in varying amounts, sometimes claiming that the invented parts of the tale made for a higher truth, sometimes disclaiming any responsibility whatsoever because the author is not the author. In *Satanstoe* (1845), *The Chainbearer* (1845), and *The Redskins* (1846) Cooper delivers himself of the most adventitious personal opinions while denying in his Prefaces that he is at all guilty of any bias and claiming that he has no responsibility for what characters say or do, real or fictitious:

In the first place, we do not pretend to be answerable for all the opinions of those whose writings are submitted to our supervision [Cooper is the ostensible "editor" of the Littlepage Manuscripts], any more than we should be answerable for all the contradictory characters, impulses, and opinions that might be exhibited in a representation of fictitious characters, purely of our own creation.[88]

The Leatherstocking Tales also interweave actual historical information, easily documented, with authorial invention—*The Last of the Mohicans: A Narrative of 1757* (1826), for example, intermixing details from the actual massacre at Fort William Henry, by the Indians under Montcalm, with quasi-supernatural events in the deep forest, involving prophecies, tribal totems, men metamorphosed into animals, and invocations to the Great Manitou.

Twain, on the other hand, detested the historical romance, as practiced by Scott and Cooper, and burlesqued it in *The Prince and the Pauper* (1882). He also parodied elegiac verse and graveyard poetry in Miss Emmeline's mortuarial effusions in *Huck Finn*, ridiculed the genre of escape literature like *The Man in the Iron Mask* in the tale of Jim's "evasion" in *Huck Finn*, and lambasted the chivalric fairy tale in which the Noble Knight rescues the Royal Princess. (Sandy, in *A Connecticut Yankee*, cannot see that their "porcine highnesses" are really just hogs and not noble maidens under a spell.) In this novel, Twain mixed fact and fancy with hilarious abandon. The novel began with Twain's dream of being

a knight errant in armor in the middle ages. Have the notions & habits of thought of the present day mixed with the necessities of that. No pockets in the armor. No way to manage certain requirements of nature. Can't scratch. Cold in the head—can't blow—can't get at handkerchief, can't use iron sleeve. Iron gets red hot in the sun—leaks in the rain, gets white with frost & freezes me solid in winter. Suffer from lice & fleas. Make disagreeable clatter when I enter church. Can't dress or undress myself. Always getting struck by lighting. Fall down, can't get up.[89]

Twain ransacked Lecky's *A History of European Morals*, Forneron's *The Court of Charles II*, and Taine's *The Ancient Regime* in order to ground the work on historical actualities. But the facts merely provide Twain with multiple opportunities to indulge his wildly improbable fantasies. Thus we see Hank setting up the Kingdom on a capitalist basis, inventing electricity, factories, printing presses, telephones, and gatling guns. He organizes the mailed and belted knights into baseball teams and mounts them on bicycles as travelling salesmen, complete with sandwich signs advertising his new toothpaste. Intermixed with these improbabilities are dramatizations of historical actualities including peasant life, affairs at court, and the ecclesiastical Inquisition.

Other older narratives mixing historical fact and authorial fancy include Simms's *The Yemassee* (1835), Hawthorne's *The Scarlet Letter* (1850), and Meville's *Billy Budd* (1924), the latter drawing extensively on the naval court of inquiry into the *Somers* mutiny. Crane's "The

Open Boat"—which he called "A Tale Intended to be after the Fact: Being the Experience of Four Men from the Sunk Steamer 'Commodore' "—adumbrates the new journalism of Tom Wolfe, Capote, and Mailer; we might even call it the first nonfiction short story.

In the field of older historical fiction, the *setting* of such stories is not as commonly fictitious as the characters. To name a real place in traditional fiction was thought of as a commitment to the task of representing it, at least in some measure. James's remark about Balzac does well enough in accounting for what the older novel tried, in its setting, to do. In representing a *ville de province*, James wrote, Balzac "tackled no group of appearances, no presented face of the social organism (conspicuity thus attending it), *but* to make something of it. To name it simply and not in some degree tackle it would have seemed to him an act reflecting on his general course the deepest dishonour."[90]

Even so, there are many instances in early American fiction of writers who created alternate worlds and invented imaginary landscapes. As Kuehl observes, some alternate worlds are disguised actual places, some have the names of real places but are so bizarre as to accent the invention, and some settings are utterly fantastic. In the first category, disguised actual places, England became Dominora and the United States became Vivenza in Melville's *Mardi;* in the Leatherstocking Tales, Cooperstown became Templeton; Hannibal, Missouri, became St. Petersburg in Twain's *Adventures of Huckleberry Finn;* Port Jervis, New York, became Whilomville in *Whilomville Stories* (1960); Clyde, Ohio, became Winesburg in *Winesburg, Ohio* (1919) and Oxford, Mississippi, became Jefferson in *As I Lay Dying* (1930). At times the actual fades into the fanciful with cavalier abandon, and fancy impersonates reality when the writer affects even a cartographic description. The author of *Absalom, Absalom!* (1936) draws us a map of the mythical Yoknapatawpha County ("William Faulkner, Proprietor"). And Anderson gives us a map of the street-layout of Winesburg in the novel. To divert attention from its being Clyde, Ohio (although the map lists some real Clyde businesses), Anderson claimed that Winesburg was a mythical town, only to discover (after book publication) that there was a *real* Winesburg, Ohio, that the inhabitants of the place "declared the book immoral," and that they insisted that "the actual inhabitants of the real Winesburg were a highly moral people."[91]

In the second category, a number of older fictional settings have the names of real places but are so bizarre that we invariably understand them to be projections of a peculiar imagination. Charles Brockden Brown's plague-stricken Philadelphia in *Arthur Mervyn* (1798) seems more of a gothic charnel house than a represented city, while Poe blended sites that never were on land or sea with equally make-believe ones called Hungary, Venice, London, Paris, and Toledo. So valuable were the horrific associations of Walpole's *The Castle of Otranto* that, in *The Asylum; or, Alonzo and Melissa* (1811), Isaac Mitchell imprisons his heroine in a moldering gothic castle—set, improbably enough, on Long Island Sound. Then, recognizing that the reader might have a natural sightseer's curiosity about the old pile, Mitchell contrived to explain how the castle was destroyed after the American Revolution—thus preventing the idle from looking it up. (How a medieval castle could have been built in the New World, before the discovery of America, Mitchell does not say and could care less.)

In *Typee* (1846) and *Omoo* (1847), Melville likewise created a group of Pacific islands so incredible to his well-read audience, that, with *Mardi* (1849), "the thought occurred to me, of indeed writing a romance of Polynesian adventure, and publishing it as such; to see whether the fiction might not, possibly, be received for a verity: in some degree the reverse of my previous experience."[92] Hawthorne's forests are invariably allegorical sites of the encounter with evil (à la Dante and Bunyan). In "Young Goodman Brown" (1835) the setting might as well be the unconscious mind of the author or title character as any real copse outside of Boston.

In fact, the romance regularly sought to blur the distinction between the real and the invented place by discovering a neutral territory, a place like unto a reality that we know but markedly different. In *The Scarlet Letter* Hawthorne defined the proper setting of the romance as resembling his study, where the objects of the room, illuminated at night by the fire and moonlight, are "so spiritualized by the unusual light, that they seem to lose their actual substance, and become things of the intellect." The child's shoe and the doll are "invested with a quality of strangeness and remoteness, though still almost as vividly present as by daylight. Thus, therefore, the floor of our familiar room has become a neutral territory, somewhere between the real world and fairy-land, where the Actual and the Imaginary may meet, and each imbue itself with the nature of the other."[93] Hester's Boston, Zenobia's Blithedale, Irving's Sleepy Hollow, and Poe's Toledo are just such "fairy precincts," the term Hawthorne used for the Italy of *The Marble Faun* (1860).

The third type of setting in earlier fiction, the utterly fantastic place, most often occurs in science fiction stories. In American writing, such settings may be either utopian (like Jeff Hayes's *Paradise on Earth* [1913]), or dystopian (like the destroyed world of Jack London's *The Scarlet Plague* [1915]). Lost tribes, hidden valleys, and societies living in the interior of the earth predominate. The moon, Mars, and other planets are favorite exotic landscapes—as in George Tucker's *A Voyage to the Moon* (1827), G. W. Pope's *Journey to Mars* (1894), and Mark Ticks's *To Mars via the Moon* (1911). Most of these feature formulaic adventures, mixed with social satire, typical of the Tralfamadorian novels of postmodern antirealist Kurt Vonnegut—*The Sirens of Titan* (1959) and *Slaughter-House Five* (1969). Poe knew Tucker's work, and *Pym* was clearly derived from *Symzonia: A Voyage of Discovery* (1820), a celebration of democracy and other social ideas doubtless written by John C. Symmes of Ohio. It was Symmes who proposed in 1818 that the hollow earth could be entered through a hole. "Symmes's Hole," one of the pseudoscientific jokes of the century, sparked a number of science fictions set in Antarctica, including (besides Poe's *Pym*) James DeMille's *A Strange Manuscript Found in a Copper Cylinder* (1888), William Bradshaw's *The Goddess of Atvatabar* (1892), and Robert A. Bennet's *Thyra: A Romance of the Polar Pit* (1901). Some of them even resurrect Pym, as living now in the interior of the earth. As Karl Mannheim has remarked in *Ideology and Utopia* (1929), utopias represent "situationally transcendent ideas" that express "unrealized and unfulfilled tendencies" of the age and so dramatize the feared or hoped-for condition, whether projected spatially in Edenic or nightmarish settings or temporarily in dream visions or time travel back to a golden age or forward into a hideous future.[94]

Cantell A. Bigly's *Aurifodina; or, Adventures in the Golden Region* (1849) finds utopia in the Western wilderness, as does W. H. Bishop in *Garden of Eden, U.S.A.* (1895), both glorifications of American democratic freedoms. R. Elton Smile's *The Manatitlans* (1877), on the other hand, creates a Paraguay as exotic as that of Donald Barthelme, complete with a miniaturized human race living in the petals and pistils of a flower. Inez Haynes Gillmore and Charlotte Perkins Gilman perpetrate feminist utopias in *Angel's Island* (1914) and *Herland* (1915), respectively, Gilman's featuring a lost world without men— where women, thank Heaven, reproduce parthenogenetically. And William Dean Howells indulged his Christian Socialist fantasies about absolute brotherhood in *A Traveller from Altruria* (1894) and *Through the Eye of the Needle* (1907). But of these subliterary works we need only say that the older dystopian imagination underlies the tradition of fantastic settings we discover in contemporary American antirealism.

Many of the older American utopias attacked current social and economic conditions, which were viewed as irrational, inhuman, or otherwise destructive to human well-being. On the whole, however, they assumed the rationality of the world, and the inevitability of melioration if only, say, the Socialists got the power. Few early American writers were so despairing as to consider the world itself as governed by insanity. But if contemporary antirealists find in the insane asylum a figure for the condition of the world, they are simply following metaphoric possibilities first developed by a few American predecessors. Kesey and Hawkes, for example, present us as readers with the same problem faced by the narrator of Poe's "The System of Dr. Tarr and Prof. Fether" (1845). He fancies that his "long acquaintance with the metaphysics of *mania*" has taught him to separate the sane from the insane and to detect how madmen disguise their illness by a show of rational lucidity. In this tale, the narrator's grand tour brings him to the neighborhood of "a certain *Maison de Santé*, or private Mad-House," about which he had heard much, in Paris, from his medical friends. Securing a letter of introduction to Monsieur Maillard, who runs the asylum, he enters the "fantastic *château*, much dilapidated, and indeed scarcely tenantable through age and neglect" which naturally fills him "with absolute dread." Still, he is avid to see this progressive institution where patients "were left much apparent liberty" and were "permitted to roam about the house and grounds, in the ordinary apparel of persons in right mind." To cure a patient's delusion, the "soothing system" is employed: a delusion is encouraged by the doctor to the point where even the madman sees it as ridiculously delusional and so renounces it. The policies of M. Maillard also include setting "each lunatic to guard the actions of all the others," for "to repose confidence in the understanding or discretion of a madman, is to gain him body and soul." M. Maillard, in the most lucid and engaging manner, apologetically explains to the narrator, at a dinner held in his honor, that the "soothing system" has unfortunately been changed to one of conventional restraint because some lunatics had recently tried to overthrow the system and to imprison the keepers. Throughout the dinner, the relatives of M. Maillard seem exceedingly odd to the narrator. But, on the theory that everyone has his eccentricities, and besides this is France, the narrator fails to realize that the revolution had indeed *already succeeded:* the lunatics have now replaced the staff and imprisoned the keepers. The lunatic who had instigated the earlier revolt was in fact M. Maillard himself, the former superintendent of the asylum, who had himself gone mad and so become a patient. The resolution of the tale, which involves the "real" staff violently regaining control of the asylum, suggests the thin line that separates sanity from insanity and the madness of some methods of treating the insane. If one cannot tell the sane from the insane, the implication is inescapable that the world itself is a madhouse.[95]

The suspicion that irrationality lies at the heart of experience—so common in the postmodern antirealism analyzed by John Kuehl—is closely allied to paranoid delusions of persecution and to the terror of believing that we are victims of some enormous conspiracy. The conspiracy theme that Kuehl elaborates is an old one. Puritan writers were perfectly confident of one gigantic conspiracy—that of Satan, who roamed the earth, going to and fro, seeking whom he could devour, seducing men into the corruptions of disbelief. Cotton Mather, for one, asked his Boston congregation "How many doleful Wretches, have been decoy'd into *Witchcraft* it self, by the opportunities which their *Discontent* has given the *Devil*, to visit 'em and seduce 'em?"

Moreover, even Indian warfare was a conspiracy of Satan, who was incarnate in the Red Man: "The *Devils* are stark mad, that the *House of the Lord our God,* is come into these Remote Corners of the World; and they fume, they fret prodigiously." By the time of the Age of Reason, however, recourse to satanic conspiracies subsided. Thomas Paine spoke for his countrymen in remarking about the revolutionary battles with England that "Neither have I so much of the infidel in me, as to suppose that [God Almighty] has relinquished the government of the world, and given us up to the care of devils."[96]

On the whole, then, dark conspiracies in American fiction since the Revolution are local and usually involve English espionage (as in Cooper's *The Spy* [1821]) or secret societies like the Jesuits (as in Hawthorne's *The Marble Faun* or Frederic's *The Damnation of Theron Ware*), the Bavarian Illuminati (as in *Wieland* [1798]), or the Masons (in "The Cask of Amontillado"). But early army life also came to arouse paranoid feelings. In *The Red Badge of Courage,* Henry is described as caught in "a mighty blue machine," and, as he runs with the regiment, he feels that he is trapped in a moving box, enclosed by "the iron laws of tradition." His mechanical firing suggests that overtone of naturalistic determinism in which the individual is always acted upon by conspiratorial forces beyond his control. A similar sense of an insane conspiracy arises in Hemingway's world, where senseless war is the recurrent figure of the human condition. In Lt. Frederick Henry's chaotic retreat from Caporetto, in *A Farewell to Arms,* we see a style of paranoia that is fully fleshed out in Joseph Heller's *Catch-22:* all is *nada.* Emerson paradoxically sets the tone for most of these institutional conspiracies by indicting society itself as "in conspiracy against the manhood of every one of its members."[97]

The paranoid idea of some vast conspiracy enters prominently into many of Poe's stories, for he specialized in the deranged intellection of madmen. In "The Imp of the Perverse" (1845) Poe's insane murderer finds the conspiracy against mankind to have been fomented by God, who implanted in us a perverse propensity for self-destruction, here personified as "The Imp of the Perverse." But a moment later the madman is certain that "this overwhelming tendency to do wrong for wrong's sake" represents "a direct instigation of the archfiend."[98] God or Satan—it makes little difference to the paranoid.

Melville's doubts also devolve into a paranoid "desperado philosophy" in *Moby-Dick*, where he theorizes that the ills that afflict man—particularly "this whole voyage of the Pequod, and the great White Whale its object"—may be effects of a cosmic conspiracy plotted by God, the Cosmic Joker. "There are certain queer times and occasions in this strange mixed affair we call life when a man takes this whole universe for a vast practical joke, though the wit thereof he but dimly discerns, and more than suspects that the joke is at nobody's expense but his own."[99] And, as we have seen, the deranged late Twain saw all life as a nightmare conspiracy against man by a satanic God. A saving sanity inheres in one of Frost's unnamed couplets from *In The Clearing* (1962): "Forgive, O Lord, my little jokes on thee, / And I'll forgive thy great big joke on me." But this wholesome reconciliation to fate is usually absent from the postmodern imagination.

It is but a small step from the view that life is a nightmare of insane horrors to the view that the world deserves annihilation—the theme that climaxes Kuehl's superb study of the postmodern imagination. Even in this feeling, antirealists arrogate unto themselves one of the powers of God, that of destruction. But if we ask whether there is anything new in the annihilation of humanity in Vonnegut's *Cat's Cradle* (1963) or Pynchon's *Gravity's Rainbow* (1973), the answer would appear to be no. Certainly, their destructive rage is not unique in American writing.

It is true that the preoccupation with entropy in the apocalypticists West, Pynchon, and Gaddis hinges on a contemporary conception of the Second Law of Thermodynamics—a scientific idea rarely explored by previous literary pessimists. But the notion of continuous world deterioration does appear in the eighteenth century in Pierre Laplace's Nebular Hypothesis, according to which the burning gases of the sun are being self-consumed and the world is therefore condemned to increasing frigidity and eventual extinction. Poe was, in certain moods, confident of the gradual extinction of the world by this means, remarking in *Eureka* that "The Nebular Theory of Laplace has lately received far more confirmation than it needed, at the hands of the philosopher, Comte."[100] But in "The Power of Words" he claimed for the "Angelic intelligence" (that is, the writer's imagination) an entropic "power of retrogradation" that "is of course the prerogative of the Deity alone."[101] Shifting the ground from astronomy to biology, we note that, while nineteenth-century Darwinian science implied progress toward greater spirituality for the human animal, almost simultaneously it was recognized that, if life could evolve, it might also *devolve*: that an entropic regressionary atavism might terminate life in the original slime from which it had emerged. Frank Norris's *McTeague* (1899) and Jack London's *The Call of the Wild* (1903) both dramatize this backward motion toward the source.

But much more vivid than the world's ending in ice is its end in fire. The notion of Armageddon and the Apocalypse is rooted in American Christian thought, from the Puritans onward, and Edwards's "Sinners in the Hands of an Angry God" is only typical of a train of thought that saw annihilation as the appropriate culmination of man's having spoiled the purity of Creation and produced a fallen world. Such early writings as John Cotton's sermons, Edward Johnson's *Wonder-Working Providence* (1654), Michael Wigglesworth's *The Day of Doom* (1662), and Joseph Morgan's *The History of the Kingdom of Basaruah* (1715) inaugurate the tradition of American apocalypses.

Jay Martin has observed that "the sense of catastrophism recurs repeatedly in the history of consciousness, and the fear of the end of the world is an aspect of modern anxiety." But, as he remarks, "catastrophism had a particularly strong appeal in America through its association with the premillennial impulse which guaranteed a purposeful and fruitful catastrophe."[102] Indeed, as Charles Nordhoff remarked in *The Communist Societies of the United States* (1875), so widespread was the millenarian craze among the Zoarites, Shakers, Icarians, and other such religious cults that many appeared "to look forward with quite a singular pleasure to the fiery end of all things."[103]

Hawthorne satirized Armageddonism in "Earth's Holocaust" (1844) although the object of his ridicule there was as much the transcendental reformers as exotic Christian sects awaiting the Second Coming. In any case, the lust for otherworldly purification in the religious reformers of the time leads them to ignite a bonfire upon which they cast all of the worldly monuments of civilization and learning that have lifted man out of his age-old barbarism. The Devil appears at the end of the tale, his eyes glowing "with a redder light than that of the bonfire," to mock these reformers because they have forgotten to incinerate the human heart: "And, unless they hit upon some method of purifying that foul cavern, forth from it will re-issue all the shapes of wrong and misery—the same old shapes, or worse ones—which they have taken such a vast deal of trouble to consume to ashes."[104]

Melville's *Moby-Dick* likewise terminates in an apocalypse, as the catastrophic end of Ahab's hubris in daring to defy the Omnipotent. In this tale crippled Ahab becomes Antichrist, false prophet, apostate, Satan. He is repeatedly warned against pursuing the white whale, yet persists, though Fedallah, the Parsee, prophesies his death. Before Moby Dick appears, Ahab, undaunted by the lightning omen, challenges God, whom fire symbolizes. There ensues a three-day chase, ending with the drowning of captain and crew when the whale annihilates the *Pequod,* a ship that clearly symbolizes the federation of mankind. That this catastrophe has a positive aspect—that of renewal/rebirth (as found in all biblical apocalypses)—Melville makes clear, for Ishmael survives on Queequeg's "coffin life-buoy," which reflects the fellowship established between them back at the Spouter Inn. Whereas the monomaniacal Ahab abandons wife and child, then leads the whole crew to their doom, the humanistic Ishmael, having borne witness, reports these perverted acts.

Moby-Dick offers us what might be called a local apocalypse. But toward the end of the nineteenth century, entropic notions of the inevitable decay and deterioration of culture were often accompanied by prophecies of the end of all life. Brooks Adams's *The Law of Civilization and Decay* (1895), Max Nordau's *Degeneration* (1895), Henry Adams's *The Education of Henry Adams* (1907), and Spengler's *The Decline of the West* (1918) all announced the end of the world, whether by bang or whimper, or at least the end of Western civilization, a pessimism that finds its way into the early T. S. Eliot's work. Much of the theme of degeneration hinged upon a popular notion of entropy, but as Jay Martin has remarked, there was some resistance to the entropic idea underlying this widespread pessimism. "Irritated by Adams's insistence on degradation, for instance, William James pronounced the Second Law of Thermodynamics irrelevant to human history, asserting that, to the contrary, 'there is nothing in physics to interfere with the hypothesis that the penultimate state might be the millennium.' "[105] But James's was a minority view swallowed up in the anti-Christian pessimism of the times.

In *A Connecticut Yankee,* Hank Morgan tries to create a millenial kingdom in Camelot, featuring all the scientific marvels of nine-teenth-century physics. Twain even goes so far as to name "the crea-tors of this world—after God" as "Guttenberg [inventor of the print-ing press], Watt [steam engine], Arkwright [cotton spinner], Whitney [cotton gin, firearms], Morse [telegraph], Stephenson [locomotive], Bell [telephone]."[106] But, despite his scientific know-how, Morgan is unable to alter human nature, defeat superstition, and nullify tradi-tional religion. Condemned as a godless heretic by the Inquisition, Hank, aided only by his friend Clarence and fifty-two boys, defeats sixth-century English chivalry at the Battle of the Sand-Belt (Arma-geddon) through fire (dynamite, electrified fences, gatling guns) and water (a diverted mountain brook). However, the postscript suggests that this victory was Pyrrhic, since the disguised Merlin soon enchants Hank ("Ye were conquerors; ye are conquered!) and dies laughing. The resultant ambiguity leads David Ketterer, in "Epoch-Eclipse and Apocalypse: Special 'Effects' in *A Connecticut Yankee*," to conclude that "[T]he apocalyptic solution implied in *A Connecticut Yankee*" and else-where "is that all reality is a dream."[107]

That longing for the termination of the universe, because all exis-tence is a nightmare, we find in many of Poe's works. And with Poe this introduction must conclude. For, as Allen Tate has rightly re-marked, Poe is thus the "man we must return to: a figure of transi-tion, who retains a traditional insight into a disorder that has since become typical, without being able himself to control it."[108] In "The Fall of the House of Usher," the madman Roderick deteriorates, like his house, in an entropic "kingdom of inorganization"[109] and col-lapses into the miasmic tarn. The entropic sense is also evident in three of Poe's dialogues, "The Colloquy of Monos and Una" (1841), "The Conversation of Eiros and Charmion" (1839), and "The Power of Words" (1845). (All three are revelations of post-Holocaust con-sciousness.) In the first, "the Earth's records had taught [Monos] to look for widest ruin as the price of highest civilization" so that he "could anticipate no regeneration save in death."[110] In the second, we learn that it was a comet that caused the end of the world in "a combustion, irresistible, all-devouring, omni-prevalent, immediate;— the entire fulfillment, in all their minute and terrible details, of the fiery and horror-inspiring denunciations of the prophecies of the Holy book," with "the whole incumbent mass of ether in which we existed, burst[ing] at once into a species of intense flame, for whose surpassing brilliancy and all-fervid heat even the angels in the high Heaven of pure knowledge have no name."[111] But in the third post-Holocaust dialogue, "The Power of Words," the artist as God has now, through his language alone, called another physical world, a better star, into being.

These dialogues anticipate the full-scale decreationism of *Eureka* (1848), where the Newtonian-Laplacean universe, being at the maximum point of diffusion, is beginning to contract back again into the original unity of God's Oneness: *"In the Original Unity of the First Thing lies the Secondary Cause of All Things, with the Germ of their Inevitable Annihilation"*[112]—an annihilation, for this romantic antihumanist, devoutly wished yet morbidly feared. Even so, as Daniel Hoffman has remarked, "Poe must extinguish the entire world. He must consume it in fire."[113]

It is the condition of the romantic imagination continually to call, as Emerson did, for the "transfer of the world into the consciousness."[114] For Emerson, the subjectivization of actuality merely confirmed an objective truth—"a rule of one art, or a law of organization," that essential unity underlying all forms of existence.[115] For Poe and other antirealists, however, the incorporation of the world into consciousness is a desperate effort to resolve the "inorganization" of the world into a unity seemingly provided only by imagination. Poe's solipsistic sense of the fragmentation of the world and his imaginative effort to reunify it is conceptually akin to the pluralistic universe of William James and Henry Adams, where, as *The Education* puts it, "Chaos was the law of nature; Order was the dream of man."[116] The view that world order is a human invention leads directly to the aestheticism of the fictive heterocosms of contemporary antirealists like Burroughs, Coover, and Hawkes. Wallace Stevens best formulated this aesthetic skepticism that emerges out of the loss of a sense of order in the twentieth century.

The paramount relation . . . between modern man and modern art is simply this: that in an age in which disbelief is so profoundly prevalent . . . , the arts in general, are, in their measure, a compensation for what has been lost. Men feel that the imagination is the next greatest power to faith: the reigning prince. Consequently their interest in the imagination and its work is to be regarded not as a phase of humanism but as a vital self-assertion in a world in which nothing but the self remains, if that remains.[117]

Once a conception of a real *universe*, exterior and anterior to consciousness, was lost, the imagination came to be a substitute for faith, a religion of art came to substitute for revelation, and an abandoned humanism disappeared into a mere aesthetic self-assertion. At least, for the modernists, art was some kind of compensation for lost certitude. Something of that modernist aestheticism survives into the postmodern imagination. But increasingly, the situation of the postmodern writer, as we shall see in Kuehl's account, is like that described by Ronald Sukenick: not even literature is the compensation that it once was:

The contemporary writer . . . is forced to start from scratch: Reality doesn't exist, time doesn't exist, personality doesn't exist. God was the omniscient author, but he died; now no one knows the plot, and since our reality lacks the sanction of a creator, there's no guarantee as to the authenticity of the received version. Time is reduced to presence, the content of a series of discontinuous moments. Time is no longer purposive, and so there is no density, only chance. Reality is, simply, our experience, and objectivity is, of course, an illusion. Personality, after passing through a stage of awkward self-consciousness, has become . . . a mere locus for our experience. In view of these annihilations, it should be no surprise that literature, also, does not exist—how could it? There is only reading and writing . . . ways of maintaining a considered boredom in the face of the abyss.[118]

But if the literary techniques of postmodernism are not especially original; and if their worldview resembles familiar older nihilisms, Barth, Barthelme, Hawkes, Nabokov, and the others have captured subjective experience in a striking and original way. One's inclination is to see them in the light of Valéry, who remarked apropos of Poe that "The glory of man, and something more than his glory, is to waste his powers on the void. . . . Thus it would seem that the history of thought [and here one would add, the performance of postmodern antirealism] can be summarized in these words: *It is absurd by what it seeks; great by what it finds.*"[119]

PART I

The Author as God

Metafiction has come to define self-conscious writing, in which the relationship between the world of words (fiction) and the world of phenomena (reality) is explored, the assumption being that artistic heterocosms are not only as valid as God's cosmos, but, because they escape the sameness associated with His text (existence), prove more interesting to render. "The writing of story" serves "the story of writing" in such *oeuvres*, whose creators insist on their own fictionality and defend historical collaboration/plagiarism. Whereas autoreferential authors like Nabokov, Sorrentino, and Barth allude to themselves, if only obliquely, other antirealists under consideration appear disguised through raconteur masks. That metafictional productions also frequently employ frames should be apparent from the works discussed during the first section, "Reflexivity": "The Magic Poker," *Lolita, Pale Fire, Mulligan Stew, The Friday Book, Dunyazadiad, Giles Goat-Boy,* "Lost in the Funhouse," and *Letters.*

In the next section, "the story of writing" dominates, with verbal art and game-playing strategies becoming synonymous. Besides inspiring the manipulation of syntax and punctuation, the ludic impulse in contemporary prose has given us notable alphabetical experiments—for example, *Splendide-Hôtel* and *Alphabetical Africa* (lipogram)—and notable typographical/graphical experiments—for example, *Double or Nothing* and *Willie Masters' Lonesome Wife.* This playful spirit has motivated our fabulators to mix genres and styles, sometimes satirically *(Darconville's Cat),* but most often parodically *(Mulligan Stew).* Parody, which defamiliarizes conventional forms, dominates antirealism, since, according to Nabokov, it connotes "game," while satire means "lesson." Thus, Hawkes parodies the American western *(The Beetle Leg)* and the crime thriller *(The Lime Twig),* as Coover ("The Magic Poker," "The Gingerbread House") and Barthelme *(Snow White)* parody the fairy tale. Besides such popular types, ancient myths (and traditional forms) may be parodied too, one example being *The Beetle*

Leg's burlesque of the pagan god Osiris and the Christian Fisher King.

Part I closes with "Maximalism versus Minimalism" to demonstrate the wide range that postmodern antirealistic American fiction commands. The movement has generated gigantic novels in the learned wit vein and lean novels in the *mot juste* vein. The differences between a "putter-inner" like William Gaddis and a "leaver-outer" like Donald Barthelme are illustrated through analyses of *The Recognitions* and *The Dead Father*. But though their prose styles seem antithetical, the former depending on amplification and the latter on condensation, both books celebrate language, as do other experimental texts. Indeed, the celebration of language (and literature) is probably the most positive element in fictional works molded by authorial gods.

Reflexivity

When we analyze the new style we find it contains certain closely connected devices. . . . to see to it that the work of art is nothing but a work of art . . . to consider art as play and nothing else.—JOSÉ ORTEGA Y GASSET

Modernism criticizes from the inside, through the procedures themselves of that which is being criticized. . . . Realistic, illusionist art had dissembled the medium, using art to conceal art. Modernism used art to call attention to art.
—CLEMENT GREENBERG

The novel is thus no longer a mirror taken out for a walk; it is the result of internal mirrors ubiquitously at work within the fiction itself. It is no longer representation, but self-representation.—JEAN RICARDOU

Twentieth-century art has tended to *search itself* rather than exterior reality for beauty of meaning or truth, a condition that entails a new relationship between the work of art, the world, the spectator, and the artist.—ROGER SHATTUCK

No aspect of antirealism is more universal or timeless than self-consciousness. Contemporary reflexive fiction has roots at least as far back as Cervantes's *Don Quixote,* where the author, who pretends to be Cid Hamete Benengeli, ridicules chivalric literature, and Sterne's *Tristram Shandy,* where the author, who was called the English Rabelais, also mocks conventional writing. Among other early foreign metafictionists are Henry Fielding and Denis Diderot. Nineteenth-century American works in this tradition include *The Scarlet Letter,* "Song of Myself," *Huckleberry Finn,* and *Billy Budd.*

A later American, Ernest Hemingway, stated during his *Green Hills of Africa* (1935), "The writer has attempted to write an absolutely true book to see whether the shape of a country and the pattern of a month's action can, if truly presented, compete with the work of the imagination." One year before, *A Cool Million* was narrated by an "I" who characteristically declared, "It is with reluctance that I leave Miss Prail in the lecherous embrace of Tom Baxter to begin a new chapter." Antirealistic Nathanael West belongs—as Hemingway does not—to the old metafictional line that Beckett, Gide, Huxley, Joyce, Pirandello, Proust, Queneau, Unamuno, and others revived throughout the modern era. This trend has grown so much since their time that it may now be considered the hallmark of postwar experimental prose. Practitioners range from Christien Brooke-Rose, Lawrence Durrell, John Fowles, B. S. Johnson, Doris Lessing, Iris Murdock, Muriel Spark, and D. M. Thomas in England, to Michel Butor, the *nouveaux romanciers*, Robert Pinguet, Nathalie Sarraute, the Tel Quel group in France, to Italo Calvino, Umberto Eco, the *Gruppe 63* in Italy, to Jorge Luis Borges, Julio Cortazar, and Gabriel García Márquez in South America. North American adherents include Walter Abish, John Barth, Donald Barthelme, Richard Brautigan, William Burroughs, Robert Coover, Coleman Dowell, Raymond Federman, William Gaddis, William Gass, John Irving, Steve Katz, Joseph McElroy, Vladimir Nabokov, Joyce Carol Oates, James Purdy, Ishmael Reed, Gilbert Sorrentino, Ronald Sukenick, and Kurt Vonnegut, Jr. Even Ralph Ellison *(Invisible Man)* and John Hawkes *(Second Skin; The Blood Oranges)*, though not fundamentally metafictionists, and Norman Mailer *(The Armies of the Night; Why Are We in Vietnam?)* and Philip Roth *(My Life as a Man)*, though not intrinsically antirealists, have used reflexivity.

According to Patricia Waugh, Gass invented the label metafiction in *Fiction and the Figures of Life* (1970). She defines it as

a term given to fictional writing which self-consciously and systematically draws attention to its status as an artefact in order to pose questions about the relationship between fiction and reality. In providing a critique of their own methods of construction, such writings not only examine the fundamental structures of narrative fiction, they also explore the possible fictionality of the world outside the literary fictional text.[1]

Consequently, the metafictional novel "becomes the story of writing as much as it is the writing of story" (136).

The main characteristics of metafiction are the irrelevance of the individual author and the assumption that literature is collaborative/plagiaristic; the borrowing of characters from one's own and others' work; the fictionalization of the author, who appears in the "unreal" domain of the characters, and the actualization of the characters (often writers), who appear in the "real" domain of the author; the treatment of history as fictitious; the inclusion of unreliable documentation; the projection of linguistic heterocosms or substitute worlds; the tendency to unmask and defamiliarize dead conventions through parody; the employment of arbitrary beginnings and multiple endings; the introduction of frames and tales-within-tales, leading to circularity and *regressus in infinitum;* and the focus on fiction as process rather than product.

Though these traits seldom, if ever, all come together, many regularly recur. Thus, "Mr. Burroughs presence on earth is . . . a joke" in *Nova Express;* Mr. Gaddis ("Willie") is "—writing for a very small audience" in *The Recognitions;* and Mr. Vonnegut is "an old fart with his memories and his Pall Malls" in *Slaughterhouse-Five.* Authors frequently recycle characters (e.g., Burroughs's Doctor Benway and Pynchon's Pig Bodine), make intertextual references to their own work (e.g., Burroughs's direct allusion to *The Ticket That Exploded* in *The Soft Machine* or to *Naked Lunch* in *Nova Express* and Gaddis's indirect allusion to *The Recognitions* in *J R* or to *J R* in *Carpenter's Gothic*), and even mention each other. As they invade the sphere of characters, characters invade theirs. Federman, discussing *Double or Nothing,* observes: "[T]he protagonist argues with the creator of the fiction because he doesn't like the name he was given, or the way his story is being told and shaped."[2] And Coleman Dowell comments during *White on Black on White:*

(In the typescript of this section, that last sentence is strongly marked out and I know it was Cayce, not Ivy, who censored, though I can imagine her pencil hovering uncertainly over the concluding image—deformity, etc., wondering if it is a racist remark. For my own reasons I am over-ruling Cayce as I have done in other sections of censorship, the sole despotism I can ever practice with this terrific independent man.)[3]

Like Federman and Dowell, Robert Coover concentrates on the writing process. Ms. Waugh says "The Babysitter" and Donald Barthelme's "Views of My Father Weeping" "offer a set of alternative stories as one story, which can be explained neither as happening *simultaneously* (because they can only be substituted for each other) nor as happening *in sequence* (because they cannot be combined, according to normal logic: they erase or cancel out each other)" (137).

"The Magic Poker," which also appears in *Pricksongs & Descants* (1969), is a narrative about a writer writing a narrative, whose first sentence, "I wander the island, inventing it,"[4] initiates the heterocosm motif. Lying on the grass, Coover's narrator compares himself to the magic poker (compare Barth's Genie and Sorrentino's Magician), and creates this substitute world. He has been "thorough, a real stickler for detail" (23), so the heterocosm should function autonomously. Artistic powers are vast—"perhaps tomorrow I will invent Chicago and Jesus Christ and the history of the moon . . . as I have invented you, dear reader" (40)—but morally ambivalent—"my beneficence and cruelty" (25). If anything, cruelty predominates, with the narrator even more destructive than the caretaker's son, his fabricated counterpart. Their antipode, the tall man, "affirms reason," though "nature reclaiming her own" makes the "artifice of imposed order" (28) useless. When the narrator sees things "getting out of hand," he, too, chooses the positive (archetypal poker) over the negative (befouled teakettle) because the earth, already "littered" by "our contentious artifice," does not need savage songs (30). The heterocosm may grow increasingly real, occupying a "place in world geography" (40), yet writers exercise limited options. They are not omnipotent. Indeed, this narrator sometimes forgets his "arrangement is . . . invention" and takes "historical denouement" for "aesthetic design" (33). Further, he fears involvement, wonders whether the caretaker's son created him, knows that stories conclude midway, and observes how distortedly one imaginative character paints.

"The Magic Poker's" tale-within-a-tale constitutes surrealistic allegory structured on the well-worn arrival-departure pattern. A quaternion of two women and two men develops. The romantic girl in gold pants, who has had "three wrecked marriages" (29), is attracted to the contemplative tall man, as her unmarried sister, Karen, lusts after both him and the bestial caretaker's son. They roam about a wasted landscape, where phallic symbols abound. Virtually nothing happens prior to the unexplained death of the caretaker's son. Meanwhile, a ghostly grandmother tells ghostly children "the story of 'The Magic Poker,' " beginning several accounts with "Once upon a time." Her fourth version—prepared for earlier when the tall man was conjured—mythicizes present events and travesties traditional fairy tales. Nobody can remove the tight gold pants from the thrice-wed

Princess (romantic girl), so the King issues the predictable proclamation. Aided by the Magic Poker, the Caretaker's son finally succeeds,
but the Princess kisses the poker and "a handsome Knight" (tall man)
materializes to slay the "little gnome-like creature." He exclaims, " 'I
have slain the monster and rescued your daughter!' " yet the King,
considering him foolish, reacts, " 'You have made her a widow' " (43).

Elsewhere, in *The Origin of the Brunists* and *The Public Burning*,
Coover encloses his narratives, as do many other antirealists, none of
whom uses framing devices more skillfully than Vladimir Nabokov.
Lolita, which enacts the erotic entanglement between a decadent European nympholept and a vulgar American nymphet, originally contained foreword but no afterword, much like works employing prologues without epilogues, introductions without conclusions. The
Foreword, signed "John Ray, Jr., Ph.D. / Widworth, Mass. / August
6, 1955,"[5] attempts to authenticate and legitimatize "the Confession
of a White Widowed Male." Establishing authenticity, Dr. Ray tells us
that author "Humbert Humbert"—a self-invented cognomen—"died
in legal captivity, of coronary thrombosis, on November 16, 1952 . . .
before his trial"; that Clarence Choate Clark, Esq. asked Ray "to edit
the manuscript"; that except for correcting "obvious solecisms" and
suppressing "a few tenacious details," he kept H. H.'s "remarkable
memoir . . . intact"; and that the characters, though bearing fictitious
names, are "real." Dr. Ray includes documentation, mixing facts (e.g.,
Hon. John M. Woolsey's December 6, 1933 decision about *Ulysses*)
and nonfacts (e.g., crime references "in the daily papers for Septem-
ber-October 1952"). Keenly aware of public opinion, the editor also
legitimatizes *Lolita*. We learn that the text holds no "four-letter words,"
yet retains erotic scenes "functional . . . in the development of a tragic
tale moving toward "a moral apotheosis"; that H. H.'s "case history
. . . will become . . . a classic in psychiatric circles"; and, most important, that the characters reveal "dangerous trends," "potent evils."
Ray, having cited "his own books and lectures," piously concludes:
" 'Lolita' should make all of us—parents, social workers, educators—
apply ourselves with still greater vigilance and vision to the task of
bringing up a better generation in a safer world."

Ostensibly, then, John Ray, Jr., Ph.D., wrote the Foreword to *Lolita*,
just as Charles Kinbote wrote the Foreword to and Commentary on
Pale Fire, and a third, anonymous editor wrote the parenthetical

notes in *Ada*. Actually, however, "the authorial voice—'an anthropo-morphic deity impersonated by me' " (xxxi)—can be detected sub-verting these pedants. The current editor, whose name derives from the "English naturalist famous for . . . systems of natural classifica-tion" and so familiar to "a distinguished lepidopterist" like Nabokov (327), mentions "Vivian Darkbloom," without sensing anagrammatic significance. "Such phenomena undermine the narrative's realistic base by pointing beyond the book to Nabokov, the stage manager, ventriloquist, and puppeteer" (325), argues Alfred Appel, Jr.

Perhaps distrusting our ability to discern "such phenomena," the author composed an afterword which "appeared in the 1957 edition of *The Anchor Review*, the novel's American debut" (438), and which closed its open frame. Resembling numerous other frames—for ex-ample Introduction/Appendix *(Naked Lunch)*; One/Ten *(Slaughter-house-Five)*, "Vladimir Nabokov on a book entitled *Lolita*" is autobio-graphical. Here, Nabokov destroys the authentication/ legitimization established during the Foreword. He confesses "my impersonation of suave John Ray," then records Lolita's genesis from "newspaper story about an ape in the Jardin des Plantes" to prototypical "short story some thirty pages long" to "new treatment of the theme . . . in En-glish." This last transpired between 1949 and 1954 and involved "inventing America" through "individual fancy" and limited "average 'reality,' " a word that signifies "nothing without quotes." Whereas editor Ray felt H. H.'s "aphrodisiac scenes must be justified, author Nabokov, whose typescript had shocked "four American publishers," denies pornography altogether because it "connotes mediocrity, com-mercialism, and certain strict rules of narration"; whereas the editor trusted psychology, the author scorns "Freudian voodooism"; and whereas the editor was moralistic, the author is artistic: "I am neither a reader nor a writer of didactic fiction, and, despite John Ray's assertion, *Lolita* has no moral in tow. For me a work of fiction exists only insofar as it affords . . . aesthetic bliss."

There are three *Pale Fires:* Vladimir Nabokov's novel, published in 1962; John Shade's poem, written during July 1959; and Charles Kinbote's annotated edition of the latter, dated "Oct. 19, 1959." The annotated edition frames the poem with Foreword and Commentary, while the novel frames the annotated edition with epigraph and Index. Though we encounter three writers, one covertly (Nabokov) and two overtly (Shade and Kinbote), we never doubt that the "anthropomorphic deity impersonated by me" controls the entire text. Thus, Shade, the poet, remarks "Hurricane / Lolita swept from Florida to Maine,"[6] and Kinbote (see Index under *"Botkin,* V., American scholar of Russian descent") criticizes Prof. Pnin (compare *Pnin,* 1953). Reflecting Nabokov's principal nonliterary commitments, both recognize the Vanessa butterfly and play chess, a game Kinbote seems quite knowledgeable about. Moreover, he alludes to "Boswell's *Life of Dr. Johnson"* (154), which, as the *Life of Samuel Johnson,* gave the author his epigraph.

Charles Kinbote may be the craziest first-person narrator in postwar antirealistic American fiction, triumphing over such stiff competition as Chief Broom of *One Flew Over the Cuckoo's Nest,* Bukka Doopeyduk of *The Free-Lance Pallbearers,* Jacob Horner of *The End of the Road,* and even Zizendorf of *The Cannibal.* His biography adumbrates circumstances described by Nabokov during *Speak, Memory: An Autobiography Revisited.* There, we encounter Kinbote-like associations: "my great-grandfather . . . participated . . . in an expedition to map Nova Zembla . . . where 'Nabokov's River' is named after my ancestor." We hear too about "a certain night in 1922 at a public lecture in Berlin, when my father shielded the lecturer . . . from the bullets of two Russian Fascists and, while vigorously knocking down one of the assassins, was fatally shot by the other,"[7] an incident that inspired John Shade's murder. And though Kinbote, "a soft, clumsy giant" (17) called "elphantine tick," "king-sized botfly," "macaco worm," "monstrous parasite" (171–72), does not physically resemble athletic Nabokov, he "may turn up yet, on another campus, as an old, happy, healthy, heterosexual Russian, a writer in exile" (300–301).

This homosexual, paranoiac, pedantic, religious, voyeuristic editor represents the antithetical self. Accordingly, his attitude toward art embodies everything Nabokov detests. Kinbote castigates Shade on several grounds and ridicules fellow-Shadeans because they consider him insane. Both Foreword and Commentary contain unprofessional personal allusions to migraine headaches, erotic liaisons, and so forth. Socially rejected by Sybil Shade, he accuses her of making husband John "tone down . . . the magnificent Zemblan theme . . . I kept furnishing" (91). "Pale Fire" becomes his poem, and, consequently, he distorts or is tempted to distort the text, which, "without my notes" lacks "human reality" (28). These notes already enact the "old-fash-ioned melodrama" Kinbote may someday write, involving "a lunatic who intends to kill an imaginary king, another lunatic who imagines himself to be that king, and a distinguished old poet who stumbles ... into the line of fire" (301). Meanwhile, through Shade's domestic poem and Kinbote's solipsistic edition—the first pedestrian and the second demented—Nabokov paradoxically contrives a brilliant arti-fact. And so the author, not the commentator, "has the last word" (29) after all.

Nabokov appears often during *Mulligan Stew*, an impressive au-tochthonous reflexive novel Gilbert Sorrentino published in 1979. One character is "doing a book on Nabokov";[8] one refers to "a Nabokov mot" (82); and one mentions "a plot of Nabokov's" (223), believing the latter abetted "my failing career" via coded *New York Review* letters (357). *Something Said,* where Sorrentino could practice the self-expression purposely exorcised from his creative *oeuvre,* treats other metafictionists, among them Coleman Dowell, William Gaddis, William Gass, García Márquez, Raymond Queneau, and Italo Cal-vino, whose "labyrinthine and convoluted" *If on a winter's night a traveler* "parodies ... an entire battery of modern and postmodern literary techniques" and represents "objective reality" as much as "the linear, plotted, sequential narrative of the conventional novel." Pre-dictably, Sorrentino " 'understand[s]' Italo Calvino better than ... John Cheever" and feels "closer to Laurence Sterne than ... to Henry Thoreau."[9] Like *Tristram Shandy* and *If on a winter's night a traveler, Mulligan Stew* typifies the linguistic heterocosm:

> By making it a collection of written documents, I cut it off completely from any sense of it being a story that reflects the real world. . . . I wanted it to be an artificial world. It's an abstract world. It doesn't reflect, it doesn't imitate, it doesn't mirror reality. It *is,* in terms of literature, *a* reality and that's all it is. It's as if it were in an airless box, existing in a kind of vacuum. My hope is that as soon as you put your foot into the book, you are in another world.[10]

Sorrentino's metafictional masterwork also employs framing de-vices. The book is sealed inside the title page by epigraphs, three at the start, drawn from Flann O'Brien/Philip Vogel/James Joyce, and one at the finish, taken from Emile Fion criticizing Cézanne for attempting "to go beyond the sublime balances of nature." Prior to the title page, an additional, unclosed frame advertises its separateness through thicker-textured, bluish-grey paper. This frame contains twelve letters of rejection, some sent by fictional characters such as Flo Dowell (*The Good Soldier*), Chad Newsome (*The Ambassadors*), and Claude Estee (*The Day of the Locust*). Several factual errors appear in these letters: the author's Christian name becomes "Robert," his surname, "Sorrento"/"Sorrantino," while an earlier novel, *Imaginative Qualities of Actual Things*, becomes IMAGINARY QUALITIES AND THINGS / IMAGINARY QUANTITIES OF THINGS. Next we get a communication "Gil" to "Barney" (i.e., Rosset, Grove Press president), which begins, "The xerox copies of the rejection letters that I have enclosed are self-explanatory, and will inform you as to the fate of my poor but honest *Mulligan Stew* over the past three years." Then comes an enthusiastic, if ludicrous READER'S REPORT (signed "Horace Rosette") "strongly" recommending publication. Exchanges between Hasard House and Grove Press ensue, wherein Hasard House refuses to distribute the Grove Press volume. Blending fact and fancy, *Mulligan Stew*'s unclosed outer frame thus exposes the literary environment that inspired the incredible *potpourri* awaiting us.

"The idea of a novel about a writer writing a novel is truly *old hat*. Nothing further can be done with the genre" (224), ironically asserts protagonist Antony Lamont while Gilbert Sorrentino defamiliarizes this outworn convention, focusing on him as a hack writer and on *Guinea Red / Crocodile Tears* as a bad book. The plot of its story-within-a-story may be quickly summarized. Narrator Martin Halpin awaits the police after murdering Ned Beaumont. Meantime, he recounts the moral decline of his friend and associate, hastened by two trollops, Corrie Corriendo and Berthe Delamonde, whose promotional pornographic literature occupies BURST LOVELETTERS, an epistolary chapter. They prompted Beaumont to abandon an adulterous affair with Daisy Buchanan when she became serious over him and her husband urged divorce. Later, Halpin replaced Beaumont as the wanton wife's lover.

Though author Lamont, narrator Halpin, and others provide the only actual voices of *Mulligan Stew*, Sorrentino, fictionalized throughout, makes numerous indirect, Nabokovian appearances. The name "Sorrentino," diversely rendered ("Sorento," "Sonnertino," "Soterroni," "Sorentain"), recurs, besides the titles of the two reflexive works that prefigured *Mulligan Stew: Imaginative Qualities of Actual*

Things (1971), likewise distorted *(Quantities of Imagistic Things)*, and *Splendide-Hôtel* (1973).[11] Rosette inhabited both before writing the Grove Press READER'S REPORT. He has edited *"Bridges: Poets Express Their Love,"* and eventually occupies the library Halpin discovers. Logic does not necessarily govern such intertextuality:

> Sheila Henry (her married name) is also a character in Sorrentino's third novel, *Imaginative Qualities of Actual Things*, where she did *not* have a brother named Antony Lamont. But in *Stew* Sheila is remarried. To whom? Dermot Trellis (!!), who is Lamont's rival in avant-garde American fiction. . . . Whose Lamont is this? and how could a character from another Sorrentino novel be his sister while he is the brother-in-law of the man who invented him in someone else's book?[12]

"Someone else's book" was *At Swim-Two-Birds* (1939) by Flann O'Brien, supplier of one epigraph and, under another name, *Mulligan Stew* dedicatee: "To the memory of Brian O'Nolan / ——— his 'virtue *hilaritas.*' " O'Brien thought characters "should be allowed a private life, self-determination and a decent standard of living."[13] He created the young man who created Dermot Trellis (author) who created Antony Lamont (character). As the above quotation indicates, these last two are related in *Mulligan Stew*, where they become personal and professional enemies. Lamont, the "writer writing a novel," steals too, since Martin Halpin (of *Finnegans Wake*), Ned Beaumont (of *The Glass Key*), and the Buchanans (of *The Great Gatsby*) all enter *Guinea Red/Crocodile Tears*. Such "plagiary" reflects Sorrentino's metafictional credo: "With Butor and other writers, I do not believe in Originality but consider writers a kind of 'collaborative' band, each adding a stratum to the work done by others, each stratum possible only because of that work. My novel *Mulligan Stew* is not truly intelligible unless it is seen as dependent on the work of Joyce and Flann O'Brien."[14]

If the *Washington Post* can be trusted, Lamont's "prize-winning . . . elementary school" essay, "What I Can Do To Help The War Effort" (94), actually earned youthful Sorrentino an award. We are not surprised, therefore, that Lamont claims chapter twelve of *Guinea Red/Crocodile Tears*, LIKE BLOWING FLOWER STILLED (389–99), was written by his characters. However, the most interesting material concerning the involvement between author and authored appears in the journal that narrator Halpin keeps. The installment on pages 150–55 is illustrative. Ned Beaumont had convinced him "Lamont loses control over our 'present' substances, re-creating us, as he does, in the past." Because Ned plays a corpse during the present, they may switch roles, alternating days off. The absent-minded writer, easily fooled, "has no idea what we look like, nor what clothes we are wearing, since he never bothered to describe us . . . a modern prerogative." Actual desertion would be dangerous, though, since deserters wind up working adventure/confession stories, "badly paid and treated with enormous contempt," so these two must wait and see how Lamont's "ridiculous novel" develops.

Once while Beaumont took his place, Halpin walked through a static, one-dimensional landscape until arriving at an unfinished town, begun, then abandoned by some American novelist turned journalist. There he met Clive Sollis, who had once "slaved" for Lamont. Both had served James Joyce too, but neither remembered the other. Whereas Sollis had found Joyce annoying, Halpin considered him fair and kind. Sollis claimed Lamont had ruined his brilliant career, and thus he can now perform only "English rotters." Should Halpin remain, Lamont would never know, as the town "existed in a typescript locked away in a trunk in a Poughkeepsie attic." Its inhabitants, having fled various stories, often caused authors to digress and to dissipate. Sollis did not care, feeling "the better the author, the more difficult" the employer. Contrariwise, "he had yet to meet a malcontent from the pages of a 'commercial' novel or slick-magazine short story." That world consists of "kisses," "nice clothes," "happy divorces," and "polite sex."

Another disciple of Nabokov, John Barth, is our best-known and most gifted contemporary self-conscious prose artist. His critical views are fully articulated in *The Friday Book* (1984). As if to flaunt Barth's dominant motif, this collection features an elaborate unclosed frame that presents, then mocks, production front matter. Official half-title page, title page (verso: Books by John Barth), copyright page, and dedication (For Shelly) precede a second, unorthodox half-title page (THE FRIDAY BOOK, / OR, / BOOK-TITLES SHOULD BE / STRAIGHTFORWARD / AND SUBTITLES AVOIDED / Essays and Other Nonfiction). Next we encounter three short pieces: The Title of This Book (ix–xii); The

Subtitle of This Book (xiii–xiv); and Author's Introduction (xv–xvi), which concludes J. B. / Baltimore/ Langford Creek, Md. 1983/84, and, referentially, "James Joyce made these subscripts fashionable. . . ." Finally, Table of Contents and Epigraphs (signed "—J. B.: 'Epigraphs,' in *The Friday Book*"; "—Ibid."), also footnoted, appear. The epigraphic comment rounding off the open frame advises us to eliminate epigraphs, especially when counterpointed, and, indeed, all preliminaries so we may *"for the love of God get on with the story."*[15]

From front matter to last piece treating *The Thousand and One Nights*—"a fit note to end . . . upon" (258)—*The Friday Book* emphasizes frames and tales-within-tales. Its author contends this "phenomenon is ancient, ubiquitous, and persistent; almost as old and various . . . as the narrative impulse" (221). Once a Johns Hopkins University book-filer (compare Borges, the librarian), he has detected "nearly 200 specimens of frame-tale literature" (86). These enabled him during a 1981 lecture called "Tales Within Tales Within Tales" to categorize such literature and to understand "relations . . . between . . . framed and framing stories" (232). Influenced by Tzvetan Todorov, he affirms that "not only is all fiction fiction about fiction, but all fiction about fiction is . . . fiction about life" (236).

Barth's affection for Scheherazade spans his collection, forming what could be considered a closed inner frame. The Title of This Book (front matter) discusses the genetic complexity of the Islam classic:

> *Book of the Thousand Nights and a Night* . . . refers immediately neither to the book thus titled nor to the period of Scheherazade's liaison with King Shahryar, but rather to a book *described* by the book thus titled, itself entitled *The Marvels and Wonders of the Thousand Nights and a Night*, which book in turn, the text itself explains, is a popular edition of yet another book (in thirty volumes) called *The Stories of the Thousand Nights and a Night. That* is the original book of the scribes' transcription of the tales told by Scheherazade to the king, plus the tale of Sheherazade telling those tales to the king. (x)

More than 250 pages later, "Don't Count on It: A NOTE ON THE NUMBER OF THE 1001 NIGHTS" (last piece), while analyzing the latter's chronological difficulties, returns to this oral aspect: 'Scheherazade tells by my count 169 primary tales; she moves to the second degree of narrative involvement on no fewer than nineteen occasions, to tell 87 tales within the primary tales, and to the third degree on four occasions, to tell eleven tales-within-tales-within-tales—267 complete stories in all" (268). We are reminded throughout *The Friday Book* that Barth ranks *The Thousand and One Nights* above all other literary artifacts because of the character of the storyteller, the circumstances of the narration, the use of the framework, and the antiquity of the yarns.

Though his own "Menelaiad" *(Lost in the Funhouse)* outdoes *The Thousand and One Nights* to reach the seventh narrational level—a *regressus in infinitum* unique even for Barth (compare "Tales Within Tales Within Tales," 218–38)—the *Chimera* "triptych" (1972) most successfully manipulates the Chinese box method he learned from enclosed yarns. Its third novella, *Bellerophoniad,* is more *directly* auto-referential than the first, *Dunyazadiad,* or the second, *Perseid,* since the author discusses the impact the wandering-hero myth had on his work, finds "pet motifs" in *The Greek Myths,* alludes to writer's block when composing *Letters,* and so forth. However, the much shorter *Dunyazadiad* better illustrates Barth's "endless love affair" with Scheherazade (98). She provides both the form and content of this novella, whose tripartite structure discloses several narrators: (1) her sister Dunyazade ("Doony") as "I" speaking a monologue to auditor-groom Shah Zaman that recounts what happened between Scheherazade and his brother, King Shahryar, from Scheherazade's point of view; (2) Shah Zaman as "I" speaking a monologue to Dunyazade, " 'in exchange for the one you've told me,' " [16] that expresses the male perspective and is framed by third-person passages; and (3) un-named Barth as "I" informing us that "Dunyazade's story begins in the middle; in the middle of my own, I can't conclude it" (64).

"Dunyazade's story" and "my own" have been linked all along. During the first part, Scheherazade asks Doony to " 'pretend . . . you and I and Daddy and the King are . . . fictional characters' " (15–16). Then another figure called "Genie" and resembling Barth appears: "Light-skinned fellow of forty or so, smooth-shaven and bald as a roc's egg. His clothes were simple but outlandish; he was tall and healthy and pleasant enough in appearance, except for queer lenses" (16). "A doctor of letters" and "a writer of tales," Genie, whose personal and professional lives signify "disorder," comes from America, where the only serious readers now comprise "critics, other writers, and unwilling students." He wishes "neither to repudiate nor to repeat . . . past performances"; instead, he wants "to go beyond them" and "at the same time go back to the original springs of narrative" (17). Though Scheherazade, living centuries ago, has not yet told King Shahryar any tales, Genie, living centuries later, considers her his "favorite" storyteller. Thus, he can supply "The Merchant and the Genie" and others from *The Thousand and One Nights* on " 'my worktable' " in Maryland. Flattered Scheherazade gives him a gold earring, out of which he promises "to spin . . . fiction" (26). And so he does: "Using, like Scheherazade herself, for entirely present ends, materials received from narrative antiquity and methods older than the alphabet, in the time since Sherry's defloration he had set down two-thirds of a projected series of three *novellas*" (36). The series is *Chimera* and the unfinished third *Dunyazadiad*, the story we are reading. Meanwhile, Genie and Scheherazade, whom he has loved more passionately than "real" women since he was "a penniless student pushing book-carts through the library-stacks" (20), discuss the relationship between narrative and sexual art, the dominant motif here and elsewhere. They find that plot mirrors intercourse: exposition = foreplay; rising action = coitus; climax = orgasm; denouement = release. Teller and told become erotically involved, according to Genie, as during *The Thousand and One Nights*, with the teller always representing masculinity and the listener/reader, femininity, "regardless of . . . actual gender" (34).

The *Chimera* triptych, which *Dunyazadiad* initiates, is Barth's most elaborate Chinese box experiment, but *Giles Goat-Boy or, The Revised New Syllabus* (1966) contains his most complex single framework. The opening frame consists of "Publisher's Disclaimer," and "Cover-Letter to the Editors and Publisher." Immediately, The Editor in Chief asks "[t]he reader . . . to believe in the sincerity and authenticity of this preface." He mentions both *"our* title-page" (changed "by us" from *R. N. S.* to *Giles Goat-Boy*), bearing the name John Barth ("professor and quondam novelist"),[17] and the enframed title page, bearing the name of another author/authors: *R. N. S. / The Revised New Syllabus of George Giles our Grand Tutor / Being the Autobiographical and Hortatory Tapes Read Out at New Tammany College to His Son / Giles (,) Stoker / By the West Campus Automatic Computer And by Him prepared for the Furtherment of the Gilesian Curriculum.* Four editorial reports follow, two negative, one positive, one neutral. Editors A and C vote to reject

the manuscript, the first on moral/aesthetic and the second on aes-
thetic/commercial grounds, while B votes to accept it as a tax write-
off and D "doesn't care." These reports, like the unclosed outer
frame of *Mulligan Stew,* expose the publishing world. "[N]o longer
the ranking member," retired A regrets the firm's loss of "moral
prestige" and laments "recent policy" (xi), yet B reveals A was de-
posed after a similar moralistic report and says the elderly fellow
harbors "private antipathy" toward *Giles Goat-Boy* because his daughter fled college with an irresponsible bearded poet. A and B are
accused of "personal motives" by C, who claims to be "relatively
objective," and neurotic D resigns. The Editor in Chief returns for
the last word, admitting A "gave me my first job" and D, "where-
abouts unknown," represents "my only son." A footnote concludes
"Publisher's Disclaimer": "[W]e have exercised as discreetly as possible our contractual prerogative to alter or delete certain passages
clearly libelous, obscene, discrepant, or false" (xvi).

"The manuscript enclosed is not *The Seeker,* that novel I've been
promising you for the past two years" (xvii) [18] begins Cover-Letter to
the Editors and Publisher. Instead, J. B. has sent them "the extraordinary document" left him "several terms ago" by a twenty-year-old
man affecting "a walkingstick as odd as the rest of his get-up" (xvii–
–xix). Neither writer nor student, ambivalently called Stoker Giles/
Giles Stoker convinced the thirty-year-old "artist, teacher, lover, citizen, husband, friend" that what the latter had accomplished "was
wrong . . . a procession of hoaxes" (xxiii). Consequently, J. B. must
study the New Curriculum, graduate, and "establish Gilesianism here"
(26), where he then conducted "fiction-writing seminars." The converted professor will eventually devise a three-point plan, but meanwhile Stoker provided a brief history of father George Giles, Grand
Tutor at New Tammany College. Interested in disseminating the
latter's message, the son had employed the WESCAC computer, which
"declared itself able and ready . . . to assemble, collate and edit"
information already stored up, interpolating "all verifiable data from
other sources" (29). Subsequently, Stoker "corrected the mistaken
passages" in this "first-person chronicle" (xxvi), and later still J. B.,
whose own typescript "got mixed with it by a careless janitor" (xxix),
contributed "emendations and rearrangements." James L. McDonald
comments:

By explaining and analyzing the composition of the *R. N. S.*, the frame renders its authorship problematical, making the reader unable to hold any single person responsible. . . .
    Thus the *R. N. S.* is the product of many authors: Giles himself (?), certain pupils, Stoker, WESCAC, an unnamed janitor, J. B., and the editors. The emendations go far beyond casual editorial changes: 'mistaken pages' have been corrected; 'false' pages have been altered or deleted; artistic 'judgment' has been exercised. The very substance of the narrative has been manipulated, 'Revised.'[19]

Like the two-part opening frame, the three-part closing frame of *Giles Goat-Boy* treats authorship problematically. Posttape or the last recording George Giles fed WESCAC, which recounts what happened during "the interval between my 'triumph' of twelve years back . . . and my present pass" (700), is termed "spurious" by Postscript to the Posttape, where J. B. cites "internal evidence against its authenticity" (709) and notes "the hopeless, even nihilistical tone of the closing pages." But if J. B. doubts George Giles authored Posttape, his "Ed." doubts J. B. authored Postscript to the Posttape, since Footnote to the Postscript to the Posttape divulges "The type of typescript pages of the document entitled 'Postscript to the Posttape' is not the same as that of the 'Cover-Letter to the Editors and Publisher' " (710).

Authorship, whether collaborative *(Chimera)* or problematical *(Giles Goat-Boy)*, fascinates Barth. During *The Friday Book*, he continues to "regard the Almighty as not a bad novelist, except He is a realist" (219). "God's text" ("our reality") (221) was botched, yet humanly manufactured heterocosms remain "distinct, harmonious, and radiant" (19). The artistic worlds Barth invented are influenced by music, for "At heart I'm an arranger still, whose chiefest literary pleasure is to take a received melody—an old narrative poem, a classical myth, a shop-worn literary convention . . . and, improvising like a jazzman within its constraints, reorchestrate" (7). "Artists are ethical nihilists," indifferent toward external values, *and* "anti-nihilists" fashioning new universes (24), so Barth can say, "Muse, spare me (at the desk, I mean) from social-historical responsibility, and in the last analysis from every other kind as well, except artistic" (55).

Understandably, then, he praises Jorge Luis Borges throughout *The Friday Book*, but especially during "The Literature of Exhaustion," written seventeen years earlier. "Pierre Menard, Author of the Quixote" shows the South American transcending "an intellectual dead end": "Borges *doesn't* attribute the *Quixote* to himself, much less recompose it like Pierre Menard; instead, he writes a remarkable and original work of literature, the implicit theme of which is the difficulty, perhaps the unnecessity of writing original works of literature" (69). His attitudes and practices reflect Barth's, since he too asserts "the fictitious aspect of our own existence"; utilizes the *regressus in infinitum;* employs mirrors, doubles, labyrinths; and believes " 'all writers are more or less faithful amanuenses of the spirit, translators and annotators of pre-existing archetypes' " (73).

Despite separating *The Floating Opera* (1956) and *The End of the Road* (1958), as "Two short novels, relatively realistic and contemporary," from *The Sot-Weed Factor* (1960) and *Giles Goat-Boy* (1966), as "two very long novels . . . irrealistic and non-contemporary,"[20] Barth has always been a reflexive writer. Todd Andrews, who states, "If you do not understand by now that the end of my *Floating Opera* story must necessarily be calm and undramatic, then you have understood nothing at all, and once again I'm cursed with imperfect communication,"[21] and Jacob Horner, who states, "Here is what she told me, edited and condensed,"[22] are self-conscious narrators. However, Barth's contention, *"Whatever else it is about, great literature is almost always also about itself,"*[23] does not become dominant until we encounter the author/reader strategy of *The Sot-Weed Factor* (part IV) and the closed frame of *Giles Goat-Boy,* where "a girl . . . has got to the precise place in the book . . . she is described reading."[24]

The works following *Giles—Lost in the Funhouse* (1968), *Chimera* (1972), *Letters* (1979), and *Sabbatical* (1982)—appear markedly autoreferential. For instance, during the last, which contains much literary talk and many literary allusions, protagonists Fenwick and Susan Turner invoke the author and thus reside inside and outside the tale they are simultaneously living/writing. This tale suggests the wandering-hero pattern of "summons, departure, threshold-crossing, initiatory trials, et cetera," a pattern that may be bent "to fit our story, so long as we don't bend the story to fit the pattern."[25]

Also reflexive, *Lost in the Funhouse* represents Barth's most experimental book. A bipartite open frame, *Author's Note* and *Seven Additional Author's Notes,* introduce it. *Author's Note* declares the fourteen short pieces included form "a series" and classifies each according to the categories announced by the subtitle, *Fiction For Print, Tape, Live Voice.* "The regnant idea is the unpretentious one of turning as many aspects of the fiction as possible—the structure, the narrative viewpoint, the means of presentation, in some instances the process of composition and/or recitation as well as of reading or listening—into dramatically relevant emblems of the theme,"[26] explains *Seven Additional Author's Notes* before briefly analyzing six individual selections.

The title story has a simple plot: Thirteen-year-old Ambrose Mensch, who had figured earlier in the volume and will become the correspondent immediately preceding "The Author" in *Letters,* arrives via automobile at Ocean City with his family and Magda G—— on an Independence Day during World War II, when and where he enters the labyrinthine funhouse, which symbolizes both existence ("God's text") and art (our texts) and thus decides to "construct funhouses for others and be their secret operator—though he would rather be among the lovers for whom funhouses are designed" (94).[27]

Paradoxically, the narrator, while demonstrating an exhaustive knowledge of realistic writing that compels him to summarize "conventional dramatic narrative" through Freitag's Triangle (91), cannot render this simple plot traditionally, and so "Lost in the Funhouse" *seems* disjointed and badly written. He informs us:

The function of the *beginning* of the story is to introduce the principal characters, establish their initial relationships, set the scene for the main action, expose the background of the situation if necessary, plant motifs and foreshadowings where appropriate, and initiate the first complication or whatever of the "rising action." Actually, if one imagines a story called "The Funhouse," or "Lost in the Funhouse," the details of the drive to Ocean City don't seem especially relevant. The *beginning* should recount the events between Ambrose's first sight of the funhouse early in the afternoon and his entering it with Magda and Peter in the evening. . . . So far there's been no real dialogue, very little sensory detail, and nothing in the way of a *theme.* And a long time has gone by already without anything happening. (73–74)

Unable to shape "Lost in the Funhouse" through illusionist principles, the narrator despairs, "I'll never be an author" (83). However, irony arises from the discrepancy between what he executes as ostensible storyteller and what Barth achieves as actual raconteur. The narrator, who is only one character in this heterocosm, produces an unsuccessful realistic account of the Ocean City episode that becomes

Barth's successful irrealistic account of his account. By attacking realism while embracing irrealism, the title story implies the dual Barth/
Mensch conversion from traditional to avant-garde art.

Their symbiotic connection crystallizes during *Letters*, perhaps our
most accomplished metafictional novel. Its "Author" writes to Ambrose Mensch on August 3, 1969, "Time was when you and I were so
close in our growings-up and literary apprenticeships, so alike in
some particulars and antithetical in others, that we served each as the
other's alter ego and aesthetic conscience; eventually even as the
other's fiction."[28] Like J. B. *(Giles Goat-Boy)* and John Barth, Mensch,
whose pseudonym is Arthur Morton King, abandoned a manuscript
called *The Amateur*—partially reproduced on pages 153–89 of *Letters*
—which contributed much to *Lost in the Funhouse:*

> *[T]he rest of* G, *together with all of* H *and* I, *are missing from this recension of Arthur
> Morton King's* Menschgeschichte, *having been given years ago as aforetold to your
> Litt.D. nominee.* G *came to light as a first-person piece called "Ambrose His Mark";*
> H *first saw print as the story "Water-Message";* I *(in my draft but a bare-bones sketch)
> was fancifully elaborated into the central and title story of* B's Lost in the Funhouse
> *series, where the others rejoin it to make an "Ambrose sequence."* (165)

Later, Barth receives from Mensch a "ground plan for that Perseus-
Medusa story" and "alphabetized instructions" for both *Chimera*
("midlife crises and Second Cycles") and *Letters ("reenactment")*, to be
published separately rather than together: Opus #6 (three novellas);
Opus #7 *(Letters)* (652–53). His "alter ego and aesthetic conscience"
will also supply the acrostic beginning (title page) of the latter. A
seven-month calendar (March–September, 1969) and a fixed sequence of correspondents (Lady Amherst, Todd Andrews, Jacob
Horner, A. B. Cook, Jerome Bray, Ambrose Mensch, and The Author), it spells *"An old-time epistolary novel by seven fictitious drolls &
dreamers, each of which imagines himself actual."* The acrostic, sent on
September 22, helps to answer the previously quoted August 3 mis-
sive seeking "advice and assistance" (653). There (as elsewhere), Barth
had described his new 88-letter project that would revolve around
the number seven:

> Its working title is LETTERS. It will consist of letters (like this, but with a plot)
> between several correspondents, the capital-*A* Author perhaps included, and
> preoccupy itself with, among other things, the role of epistles—real letters,
> forged and doctored letters—in the history of History. It will also be con-

cerned with, and of course constituted of, alphabetical letters: the atoms of which the written universe is made. Finally, to a small extent the book is addressed to the phenomenon of literature itself, the third main sense of our word *letters*. (654)

Like several previous fictions, the 1979 novel employs a complex framework. The open outer frame comprises the initial six epistles (pp. 3–42). There follows the first of two "Author to the Reader" sections, which announces: "Gentles all: LETTERS is now begun, its correspondents introduced and their stories commencing to entwine" (42). These sections constitute the closed inner frame. Both inner and outer frames emphasize time. In the one marked "March 2, 1969," Barth explains:

[E]very letter has two times, that of its writing and that of its reading, which may be so separated, even when the post office does its job, that very little of what obtained when the writer wrote will still when the reader reads. And to the units of epistolary fictions yet a third time is added: the actual date of composition, which will not likely correspond to the letterhead date, a function more of plot or form than of history. (44)

We learn 727 pages later that the second section, "Sunday, September 14, 1969," was drafted on July 10, 1978 and typed on October 5, 1978. After exclaiming *"Sic transit! Plus ça change!"* the Author concludes his *Envoi* with "the end" (772).

Barth's masterwork owes a debt to more collaborators than Ambrose Mensch. Besides protagonist Lady Amherst (new character), who provided "the general conceit of 'doctored letters,' "

[f]rom "Todd Andrews" (the lawyer-hero of my first novel, *The Floating Opera*) came both the notion of free-standing sequelae and the Tragic View of history, to which in fact I subscribe. From "Jacob Horner" (novel #2, *The End of the Road*) comes what might be called an Anniversary View of history, together with certain alphabetical preoccupations and the challenge of "re-dreaming" the past, an enterprise still not very clear to me. (431)

Thus, the writer-as-plagiarist becomes an important theme during *Letters*. Though Barth spurns the collaborative claims of A. B. Cook VI (an imposter with fradulent documents, according to H. C. Burlingame VII), novel #3 was inspired by presumed ancestor Ebenezer Cooke's *Sot-Weed Factor* and fed by additional sources like the *Archives of Maryland*. Cook readily accepts a role in *Letters*, but not Horner, whose *What I Did Until the Doctor Came* furnished "the basis of a slight novel called *The End of the Road*" (19). He finds the Author's elaborate tale about discovering his lost typescript "less convincing" than the published book (279), which infuriated rival Joe Morgan "to the point of seriously contemplating vaticide" (364). Meanwhile, Andrews has "mixed feelings" over *The Floating Opera:* "It was decidedly a partial betrayal on your part of a partial confidence on mine," yet [I] "was gratified to see the familiar details of my life and place projected as through a camera obscura" (85). Jerome Bray, the angriest character, threatens legal "action for plagiarism" (27) regarding the "perversion . . . of our *Revised New Syllabus* of the Grand Tutor Harold Bray" (28), an "archancestor" (756). Barth refutes this and other charges two days prior to stealing the Bellerophon/Chimera idea from Bray's July 8 "P.S."

Though the Author must still function in the unscrupulous fictional world, Mensch (admirable human being), having bequeathed him the Perseus-Medusa story, fulfills his adolescent wish of joining "the lovers for whom funhouses are designed" when he marries pregnant Lady Amherst. That their union not only climaxes the private plot of *Letters* but also represents its positive pole is suggested by the Author's penultimate communication, an excerpt from "*Ye Hornebooke of Weddyng Greetyng* (Anonymous, 16th Century?)," which concludes, "Bee / Younge in hearte with / Zest to enjoy these & alle other good thyngs / Amen" (770). Conversely, the public plot or negative pole, focused on filming the Barth canon, epitomizes dissension and death otherwise marking a novel where life (procreation) triumphs over art (creation).

The correspondents of *Letters* are writers and historians, yet, as Thomas R. Edwards observes, [t]hey "mostly address nonexistent or nonfunctioning others": "Andrews writes to his dead father, Mensch to the unknown 'Yours truly' whose blank message he found in a bottle when he was a boy, Andrew Burlingame Cook IV (in 1812) to his unborn child (who turns out to be twins), the modern Andrew Burlingame Cook VI to his lost and unresponsive son, and the schizoid Horner to himself."[29] However, despite this emphasis on one-way communication, Barth's people relate intertextually during *Letters* to dramatize its central subject of reenactment.

Alternate Worlds commences with reflexivity because it best defines contemporary antirealistic American fiction. Statements like Greenberg's "Modernism used art to call attention to art" and Ricardou's "It is no longer representation, but self-representation" certainly characterize the texts Coover, Nabokov, Sorrentino, and Barth have provided for our discussion. They, even more than twentieth-century precursors, incorporate the chief traits associated with metafictional or autoreferential prose. Among these are the vision of literature as collaborative/plagiaristic, the borrowing of figures from other works (intertextuality), the relation of fictionalized authors and actualized characters, the fabrication of history and the spuriousness of documentation, the defamiliarization[30] of dead conventions through parody, the use of frames leading toward *regressus in infinitum,* the elevation of artistic process over artistic product, and so forth. To a very large extent all this makes possible the impressive postwar heterocosms epitomized here by "The Magic Poker," *Lolita, Pale Fire, Mulligan Stew, Giles Goat-Boy,* and *Letters.* Next we will see how their inherent playfulness is enhanced by games and analogous devices.

CHAPTER 2

The Ludic Impulse

I've put in so many enigmas and puzzles that it will keep the professors busy for centuries arguing over what I meant. —JAMES JOYCE

Literature is a game with tacit conventions; to violate them partially or totally is one of the many joys (one of the many obligations) of the game, whose limits are unknown. —JORGE LUIS BORGES

I discovered in nature the nonutilitarian delights that I sought in art. Both were a form of magic, both were a game of intricate enchantment and deception. —VLADIMIR NABOKOV[1]

Whereas the typical American writer between the Civil War and World War II was a journalist, the typical American writer today is a college teacher, who, unlike his predecessors, has wide formal education, including postgraduate degrees. Many resemble such intellectual moderns as Joyce and Eliot, and many even treat scholastic settings. Gore Vidal terms them "University or U-writers," who are "bored with . . . narrative, character, prose," and he believes that "[e]ventually the novel will simply be an academic exercise, written by academics to be used in classrooms in order to test the ingenuity of students. A combination of Rorschach test and anagram." Hence the popularity of John Barth, "a perfect U. novelist whose books are written to be taught, not to be read."[2]

The latter, when addressing a student body on orientation, admitted, "I hadn't quite realized how *academic*, in this special sense, my life's work . . . has been."[3] However, Barth novels are not academic just because they educate but because they reflect the pedagogic world. For instance, aptly titled *Sabbatical*, which renders the nine-month journey taken by the Turners—an ex-CIA agent/author and an associate professor of American literature/creative writing—contains passages analyzing *Manfred*, Vietnamese poetry, and *The Narra-*

tive of Arthur Gordon Pym. Like several postwar antirealistic texts, it also employs footnotes reminiscent of sometime professors Vladimir Nabokov and Jorge Luis Borges.

That Susan Turner teaches creative writing seems appropriate since creative writing is the principal subject Barth and other U-writers purvey. Its advent in American colleges around World War II (the Iowa Writers' Workshop dates from 1936) coincides with the resurgence of metafiction. Emphasizing "the story of writing as much as . . . the writing of story," the reflexive movement could be considered a vast creative writing course.

One crucial aspect of this movement becomes apparent when U-novelist Alexander Theroux asks: "Can you ignore the concept of fiction, always erudite, as game, pleasure, hobby, and puzzle?"[4] The answer is no, for the spirit of play, or the ludic impulse, involving its own rules and systems, helps the metafictionist construct his or her heterocosm.

Thanks to *Games Authors Play* by Peter Hutchinson, *Sport and the Spirit of Play in American Fiction* by Christian K. Messenger, "Games and Play in Modern American Fiction" by Robert Detweiler,[5] and others, we are now familiar with the formal and conceptual contribution games have made to our literature, particularly during the twentieth century. Who has not encountered, at least indirectly, Nabokov's famous equation of verbal art and chess?

It should be understood that competition in chess problems is not really between White and Black but between the composer and hypothetical solver (just as in a first-rate work of fiction the real clash is not between the characters but between the author and the world), so that a great part of the problem's value is due to the number of "tries"—delusive opening moves, false scents, specious lines of play, astutely and lovingly prepared to lead the would-be solver astray.[6]

When chess or metaphoric life becomes artistic strategy, we get books like *The Defense, Lolita,* and *Pale Fire.* Consequently, the "fatal pattern" in Grandmaster Luzhin's existence resembles "a game of skill," "a regular chess attack," which affects not only "those separate scenes," but "the basic structure" of *The Defense.*[7] Often during *Lolita* Humbert Humbert and Gaston Godin play chess, with queen symbolizing nymphet, an arrangement that prefigures the contest over the latter between Humbert and Clare Quilty. Mary McCarthy claims

"There is surely a chess game or chess problem in *Pale Fire,* played on the board of green and red squares," then discusses the " 'solus rex type' " and chess as "the perfect mirror-game."[8] Besides recurrent allusions to chess, *Ada* contains many games, some word-oriented: duel, Flavita, lovers' code, poker, Scrabble, snap, sun-and-shade.

Robert Coover's J. Henry Waugh "enjoyed chess but found it finally too Euclidian, too militant, ultimately irrational, and in spite of its precision, formless really—nameless motion."[9] Descended from Tiger Miller, whom games sustained throughout *The Origin of the Brunists,* Henry had experienced several paper matches—"baseball, basketball, different card games, war and finance games, horseracing, football"—and had even created "a variation on Monopoly" called "Intermonop" (44, 45) before he became proprietor of The Universal Baseball Association, Inc. His fiction-within-a-fiction is a game about the game that also inspired Philip Roth's *The Great American Novel* and Bernard Malamud's *The Natural.* "Beyond each game," one player, seeing another game "and yet another, in endless and hopeless succession," wonders, "The game? Life? Could you separate them?" (238) Both are dangerous during "Panel Game," where a live audience watches while the Moderator hangs a loser named the Unwilling Participant or Bad Sport.

This spirit of play has produced diverse linguistic experiments conducted by metafictionists like Coover, Burroughs,[10] and Barthelme, involving the manipulation of syntax and punctuation. Typical examples include Barthelme's "Our Work And Why We Do It" *(Amateurs),* which uses sentence fragments, while his "Sentence" is an eight-page unfinished sentence "moving . . . down the page aiming for the bottom."[11] A second *City Life* story, "The Glass Mountain," consists of 100 consecutively numbered statements; a third, "The Explanation," of questions and answers; and a fourth, "Bone Bubbles," of fifteen sixteen-line unpunctuated paragraphs, paving the way for Ronald Sukenick's 114-page novel, *Long Talking Bad Conditions Blues, sans* commas, semicolons, colons, or periods. It concludes with, "things didn't have beginnings and endings in that sense they just start and then they stop."[12]

Published one year apart, Gilbert Sorrentino's *Splendide-Hôtel* (1973) and Walter Abish's *Alphabetical Africa* (1974) go way beyond acrostics and anagrams in their experimentation with letters. The earlier "is a work of criticism"[13] focused generally on the verbal imagination and particularly on two poets: Arthur Rimbaud and William Carlos Williams. Title and epigraph *(Et le Splendide-Hôtel fut bâti dans le chaos / de glaces et de nuit du pôle")* come from "Après le Déluge" *(Illuminations)*, but the organization was suggested by "Voyelles," where Rimbaud assigned a color to each vowel: "A black, E white, I red, U green, O blue." Sorrentino retains these associations, adding his own favorite color orange under "R" and yellow under "Y." He calls *Splendide-Hôtel's* A–Z structure "haphazard . . . a metaphor, a literary device of exceptionally limited use" (14), and says "Rimbaud was at the construction site" (22). Game allusions—chess, baseball, croquet—abound because this work is a "shaped and polished artifact, a game of— nouns and verbs" (14).[14]

Whereas the alphabet enabled Sorrentino to explore private and public topics achronologically through essays, poems, and letters, it furnished Abish with the most constrictive form yet practiced by any contemporary antirealistic American novelist. His 152-page first novel is a lipogram, in which words are chosen to avoid the use of one or more specific alphabetical characters. Dating back to classical times, the lipogram still inspires OuLiPo (Ouvroir de Littérature Potentielle) and books like Georges Perec's *La Disparition*.

Abish told Jerome Klinkowitz that *Alphabetical Africa* could not have been written without the precedent of "Minds Meet," a story whose short sections were "built around the key word in the alphabetically arranged subtitles" ABACK, ABANDONED, ABASED, ABATED, ABBREVI-ATED, ABERRANT, ABEYANCE, ABHORRENT, ABILITY, ABOVE, ABSENT, AB-STAIN, APART, AUSPICIOUS. These motivated their respective sections, "defining and limiting each occurrence."[15] They carried the author's message or theme—his "concern with the formation of ideas in a literary context"—that read, "Is there any other way to live?" (99).

Thus, "Minds Meet" broke ground for the even more inhibitive *Alphabetical Africa,* where the first chapter includes only words starting with "a"; the second, only words starting with "a" and "b"; the third, only words starting with "a," "b" "c," and so forth. By the twenty-sixth chapter, Abish was able to use the whole alphabet, but during the twenty-eighth he reversed the process when eliminating "z," and so began to work back toward chapter 52, which, like one, is designated "A." The novel, therefore, "constructs and then decon-structs itself" (99), as juxtaposition of initial and last sentences indi-cates: "Ages ago, Alex, Allen and Alva arrived at Antibes." / ". . . another Alva, another Alex another Allen another Alfred another Africa another alphabet." Klinkowitz learned from Abish that the accretion-contraction method mirrored various fictional situations, particularly "the shrinkage of the African continent" (99). Paradoxi-cally, the lipogram's severe limitations made *Alphabetical Africa* an original creation for even the author:

> I was fascinated to discover the extent to which a system could impose upon the contents of a work a meaning that was fashioned by the form and then to see the degree to which the form, because of the conspicuous obsta-cles, undermined that very meaning. For example, I could not introduce the first person singular until I had reached the ninth section. Frequently, I intended to follow one direction and was compelled to follow another. (96)

However, the ludic impulse has produced more than linguistic triumphs like *Alphabetical Africa* during the postwar period. "Nothing is now safely out of the book," according to William Gass, since "[t]hese days, the text is oozing out into the very shapes of the letters . . . out into the space of the print, into the nature of the page—in placement, drawing, type size, bindings, cover." [16] What L. Moholy-Nagy terms "The New Typography" evidently began with Apolli-naire's ideograms and continued when the futurists and the dadaists abandoned "the rigid horizontal order of typesetting" to employ "typographical material as a flexible element in pictorial composi-tion." [17] Contemporaneous concrete poetry, which rearranges type or uses diverse typefaces, and the *nouveau nouveau roman* of Maurice Roche, which must be read backward, upside down, and vertically, make the typographical experiments of American writers such as Burroughs (see *Minutes to Go*) and Sorrentino (see *Blue Pastoral*) seem unexceptional.

Raymond Federman's *Double or Nothing* (1971) remains our most brilliant typographical novel. Framed, it opens with THIS IS NOT THE BEGINNING (preceded by an epigraph from Robert Pinguet) and closes with SUMMARY OF THE DISCOURSE (followed by WARNING). As in *Splen-dide-Hôtel, Alphabetical Africa,* and numerous reflexive works, narrator equals writer, though here we find Chinese box complexity worthy of Barth. Initially, three figures are introduced: the recorder or first person, the inventor or second person, and the protagonist or third person. "Someone to control organize supervise . . . the activities and relations of the other three persons" dominates FOOTNOTE on p. oooooooo.o. This turns out to be Raymond Federman, the fourth person, who will finish *Double or Nothing* while narrator one—"a rather stubborn and determined middle-aged man"—and narrator two—"a somewhat paranoiac fellow"[18]—never get beyond the planning stage.

Writer supervising writer recording writer inventing protagonist is only one of many self-conscious phenomena in "a real fictitious discourse." For example, pages 70–71 speculate on possible endings, which might include "He decides to give up everything and go back to France," "Tries to find another girl," "Drops out of life," and pages 81–85 discuss possible names provided by teller, by reader, by both. On page 99 the narrative voice worries about having "too many CHARACTERS" ("they'll drop out / they'll fade away / they'll disappear / they'll die maybe"), about point of view (FIRST PERSON is more restrictive more subjective more personal harder/ THIRD PERSON is more objective more impersonal more encompassing easier"), about structure ("one night scene / then / one day scene"). Elsewhere, this voice insists the protagonist not "be confused . . . with me," also "A pure invention" (114). Yet during their circular journey, their old-fashioned quest, "we are coinciding merging into one another more and more" (172), so that protagonist, inventor, and recorder become excited over the same sexy girls. Nevertheless, AUTHOR Federman, who pens the last words, maintains autonomy, for he "is solely responsible."

Because its title signifies a wager, its inventor embodies a gambler, and its text invokes a world of poker/dice, the reader readily accepts *Double or Nothing*'s playfulness. Richard Kostelanetz noted

a form is established for each page—usually a visual shape, but sometimes a grammatical device such as omitting all the verbs. . . . Over these individually defined pages which reveal an unfaltering capacity for formal invention, [Federman] weaves several sustained preoccupations. . . . In *Double or Nothing*, as in much other visual fiction, the page itself becomes the basic narrative unit, superceding *[sic]* the paragraph or the sentence, the work becoming a succession of extremely distinctive, interrelated pages. No other "novel" looks like it; none of the other visual fictions is so rich in traditional content.[19]

Federman's "distinctive, interrelated pages" contain such "capacity for formal invention" that describing them all would be virtually impossible. His book, which also evidences much unorthodox pagination and many blank sheets (one blue), makes us read from bottom to top and right to left as well as from top to bottom and left to right. The inexhaustible visual shapes mentioned by Kostelanetz often take the form of objects and thus resemble not only Apollinaire's *Calligrammes* (1918), but seventeenth-century emblematic verse like Herbert's "Easter Wings" and Herrick's "The Pillar of Fame." Beginning with the unnumbered page following ooooooooo.o, where cross, inverted triangle, triangle, and rectangle appear in a centered column amid the reiterated word "noodles," these shapes extend throughout *Double or Nothing:* for example, the ladder, whose steps read UP & DOWN on page 34.0; the "L" devoted to LOULOU on page 122; and the maze ending, "It's like an attack" on page 138.

Gass's own *Willie Masters' Lonesome Wife* (1968), combining typographical and graphical experimentation, illustrates even better how "nothing is now safely out of the book," how the text has invaded "placement, drawings, type size, bindings, cover." This remarkable fiction constitutes an elaborate conceit to link narrative and sexual art several years before Barth articulated the erotic involvement between male teller and female told in *Chimera,* though here the genders are reversed. Gass subsequently observed: "A novel of mine . . . regards its text as the body of a woman of generous morals and much misuse, so that I once felt it might be appropriate to provide those who thought to enter it with a condom which would serve double duty as a book mark, so safeguarding their journey. But the symbol was too sexist, the publisher too chary." [20]

The notion of the masculine reader entering, then exiting from the feminine book, is reinforced by the naked breasts and buttocks adorning, respectively, front and back cover. The glossy white paper chosen for these photographs reappears during the fourth and final section, where protean actress Babs Masters plays only herself in a monologue free of typographical and structural innovations. Once again we are identified with the lady's failed lovers, whom crippled Willie has epitomized, because we are the world and she, language. Babs's twenty-seven line advocacy of "democratic style" bears several coffee or liquor stains, the last containing the command, "YOU HAVE /

FALLEN / INTO ART / —RETURN TO / LIFE." This leads toward yet another blemish on the opposite page; significantly, it encircles the navel below a large, firm bosom.

First and third sections use similar dull paper, the first all blue, the third all red. Like section four but unlike two, they both display erotic photographs. The final blue picture depicts the female protagonist masturbating, a pervasive motif that ultimately includes Gass as neglected experimental writer. After the front matter, section one introduces Babs's dead father, absent husband, various affairs, and sexual obsessions. Here, the pronominal shifts, the literary allusions, and the key phrase, "imagination imagining itself imagine" also commence. Most ingenious is the right-hand page rendered backward on its verso.

Structural inventiveness marks the red section, where three separate "stories" soon synchronize. Identified through appearance, one employs ordinary typeface, one uppercase letters, and one dialogue. The ever-diminishing first story reads down the page, while the ever-expanding second and third stories read across each pair at top and bottom. These two vanish when a fourth story in bolder face emerges to read down the page as well, but alternately below the first. Marginal distractions occur: coffee or liquor stains, italicized phrases, glosses. Then, after the nude centerfold, interruptions begin: a double column, a discolored fragment, a passage framed slantwise with "You've been had, / from start to finish." Finally, the uppercase story resumes, and since Babs narrates this, it bridges red section three and white section four.

Unpaginated like the rest of *Willie Masters' Lonesome Wife*, only the chartreuse-colored, rougher-textured section has no erotic photographs. Typographical innovations flourish, however, providing standard and italic, plain and fancy, large and small, light and dark typefaces. One line runs off the page and many look uneven or distorted. Musical notes, placards, glosses, and huge asterisks materialize. There are a balloon speech, a partially obliterated fragment, and both a human eye and a Christmas tree shaped by words. Diverse kinds of discourse compete: for instance, the surrealistic play starring Ivan and Olga and the pornographic page 121 from PASSIONS OF A STABLEBOY. Most notable, though, seem the twenty-five footnotes that dominate section two. These sometimes incomprehensible, unfinished, misplaced, verbose, esoteric, and subjective commentaries overwhelm what little narrative Gass permits. His last few pages, which juxtapose love and language, end with the lament, "Oh you unfortunate animals—made so differently, so disastrously—dying." Obviously, then, like *Double or Nothing, Willie Masters' Lonesome Wife* represents the "new fiction," whose "visual dimensions are not auxiliaries to language, as in certain Wright Morris photographic works, but entwined within the verbal material."[21] Such visualized texts would also include the *Cyclops* publication of Burroughs's *The Unspeakable Mr. Hart* (drawings by Malcolm Neil) and *The Book of Breething* (drawings by Bob Gale), as well as Barthelme's *City Life* and Vonnegut's *Breakfast of Champions.*

The spirit of play that has inspired the linguistic experiments and the typographical/graphical innovations characteristic of contemporary metafiction has motivated many antirealists to blend genres, juxtaposing journal entries, stories, essays, letters, poems, popular songs, excerpts from newspapers, magazines, documents, and so forth. Among the most impressive orchestrators of such medleys are Gilbert Sorrentino and Alexander Theroux.

Several Sorrentino fictions—*Imaginative Qualities of Actual Things, Splendide-Hôtel, Crystal Vision, Blue Pastoral*—combine various modes, but *Mulligan Stew* (1979) is nothing else.[22] Rejection letters at the outset to Fion quotation at the end, this work remains *strictly* an assemblage of literary and subliterary forms, whose stylistic range rivals its model *Ulysses.*

Fourteen chapters scattered throughout the text comprise Antony Lamont's absurd novel-within-a-novel. Partly because he exhibits three versions of chapter 1, FALLEN LUCIFERS, we believe the complaints he makes about the difficulty experienced in composing *Guinea Red / Crocodile Tears.* The last few chapters indicate that the trouble entails more than incompetence, that, indeed, the self-styled avant-garde author has gone berserk. Lamont denied writing the twelfth, LIKE BLOWING FLOWER STILLED (a travesty of Shakespeare), which he attributes to his characters. In chapter 13, DISLOCATED REASON, where Halpin asks, "What is truth? What is reality? Have I invented this entire tale? Were the bizarre people I have been involved with all inventions to excuse my terrible deed?"[23] everything grows doubtful. And, finally, referring to Lamont and the last chapter, MAKING IT UP AS WE GOES ALONG, Halpin's Journal comments, "What went through his mind when he discovered Ned gone? I don't even want to think of it. There I stood, speaking first as myself and then as Ned—on and on, totally incoherent conversation, totally garbled, totally crazy!" (439).

Throughout the Journal, Halpin considers Lamont to be an "unbearably pretentious *hack*" (25), whose story and dialogue are silly. He resents being given a "grossly vulgar 'life,'" while Beaumont resents always playing the fool. Insane Lamont never describes them or their cabin quarters. To Halpin, "It is quite clear now that not only is Lamont a very bad writer, he has no clear idea of what he is doing in this book" (88). The same thing may be said about his four published novels, if we may believe the negative reviews found by Beaumont and quoted by Halpin. Excerpts of three, plus the story "O'Mara," appear elsewhere during *Mulligan Stew*, which also offers samples of the equally wretched work of arch-rival, brother-in-law Dermot Trellis.

Halpin's Journal, Lamont's Scrapbook and Lamont's Notebook recur to give Sorrentino's farrago coherence. Generic themselves, they house several forms besides fiction. For example, Halpin's Journal features two interviews: CHATS WITH THE REAL MCCOY and *Art Futures* Interview of the Month; FLAWLESS PLAY RESTORED: The Masque of Fungo and *A Garland of Impressions & Beliefs Culled from a Lifetime by E. B., A Disappointed Author*, while Lamont's Notebook presents Vance Whitestone's INTRODUCTION to Trellis's *The Red Swan* and *An Anonymous Sketch*. The Scrapbook appears inexhaustible, disclosing promotional materials, newspaper items, and the like.

Mulligan Stew is almost as dependent on correspondence as John Barth's *Letters*, published during the same year. Sixteen missives to and from publishers launch the book, and one chapter, BURST LOVE-LETTERS, contains thirty-five missives involving all the principal characters in the Sorrentino novel except Halpin. Additional epistles saturate the text, some accompanying enclosures: for example, Lamont's prize-winning elementary school essay, WHAT I CAN DO TO HELP THE WAR EFFORT, *BP's Feature Review* of THE RED SWAN, and RECENT STUDIES IN CONTRAVARIANT BEHAVIOR PROCESSES IN COMPLEX

RESOLUTIONS *by Morton D'ovington, Ph.D.* One correspondent, Lorna Flambeaux, mails Lamont her twelve-poem pornographic volume, THE SWEAT OF LOVE, concluding with Summerfuck: A Dramatic Eclogue.

This "stew" of literary and subliterary forms required Sorrentino, as it has Barth, Barthelme, Coover, Gaddis, and others to adopt several styles, an ability he praised in Raymond Queneau's *Exercises in Style* (1947): "We then read it ninety-eight more times, each retelling deploying a different style, from word games and permutations through slang, jargon, and cant, to narrational attitudes toward the subject matter, modes of formal rhetoric, and other linguistic tactics."[24] However, that it was Joyce who had most inspired him becomes evident during the analysis made by Max Eilenberg of FLAW-LESS PLAY RESTORED: The Masque of Fungo, the most ambitious attempt at generic defamiliarization or making it new we encounter in the Sorrentino *potpourri*.[25]

Reviewing *Mulligan Stew*, Hugh Kenner wrote, "for another such virtuoso of the List you'd have to resurrect Joyce,"[26] an assessment that emphasizes the single most dominant form the author employs, as *Steelwork, Imaginative Qualities of Actual Things, Splendide-Hôtel, Crystal Vision,* and *Blue Pastoral* attest. The list or catalog boasts a long tradition, extending from the Bible and epic through *Song of Myself* and *Ulysses*. Several postwar antirealistic American writers continue that tradition—Abish, Barthelme, Coover, and Sontag—, but no one more successfully than Gilbert Sorrentino. Nor has anybody, with the exception of William Gass in *Habitations of the Word* (175–84), better articulated this phenomenon. Sorrentino told an interviewer he first used the list to take "the place of description, character, and action," since stripping "verbosity from the usual narrative paragraph" and thus deflating "pretentions" leads to comedy and truth. Having already discovered how important nouns were in poetry, as had William Carlos Williams and Jack Spicer, after *Splendide-Hôtel* lists interested Sorrentino because "the substantive seemed to define a kind of absolute reality about the world." Long noun catalogs provide rich and dense texture, for they function "like a data bank," enabling the novelist to repeat items verbatim, altered or parodied. Consequently, there arises "the possibility of creating an enormously layered fabric . . . which is the world of *Mulligan Stew*."[27]

Nearly all its lists are associated with Halpin, and because his journal terminates the novel with "a list of gifts given by writers to characters" (439), we realize just how highly Sorrentino regards this form. He has claimed, "The final list of gifts in *Mulligan Stew* are gifts that go to many, many people whom I have known, all of whom are disguised,"[28] but he reserves his last present for us: "And to all you other cats and chicks out there, sweet or otherwise, buried deep in wordy tombs, who never yet have walked from off the page, a shake and a hug and a kiss and a drink. Cheers!" (445).

Like Gilbert Sorrentino, Alexander Theroux is both master of the medley and "virtuoso of the List." His remarkable *Darconville's Cat* (1981) charts the tragicomic love affair between aristocratic twenty-nine-year-old schoolmaster Alaric Darconville and beloved freshman, the Lolitaesque Isabel Rawsthorne, who meet at a Southern college for women. Brief scattered lists reflect their courtship; then, after they separate geographically and emotionally, three long, inimitable catalogs ensue. The first encompasses ten-page chapter 68, The Misogynist's Library. These books belong to diabolical eunuch Dr. Abel Crucifer, Harvard professor emeritus and author of *Christianity and the Ages Which It Darkened,* now living alone atop Adams House. The second dominates twenty-two page chapter 82, The Unholy Litany. Here, while the phonograph plays the *Dies Irae,* Crucifer recites nearly 500 phrases indicting female malefactors that begin with "from" and conclude with *"libera nos, Domine,"* the initial one *"—from Eve and her quinces, libera nos, Domine"* serving as model. Meantime, his reluctant disciple Darconville experiences such despair over this "queerest litany ever heard"[29] that he becomes comatose. Finally, the third misogynistic list, which occupies nine-page chapter 93, Why Don't You—? harbors thirty-eight paragraphs of commands, all involving torture.

Mulligan Stew possesses no voice outside the collage of literary and subliterary forms constituting its structure, but *Darconville's Cat,* an otherwise rather conventional third-person narrative, also contains a vast range of literary forms. Besides the lists and epigraphs that evoke multiple genres, there are excerpts from the treatise by Dr. Crucifer and references to the monograph by Cardinal Theroux-d'Arconville entitled *The Shakeing of the Sheets.*[30] The author also includes: academic address, fuel-burner, fable, questionnaire, essay on Love, examination, blank verse playlet, sermon, classical oration after Quintillian (Exordium, Propositio, Partitio, Narratio, Concessio, Argumentation, Confirmatio, Reducto ad absurdam, Admonitio, Confrontatio, Peroratio), A Digression on Ears, diabolical pact in reversed Latin, malediction, discourse on Hate, letters, poems, footnotes, diary entries, and others. These appear while the protagonist completes two works: *Rumpopulorum* ("my grimoire of dark invocations, mystic runes, mantic spells" [335]) and "a fable about Isabel Rawsthorne and himself" (686).

Darconville's Cat, no less than *Mulligan Stew*, expresses its multiple genres through multiple styles. Thus, the protagonist assumes different literary voices—each with a distinct rhetoric—depending on the context. One composes a Shakespearean sonnet for Isabel; one blasts rival Gilbert van der Slang through digression; and one summons the underworld. Antagonist Abel Crucifer is likewise gifted, for we hear the man who penned an eccentric treatise deliver an urgent oration, draw up an almost unreadable diabolical pact, and, mirroring the earlier piece on Love, present an equally brilliant discussion of Hate.

Obviously, *Mulligan Stew* and *Darconville's Cat* realize their aims by exercising myriad genres and styles, but while the first impresses us as a parodic book with satiric overtones, the second seems to be a satiric book that utilizes parody. Through imitative mockery, *Mulligan Stew* ridicules avant-garde fiction and the publishing industry. Even Sorrentino's own previous efforts become fair game, according to Eilenberg:

> Lamont is a sorry author, then, but behind him lurks a recognisable, if grotesquely parodied Sorrentino. ... *Fretwork* has the same characters as *Imaginative Qualities;* excerpts from *Three Deuces* parody *The Sky Changes,* and *Rayon Violet* hideously rewrites *Steelwork.*
> The parodic references abound. Lamont's attacks on Trellis, for instance, evince the same concerns as Sorrentino's *Kulchur* reviews.[31]

Though satire remains the dominant tone of *Darconville's Cat*, it too burlesques traditional literary and subliterary forms, and so Theroux, like Sorrentino, defamiliarizes "fictional conventions . . . become automatized and inauthentic," thereby freeing "new and more authentic forms."[32] He ridicules "rhetoric that would have taxed Quintillian" (33) in the welcoming address of Quinsy College President Greatracks, and he derides the cant of Dr. W. C. Cloogy of the

Wyanoid Baptist Church. However, these nonsensical treatments cannot quite match the comedy attained through the selections representing "I Knew Rhoda Rumpswab by 16 People," the author's version of pornographic writing. Humor here is more than linguistic, encouraging the indecorous reactions attributed to the female undergraduates who occupy Clitheroe 403.

Vladimir Nabokov, whose *Lectures on Literature* analyzes parody in *Ulysses* (see p. 285ff.), considered himself a parodist rather than a satirist because, for Nabokov, parody connoted "game" and satire, "lesson." Though the above discussion of *Mulligan Stew* and *Darconville's Cat* indicates how inseparable these two can be, and though texts like *Lolita* and *Pale Fire* clearly manifest satirical elements, his acceptance of the one and rejection of the other illustrates the postwar antirealistic commitment to the ludic world. Alfred Appel, Jr., makes this commitment apparent during *The Annotated LOLITA,* where parody is "willful artifice" and "verbal vaudeville."[33] Through it, *Pale Fire* embodies "a grotesque scholarly edition" and *Lolita,* "a burlesque of the confessional mode, the literary diary, and the Romantic novel," which also echoes Poe's "William Wilson" and Eliot's "Ash Wednesday."[34]

Nabokov's aesthetic descendants often parody the fairy tale and the detective story among popular forms, and, among "serious" ones, everything from established genres to ancient myths. It was noted previously how Robert Coover's "The Magic Poker" travestied the fairy tale by repeating "Once upon a time" and introducing a cast of familiar characters that enacts the royal proclamation, " 'Whosoever shall succeed in pulling my daughter's pants down, . . . shall have her for his bride!' "[35] Another *Pricksongs & Descants* piece, "The Gingerbread House," badly distorts "Hansel and Gretel." Here, the children are divested of individuality and become "the boy" and "the girl"; their woodcutter-father is now "the old man," but witch remains witch and stepmother disappears. Forty-two numbered paragraphs with copious iterative imagery replace the linear narrative of the Brothers Grimm, which shows good triumphing over evil and concludes, "they lived together as happily as possible." Later, the perverse "Gingerbread House" suggests that sexual initiation lay just beyond an ominous heart-shaped door.

Several other antirealistic texts parody the fairy tale—for example,

The Crying of Lot 49 ("Rapunzel") and *Hind's Kidnap* ("Jack and the Beanstalk")—the best known being Donald Barthelme's first novel that mocks its Grimm/Disney model.[36] If the latter is obsessively symmetrical, *Snow White* (1967) is inordinately disjunctive. The very different plot of the Barthelme version, while comprehensible enough, reaches us through nontraditional methods. Third-person narrative viewpoint has been superseded mostly by recurrent alternation between first-person plural and first-person singular voices conveying story fragments that range from one sentence to several pages in a tripartite structure. They sometimes project incoherence by unorthodox spacing and absent capitalization/punctuation, and often they frame omniscient uppercase, boldfaced passages focused on either central characters or related topics such as THE SECOND GENERATION OF ENGLISH ROMANTICS, THE REVOLUTION OF THE PAST GENERATION IN THE RELIGIOUS SCIENCES, THE HORSEWIFE, THE VALUE THE MIND SETS ON EROTIC NEEDS, 19TH CENTURY . . . RUSSIA[N] LITERATURE, ANATHE-MATIZATION. The last section of part I stands alone, containing fifteen questions. Here, reflexivity dominates:

"In the further development of the story, would you like more emotion ( ) or less emotion ( )?"; "Has the work, for you, a metaphysical dimension? Yes ( ) No ( )." A few queries echo the nonsensical tone of Barthelme's novel: "Would you like a war? Yes ( ) No ( )"; "In your opinion, should human beings have more shoulders? ( ) Two sets of shoulders? ( ) Three? ( )."[37] These numbered interrogatives appear among the many lists *Snow White* includes.

It also includes minimal plot material from the Grimm original as exposition. Thus, the heroine, whom the dwarfs found "wandering in the forest" (87), fears "MIRRORS / APPLES / POISON COMBS" (17), while her nemesis, witch Jane, was once " 'fairest of them all' " (40). Even the past tends to be reordered, however, with Snow White having been educated at Beaver College and the dwarfs having been " 'born in National Parks' " (62).

Barthelme defamiliarizes the present too. Now twenty-two years old, still possessing hair "black as ebony" and skin "white as snow" (3), the dissatisfied protagonist is " 'tired of being just a horsewife!' " (43) and angry over "male domination of the physical world" (131). She therefore no longer makes love to the dwarfs in the shower. This independence takes various forms when Snow White writes a dirty poem, becomes a radical, seduces a psychiatrist, or awaits a prince, "long hair streaming from the high window" (80) Rapunzel-like.

One dwarf, leader Bill, seems as bored as she, so his reactions are more ambiguous than those of Clem, Dan, Edward, Henry, Hubert, and Kevin. Rich through washing buildings and manufacturing Chinese baby food, they continue to give their mistress gifts, yet, at the same time, resent the current "confusion and misery" (87–88) enough to dream about cooking her. Such "anger and malevolence" (109) is actualized, if diverted, as the drinking, thieving, lusting dwarfs pelt a visitor, attempt rape, and destroy property. They find Bill, whose lack of leadership several sequences illustrate, "guilty of vatricide and failure." With prospective new tenant Hogo de Bergerac's help, the dwarfs hang him and make Dan leader. "Now there is a certain degree of equanimity. We prize equanimity" (180).

Formerly just "Roy," Hogo represents the most vivid character Barthelme adds to the fairy tale cast. His possessions vindicate the repeated epithet "loathsome": "cobra-green Pontiac convertible," "Iron Cross t-shirt" (32), "book of atrocity stories" (64), and cruel weapons like the quirt used on Bill. Had Snow White succumbed to Hogo's " 'cunningly-wrought dark appeal' "—' "Prussian presence . . . chromed chains . . . tasteful scars' " (170–171)—he would have stolen the young woman from the dwarfs, as he would have betrayed them earlier with the Internal Revenue Service. Two other unprecedented characters deserve mention: Fred, "the acid rock bandleader" (90), and the President, always worried about these Americans because of "the falling Dow-Jones index" (81).

Hogo also betrays old flame Jane, the witch, and old friend Paul, the prince, who are markedly different from their archetypes, the stepmother-queen and the king's son. During this urban fantasy, her sadistic boyfriend lives behind "chain-link-fence walls" (127), and her protective mother inhabits a "magnificent duplex apartment on a tree-lined street in a desirable location," where Jane frequents "the rare-poison room" (158). She demonstrates supernatural powers when swinging "from the lianas" (32) and invoking simian familiars. Both Jane and Paul are pretentious; the former claims the name Villiers de l'Isle-Adam and the latter " 'has the blood of kings and queens and cardinals' " (170). He composes poetry ("a palinode") and paints pictures ("a dirty great banality in white" [48]), yet must visit the unemployment office and work for *Cat World*. An inveterate bather, as Jane is an inveterate letter-writer, monkish Paul joins the Abbey Theleme out West. His one gallant gesture—intercepting the poisoned vodka Gibson " 'cello-shaped' " witch gives to "viola da gamba-shaped" heroine (152)—kills him. They attend the cremation ceremony together, while a secret lover, Amelia, sits alone. Though "fond [only] of his blood," Snow White "continues to cast chrysanthemums on Paul's grave" (180).

At the end of part 2, she complains about the world " 'for not being able to supply a prince. For not being able to . . . supply the correct ending of the story' " (132). This adumbrates Barthelme's reversal of the stereotypical fairy-tale termination ("They lived happily ever after"), which is as formulaic as the fairy-tale inception ridiculed by Coover ("Once upon a time"). "Snow-White and the Seven Dwarfs" offers us " 'the correct ending' " because prince and princess survive wicked stepmother-queen, but *Snow White* lets Jane, Hogo, and the dwarfs destroy Bill, Paul, and even the title character. Thus, Barthelme concludes: "THE FAILURE OF SNOW WHITE'S ARSE / REVIRGINIZATION OF SNOW WHITE / APOTHEOSIS OF SNOW WHITE / SNOW WHITE RISES INTO THE SKY / THE HEROES DEPART IN SEARCH OF / A NEW PRINCIPLE / HEIGH-HO" (181).

The ultimate harmony the Brothers Grimm impose through love and marriage becomes inverted during the fragmented 1967 novel. It dramatizes *Waste Land* dissonance by lack of communication, showing, on the most immediate level, sexual alienation. Besides Snow White's unhappiness over numerous suitors, Jane's broken relationship with Hogo, and the dwarfs' hostility toward females, there emerges a voyeuristic pattern inseparable from the important window motif. For example, nobody climbs up the Rapunzel-like hair, yet most men ogle that once magical ladder, as the sequence *"Reaction to the hair"* indicates. Paul even builds an "underground installation," which contains " 'mirrors and trained dogs,' " so he may " 'keep . . . constant surveillance' " (156–57).

Dissonance dominates the linguistic level too, where, according to Lois Gordon, "these people are less flesh and blood than verbal constructs, informational machines, or automatons."[38] They often speak jargon. Snow White states about Paul's canvas, " 'I find it extremely interesting as a social phenomenon . . . to note that during the height of what is variously called, abstract expressionism, action painting and so forth, when most artists were grouped together in a school, you have persisted in an image alone' " (48), while Bill states about his " 'penetrating study' " (51), " 'My survey of the incidence of weeping in the bedrooms of members of the faculty of the University of Bridgeport was methodologically sound but informed, you said, by too little compassion' " (52). However, Barthelme mocks more than art criticism, academic lingo, and other pretentious vocabularies. To Gerald Graff, "[t]he self-parodic form of *Snow White*," which employs ostentatious prose, "emphasizes the disjunction . . . between genuine feelings of alienation and the fashionable literary and cultural languages" explaining them.[39] Jargon—"filling," "stuffing," "sludge," *"dreck,"* and "blague"—becomes the central subject in this work (see chapter 3, "Maximalism versus Minimalism").

Parodies of the detective story abound too, as Burroughs, Pynchon, and McElroy demonstrate. John Hawkes's *The Lime Twig* (1961), based on Graham Greene's *Brighton Rock* (1938), is especially vivid. Its action occurs ten years after World War II. William Hencher, having once lived there with his now deceased mother, returns to the boarding house presently occupied by Michael and Margaret Banks (compare "Mary Poppins"). Coveting the place, he joins the Aldington racetrack mob, whose members were also perverted during the war. They ensnare the Bankses as easily as limed branches ensnare birds. Michael represents the perfect dupe, for drab postwar England has spawned the recurrent dream about Rock Castle, a racehorse Hencher urges him to steal. This dream, promising violent sexual fulfillment that husband and wife both unconsciously crave, leads to their nightmarish deaths.

Among other things, *The Lime Twig* parodies underworld sensationalism via the trampling of Hencher, the drugging of Sparrow, the crushing of Michael, the smashing of the flat, the slitting of Cowles's throat, the beating of Margaret, and the shooting of Monica. Inexplicable events occur to subvert the logic detective fiction demands. Annie, "a girl [Michael] had seen through windows in several dreams unremembered,"[40] appears without explanation at the widow's parlor, where they make love and she enigmatically warns him against Hencher. Later, at the paddock, Annie kisses a jockey she scarcely knows. Almost as unbelievable as these events are the criminals, victims, and law officers of *The Lime Twig*. The criminals number Larry, the head mobster, Sparrow/Thick, his henchmen, and Little Dora/Sybilline, his molls. Henchmen and molls make absurdly opposite pairs. Sparrow/Thick caricature the small, defective bodyguard serving out of gratitude and the gross, brutal executioner hired for money. When capricious Larry chooses Little Dora over sister Syb, proposing " 'A bit of marriage, eh?' " (165). he unaccountably selects ugliness rather than beauty. Victims (childlike females, obese males), though familiar, seem excessively helpless, while law officers, also familiar, seem excessively incompetent. The Violet Lane detectives that discover the body of Hencher at Highland Green during the last chapter prefigure Inspector Pardew and the two policemen in *Gerald's Party* (1986), the most brilliant crime parody since Hawkes, to whom Robert Coover dedicated his novel.[41]

Antirealistic fiction, feeding on mixed genres and styles, may mock popular and serious forms simultaneously.[42] Thus, besides the detective story, *The Lime Twig* ridicules the Circe/Icarus legends. An earlier book, *The Beetle Leg* (1951), employs manifold derision too, as it combines parody of the popular American western and the serious Osiris/Fisher King myths. This work achieves structural coherence through a motif—the search—instead of sequentially arranged incidents, a motif affecting every character, whose personal quest the communal quest for lost Mulge Lampson mirrors. Extreme literary stereotypes, *all* the females are betrayed. Ma, the pioneer woman with an enormous deep dish skillet, and Lou, the sophisticated outsider with perfume, slacks, and diamonds, both seek faithless husbands. Deserted frontier mother Hattie cuts off two sons prior to her death and afterward dominates one from the grave. Thegna, the Norwegian cook, loves asexual Bohn unrequitedly, while Maverick, the Mandan, suffers symbolic rape at the hands of sadistic Cap Leach. Other actions magnify feminine isolation: Lou confronts Thegna over errant Camper, then joins a card game that should involve men but involves four companionless old ladies. Meantime, the men, representing extreme literary stereotypes too, are *all* impotent. Bizarre factions clash. The Sheriff's posse includes a devoted deputy, a senile misogynist, a celibate cowboy, a crippled ex-bronc rider, a lecherous quack-doctor, and a perennial greenhorn. They track down the hermaphroditic Red Devils motorcycle band, who caricature outlaws and

Indians through innocuous misdeeds. An inevitable ambush climaxes when the posse fires rock salt into the buttocks of their apple thief adversaries.

Simultaneously during *The Beetle Leg* Mulge becomes more than a local figure with sporadic mythological associations, for his fate burlesques that of the pagan god Osiris and the Christian Fisher King. Conceived by an adulterous liaison between Hattie Lampson and Cap Leech, their older son dies at about thirty, although not from wounds or illness. Brother Luke's hostility toward him resembles Typhon's toward Osiris, yet the death of Mulge is accidental, not fratricidal. Both are trapped in water—king-god above, anti-king-god below— and both are buried in doubtful places. Mulge neither gets resurrected like Osiris-Christ nor restored like the Fisher King. Anything but a vegetation deity, he bears no sexual wound, occupies a gravesite that takes "seeding badly,"[43] and leaves secular relics very different from the religious relics attributed to the Egyptian divinity. Nonetheless, he shares the ritual fault of such mythological characters. As Osiris married sister Isis, Mulge marries mother-surrogate "Ma"; then, on their honeymoon, he abandons her, and his real mother, for the previously deceived Thegna. "No one ever even thought they had done one thing to shame us, at least not before the older married" (8–9), says the Sheriff. This shame, this sexual crime is accentuated when Hawkes reveals that Ma was accompanied across the desert by several ancient females wishing "to see one woman their own age brought to bed" (82).

Mulge debases the mythical water-god, while Ma, who wears "black summer and winter" (119) and "actively pined away and opened many graves" (117), debases the Weeping Women. A divining rod leads her over "sacred ground," as she cries, " 'Oh, Mulge. Where are you, Mulge?' " (116) on a search which, like ceremonial marriage rites involving water, Tarot pack, and Medicine Man, travesties its models. Leech and Luke, *The Beetle Leg*'s medicine men, have become the reverse of Gawain-type healers. Nor do Luke and Camper make successful fishermen, the first hooking only a dead child and the second nothing at all. Ironically, these questers never ask the right questions, and the waters are freed to produce Mircea Eliade's annihilative, rather than Jessie L. Weston's restorative flood.

The spirit of playfulness among contemporary American metafictionists and other antirealistic writers involves more than artistic strategies structured through games like chess and baseball. Indeed, it covers everything from linguistic experimentation to the way print and picture appear on a page or motivate a book. It even covers the prevalent tendency nowadays toward orchestrating literary medleys that combine various generic and stylistic modes, not all of which are prosaic/fictional. Their tone often mixes satire and parody, but the latter, "designated to ridicule in nonsensical fashion,"[44] predominates because parody conveys a ludic tone aimed, sometimes simultaneously, at both popular and serious forms. Such playful devices serving defamiliarization help to make the ordinary seem strange, one hallmark of alternate worlds designed by cosmic jokers.

CHAPTER 3

Maximalism versus Minimalism

Many of us are familiar with Keats's advice to Shelley: "Curb your magnanimity and be more of an artist, and 'load every rift' of your subject with ore." Less familiar, perhaps, is the debate between H. G. Wells, who, in "The Contemporary Novel" (1911), argued for discursive fiction, and Henry James, who, in "The New Novel" (1914), advocated "selection over saturation." Later, Scott Fitzgerald jotted on the margin of his copy of Thomas Wolfe's *Of Time and the River,* "All this has been about as good as Dodsworth for chapter after Chapter," and "trite, trite, trite, trite, page after page after page." Replying to Fitzgerald's objections, Wolfe claimed, "A great writer is not only a leaver-outer, but also a putter-inner," citing as evidence Shakespeare, Cervantes, and Dostoyevski.[1]

For John Barth, the coexistence of putter-inners and leaver-outers —now called maximalists and minimalists—seems commensurate with storytelling itself. "Against the large-scale classical prose pleasures of Herodotus, Thucydides and Petronius, there are the miniature delights of Aesop's fables and Theophrastus' 'Characters,' " and against "the low-fat rewards of Samuel Beckett's 'Texts for Nothing' " there are "the high-calorie delights of Gabriel García Márquez's 'One Hundred Years of Solitude,' " observes Barth.[2] *The Tidewater Tales* (1987) reflects this preoccupation with literary extremes, since the 655-page book focuses on a professor of "Everdiminishing Fiction," whose favorite poet is Emily Dickinson, and his pregnant oral historian wife, whose favorite poet is Walt Whitman.

The way minimalists and maximalists use language epitomizes their differences. Barthelme speaks for leaver-outers through Dan addressing fellow dwarfs at the plant during *Snow White.* He invokes one Klipschorn on " 'the "blanketing" effect of ordinary language . . . the part that . . . "fills in" between the other parts.' " This "filling" or "stuffing" ("*dreck*" and "*blague*" elsewhere) is characterized by "endless" and "sludge" qualities, the first dominating human exchanges and the second connoting " 'heaviness . . . similar to . . . motor oils.' " Because language " 'may be seen as a model of the trash phenomenon' "—" 'the everted sphere of the future' "—the plant pays special attention to it. Dan tells the dwarfs " 'that the per-capita production of trash in this country is up from 2.75 pounds per day in 1920 to 4.5 pounds per day in 1965 . . . and is increasing at the rate of about four percent a year." Not disposable, it has, nevertheless, become, as " 'plastic buffalo humps,' " the plant's " 'great moneymaker.' "[3] Therefore, Barthelme detects the same entropic process novelists like Pynchon and Gaddis dread, but while they record and so expose "the trash phenomenon" through inclusive styles, he banishes this wasteful proliferation through the elliptical syntax typical of minimalist prose.

Nowhere is such syntax better represented than in his second full-length fiction, *The Dead Father* (1975), which, though far more absurd, resembles Faulkner's *As I Lay Dying* (1930), for its plot involves family members (and others) transporting their half-dead, half-alive parent across alien territory toward some great burial hole. A cursory glance at the words beginning nearly every chapter of *The Dead Father* reveals short, sometimes fragmentary sentences without subordinate clauses, qualifying phrases, or adjectival/adverbial embellishments. These sentences eschew the verbosity and "sludge" that constitute "the trash phenomenon." Chapter 3 opens:

A halt. The men lay down the cable. The men regard Julie from a distance. The men standing about. . . . Edmund lifts flask to lips. Thomas removes flask. Protest by Edmund. Reproof from Thomas. Julie gives Edmund a chaw of bhang. Gratitude of Edmund. Julie wipes Edmund's forehead with white handkerchief. The cable relaxed in the road. The blue of the sky. Trees leant against. Bird stutter and the whisper of grasses.[4]

This passage could have been written by Beckett, Ionesco, or Pinter as an absurdist stage direction. So too could Barthelme's duologues, which echo their staccato, repetitive, disconnected, cliché-ridden, nonsensical speech. A sample from one of the four between Julie and Emma, who mirror the interdependent, complementary pairs associated with plays like *Waiting for Godot, The Bald Soprano,* and *The Dumbwaiter,* is typical:

Where can a body get a bang around here?
Certain provocations the government couldn't handle.
A long series of raptures and other spiritual experiences.
He was pleased.
Beside himself.
Something trembling in the balance.
Codpiece trimmed with the fur of silver monkeys.
He was pleased.
Feeling is what's important. (147–48)

Such sentences are diametrically opposed to the "amplified prose" of Alexander Theroux or what has been called the "loose baroque prose" of William Gaddis.[5] Yet, however different Barthelme's elliptical style is from the discursive writing of his expansive contemporaries, he shares their love of wordplay, as comically imaginative coinages like "roaratorious," "murderinging," "inwardize," "conceptioning," "supposititious," "presuppositionless," "castigatorious," and "nonflogitiousness" prove. That Barthelme was influenced by James Joyce becomes clear from two monologues indebted to *Finnegans Wake,* one of which begins:

The grand Father's bein' all hauly-mauly by the likes of us over bump and bumbust and all raggletailed and his poor bumleg all hurty and his grand aura all tarnagled . . . the grand Father the moon-hanger the eye-in-the-sky the old mester the bey window the bit chammer the gaekwarder the incaling the khando kid the neatzam the shotgun of kyotowing the principal stadtholder the voivode the top wali . . . (92)

Alexander Theroux, who finds "everything after Joyce an impertinence," speaks for the putter-inners or maximalists when he confesses, "I have a very amplified prose style. . . . I come down on the side of *amplificatio*—as did Burton, Montaigne, Rabelais, Stern."[6] Later, during "Theroux Metaphrastes: An Essay on Literature" (1975), he celebrates this inclusiveness:

Mine, then as now, was a love affair with a prose that moved sideways as well as forward, a "logic of passion," to alter Coleridge somewhat, combined with a "logic of grammar" that drifted out in recondite, non-colloquial inkhorn terms—often pictorial—that carried within it not only humor but refining and elevation, as well. It showed lofty sentiments in lofty sentences. Elaborateness in composition is no mark of trick or artifice in an author, nor is the majestic, the *os magna sonatorum*. Latin never died. It became simply ignored.[7]

"Recondite, non-colloquial inkhorn terms" pervade *Darconville's Cat* (1981). For example, the brief paragraph that begins the ninety-third chapter contains several obsolete or obscure words:

"STAB HER with a bung-starter! Mail her a poison suit! Employ the *scaphism!* Hurl her down the *Gemonian* steps with tincans tied to her ears! Whittle her nose into a dowel! *Exenterate* her with an oilclothcutter's knife! *Glume* back her scalp and paint the skull with a crimson A! *Incrassate* her into jellies! *Conglutinate* her buttocks with hot solder! . . . *Ablende* her eyeballs!"[8] (Emphasis added)

Often too, we come upon "lofty sentiments in lofty sentences," vividly illustrated by the conclusion of an earlier chapter titled Love:

"Proud would you be her phaeton, her gig, her shoe-latchet snapped shut to walk her safely in the fittest steps toward paradise, to the snows of Monte Rosa, to the heights of Horeb where each dream dreamt is only yet another dream dreamt among dreams. You have been given the gift of love. You believe it only when you realize it, and yet at that very stroke you cannot but have removed its momentous secret far beyond the hollow formulae, abstract terms, and words such as these that since the beginning of time have stammered after it, pitifully, in the desolation of vain human syllables."[9]

Though the manner in which a leaver-outer like Barthelme and a putter-inner like Theroux employ language marks their opposition, the one associated with stripped-down vocabulary, syntax, rhetoric, and the other with "[e]laborateness in composition," we shall see when we return to minimalism and *The Dead Father* that there are important additional differences between condensed and inflated fiction, involving allusions, myths, actions, landscapes, and characters. Meanwhile, because of its complexity, maximalism must be elucidated.

Maximalists like Theroux, whose *Darconville's Cat* has been called "the finest example of learned wit ever produced in American literature," often belong to the Tradition of Learned Wit, which extends "back through the Augustan satirists to Burton, Cervantes, Erasmus, and Rabelais, and ultimately back to classical satirists such as Lucian and Petronius." Having crossed the Atlantic from England during the eighteenth century, this tradition inspired many antecedent American works, including Brackenridge's *Modern Chivalry,* Irving's *A His-*

tory of New York, and Melville's *Moby-Dick.* Since World War II, it has
flourished here in *Darconville's Cat* and *The Recognitions,* for example.[10]

These and other contemporary big books, mega-novels, total novels *(Ada, Giles Goat-Boy, Gravity's Rainbow, J R, Letters, Miss MacIntosh,
My Darling, Mulligan Stew, The Public Burning, The Sot-Weed Factor,
Women and Men)* may, more or less, be called Menippean satires after
the Greek cynic Menippus because they treat "mental attitudes rather
than fully realized characters," use "plot freely and loosely to present
a view of the world in terms of sharply controlled intellectual patterns," and compile "vast accumulations of fact."[11] Distinguished by
incidental verse, stylized figures, pedantry, dislocated form, fantasy,
and moral earnestness, the Menippean satire, according to Northrop
Frye, generated a subspecies, the "encyclopedic farrago," and that
led to Rabelais's *Gargantua and Pantagruel,* Burton's *Anatomy of Melancholy,* and Sterne's *Tristram Shandy.*[12] Edward Mendelson contends

all encyclopedic narratives are eventually recognized not only as books which
have industries attached to them, but also as *national* books that stand as
written signs of the culture of which they are a part. . . . [They] are meto-
nymic compendia of the *data,* both scientific and aesthetic, valued by their
culture. . . . All are polyglot books. . . . At least six such books are familiar to
literary history: Dante's *Commedia,* Rabelais' five books of *Gargantua and
Pantagruel,* Cervantes' *Don Quixote,* Goethe's *Faust,* Melville's *Moby-Dick,* and
(a special case) Joyce's *Ulysses.*[13]

We are all familiar with the history of our most brilliant "national"
book *Moby-Dick,* how the novel received mixed reviews; how Melville
stopped writing imaginative prose; how his masterpiece was not revived until the 1920s. Virtually the identical thing happened to William Gaddis's first book. This should surprise no one, for the works
have so much in common that *Moby-Dick* even appears in *The Recognitions* as a story written by the counterfeit Melville, Mr. Feddle.
Published about 100 years apart, these enormous fictions teem with
abstruse information and literary, historical, and religious allusions.
Similar form and content made the earlier work a precursor of
modernism, the latter a templet of postmodernism. Consequently,
they suffered the same fate: neglect.

Though Mendelson and others regard *Gravity's Rainbow* as the
supreme instance of current encyclopedic narration, an even better

case can be made for *The Recognitions*.[14] However, there are so many likenesses between Gaddis's big books—*The Recognitions* (1955, 956 pages); *J R* (1975, 726 pages)—and those of Pynchon—*V.* (1963, 463 pages); *Gravity's Rainbow* (1973, 760 pages)—that an article has been devoted to this subject.[15]

The Recognitions and *Gravity's Rainbow* qualify as *national* tales, with the Gaddis protagonist Wyatt Gwyon and the Pynchon protagonist Tyrone Slothrop descending from old New England Protestant families. Since both authors owe a debt to previous Americans—Herman Melville in the case of Gaddis and Henry Adams in the case of Pynchon—they extend our native tradition, albeit obliquely. Yet *The Recognitions*, which embraces Spain, Paris, Central America, and Italy, and *Gravity's Rainbow*, which treats Germany, England, Southwest Africa, and Central America, are international too. Accordingly, the two novels incorporate several foreign languages, including uncommon tongues like Hungarian (Gaddis) and Herero (Pynchon).

The most salient feature of such narratives embodies the concept "encyclopedic" or "relating to all branches of knowledge." This certainly describes *Gravity's Rainbow*, for it provides information about science and technology, psychology, history, religion, film, and literature. More comprehensive still is *The Recognitions*, whose range of erudition appears to be unmatched among postwar American fictions, *Darconville's Cat* notwithstanding.

Even after Steven Moore's *A Reader's Guide to William Gaddis's "The Recognitions"* helps us to untangle the labyrinthine plot, we are faced with a welter of recondite data: "literary allusions, book titles, historical references, obscure subjects, hagiographies, details from church history, mythology, and anthropology, foreign phrases in over a half-dozen languages."[16] More than half of the *Guide* is devoted to annotating this material,[17] which, Moore feels, is anything but a pretentious display, as some reviewers had charged. His own detailed psychological interpretation establishes the deeper significance of several related sources. He considers *The Recognitions* "an account of personal integration amid collective disintegration" (11). Wyatt's "quest for authenticity in life and art" (4) becomes more psychological than physical, so "much of the novel's symbolism is a projection of latent contents in Wyatt's unconscious" (6). Contrary to most critics, Moore views this quest as a return to the lost and dishonored mother instead of to the father, since "the integration of the personality . . . can result only from an acknowledgment of the supremecy *[sic]* of the White Goddess" (7). In *The Recognitions,* which was influenced by C. G. Jung (and alchemy) as well as Robert Graves, Wyatt must confront and accept his anima, or the emotional, intuitive, irrational distaff elements of the male psyche. This psychological interpretation of *The Recognitions* indicates that its referential material—here *The White Goddess* and *Integration of the Personality*—is used in complex and profound ways. Thus, we are reminded of Eliot's famous dictum: "Immature poets imitate; mature poets steal; bad poets deface what they take, and good poets make it into something better, or at least something different." As a "mature poet," Gaddis steals even from the master himself, who would have appreciated the irony.[18]

The sources of the epigraphs affixed to every chapter of *The Recognitions* suggest the scope of its allusiveness: Goethe, *Faust II;* Paul Eudel, *Trucs et truqueurs;* the Clementine *Recognitions* (twice); Rimbaud; Emerson, Dostoyevski, *The Brothers Karamazov* (twice); Raymond Lully, *Codicillus;* Thomas De Quincey; Kyd, *The Spanish Tragedy;* Darwin, *The Origin of the Species;* Joseph Quincy Adams, ed., *The Harrowing of Hell;* Julian [the Apostate]; Ackerley, *Hindoo Holiday;* Lope de Vega, *Amar sin saber a quien;* Blake; and II Kings 4:26. There are hundreds of references in the book—real and unreal, direct and indirect, past and present—to literature, music, painting, philosophy, religion, sculpture, and so forth. Among the important allusions that recur, we find Bosch *(The Seven Deadly Sins);* Clement *(Recognitions);* Dante *(The Inferno);* El Greco; Eliot *(The Waste Land, Four Quartets,* other poems); the Flemish masters (the van Eycks, van der Goes, van der Weyden); Fox's *Book of Martyrs;* Goethe *(Faust);* John Huss; Ibsen *(Peer Gynt);* Melville *(Moby-Dick);* Mithras; Mozart; Rilke *(Duino Elegies);* Thoreau; and Titian.

Gaddis's central concern is authenticity. In exploring this, *The Recognitions* becomes an extended metaphor, with the vehicle Art/Religion, and the tenor Life. Several artistic modes are represented, but painting dominates. Thus, the critics have written extensively about the connections between Wyatt Gwyon and the notorious Han van Meegeren; the significance of *The Seven Deadly Sins* and its warning "Cave, cave, Dominus videt" ("Beware, beware, the Lord sees"); and, above all, the role played by the Flemish masters.

Various modes of religious experience are represented too: Calvinism, Catholicism, Gnosticism, Mysticism, and Mithraism. Two interrelated religious legends contribute to the structure, as well as the meaning, of *The Recognitions*. In Gaddis's notes to the novel, he wrote, "When I started this thing . . . it was to be a good deal shorter, and quite explicitly a parody of the FAUST story, except the artist taking the place of the learned doctor."[19] Faustian elements appear throughout the text; for example, a character named Otto says, " 'Faust sold his soul to the devil,' "[20] precisely what occurs the moment Wyatt-Faust agrees to forge paintings for Brown-Mephistopheles, who, like the Goethean villain, is associated with a dog.

During the most reflexive passage of *The Recognitions*, another character, Basil Valentine, links *Faust* and the Clementine *Recognitions*, the third-century theological tract falsely ascribed to Clement of Rome and the source of Gaddis's title, two epigraphs, and many references. He is conversing on the telephone with an unidentified interlocutor:

—A novel? But . . . yes, perhaps he can, if he thinks it will do any good. But you can tell your friend Willie that salvation is hardly the practical study it was then. [. . .] *The Recognitions*? No, it's Clement of Rome. Mostly talk, talk, talk. The young man's deepest concern is for the immortality of his soul, he goes to Egypt to find the magicians and learn their secrets. It's been referred to as the first Christian novel. What? Yes, it's really the beginning of the whole Faust legend. [. . .] My, your friend is writing for a rather small audience, isn't he.[21]

Parodic parallels between Clement's ancient and "Willie" Gaddis's modern *Recognitions* abound. Both treat a peripatetic youth seeking salvation. Their journeys take Clement to Palestine (not Egypt) and Wyatt to Munich, Paris, New York, Madrid/San Zwingli (Escorial). As Clement becomes a disciple of St. Peter, who teaches him about Christianity, Wyatt follows Mr. Yak, the disguised counterfeiter Frank Sinisterra, who involves him in a ghoulish scheme. Ancient and modern *Recognitions* contain devil figures, the first, Simon Magus (magician), and the second, Recktall Brown (businessman). While Clement is finally reunited with his family, Wyatt's quests for mother and father prove abortive. And while Clement achieves salvation through the love of God, Wyatt may be redeemed only through the love of man.[22]

Not only William Gaddis, but Alexander Theroux, Thomas Pynchon, and other postwar authors of maximalist fiction are "writing for a rather small audience." The length of their novels, the complexity of their styles, and the abstruseness of their allusions have conspired to keep books like *The Recognitions, Darconville's Cat,* and even *Gravity's Rainbow* virtually unknown except in select academic circles. Contrariwise, the leaver-outers currently publishing minimalist fiction, though sometimes antirealistic, enjoy a wider readership.

Frederick R. Karl analyzes "The Possibilities of Minimalism" in *American Fictions 1940/1980:*

> The minimalist writer must assure the audience that he, the writer, knows far more about the subject than he is including; that beyond him, in some spatial realm, there is the rest, undefined perhaps, but *there.* Often, the writer makes as his point of reference not the line he develops but the beyond; what is not as dominant as what is, and possibly more significant. . . . Sequential narrative line and routine characterization, as well as plotting, are either diminished or undermined altogether. . . . The author brings us close to boredom, withdrawal, rejection of the work itself. Further, minimalist fiction is nearly always based on a pessimistic view of life, where all the normal goals or controls no longer obtain. It depends heavily on irony, itself a form of negation.[23]

Before European writers like Camus and Beckett, who have excelled in this tradition, there were American leaver-outers like Stephen Crane, Willa Cather, and Ernest Hemingway. Crane's disciple Cather had said: "It is the inexplicable presence of the thing not named, of the overtone divined by the ear but not heard by it, the verbal mood, the emotional aura of the fact or the thing or the deed, that gives high quality to the novel or the drama, as well as to poetry itself."[24] Hemingway later added: "If a writer of prose knows enough about what he is writing about he may omit things that he knows and the reader, if the writer is writing truly enough, will have a feeling of those things as strongly as though the writer had stated them. The dignity of movement of an iceberg is due to only one-eighth of it being above water."[25]

Few would quarrel with Karl's contention that "[t]he 1960s and 1970s have produced a small body of minimalists, of whom Donald Barthelme is the most practiced, and his *The Dead Father* the most expert example," yet many would question the assertion that "[m]uch minimalist fiction tries to be innovative" despite the authors Karl records: "Wurlitzer, Tuten, Sontag, McGuane, Adler ... Brauti-gan."[26]

At any rate, Barthelme's innovative second novel contains allusions, but these tend to be scattered rather than focused, isolated rather than clustered. Robert Burton, Albert Schweitzer, Lenin, Franz Joseph Haydn, Martin Luther, John Wilkes Booth, Aristotle, and Pascal are sprinkled throughout the text unconnected. However, Lord Raglan's appellation and epic lists recur besides revelatory passages such as "Sword play of this quality has not been seen since the days of Frithjof, Lancelot, Paracelsus, Rogero, Artegal, Otuel, Ogier the Dane, Rinaldo, Oliver, Koll the Thrall, Haco I, and the Chevalier Bayard"[27] to *imply* a mythic context one critic neatly summarizes:

> Barthelme accomplishes the "cosmopolitanization" or global application of the Dead Father figure by comparing him to the Judeo-Christian concept of God; the Greco-Roman concepts of Zeus, Orpheus, and Jason; the Serpent-god of Indian mythology; the All-Father, Odin of Norse mythology, and the Norse pessimism expressed in the belief in the Day of Ragnarok or "Twilight of the Gods"; the German "voivode" (voevode) or "devil"; and the medieval English vegetation myths of the dying god and the Fisher King.[28]

Whereas *The Recognitions* enacts several interrelated myths, *The Dead Father* treats just one in sustained fashion. The Quest of the Golden Fleece commences on page 9 and terminates on page 176. Some references are explicit: "That was when I was young and full of that zest which has leaked out of me and which we are journeying to recover for me by means of the great revitalizing properties of that long fleecy golden thing of which the bards sing and the skalds sing and the Mestersingers sing" (38–39). The title character speaks these words, thinking his trip promises renewal, but for the others, it remains a funeral procession. Reminiscent of the Bundren family, they cannot live until they have buried their tyrannical parent; meanwhile, like Addie, the Dead Father, "is dead only in a sense" (14). Barthelme's book, no less than *As I Lay Dying*, mocks myth, since the Golden Fleece turns out to be feminine pubic hair.[29]

Additional patterns of recurrence help structure *The Dead Father*. Among them are the four repetitive conversations between Emma and Julie (chapters 3, 8, 13, 18); the Dead Father's three rampages (chapters 1, 7, 11); his loss of buckle (chapter 6), sword (chapter 11), passport (chapter 19), keys (chapter 21); occasional sex play involving Julie and Thomas (chapters 1, 4, 19); and intermittent appearances of a mysterious horseman who is actually "Mother."

Antirealistic minimalist fiction often proceeds episodically.[30] Thus, *The Dead Father*, a 177-page novel, contains a prologue and twenty-three chapters. Its dramatic action is skeletal, consisting of only departure, dubious "trials," and arrival. Rather, digressions become central: the Hilda/Lars encounter, the porno film, the bartender incident, the Dead Father's tale about the Pool Table of Ballambangjang, Thomas's "dramatic narrative" about kidnaping, the survival speech, the Dead Father and the lady lawyer, and the dance. Most important, *A Manual for Sons*, was translated by Peter Scatterpatter. This text-within-a-text extends from page 111 to page 146, one-fifth of the total volume. Like eighteenth-century fiction, the manual has thematic relevance, while interrupting the action, as the contents hint: for instance, "Mad fathers," "The leaping father," "Dandling," "A tongue-lashing," "The falling father," "Lost fathers," "Sexual organs," " 'Responsibility.' " Scatterpatter's twenty-three entries duplicate the book's twenty-three chapters and confirm its episodic nature.

Obviously, plotting in *The Recognitions* and other gigantic novels is far more elaborate than in *The Dead Father*. Whereas Gaddis creates multiple stories that are rich and concrete, Barthelme constructs just one bare, abstract tale; and whereas Gaddis gives us a discernible, if complex, time scheme, Barthelme never clarifies during which day, month (June?) or year *The Dead Father* occurs. Space here seems almost as vague as time, contrasting sharply to the vivid Spain, New England, Paris, New York (Greenwich Village), Central America, and Italy of *The Recognitions*. A single irrelevant setting receives detailed description in *The Dead Father:* "The cathedral. Bronze doors intricately worked with scenes. Row of grenadiers in shakos. Kneeling. Interior of the egg. Painted brick, white, curving. Rug or quilt of blue and red slipping toward the edge. In the walls of the cathedral. Windows over the edge. Dies irae, dies illa" (84–85). Otherwise, origin, road, and destination remain indistinct. The two-week (?) journey begins at "our city," an anonymous metropolis that has few place names (Avenue Pommard, Boulevard Grist, the Gardens, Belfast Avenue), and ends—why, we do not know—at some "large gap in the earth" (174) "many kilometers" away. Barthelme's expedition meanwhile drags across a landscape alternately rural and urban, desolate and crowded, where mysterious creatures appear: the "man tending bar in an open field" (28), the "People taking pictures" (76), musical apes (99), and "hundreds . . . holding black umbrellas" (174). Oddest are the Wends, whom the Dead Father ruled until 1936. Their leader explains, "Wends have no wives, they have only mothers. Each Wend impregnates his own mother and thus fathers himself. We are all married to our mothers, in proper legal fashion" (73).

Vague itself, this timeless and spaceless world invokes many times and places to achieve a universal context suitable for the father archetype. The old ("hussar," "ukase," "duel," "tights," "robes") becomes juxtaposed with the new ("zip codes," "blue jeans," "car wash," "Kool-Aid" "credit cards") and the mythical ("sagas," "underworld," "Aphrodite") with the historical ("Congress of Vienna," "Romantic Movement," *"Le Monde"*). Concurrently, *The Dead Father* refers to Yorkshire, Barcelona, Warsaw, Africa, Denmark, Miami, Moscow, Borneo, Saxony, Darmstadt, Punjab, and other places, and therefore it is understandable that the characters' own unspecified city has French and Irish street names.

As might be expected, minimalist narratives treat fewer people than encyclopedic ones. *The Recognitions* may not match the 300 individuals Scott Simmon detected in *Gravity's Rainbow*, but the earlier novel supports a huge cast. On the other hand, besides the title figure, *The Dead Father* contains just four principals: son Thomas; his girlfriend, Julie; his brother, Edmund; and their companion, Emma. Unlike numerous Gaddis/Pynchon characters, no Barthelme person possesses a surname, while the even more allegorical Dead Father and ubiquitous spouse remain anonymous. Sire asks son, "What was her name?" and son replies, "Her name was Mother" (170).

Discounting the previous exploits of the Dead Father, we see that only Thomas is given biographical data, however scant: Born in "our city" thirty-nine years ago, he attended school, suffered childhood adversities, acquired higher education, entered military service, studied sociology, married frequently, fathered one child, tried commerce, joined a monastery, and read philosophy. Though somewhat more complicated than those of his fellow travelers, Thomas's relationships are also mechanical, as this excerpt from the lengthy lovemaking passage in chapter 19 illustrates:

Thomas lying on his back, cruciform. . . .
Julie smokes with one hand (second finger) moving up and down between
her legs.
Various movements on Thomas's part. Trying to see.
Julie smokes. Offers cigarette to Thomas.
Thomas raises head, takes cigarette between lips. Two puffs.
Julie removes cigarette. Hand between legs.
Julie smokes looking at Thomas.
Thomas remains in Position A, as per the agreement. (159–60)

Most antirealists treat similar dehumanized erotic behavior, yet
minimalism and maximalism remain dichotomous. The first has fewer
of nearly everything. Whereas maximalist fictions (big books, mega-
novels, total novels)—descended from Menippean satire and encyclopedic farrago—employ inclusive styles, minimalist fictions, representing an equally venerable opposite tradition, tend to be exclusive.
And whereas maximalist fictions teem with recondite data, which
includes numerous allusions and myths, minimalist fictions, though
not devoid of such material, use it sparingly. Putter-inners are much
less vague than taker-outers about time, space, and so forth, while
much more copious about plot and character, because putter-inners
believe "more is more" and taker-outers believe "less is more."

"[T]he dialogue between maximalist and minimalist" may be "as
old as storytelling," but Barth feels compelled to cite several factors
that explain the present minimalist vogue: "Vietnam War," "energy
crisis," "decline in reading and writing skills," "ever-dwindling readerly attention span," "literary antecedents," "American advertising."[31] Another John, named Rockwell, finding minimalism everywhere during the 1960s and 1970s—"popular music and jazz, films,
plays, poetry and novels," even "nouvelle cuisine"—terms the movement "a variant of the overall Modernist reaction against late Romantic Victorian plush."[32] However, to antirealists, Dan's analysis in Barthelme's *Snow White* carries greater weight, since the equation between
linguistic "filling"/"stuffing" and the "trash phenomenon," which requires the banishment of wasteful proliferation through elliptical
expression, invokes the all-important entropy motif treated during
chapter 10. This motif has also inspired maximalist books like *J R*
whose "form and style" duplicate rather than obliterate "the runaway
system it is about." There, according to Thomas LeClair in "William
Gaddis, *JR*, and the Art of Excess," the author imitates what he hates,

embracing such entropic matter as jargon, double-talk, noise, destruction, deterioration, sickness, sameness, fragmentation, garbage, and excrement. *J R* and other maximalist novels "deform old modes and create new models" because "representation and metonymy have failed" and "radical new communication is necessary for survival."[33]

Antirealistic minimalism shares much besides defamiliarization with antirealistic maximalism. For instance, *The Dead Father* resembles *Darconville's Cat* and additional encyclopedic works by its juxtaposition of various literary forms: epic list, duologue, monologue, tall tale (called "dramatic narrative"), manual, and speech. That these are often parodied the following epic list demonstrates:

> The Dead Father was slaying, in a grove of music and musicians. First he slew a harpist and then a performer upon the serpent and also a banger upon the rattle and also a blower of the Persian trumpet and one upon the Indian trumpet and one upon the Hebrew trumpet and one upon the Roman trumpet and one upon the Chinese trumpet of copper-covered wood. (11)

Though radical dissimilarities separate postwar writers associated with maximalism and those associated with minimalism, the antirealists belonging to both schools glorify language, as the above passage hints. Reminiscent of their spiritual father, the old artificer James Joyce, our putter-inners and leaver-outers alike create rhetorical heterocosms confirming the statement *"Whatever else it is about, great literature is almost always also about itself."*[34]

PART II

The Universe as Madhouse

Self-conscious or not, the alternate worlds that constitute the antireal-istic universe make it appear irrational. Many factors are involved, four of which receive treatment in part 2, chapter 4 "Fragmentation/Decentralization"; chapter 5 "The Grotesque and the Devil"; chapter 6 "Imaginary Landscapes"; and chapter 7 "Absurd Quests."

With regard to fragmentation, *The Waste Land* is the seminal mod-ern text, influencing both those who share the Eliotic "rage for order" like William Gaddis and Coleman Dowell and those who fear order as systemic like William Burroughs and Thomas Pynchon. Dowell's *Island People* resembles *The Waste Land*, since the novel, no less than the poem, replaces transition by juxtaposition (montage, collage), invokes metamorphic voices, and explores androgynous characteri-zation. Because he fears the order Eliot, Gaddis, and Dowell miss, anarchist Burroughs destroys continuity deliberately through various devices: "the cut-up method," "the fold-in method," and spliced tape/films. The technique of mixed focus, derived meanwhile from John Dos Passos, whose multiple perspectives necessitated multiple plots, forced fiction to become decentralized and decentralization, parallel-ing fragmentation, also reflects disjointed contemporary life in works such as *The Recognitions,* where the ostensible protagonist has a tragic and comic counterpart, and *Gravity's Rainbow,* where one story line is only slightly more important than four others. These massive heter-ocosms resemble *The Waste Land* too, for they explore spiritual ma-laise and loveless involvement on an international scale.

The figures, objects, and situations filling our fractured universe are grotesque, a fact that fictions by John Hawkes and Flannery O'Connor—*The Cannibal* and *Wise Blood*—well illustrate. Malformed and estranged, their people, like many other American characters past and present, often embody the diabolical, which helps confirm one famous definition of the grotesque: "An Attempt to Invoke and

Subdue the Demonic Aspects of the World." Hawkes's article, "Flannery O'Connor's Devil," and the correspondence between them indicate Satan may be either sacred or secular. Other texts discussed in the context of the grotesque/diabolical include *Darconville's Cat, Miss MacIntosh, My Darling, Miss Lonelyhearts,* and *The Recognitions.*

This universe is as elusive as it is discontinuous and bizarre, since location, the bedrock of realistic fiction, waxes more mental than physical in antirealistic compositions. Three settings emerge from native literary history: the fantastic, the disguised, and the actual. Current instances appear, respectively, during *Cities of the Red Night* (Burroughs), *Mrs. October Was Here* (Dowell), and "Paraguay" (Barthelme). All three types—Ba'dan, Tasmania, and Paraguay—may be discovered both within and without the verifiable world. "Tlön, Uqbar, Orbis Tertius" and *Pale Fire* by two past masters of fabulous places, Jorge Luis Borges and Vladimir Nabokov, prepare us for *Ada,* where the latter makes the real unreal and the unreal real, and where nationalities, languages, and hybrid locales commingle on his psychic map. Chapter 6 closes with John Hawkes, a present master, whose texts—especially *Second Skin* and *The Blood Oranges*—are analyzed, and whose views regarding imaginary landscapes are illustrated.

Absurd quests and grotesque questers dot these landscapes. Like *The Great Gatsby, Giles Goat-Boy* mocks the heroic monomyth in detail, yet because *Giles* is a post–World War II novel, it lacks Gatsby's plausibility and circularity (i.e., "departure," "initiation," *and* "return"). *Blue Pastoral,* the most ridiculous autochthonous journey since *The Dream Life of Balso Snell,* takes Wandering Jew "Blue" Serge Gavotte across the United States after "the Perfect Musical Phrase." Its author, Gilbert Sorrentino, shares self-consciousness and academic satire with John Barth; however, he largely ignores the monomyth that Barth and Fitzgerald mock, defamiliarizing instead diverse literary and subliterary genres and styles—particularly connected to the pastoral—through parody, burlesque, and travesty, until, finally, his own mad tale deconstructs. Two additional inconclusive contemporary searches receive extended treatment during chapter 7: *Hind's Kidnap* and *V..* Though these nonmetafictional narratives seem more realistic than *Giles Goat-Boy* or *Blue Pastoral,* both contain absurd elements, and though their orphan protagonists seek self-identity via father figures, this traditional motif does not supersede the conspiracy/paranoia theme that Joseph McElroy and Thomas Pynchon explore. *V.* further foreshadows part 3 when its entropic world, haunted by "the ultimate Plot Which Has No Name," anticipates Armageddon/apocalypse.

CHAPTER 4

Fragmentation/Decentralization

—That's what it is, a disease, you can't live like we do without catching it. Because we get time given to us in fragments, that's the only way we know it. Finally we can't even conceive of a continuum of time. Every fragment exists by itself, and that's why we live among palimpsests, because finally all the work should fit into one whole, and express an entire perfect action, as Aristotle says, and it's impossible now, it's impossible because of the breakage, there are pieces everywhere.—*The Recognitions*

Although the above speaker does not quote T. S. Eliot in his comment to another about "this modern disease," the poet, whose formal and conceptual preoccupation with fragmentation affected almost every subsequent antirealistic American prose writer,[1] had a profound influence on *The Recognitions*. One critic has pointed out how "Gaddis' Debt to T. S. Eliot" included shifting points of view, juxtaposition of past and present, spatialization of events, arid landscapes, mourning women, questers, imposters, fertility figures, chapels, bells, burials, and resurrections. According to her, the protagonist's progress toward integration mirrors the harmony of the *Four Quartets*, while civilization's regression toward disintegration echoes the cacophony of *The Waste Land*.[2]

"These fragments I have shored against my ruins" (l. 431) all but concludes the latter, which is probably the most memorable collection of poetic fragments since *On Nature* by Empedocles.[3] Among the many forms fragmentation takes during *The Waste Land*, those involving structure and characterization are especially prominent.

The poem consists of five sections, ranging from 139 lines ("The Fire Sermon") to 10 lines ("Death by Water"). Discontinuous as a five-part whole, these sections contain seemingly unrelated passages. Whatever coherence we find comes partially through standard organizational devices. Eliot has admitted in his Notes that "Not only the title, but the plan and a good deal of the incidental symbolism of the poem were suggested by Jessie L. Weston's book on the Grail legend: *From Ritual to Romance*," so we catch intermittent glimpses of the Fisher King and the archetypal quest. Accompanying this vestigial narrative is a recurrent, though erratic, seasonal cycle, beginning with spring or autumn, skipping summer, and ending with winter. Related images also appear to create unified patterns.

Less orthodox are two other organizational devices: associational flow and juxtaposition. Associational flow pervades *The Waste Land*, one instance being "The Fire Sermon," where, after the suitor deserts the typist, she "puts a record on the gramophone" that leads to the music Ferdinand hears that leads to "The pleasant whining of a mandoline" (l. 261). Even more important, juxtaposition warrants considerable discussion by Roger Shattuck:

> The modern sensibility, however, began to proceed not so much by untrammeled expansion of the unities as by a violent dislocation of them in order to test the possibility of a new coherence. . . . a work of art began to co-ordinate as equally present a variety of times and places and states of consciousness. . . . This factotum word is *juxtaposition:* setting one thing beside the other without connective. The twentieth century has addressed itself to arts of juxtaposition as opposed to earlier arts of *transition*.
>
> Transition refers to those works that rely upon clear articulation of the relations between parts at the places they join: connection at the edges (though other, inner connections may exist as well). . . .
>
> The arts of juxtaposition offer difficult, disconcerting, fragmented works, whose disjunct sequence has neither beginning nor end.[4]

"The arts of juxtaposition" in *The Waste Land* include the cinematic technique of montage, whereby several shots are superimposed to form a single image, and the artistic technique of collage, whereby diverse materials not normally associated with one another are pasted on a single surface. Thus, during The Fire Sermon, while Eliot's protean protagonist visits the Thames, the dull canal, London (typist quarters, Strand, Lower Thames Street), the Thames again (Greenwich, Isle of Dogs, Richmond, Margate Sands) and Carthage, we get quotations from or allusions to various literary worlds. Juxtaposition of these, which span contemporary England to ancient India, abolishes spatial/temporal differences, creating "a new coherence" that makes "equally present" several "times and places and states of consciousness."

The Waste Land protagonist, "if it exists at all, is changing and

discontinuous," argues Robert Langbaum.[5] Fragmentation of character, then, owes much to the metamorphic process evident here as
well as in other modern poetic sequences (e.g., *The Cantos*), novels
(e.g., *Finnegans Wake*), and even dramas (e.g., *A Dream Play*). That
characterological fragmentariness involves transformation from one
sex to another besides one voice to another receives support in the
note for l. 218, where Eliot quotes Ovid on the physical changes
experienced by Tiresias because of sexual crimes. Hermaphroditic,
his own seer embodies the entire *Waste Land* cast. The paradox of
Tiresias's dual nature—unified or androgynous versus divided or
male/female—emerges at the very heart of *The Waste Land*, section 3,
The Fire Sermon. There, the "old man with wrinkled dugs" (l. 228)
who has "fore-suffered all" (l. 243) perceives loveless coitus performed by his two psychic components the typist and the suitor.
Eliot's Tiresian figure, like the juxtapositional method, both repli-
cates and resists twentieth-century chaos in a work whose author
maintains the "rage for order" while "London Bridge is falling down
falling down falling down" (l. 427).

Coleman Dowell resembles Eliot more than any successor with regard
to the fragmentation/metamorphosis/androgyny syndrome.[6] Citing
Island People, he admitted in a 1981 interview, "I started to use an
epigraph from *The Waste Land*, then thought the connection should
be plain enough. I used the soul-searching, the sense of the disembodied, the looking for grace, the foreign languages and civilizations."[7]

Even Dowell's compositional method seems fragmentary. During
the same interview, he said: "[W]hile I was writing *One of the Children
Is Crying*, I started *Too Much Flesh and Jabez*, finished *One of the
Children*, gave up *Jabez* and started *Island People*, stopped that and
wrote all of *Mrs. October Was Here* in six months, went back to *Island
People*, finished it, then back to *Jabez*. That's the only way I can
work."[8]

The motif of fragmentation, which dominates *Island People* (1976)
—"ALL THERE IS, IS FRAGMENTS, because a man, even the loneliest of
the species, is divided among several persons, animals, worlds"[9]—
had already appeared in *One of the Children Is Crying* (1968), where

earth/air/water/fire are symbolized by siblings, and in *Mrs. October Was Here* (1974), where the characters stand for various aspects of the creative personality. Subsequently, joined with the metamorphosis and androgyny marking *Island People*, it appeared again in *Too Much Flesh and Jabez* (1977): "Thinking to have found herself in one character [Miss Ethel] would, without warning, 'become' another: now Jim, now Jabez, now Ludie, and so on, but she had an increasing sense of insecurity in her own persona, which like an amoeba had divided into two and then gone on subdividing."[10]

The most important manifestation of fragmentation during *Island People* concerns metamorphosis, or what Miss Ethel terms "subdividing." Dowell invents a nameless protagonist, virtually identical with himself: both were Scottish, from Kentucky, island residents, dachshund owners, companions of Claudo (Carl Van Vechten), and failed playwrights working on a manuscript titled *Island People*. The protagonist then invents "New Novelist" Beatrix, who, in turn, invents the protagonist's negative mask Chris. All three are unreliable narrators. Dowell comments, "I have endowed the 'I' of this book with total recall—(though there will be a lot he will not want to recall, and will manage, sometimes, not to)" (33), and the protagonist confesses his "authorship of lies" (271). He regularly accuses Beatrix of distortion —"THIS IS NOT THE PAST IN WHICH UNACCOUNTABLY I TOOK REFUGE AND OFFERED REFUGE TO YOU" (112–13)—and as her creature, Chris, he has twisted "the facts given him by Victor over many a long afternoon" (159). Nor can minor narrators be trusted. For example, the poet-husband of Beatrix "created his own world as he wished it to be" (17).

Imaginary themselves, these figures reflect an artistic milieu. Its epitomization, Claudo Darius—"to New York what Gertrude Stein was to Paris" (186)—presides over a superficial salon reminiscent of Gaddis's Viareggio. Here and elsewhere we encounter talented personages; once real, they are now characters that, Pirandello-fashion, fracture their anonymous maker's mind. Reality is mental rather than physical, verbal rather than actual, and consequently he proclaims: "When I write 'he ran,' I see neither him nor running; I see two words" (279). As life becomes art, art becomes game, so, besides several references to famous authors, the book includes numerous genres and reflexive allusions to craft (e.g., FIRST-PERSON BIOGRAPHY,

261ff.): "Some compulsive neatness or need, some awareness of the circularity of events, perhaps, insists that I end this composition, before the coda, as it began" (308). The art-game motif has both a positive and negative side. On the one hand, through "the act of creation, we 'forgive' the objects of our imagination" (105); yet, on the other, we erect a "word-jail" (275), wherein even the "personal desire for continuity is . . . mainly literary" (269).

Separation defines *Island People*'s important architectural metaphor, initiated by the Dickinson epigraph ("One need not be a Chamber / to be Haunted / One need not be a House"), which recurs later. Such images are juxtaposed throughout to the sustained, though intermittent, story-within-a-story concerning a mid-nineteenth-century murder committed in the very edifice the protagonist occupies. Seven installments tell about a boy's love for his beautiful mother; the mother's untimely death from smallpox; the father's cold second wife; the stepmother's disappearance; the boy's flight; the bond-maid's trial and execution; the boy's return. Both Dickinson ("The Brain has Corridors surpassing / Material place") and Dowell ("his mind, which he came to inhabit like an exclusive and active ghost in an old house" [125]) connect inner and outer structures. Therefore, it is not surprising that after the protagonist, having assumed the persona of mass murderer and purged the vampiric selves causing him to complain, "I do not know now who 'I' am" (259), enters the attic, where twentieth-century son and nineteenth-century mother are united.[11]

References to hermaphroditism also pervade *Island People*, whose dust jacket shows a masculine face superimposed upon a feminine face. Passive and refined, middle-aged and bisexual, Southern and Protestant, the nameless protagonist both loves and hates his alter ego, the aggressive and primitive, young and feminist, Northern and Jewish Beatrix. She, in turn, is opposed by the protagonist's dachshund—"precious malleable strut of the earth" (35)—named Miss Gold to signify the splendid qualities absent from the succubus (i.e., "bitch" vs. "witch"). These antitheses eventually cohere, as summarized by Stephen-Paul Martin: "Like *The Waste Land*, Dowell's novel evolves through a sequence of narratives that emerge from the male and female projections of an almost-invisible central figure. The book's movement toward a final state of Grace, or 'pre-existence,' is an androgynous orchestration that concludes with a synthesis of its masculine and feminine elements."[12]

Psychic divisions are reinforced by various dichotomies: nineteenth-century past/twentieth-century present, art/life, and summer residents/winter residents. The geographical contrariety of island/mainland constitutes a second important metaphor. Dowell's action shuttles between actual settings, Shelter Island and New York City, but if his nineteenth-century house represents the human brain, his island symbolizes isolated individuals and his mainland, society, though island people may be found on the mainland too: "City apartments such as this one, owned pieces of the sky, are islands, separated from the mainland by an elaborate system of security" (147). Thus, the protagonist, embodying the writer's plight, experiences loneliness everywhere. He is, Dowell once asserted, an island striving to become a peninsula.

The four sectional headings of *Island People* (THE GAME, CAUGHT, TRIALS, THE SENTENCE), even more than the five of *The Waste Land*, indicate that its nightmarish world has *moral* continuity. Indeed, through the nineteenth-century boy, the twentieth-century man conducts "his own trial for the murder of a love—nameless, undefined" (118).

Dowell's major divisions contain fifty-three subdivisions, thirty-nine labeled, seven unlabeled, and seven (the story-within-a-story) designated by graphic design. They incorporate many genres and vary in length from five lines to thirty-nine pages. Juxtaposed arbitrarily during THE SENTENCE, these fragments form a collage consisting of thirteen units, with the seventh triparted. What confirms temporal cohesion here amid ostensible randomness is the *Memorial Day* (first unit)-"*Spring!* (twelfth unit) framework, while the total novel blends private journal dates and public occasions to project the following time scheme: Christmas, February 14 (Valentine's Day), 15, 16, 17, 18, 19, 28; March 14, 10, 15; June 22; April; May Day; Memorial Day; Independence Day; Spring. Whereas the seasonal cycle of *The Waste Land* begins in spring and ends in winter, the seasonal cycle of *Island People* begins in winter and ends in spring. Paradoxically, however, psychic integration during the novel leads toward imminent death, but psychic disintegration during the poem leads toward anticipated life.

Because *Island People* is a first-person narrative, it largely lacks the author's self-styled "organizing voice." Even so, Dowell the novelist restores unity to a chaotic world and Dowell the teacher restores morality to an immoral universe. He insists on " 'a rage for order' in my life and in my writing too. . . . If you read my whole book, you will find perfect order. . . . if you see it as a whole, all the fragments should fit together like a mosaic."[13] This mosaic results from the arts of juxtaposition, whereby present/past separate and fuse in complex temporal patterns and island/city separate and fuse in complex spatial patterns to reveal how they interact and to demonstrate that "[d]istance and time" are "the same," that "[w]e exist simultaneously with ourselves" (122).

Though William S. Burroughs also employs metamorphosis in *The Wild Boys* (1972), which treats an anarchistic youth cult whose members are misogynistic, self-generative male clones, this author does not seek harmony between the sexes. Nevertheless, he, too, is a disciple of T. S. Eliot, incorporating phrases from the latter's canon throughout his own. During an earlier novel, *Nova Express,* these mingle with additional dialogue to form a *Waste Land* composite that reads: " '*What thinking,* William?—*Were his eyes*—*Hurry up please its* half your brain slowly fading—*Make yourself a bit smart*—It's them couldn't reach flesh—*Empty walls*—*Good night, sweet ladies*—*Hurry up please it's time*—Look any place—*Faces in the violet light*—*Damp gusts bringing rain*—' "[14] (emphasis added). Another piece, the autobiographical "St. Louis Return," where Burroughs mentions former fellow resident "Tommy Eliot," alludes to several youthful poems. Among them, he has always regarded *The Waste Land* as the first great collage: "Eliot was quite a verbal innovator. *The Waste Land* is, in effect, a cut-up, since it's using all these bits and pieces of other writers in an associational matrix."[15]

Gaddis and Dowell pose their Eliotic internal "rage for order" against external fragmentation. Conversely, Burroughs, like Pynchon, finds only systemic control outside himself—death-oriented hierarchies involving the Nova Mob, the white race, the female gender, the scientific community (medicine, psychology), and the social institution (business, politics, religion). Such power groups keep us

physically enslaved to sex and drugs. Worse yet, they keep us enslaved mentally by exploiting word and image, which, during an era
of general literacy, become important control instruments: "Through
the manipulation of word and image, an illusory reality is created
and maintained. This is what Burroughs refers to as 'the God film' or
'the reality movie.' "[16] Written media, whose signs and objects are
divorced, foster addiction to the "word virus"; consequently, he dis-
mantles magazine and newspaper articles, often focused on disease,
in *Minutes to Go*, where the final contribution begins, "RUB OUT THE
WRITE WORD." However, speech may be even more dangerous than
print, as when The Subliminal Kid conquers the streets of *Nova
Express* with radio transmitters, microphones, tape recorders, and
films, introducing and intensifying conflicts.

Though Burroughs remains our most innovative postwar novelist,[17] he borrowed his principal countercountrol weapons from foreign acquaintances. An English doctor, John Dent, developed The
Apomorphine Treatment to cure addiction, while an English painter,
Brion Gysin, invented The Cut-Up Method to revolutionize syntax.
Because language lagged far behind pictorial art technically, Gysin
made collages out of printed matter during 1959, but later credited
precursor Tristan Tzara and claimed Burroughs had already used
the method unconsciously in *Naked Lunch*, a book that exhibits random order. Their collaborative *Minutes to Go*, which "contains uned-
ited unchanged cut-ups emerging as quite coherent and meaningful
prose,"[18] soon appeared (1960) and ever since Burroughs has regularly employed this and similar devices.

No place else have he and Gysin commented more lucidly on cut-
ups than in *The Third Mind* (1978), where Burroughs's "The Cut-Up
Method of Brion Gysin" tells us we may make a "new page" by cutting
an old one down and across the middle into four sections, then
juxtaposing the sections differently, while Gysin's "The Cut-ups Self-
Explained" tells us we may make a "newly constituted message" by
cutting pages lengthwise into three columns, then rearranging them
as ACB, BAC, and so forth. Both strategies, besides typographical
experiments like Pages from the Cut-Up Scrapbooks fill *The Burroughs File* (1984). The titles of its first two three-column selections
establish *The Waste Land* connection—WHO IS THE THIRD THAT WALKS
BESIDE YOU; WHO IS THE / WALKS BESIDE YOU / WRITTEN 3RD?—and a

subsequent final column concludes: "Now what have I done here in / these columns? Well the first / column is my necessary expla- / na- tions. The second column is / from the *Tangier Gazette* Jan. / 17, 1974. The third column is / composed from texts of my own / interspersed with pieces from / the *New York Times* September / 17, 1899."[19]

Also during *The Third Mind*—his "elementary manual of illusion techniques"—Burroughs discusses the scissorless cut-up, or fold-in, another means through which literature can reflect other, more ad- vanced arts:

In writing my last two novels, *Nova Express* and *The Ticket That Exploded*, I have used an extension of the cut-up method I call 'the fold-in method'—A page of text—my own or someone else's—is folded down the middle and placed on another page—The composite text is then read across half one text and half the other—The fold-in method extends to writing the flashback used in films, enabling the writer to move backward and forward on his time track—For example I take page one and fold it into page one hundred—I insert the resulting composite as page ten—When the reader reads page ten he is flashing forward in time to page one hundred and back in time to page one . . . This method is of course used in music, where we are continually moved backward and forward on the time track by repetition and rearrange- ments of musical themes.[20]

The concept of the cut-up collage also lay behind Burroughs's experiments with tape recorders. He believes that, like The Sublimi- nal Kid, anybody possessing a portable tape recorder might control mass thought, since our age is dominated by sound. Repeatedly, we are instructed how to use this mechanism. Fresh juxtapositions occur, for instance, when the operator cuts other news broadcasts into one, erasing the original words at such points. Or the operator may alter- nately record two different tapes on a third. Even so, Burroughs informed Victor Bockris, the tape recorder has never helped him compose.

Films, which utilize splices too, have contrariwise, played an in- creasingly large role in his work. *The Soft Machine* incorporates a section titled "1920 Movies" and *The Ticket That Exploded* describes "the image track." According to Eric Mottram, "Tio Mate Smiles" of *The Wild Boys* is

told in cinematic methods of metamorphosis (pan, zoom, track and montage) which are developed with new skills both here and in *Exterminator!* The camera eye and the cutting, synthesizing editor create a rapid method of shot-by-shot shorthand exemplification of information, in the manner of the metamorphic film tradition from *L'Age d'Or* to the works of Jodorowsky.[21]

Elsewhere, Mottram says *The Last Words of Dutch Schultz* was conceived cinematically, beginning "with four full-page images of a man shot in a street, the original movie shot sequence reduced to a minimum graphic immediacy of violence," followed by the words, " 'SPECIAL FEATURES OF THIS FILM,' so that the media of presentation are carefully given as an initial proposition of the work."[22] Not surprisingly, then, its author, Gysin, and Anthony Balch collaborated on three short films: "Towers of Open Fire," "The Cut-Ups," and "Bill and Tony."

Burroughs summarized the chief function of his collage technique in *The Third Mind.* "I feel the Aristotelian construct is one of the great shackles of Western civilization. Cut-ups are a movement toward breaking this down."[23] By "Aristotelian construct," he presumably meant what Brecht, who had attacked the Greek theorist earlier, called "Dramatic Theatre" (i.e., Realism) because of its commitment to plot, linear development, and so forth. Radical thinkers, both men believe traditional art mirrors and supports a reactionary power structure, which, as writers, they must challenge verbally, the playwright through Epic Theatre and the novelist through countercontrol devices. Burroughs has even claimed that his literary world, not the conventional one, embodies reality: "The montage method is much closer to the facts of actual human perception than representational writing."[24] Besides, since representational writing must entail arbitrary selection, it too may be considered cut-up.

The new literary world, where words/images are vitalized by fresh associations and where past/present/future are rendered simultaneous by structural juxtapositions, signifies anti-authoritarian democracy. Gysin implies this in *Minutes to Go* when he urges cut-ups on the reader: "Do it for yourself. Use any system which suggests itself to you. Take your own words or the words, said to be the very own words, of anyone else living or dead. You will soon see that words don't belong to anyone. Words have a vitality of their own and you or anybody else can make them gush into action."[25] Because "words don't belong to anyone," his companion cut up several writers for *Nova Express,* including Conrad, Eliot, Genet, Joyce, Kafka, Kerouac,

Rimbaud, and Shakespeare. Anarchist Burroughs, like Marxist Brecht, views literature as communal, but unlike most metafictionists, they practice what they preach by collaborating with others.

Sometimes an Eliotic rage for order subverts his paranoiac fear of order. About the fold-in technique, Burroughs said, "I edit, delete and rearrange as in any other method of composition," and about splicing tapes, "How random is random? You know more than you think. You know where you cut in."[26] He regretted fragmentation throughout *Letters to Allen Ginsberg, 1953–1957*. Equally self-conscious has been the need for unity during subsequent work, which depends less on cut-ups and more on story lines. He apprised Gérard-Georges Lemaire:

If you expect people to read your books, they must at least be given a narrative line. . . . Joyce spent twenty or thirty years of his life writing his masterpiece, *Finnegans Wake*, a book which nobody can really read. I couldn't let that happen to me. . . . *Cities of the Red Night* is a very carefully elaborated novel, put together somewhat like a roman a *[sic]* clef, with a beginning, a middle and an ending, with links and a precise story.[27]

Burroughs is rationalizing here, since, though *Cities of the Red Night* commences coherently, it concludes chaotically. Despite such assertions, then, he continues to assault an ominously ordered universe that most other Eliot descendants perceive as already broken rather than whole, and in desperate need of bonding rather than further dissolution.

Metamorphic characterization, illustrated by *The Waste Land* and *Island People*, whose protagonists constantly evolve through masculine and feminine masks, is a special instance of the modern tendency to employ multiple perspectives. Derived from earlier books like *Moby-Dick*, this tendency accelerated when reality grew more and more problematic.

Obviously, the new psychological technique of mixed focus compromised the old dramatic technique of chief character, distributing a work's protagonal energy among several figures. Less obviously, perhaps, that dispersal also affected form because it was difficult to sustain single controlling plots without individual heroes or heroines. Thus, fiction became "decentralized" and decentralization—a close relative of fragmentation—became another way authors could render disjointed contemporary life.

William Faulkner and John Dos Passos were the pre–World War II American writers who perfected multiple perspective strategies. Faulkner focused on the alternation of first-person voices during three great novels: *The Sound and the Fury* (1929), *As I Lay Dying* (1930), and *Absalom, Absalom!* (1936). Most diffuse, the second contains fifty-nine interior monologues, forty-three by seven family members and sixteen by eight outside observers. That nineteen belong to Darl Bundren is understandable, since decentralized texts, while lacking the conventional solo protagonist, usually make one character somewhat more important than the others.

Three Soldiers (1921), which shows the army damaging a trio of young Americans from widely divergent locations and vocations, intimates Dos Passos's future commitment to multiple perspectives. This interest blossomed in *Manhattan Transfer* (1925) and reached its artistic pinnacle in *U.S.A.*, a trilogy including *The 42nd Parallel* (1930), *1919* (1932), and *The Big Money* (1936). The impact of such third-person narratives on subsequent mixed focus fiction has exceeded that of the more idiosyncratic Faulkner.

Manhattan Transfer encompasses eighteen chapters and over 100 scenes within a tripartite structure. These scenes may or may not be randomly juxtaposed, as the last chapter, "The Burthen of Nineveh," indicates. There, fifteen episodes unfold, ranging from one paragraph to several pages. They constitute the following sequence, centered on (1) Mr. Densch; (2) Ellen and Little Martin; (3) Ellen and George Baldwin; (4) old man; (5) Alice and Buck; (6) Joe and Skinny; (7) Jimmy, Congo, and Nevada; (8) James Merivale; (9) Rooney and friend; (10) Anna and Dick (11) Mrs. Cunningham and Florence; (12) Dutch and Francie; (13) Phineas P. Blackhead, Gladys, and Achmet; (14) Ellen, Madame Soubrine, and Anna; (15) Jimmy and the Hildebrands. Episodes 4, 6, 9, and 11 introduce new characters and episodes 1, 5, 12, and 13 treat minor characters, leaving only seven episodes for Ellen, George Baldwin, Jimmy, Congo, James Merivale, and Anna, who represent but a handful of the previously prominent personages.

Like Darl Bundren, Ellen Thatcher and Jimmy Herf are somewhat more important than the others, so Ellen opens the book (birth) and

Jimmy closes it (departure). Their story comes to us through bits and pieces spanning about 400 pages that tell similar tales focused on bad relations between men and women. But in addition to such principals, there are people who emerge just once or recur occasionally, as well as more durable folk who drop out early or drop in late. Endless variety amid terrible sameness is the impression communicated by *Manhattan Transfer,* the decentralized form of which resembles a D. W. Griffith/Sergei Eisenstein montage. Indeed, some individual chapters alternate scenes, like superimposed camera shots, to create one image. "Went to the Animals' Fair," for example, occurs at a Brooklyn roadhouse called Seaside Inn, where five such scenes sustain two interrelated leitmotifs—the foreign assassination of Archduke Franz Ferdinand and the local murder of a female incest victim —that characterize contemporary reality. In the first, George Baldwin introduces Ellen Thatcher to Gus and Nellie McNiel, then, while they eat, he mentions his prior involvement with them, his unhappy existence, and his desire for her, yet she is distracted by a male foursome across the room. We join this foursome in scene 2; it includes Jimmy Herf, Tony Hunter, Grant Bullock, and an interior decorator named Framingham. Soon Jimmy and Bullock visit bartender Congo Jake. On the way, Jimmy spots Ellen, who rejects Baldwin in scene 3. In scene 4, we return to the bar, and there Joe O'Keefe locates Gus McNiel and Congo Jake tells Jimmy about himself. Momentarily, Ellen approaches, seeking help because Baldwin has gone crazy. After Jimmy and she converse and dance, they head toward "the murder cottage" only to confront the latter with a gun McNiel quickly seizes. Outside, Ellen again asks Jimmy about Stan Emery before she taxis home alone. Alone too sits sad Nellie McNiel watching former lover George Baldwin leave as scene 5 commences. Meantime, the men at the bar resume their discussion of the imminent war and its consequences. When Jimmy breaks away, Hunter catches up, and, distraught, confesses his homosexuality. He takes the subway, but Jimmy walks on through rainy Brooklyn, pondering this violent 1914 world. Thus, by cinematic straight-cuts between and among several scenes, Dos Passos merges private loneliness and public hysteria into one image: an animals' fair.

His characters are typical: lawyer, actress, unionist, journalist, decorator, bartender, adulteress, homosexual. Throughout *Manhattan*

Transfer and *U.S.A.*, we not only find numerous such roles, but also a wide variety of races, religions, nationalities, and classes, which the twenty-seven biographical sketches included in the latter alone make apparent. Both books constitute microcosms that mirror, if not the universe, at least Western democracy. Resembling several modern group-protagonist plays—*The Weavers, The Lower Depths, The Cherry Orchard, The Caucasian Chalk Circle, The Iceman Cometh*—the collective novel tends to be directly or indirectly radical. Therefore, the road-house sequence above contains exchanges over a socialist's slaying, war as conspiracy against the proletariat, and "failures on Wall Street." Jimmy is thinking, "The stars look down on Frederickstown. Workers of the world, unite. Vive le sang, vive le sang" when "Went to the Animals' Fair" concludes.

More effective, certain recurrent phenomena dramatize how decadent and dangerous capitalistic life has become. Murder, suicide, homosexuality, incest, adultery, divorce, promiscuity, abortion, alcoholism, gluttony, and prejudice flourish while some vehicles cause accidents and others rush toward omnipresent fires. Urban, industrialized society, where success = failure/failure = success, breeds daydreamers who wander aimlessly about labyrinthine streets. Epigraphic passages, newspaper excerpts, and snatches from popular songs all help to depict New York as a doomed city like Babylon, like Nineveh, though unlike past civilizations, with their marble columns, their broad arches, their effulgent minarets, it will be composed exclusively of functional materials: "Steel, glass, tile, concrete . . . millionwindowed buildings . . . glittering, pyramid on pyramid."

The best known instance of Dos Passos's impact on subsequent American novelists remains *The Naked and the Dead* (1948), where Norman Mailer created multiple third-person perspectives through a World War II army platoon, whose lieutenant was just slightly more significant than fellow characters. We need only scan "The Time Machine" flashback sections to realize how decentralized this text is, since there Mailer treated nine additional soldiers, and—perhaps acknowledging the influence of the *U.S.A.* biographies—saved one for Woodrow Wilson. However, mixed focus Dos Passos-style has had an even larger conscious or unconscious impact on antirealistic fiction, as Heller's *Catch-22* (1961), Coover's *The Origin of the Brunists* (1966), Stone's *A Hall of Mirrors* (1967), Dowell's *One of the Children Is*

Crying (1968), and Burroughs's *Cities of the Red Night* (1981) testify. Without his precedent, the two greatest such works during the past four decades, *The Recognitions* (1955) by William Gaddis and *Gravity's Rainbow* (1973) by Thomas Pynchon, are virtually inconceivable.

"[T]he body of the novel has not been squarely about [Wyatt], it has been about the others, and he only insofar as he was the spirit they lost," we learn from the Notes to *The Recognitions*.[28] Even so, the first three chapters convince us that the Gaddis book is another oversized *Künstlerroman*, for these 150 pages seem quite conventional, presenting the protagonist's life chronologically: his mother's death abroad; his restrictive New England childhood; his art studies at Munich, then Paris; and, in New York City, his abandonment of a promiscuous wife to forge paintings. During the third chapter, though, the author begins undermining this traditional format when ostensible hero Wyatt Gwyon suddenly becomes nameless (until he regains identity as Stephan Asche about 600 pages later) and the focus abruptly shifts toward Otto Pivner. Sporadic appearances, initiated after a lapse of almost 100 pages with Wyatt's trip to co-conspirators Recktall Brown (corrupt businessman) and Basil Valentine (corrupt art critic), keep him visible. Part 2 contains nine chapters: in two he does not materialize, in four he seems relatively unimportant, and in three he dominates. These last include 2.2, where Wyatt sees Brown, Esther (wife), Valentine, and John (divinity student); 2.3, where Wyatt travels home and back; and 2.8, where Wyatt stabs Valentine. He is missing from the first two chapters of part 3, but resurfaces as Stephan Asche during 3.3, before vanishing again during 3.4. The fifth and final chapter of this part finishes the story of Stephan, now Stephen—the name his mother had originally chosen. Significantly, the fifty-six page epilogue, which treats many others, ignores him altogether.

According to David Koenig, "Wyatt's counterparts took on increased importance in the middle part of *The Recognitions*. Gaddis intended Otto, Anselm, Valentine, Stanley, Esther, Chaby Sinisterra, and so forth, to represent facets of Wyatt. They were all to be one, or one-and-a-half dimensional versions of Wyatt's shortcomings, just as he would represent their possibilities."[29] There are several figures besides those cited by Koenig consequential enough to command scenes: Reverend Gwyon, Esme, Fuller, Recktall Brown, Mr. Pivner, and Frank Sinisterra. However, among counterparts, the superficial playwright Otto and the fanatical musician Stanley may be considered most crucial.

After the perspective moves from Esther's husband to Esther's lover in 1.3, we find the latter writing "The Vanity of Time" on a Central American banana plantation in 1.4. Later, Otto meets Esme at the Greenwich Village party and escorts her home (1.5), where he awakes the next morning (1.6), his final part 1 appearance. Absent from four chapters and practically excluded from another two, Otto is a major personage during just three part 2 chapters. He becomes as peripatetic as Jimmy Herf on 20 December 1949, visiting Agnes Deigh, taking Esme out, and accompanying Ed Feasely to the Harlem drag ball. Then 2.1 enacts an episode that rivals the grotesquery of the mummy or bread sequence later when this despicable pair steals Stanley's mother's amputated leg. Sober 2.4 handles his romantic involvement with suicidal Esme and hilarious 2.5, his abortive rendezvous with long-lost papa Pivner. We last view Otto back in Central America (3.1; epilogue). That he represents Wyatt's comic counterpart seems clear, since he now goes by a new name Gordon after the Byronic hero of "The Vanity of Time," and since the same sinister Dr. Fell who treated Wyatt for erythema grave years earlier now treats Otto for Ménière's syndrome.

Tragic counterpart Stanley remains minor throughout the parts featuring these two. He enters the book late at the 1.5 party which brings Otto and Esme together. Henceforth, during part 2, Stanley turns up, more or less briefly, only where we find Otto, as if the first were the shadow of the second. He eventually borrows some counterfeit money from him (2.5), is arrested (2.7), and forgives Otto (2.8). A devout Catholic composer, Stanley expends considerable energy in parts 1 and 2 trying to save Agnes and Anselm. He emerges as a stressed part 3 / epilogue character because Otto virtually disappears following 3.1 and Wyatt completely disappears following 3.5. His love for Esme and his attempted suicide occur aboard ship (3.4) and his death while playing the organ at Fenestrula concludes both epilogue and novel.

The center of consciousness may change during *The Recognitions*, but not its group emphasis. Because perspective shifts transpire rapidly inside chapters and even scenes, montage—"a series of brief pictures following one another quickly without apparent logical order"[30]—results, giving Gaddis's big book the simultaneity achieved by Dos Passos three decades earlier. For example, 2.1, which takes place from Monday evening, 19 December to Wednesday morning, 21 December 1949, moves from individual to individual and location to location through seventeen separate passages that cover only sixty-two pages. Passage eleven or "composite" epitomizes the consequent jumble. Edited, it reads:

Dawn . . . Fuller was busy in Mr. Brown's bathroom. . . . Esme wakened for a moment in a strange bed. . . . Esther woke, hearing sounds. . . . In the street below, young policemen raced the engines of their motorcycles. . . . In the East Fifty-first Street station-house, Big Anna sat on a bench weeping. . . . Anselm was descending the steps of the I.R.T. West Side subway, on all fours. Adeline had just closed a door behind her. . . . Herschel was not to be wakened until some hours later, by two sailors in a Chelsea hotel room.[31]

Decentralized form, the concomitant of decentralized characterization, is often reinforced by spatial fragmentation during mixed third-person narratives. Thus, *Manhattan Transfer*'s Herf and *A Hall of Mirrors*' Rheinhardt wander, respectively, around New York and New Orleans. Indebted to T. S. Eliot as well as John Dos Passos, contemporary encyclopedic novels like *The Recognitions* and *Gravity's Rainbow* may impose this peripatetic pattern on an international scale. We should be prepared, then, when the epilogue of the first evokes Rome, Barbados, New York, Paris, Budapest, Rome, and Fenestrula. A single paragraph near its end, illustrating "Spring came everywhere," cites Egypt, Rio de Janeiro, Colombia, Mexico, North Carolina, Chicago, Germany, Kuwait, Japan, and Moscow. Rightly so, for the entire twentieth-century world, and not just the United States, lacks authenticity.

If Wyatt becomes somewhat more important than other people, Manhattan becomes somewhat more important than other places. Both Gaddis and Dos Passos metropolises are microcosmic, projecting the evils of modern life, but whereas Dos Passos's sober realistic version has a political dimension that requires several classes, Gaddis's antirealistic version takes a comic spiritual attitude toward lovelessness among counterfeit artists/intellectuals. Though the group-protagonist controls their two novels, *Manhattan Transfer* emphasizes one-to-one relationships and *The Recognitions* stresses one-to-many relationships. Gaddis, therefore, puts greater weight on social gatherings, particularly at the Viareggio in Greenwich Village, "a small Italian bar of nepotistic honesty before it was discovered by exotics."[32]

Most memorable is Esther's Christmas Eve party, which runs seventy-five pages and which contains the speech calling fragmentation "this modern disease." While a crazy woman plays Handel and a seven-year-old girl from downstairs intermittently begs sleeping pills for her "Mummy," we encounter The Whole Stick Crew, according to Gaddis. Superficial chitchat reveals these unnatural culture-vultures as inimical toward both creation and procreation. Steven Moore's summary of the "chaotic" party conclusion indicates that *The Recognitions*, no less than *The Waste Land*, dramatizes spiritual *malaise* through sexual distortion:

The kitten is killed when Agnes accidentally sits on it (she then stuffs it into her purse); Maud Monk steals the anonymous baby while her husband has a homosexual encounter with Sonny Byron; Mr. Feddle, quoting Tolstoy, inadvertently puts the idea of suicide into Benny's head; Esther realizes that Ellery has made love to Adelaide during the course of the party; and Ed Feasley loses a chance to sell his father's battleship to the Argentine. Esther retreats to her bedroom with the black critic, who asks her to watch as he masturbates.[33]

Only Wyatt, who appears at his former apartment long enough to collect some clothes, is capable of connecting reality and the moral sense.

Superficially at least, the structure of *Gravity's Rainbow* resembles the structure of *Manhattan Transfer* and *The Recognitions*, but whereas they are both triparted (if we exclude the Gaddis epilogue), it has four major divisions—"Beyond the Zero," "Un Perm' au Casino Hermann Goering," "In the Zone," and "The Counterforce"—that share their predilection for epigraphs. And, whereas *Manhattan Transfer* and *The Recognitions* proceed by the conventional chapteral arrangement, *Gravity's Rainbow* is blatantly episodic, distributing seventy-three scenes among these divisions in unbalanced sequence: twenty-one, eight, thirty-two, twelve. The present action of *Gravity's Rainbow* occurs before *The Recognitions*, yet, like the 1955 novel, which focuses on spring 1949 to spring 1950, the 1973 novel spans about a year, from mid-December 1944 to mid-September 1945.

Both encyclopedic and international, these works have enormous casts, the latter very possibly containing more characters, typical and otherwise, than any previous American fiction. The manifold events they enact cohere through what Frederick R. Karl terms "the cellular method of accretion and modification":

> The cellular expansion into different forms, by way of changing the molecular structure of each cell, afforded Pynchon a method of accretion and slight modification. Just as each modification of the cell created a different molecular structure, and that in turn a new product, so Pynchon is able to hold together his basic cell—the juxtaposition of rocketry and human fate—while tampering with each unit so as to create a differential of incident.[34]

Five interconnected subplots, involving Tyrone Slothrop, Roger Mexico/Jessica Swanlake, Enzian/Tchitcherine, the Pöklers, and Katje Borgesius/Weissmann (Captain Blicero)/Gottfried constitute this structure's obviously decentralized core.[35] Reminiscent of the Jimmy Herf and Wyatt Gwyon stories, the Tyrone Slothrop subplot emerges as most important.

He and Wyatt share a similar background, coming from old New England Congregationalist families dedicated to Puritanism and mammon. While Gaddis stresses the first, Pynchon—himself purportedly a descendant of Hawthorne's Pyncheons—stresses the second. Thus, Wyatt grows up under Calvinistic Aunt May, who abhors creativity and insists he become a minister like his ancestors. If their oatmeal factory seems innocuous, the Slothrop Paper Company, which stands for "dead white" over "living green," is downright pernicious. Neither family has bred many renegades. Among the pious Gwyons, only a suicidal nine-year-old boy and the present Reverend—proponent of Mithraism and other pagan cults—appeared before Wyatt. And, among the commercial Slothrops, only a Salem witch named Amy Sprue and the colonial William Slothrop—author of subversive *On Preterition*—preceded Tyrone. This background *motivates* Wyatt to overcome guilt through *development* during *The Recognitions*, where human love will free him from the past, but during the deterministic *Gravity's Rainbow*, it dooms Slothrop. He was betrayed by both parents, Broderick and Nalline, "Blackfather" even having struck a deal with Uncle Lyle Bland involving rental of his baby body to Dr. Laszlo Jamf as payment for his college education. Visiting Harvard, Jamf, whose experiment the National Research Council funded, made infant Tyrone's erections the conditioned reflex that would eventually pinpoint rocket hits.

Though Slothrop does not materialize until scene 4 or participate after scene 67, he is somewhat more important than anyone else. His quest, which revolves around a substance called Imipolex G and which unfolds throughout all the major divisions of the book, becomes international like Wyatt's, taking Slothrop from Boston to London, the Riviera, Zurich, Nordhausen, Switzerland, Berlin, the Baltic Sea, and Peenemünde. It provides the programmed American lieutenant with numerous adventures, often coincidental, often pornographic. But whereas the parallel odyssey experienced by Wyatt leads toward a firm new identity, these adventures record Slothrop's gradual disintegration. First, he loses himself in various roles—Ian Scuffling, Rocketman, Max Schlepzig, Plechazunga, (Pig-Hero)—and then Pynchon's scapegoat-fool, so fond of imitating movie stars, gets "[s]cattered all over the Zone."

As Slothrop is absent at the beginning and ending of *Gravity's Rainbow*, Roger Mexico, another third-person perspective, is absent during parts 2 and 3. Nonetheless, he represents the positive pole of the book, combining intelligence and warmth, qualities that help make this British statistician "Antipointsman" or the reverse of Pavlovian Edward W. A. Pointsman, F.R.C.S., who runs the PISCES organization in "The White Visitation." Mexico's love for shallow Jessica Swanlake constitutes a second subplot. Their wartime affair, which includes the memorable Kent church evensong incident, soon crumbles, especially after Pointsman sends Jessica to Cuxhaven. Afraid of "his bitterness, his darkness," she abandons Roger there and announces she will marry a dull but safe boyfriend. Mexico then joins the Counterforce.

The third and fourth subplots involve relatives, the third (Enzian/ Tchitcherine) restricted to parts 3 and 4, and the fourth (Franz, Leni, and Ilse Pökler) banished from—among others—the first seventeen and last fifteen scenes. Greatly simplified, the tangled third subplot treats the Russian intelligence agent Tchitcherine's obsessive need to slay illegitimate half-black brother Enzian, the leader of the Schwarz-commandos or Herero rocket technicians, a need that dissolves through the sorcery girlfriend Geli Tripping practices. Pynchon describes the meeting between siblings before both disappear from the novel as scene 72 closes: "Certainly not the first time a man has passed his brother by, at the edge of the evening, often forever, without knowing it." In the less murky fourth subplot, German rocket engineer Franz Pökler was abandoned by wife Leni for another man and the radical Left. She and daughter Ilse were imprisoned by the SS, who kept Ilse hostage so that Pökler would continue work on rocket technology. His annual reward, a visit presumably from Ilse, ceases after the war. Nor does Leni, now prostitute Solange, ever see her child again.

Katje, Weissmann-Blicero, and Gottfried—the three figures comprising the fifth subplot—share only scene 14, where Gottfried plays Hansel and Katje plays Gretel during the sadistic sex rituals conducted by Blicero, the Witch, at a Dutch V-2 battery. Katje escapes, thanks to PISCES operative Pirate Prentice, and soon becomes Pointsman's pawn, satisfying masochistic Brigadier General Ernest Pudding as Domina Nocturna and seducing equally vulnerable Lieutenant Tyrone Slothrop as Golden Bitch. That Katje will meet Enzian, then Thanatz, confirms her role of linking character, like Ellen *(Manhattan Transfer)* and Esme *(The Recognitions)*, a role necessary to decentralized fiction whose narratives interlock. Later, Captain Blicero—the negative pole of *Gravity's Rainbow*—convinces Gottfried he must sacrifice himself in their 00000 Rocket.

Clearly, these five subplots are synecdochical, each representing the whole novel, where human love has vanished. Here, parents betray children, women betray men, and, through manipulation/conspiracy, scientists, agents, cartels, and, above all, "They" control people. Here, sexual perversion, equated with physical and spiritual death *(The Waste Lane, Island People, Cities of the Red Night, The Recognitions)*, dominates to further the separation motif, which sporadic appearances and disappearances of subplot characters reinforce. Even pervasive Slothrop is scattered about the text long before he is scattered over the Zone.

Pynchon's "little stories, parables, and *ad hoc* passages that are almost purely illustrative"[36] contribute to this decentralization. They also verify Karl's "cellular method of accretion and modification" (what Kenneth Burke had termed "qualitative progression"), whereby the "basic cell" deepens more than it expands. Associated with twentieth-century poetic sequences, such a structural strategy depends heavily on montage, and montage, we realize, defines multiple perspective novels. Thus, *Gravity's Rainbow* most resembles *Manhattan Transfer* and *The Recognitions* when, for example, it strings together fifteen mixed-focus vignettes during the last seventeen pages to help abrogate traditional dramatic concepts of chief character, central action, and so forth, concepts emerging from less problematical realities. Significantly, every novelist treated in the present chapter was influenced by T. S. Eliot, whose *The Waste Land* remains our American masterpiece of omnipresent modern fragmentation. Employing juxtaposition too, their fictions, as his poem, tend to emphasize the conceptual over the experiential, the collective over the individual, the typical over the unique, the metamorphic over the developmental, the spatial over the temporal, the urban over the rural, the international over the national, and, finally, the universal over the local. It is no wonder that such disjointed, alternate worlds are crowded with grotesque figures, objects, and situations, since the incongruous, like the imaginary and the absurd, signals a planet gone crazy.

CHAPTER 5

The Grotesque and the Devil

In "The Grotesque: An American Genre," William Van O'Connor contends that "our literature is filled with the grotesque, more so probably than any other Western literature."[1] Most of the earlier writers who reflect this tradition were romantic as opposed to realistic, puritanical as opposed to transcendental, for the grotesque was initiated here by the autobiographical works of the colonial period. Nineteenth-century practitioners include Ambrose Bierce, Charles Brockden Brown, Stephen Crane, Nathaniel Hawthorne, Washington Irving, Henry James, Herman Melville, Frank Norris, Edgar Allan Poe, and Mark Twain; their modern counterparts are Sherwood Anderson, Djuna Barnes, William Faulkner, and Nathanael West. Titles like Poe's *Tales of the Grotesque and Arabesque* and Anderson's "The Book of the Grotesque" suggest how self-conscious these people were about exercising an artistic mode already prominent during the Middle Ages.

Random examples prove that the grotesque tradition is still endemic on native ground: Ludmilla's shriveled leg in "The Second Leg" *(Minds Meet)*, the Siamese twins in "Petition" *(Lost in the Funhouse)*, the inhuman youths in *Cities of the Red Night*, the dead girl in *The Origin of the Brunists*, the homunculus in *A Bad Man*, the soldier in white in *Catch-22*, Cousin Lyman and Miss Amelia in *The Ballad of the Sad Café*, HARRY SAM in *The Free-Lance Pallbearers*, the charnel house in *Death Kit*, and the man with two noses in *A Hall of Mirrors*. *The Grotesque in American Negro Fiction*, which treats Jean Toomer, Richard Wright, and Ralph Ellison, records hundreds of similar instances. While analyzing *Invisible Man*, author Fritz Gysin observes: "Figures, objects, and situations are rendered grotesque by means of distortion, animation, and alienation." He adds:

> The grotesque figure is a human being that appears dehumanized because of physical deformity, the discordance of body and soul (or mind), incoher-

ent behaviour, the assumption of extraneous traits from the animal, vegetable, mineral, or mechanical domain or from the domain of death, or because of a combination of these features. . . .

The grotesque object is part of the mineral, vegetable, animal, or mechanical realm, which by means of transformation or independent motion assumes traits of one or more of the other realms, including human traits, so that it appears to have become animated, to possess an unusual amount of energy or even something akin to a human will, or to be the instrument of an ominous force. . . .

The grotesque situation is a state of affairs in which the incongruity of various factors evokes a concrete image of an estranged world. The violation of static laws, the disturbance of space- and time-perception, the presence or appearance of grotesque figures and objects, the contrast between expectation and fulfillment, and above all the disturbance of cause and effect may create grotesque situations, but also the juxtaposition of incompatible actions, or incompatible elements of landscape, or of incompatible moods.[2]

Though not black writers, Flannery O'Connor and John Hawkes consistently employ these criteria. O'Connor, when corresponding to "A" on 5 July 1958, asked, "Would you like to read a real surrealist novel? This boy John Hawkes who came to see me sent two of his. He is a born writer. . . . This is the grotesque with all stops out."[3] Hawkes's strangeness appealed to O'Connor because the grotesque was "the nature of my talent" (328).[4] Her letters often discuss grotesquery, making links between it and communication, comedy, and the Catholic/Christian imagination. The same subject recurs during *Mystery and Manners,* where she published "Some Aspects of the Grotesque in Southern Fiction." Even a brief comparative analysis of two early novels, Hawkes's *The Cannibal* (1949) and O'Connor's *Wise Blood* (1952), which jointly utilize distorted figures, objects, and situations, illustrate that despite certain differences, their fiction bears crucial resemblances.

Mutilated characters pervade both narratives. In *The Cannibal,* Ernst has "dueling scars,"[5] and is missing fingers; Madame Snow's son loses his leg, then depends on "steel canes" and "steel loops" (5); and the tuba-playing schoolteacher is one-eyed. Similarly, in *Wise Blood,* we meet "a one-armed man,"[6] a preacher facially disfigured, and a protagonist who blinds and lacerates himself. These stories incorporate much animal imagery. Often people exhibit bestial traits—the Duke dismembers the homosexual boy as if he were a fox (*The Cannibal,* 155); Enoch, the "hound dog" with the "fox-shaped face," dons a gorilla suit (*Wise Blood*, 27, 24)—and sometimes beasts exhibit human traits—one frozen monkey screams, " 'Dark is life' " (*The Cannibal*, 155); two bears front "each other like . . . matrons having tea" (*Wise Blood*, 54). Death imagery also permeates the Hawkes/O'Connor world. Coffinless corpses recur during *The Cannibal*, where the Merchant "was wedged, standing upright, between . . . beams" (94), and coffins themselves during *Wise Blood*, where Hazel Motes recalls those occupied by father, mother, grandfather, and younger brothers while inhabiting a cramped berth. Frequently, individuals are likened to objects. During *The Cannibal*, Herr Stintz's head resembles "a funnel in the top of a drum" (189), and during *Wise Blood*, Mrs. Flood resembles "the mop she carried upside-down" (61). They are mechanical too. Thus, the twins of *The Cannibal* march, "eyes ahead, arms in parallel motion" (5), and Sabbath Lily Hawks of *Wise Blood* possesses a head that "worked on a screw" (59). Besides the names already cited, others seem equally grotesque: for example, Zizendorf, the Census-Take, Balamir, Selvaggia, Fegelein, Stumpfegle (*The Cannibal*), and Onnie Jay Holy, Hoover Shoats, and Solace Layfield (*Wise Blood*).

Both narratives contain inanimate objects distorted through human or animal analogies. In *The Cannibal*, the town "Was as shriveled in structure and as decomposed as an ox tongue black with ants" (8); "The convoy crept . . . like a centipede" (133); "a pair of faded pink pants" lay "shriveled to the size of a fist" (138). And in *Wise Blood*, "the windshield wipers . . . made a great clatter like two idiots clapping in church" (44); the trees "looked as if they had on ankle-socks" (55); the umbrella "came down with a shriek and stabbed him in the back of the neck" (96). Occasionally, such phenomena gain symbolic significance. "The house where the two sisters lived was like an old trunk covered with cracked sharkskin, heavier on top than on the bottom, sealed with iron cornices and covered with shining fins" (61) and "a small black-haired Christ on the pillow, eyes wide and still, who trembled, and with one thin arm, motioned her away" (94) become important during *The Cannibal*, as do the Essex which "made a sound like a goat's laugh cut off with a buzz saw" (88) and the mummy which was "a dead shriveled-up part-nigger dwarf" (96) during *Wise Blood*.

Hawkes and O'Connor rely heavily on grotesque situations too.

Among those in *The Cannibal* are "the same blurred picture" shown daily "to no audience" (5); the asylum riot involving rats, monkeys, and male inmates brutalized by armed females, whose leader, Madame Snow, decapitates chickens bare-handed; and the disposal of overseer Leevey at a swamp "filled with bodies" that "never disappeared" (161). Included in *Wise Blood* are the dream about Mrs. Motes, "like a huge bat" (19), struggling to escape burial; the devoted child "strangled . . . with a silk stocking and hung up in the chimney" (32); and Sabbath mothering the mummy, whose "head popped and the trash inside sprayed out in a little cloud of dust" (102). Grotesque situations convey both thematic climaxes. The mad Duke pursues his quarry throughout *The Cannibal.* When this fox hunt finally ends, it (Jutta's gay son) is clumsily and bloodily dissected, then cooked for broth. Hazel Motes of *Wise Blood,* after noticing "the resemblance in their clothes and possibly in their faces" (110), twice runs over now nude Solace Layfield. Twitching and wheezing, the hypocritical "hired Prophet" (109) confesses before "Haze gave him a hard slap on the back and he was quiet" (111). But besides such bizarre figures, objects, and situations, both novels contain a devilish element that often —though not always—accompanies the grotesque vision.

Whenever fictions introduce and exorcise truly malevolent characters, they confirm the "final interpretation of the grotesque" proffered during *The Grotesque in Art and Literature*: "An Attempt to Invoke and Subdue the Demonic Aspects of the World."[7] Wolfgang Kayser, through a subsection titled "The Satanic Humorist as Narrator," prepares us for his famous dictum:

> In the same year in which Jean Paul, the theoretician, invoked the figure of the satanic humorist, this figure was also incorporated in a novel, where it was given the role of narrator. The narrator of Bonaventura's extraordinary *Nachtwachen (Night Watches)* of 1804 suspects that he is the son of the devil, which explains his knowledge of the vanity of human existence. He himself defines the point of view which he represents as being "satiric." (59)

With *Nachtwachen* "disillusionment is complete and irremediable, and the world is a madhouse" (60). Now meaningful things are meaningless and familiar objects are strange; now phenomena are exaggerated and insane individuals are reasonable. "Throughout the novel,"

Kayser argues, "the narrator employs the motif of the mask as the most important means of alienating the world" (61). Though as satirists Hawkes and Bonaventura both place their readers inside the book, they differ in their conception of first-person narration. In *Nachtwachen*, the protagonist wears the satanic mask; in *The Cannibal*, the author himself does. Furthermore, when pronouns were converted from third to first person, Zizendorf of *The Cannibal* was left describing material only Hawkes could know: for instance, most material in the third-person section filtered through Stella and Ernst and even some material in the first-person sections.[8] That *The Cannibal*'s principal fiend Zizendorf cannot be exorcised seems evident from the prologue, which concludes, "I will, of course, return." Evident also is the fusion of this narrator and Hawkes, who, consequently, assumes the diabolical voice later attributed to Flannery O'Connor and Nathanael West: ". . . in revision I found myself (perversely or not) wishing to project myself into the fiction and to become identified with its most criminal and, in a conventional sense, least sympathetic spokesman, the neo-Nazi leader of the hallucinated uprising . . . the teller of those absurd and violent events."[9]

Flannery O'Connor hints at the divided nature of Hazel Motes during *Wise Blood*'s short prefatory note. There, she designated her protagonist "a Christian *malgré lui*," whose "integrity" rests in being unable to rid himself of Jesus. On the one hand, he has been shaped by his fanatical "circuit preacher" (15) grandfather, and, on the other, influenced by his atheistic army friends. Having been wounded and discharged, Haze abandons Eastrod (home) and travels to Taulkinham (Babylon), where he becomes a fornicator. Worse, he now embodies the Antichrist, advocating the Church Without Christ, which signifies " 'the blind don't see and the lame don't walk and what's dead stays that way' " (60). The various false prophets he encounters, including Enoch Emery, Asa Hawks, Onnie Jay Holy (Hoover Shoats), and Solace Layfield, operate both as antipodes and counterparts. The last sports the same diabolical "glare-blue suit and white hat" and uses the same "high rat-colored car" for a pulpit. When Haze murders this double (" 'Him and you twins?' " [91]) because he " 'can't stand . . . a man that ain't true and one that mocks what is' " (111), he kills the Antichrist within. Thereby the boy frees his real nature, the Christ-figure who culminates the sight/sightlessness motif through self-blinding. "Going backwards to Bethlehem" (119) also involves putting "gravel and broken glass and pieces of small stone" (121) in shoes, wearing "three strands of barbed wire" under an "old shirt" (122), and being bludgeoned to death.

In "Flannery O'Connor's Devil," John Hawkes realizes that "the demonic aspects of the world" may be invoked, if not subdued, by both religious and secular authors. He discusses Miss O'Connor and Nathanael West, whose *Miss Lonelyhearts* influenced her *Wise Blood*, as "rare American satirists[s]":

> I would propose that West and Flannery O'Connor are very nearly alone today in their pure creation of "aesthetic authority," and would propose, of course, that they are very nearly alone in their employment of the devil's voice as a vehicle for their satire or what we may call their true (or accurate) vision of our godless actuality. Their visions are different. And yet, as we might expect, these two comic writers are unique in sharing a kind of inverted attraction for the reality of our absurd condition.[10]

West and O'Connor serve to illustrate the literary theory this essay formulates. Since our actuality is godless and our condition absurd, the satirist, bent on "demolishing 'man's image of himself as a rational creature' " (397), invokes "the devil's voice" and "the devil's 'demolishing' syntax" (399). That should surprise no one, for "in the most vigorously moral of writers the actual creation of fiction seems often to depend on immoral impulse" (398). Moreover, a relationship exists "between fictive 'authority' and 'immoral' author-impulse" (400). Something termed "the meanness'-pleasure principle," the argument continues, "fills out the devil's nihilism and defines the diabolical attitude" lying "behind the reversal of artistic sympathy" (403). According to Hawkes, West and O'Connor not only "write *about* the devil, or at least about diabolical figures," but also seem "to reflect the verbal mannerisms and explosively reductive attitudes of such figures in their own 'black' authorial stances" (400). His essay concludes by merging satanic and grotesque elements: "The voice of her devil speaks with a new and essential shrewdness about what Nathanael West called 'the truly monstrous' " (407).

Though examples are drawn from other O'Connor works—"The Life You Save May Be Your Own," "A Good Man Is Hard to Find," "The Partridge Festival," and *Wise Blood*—Hawkes dwells mainly on *The Violent Bear It Away*. There "the devil himself quite literally appears, wearing a cream-colored hat and lavender suit and carrying a whiskey bottle filled with blood in the glove compartment of his enormous car" (398). Two reproduced passages demonstrate the Hawkesian thesis, since, during the first, the devil talks both for himself and for the author, and, during the second, the demonic side of O'Connor's creative imagination becomes evident.

Throughout the essay, Hawkes allows his friend to dispute these contentions. She states, " 'I want to be certain that the devil gets identified as the devil and not simply taken for this or that psychological tendency' " and he confesses she "has pointed out the difference between her devil (Lucifer, a fallen angel) and my authorial-devil" (400). Yet, he maintains, "our disagreement may not be so extensive," because Miss O'Connor writes, " 'I suppose the devil teaches most of the lessons that lead to self-knowledge.' And further that 'her' devil is the one who goes about 'piercing pretensions, not the devil who goes about seeking whom he may devour.' " Perhaps, Hawkes reluctantly decides, "I have been giving undue stress to the darker side of her imaginative constructions, and that the devil I have been speaking of is only a metaphor" (406).

"Flannery O'Connor's Devil" was published in 1962, toward the end of her life and of her correspondence with John Hawkes, which ran from 27 July 1958 to 20 February 1964. During this exchange, they discussed, among other things, his conviction that Miss O'Connor used a diabolical voice. She made many assertions besides those quoted by Hawkes, but while she conceded "the Devil's voice is my own" (*Habit*, 464) regarding "The Lame Shall Enter First," she almost always distinguished between their two devils, as he acknowledged. Thus, on 28 November 1961, O'Connor informed him:

My Devil has a name, a history and a definite plan. His name is Lucifer, he's a fallen angel, his sin is pride, and his aim is the destruction of the Divine plan. Now I judge that your Devil is co-equal to God, not his creature; that pride is his virtue, not his sin; and that his aim is not to destroy the Divine plan because there isn't any Divine plan to destroy. My Devil is objective and yours is subjective. (456)

To O'Connor, Hawkes's "devil is an impeccable literary spirit whom he makes responsible for all good literature. Anything good he thinks must come from the devil" (507).

The letters indicate how conscious she was of her demonic figures.

Besides the devil in *The Violent Bear It Away,* we hear about Tom T. Shiftlet in "The Life You Save May Be Your Own," The Misfit in "A Good Man Is Hard to Find," the sheriff in "The Comforts of Home," and Singleton in "The Partridge Festival." Hazel Motes *(Wise Blood),* Mr. Paradise ("The River"), Manley Pointer ("Good Country People"), and Rufus Johnson ("The Lame Shall Enter First") represent additional instances.

Numerous demonic figures populate the Hawkesian canon too: Il Gufo or the hangman of *The Owl;* Herr Snow, Herr Stintz, and Zizendorf of *The Cannibal;* the Red Devils of *The Beetle Leg;* Larry Slade of *The Lime Twig;* and Tremlow of *Second Skin.* His "subjective" and O'Connor's "objective" attitude toward the diabolical role in fiction become apparent through the following juxtaposed declarations.

Hawkes (1971 interview):

The satanic stance is merely another way of trying to achieve authoritarian detachment, a kind of ruthlessness in the making of fiction. One way of dramatizing and sustaining such detachment is through attacking sacred figures or sacred institutions. . . .

Reversed sympathy seems essential to the novelistic or fictional experience. If the point is to discover true compassion, true sympathy, then clearly the task is to sympathize with what we ordinarily take to be truly repulsive in life —hence identification with the so-called criminal or rebellious mentality. I think of the art of writing as an act of rebellion because it is so single and it dares to presume to create the world. I enjoy a sense of violation, a criminal resistance to safety, to the security provided by laws or systems.[11]

O'Connor (1963 reading):

To insure our sense of mystery, we need a sense of evil which sees the devil as a real spirit who must be made to name himself, and not simply to name himself as vague evil, but to name himself with his specific personality for every occasion. . . . I have discovered that what is needed is an action that is totally unexpected, yet totally believable, and I have found that, for me, this is always an action which indicates that grace has been offered. And frequently it is an action in which the devil has been the unwilling instrument of grace. . . .

I have found, in short, from reading my own writing, that my subject in fiction is the action of grace in territory held largely by the devil.[12]

Plainly, the diabolical has an aesthetic purpose in both authors' work. For Hawkes, who favors first-person narration, it provides "authoritarian detachment," but for Miss O'Connor, who relies on third-person narration, it functions as catalyst, "the unwilling instrument of grace." One constitutes a "satanic stance," the other, "a real spirit," and one is abstract, the other, concrete. Though they are joint masters of the grotesque, secular Hawkes and religious O'Connor stand even further apart in their ideological view of the devil. Hawkes sympathizes with him, while "attacking sacred figures or sacred institutions," because his devil, an arch-rebel, forms an analogue to the artist. This, Miss O'Connor must consider blasphemous, since her devil embodies evil even when serving God. "Some time I would like to know what you think of Jack Hawkes' piece," she wrote Robert Fitzgerald. "I have argued with him for years . . ." *(Habit,* 486).[13]

"Good Country People" brilliantly displays the O'Connor vision of evil, the devil, action, and grace. Her protagonist is freakish, a thirty-two-year-old, infantile blonde—"bloated, rude, and squint-eyed"[14]— whose "highest creative act" (275) was legally converting the radiant given name Joy to the ugly adopted name Hulga. She suffers from bad eyesight, heart trouble, and the artificial leg Mrs. Freeman, through "special fondness for the details of secret infections" and "hidden deformities" (275), finds fascinating. These blemishes are physical manifestations of her warped soul, which explains why the girl dislikes dogs, cats, birds, flowers, nature, and "nice young men" (276). She holds a Ph.D. in philosophy, reads all day, and professes atheism. "Her mind," comments O'Connor, "never stopped or lost itself for a second to her feelings" (287). With Hulga, the devil becomes "the unwilling instrument of grace" and assumes the "specific personality" of tall, gaunt Bible salesman Manley Pointer. This figure wears "bright blue suit," "yellow socks" (277), and "wide-brimmed hat" (285). He first dupes the girl's mother, cliché-dominated Mrs. Hopewell (hopeless), by a pitch about "Christian service" and other hypocrisies, into regarding him as "sincere," "genuine," and "earnest" (280). No less naive, educated Hulga considers Pointer innocent, childlike, and Christian, while Pointer considers Hulga "the fantastic animal at the zoo" (286). She "seldom paid . . . close attention" (287), yet ironically claims "some of us have taken off our blindfolds" (288). After he pockets her glasses, he steals her wooden leg, and exhibits the whiskey, cards, and condoms inside his hollow Bible. Hulga—outraged, but perhaps saved—must listen when the latest exemplar of "good country people" makes the diabolical connection unmistakable: " 'One time I got a woman's glass eye this way. And you needn't to think you'll catch me because Pointer ain't really my name. I use a different name at every house I call at and don't stay nowhere long' " (291). Thus, O'Connor's devil can change identities. And her genial and glib arch-deceiver pierces pretensions. Like predecessor Nathaniel Hawthorne, she includes the centrality of a corporal defect, with its symbolic implications, and of a main character all intellect and no emotion. Such similarities are not unexpected, since her letters frequently mention that "very great writer" Hawthorne. "One of his descendants," she feels more kinship toward him than toward "any other American" (Habit, 70, 407, 457).

Devils and diabolical personages have been invoked by many American fictionists from colonial times besides Hawkes and O'Connor. Among their figures are the voice of The Devil's Dictionary, Recktall Brown of The Recognitions, Thomas Sutpen of Absalom, Absalom! and Flem Snopes of The Hamlet, Roger Chillingworth of The Scarlet Letter and Professor Westervelt of The Blithedale Romance, Peter Quint of The Turn of the Screw, Captain Ahab of Moby-Dick and the metamorphic protagonist of The Confidence Man, Dr. Crucifer of Darconville's Cat, Satan of The Mysterious Stranger, and Shrike of Miss Lonelyhearts.

Wolfgang Kayser's definition notwithstanding, both grotesque fictions without a diabolical component and diabolical fictions without a grotesque component exist. An example of the first is Marguerite Young's Miss MacIntosh, My Darling, and of the second Alexander Theroux's Darconville's Cat.

The seventeenth chapter of Young's book contains one of the most amazing transformations in American literature. Previously, protagonist Vera Cartwheel, has led us to believe that her "guardian spirit," [15] the title character, equipped with a What Cheer, Iowa background, Pilgrim's Progress, robust constitution, realistic views, and beautiful red hair, epitomizes all that is healthy and sensible. Nevertheless, on Vera's fourteenth birthday, all this becomes fraudulent when the girl invades Miss MacIntosh's bedroom to find a "monstrous stranger," "the most pitiful example I had ever seen of human nature" (239). Her red hair has disappeared, leaving a "dome like some enormous ivory ball" (238). Not only are the lady's breasts flat, but one is missing. With a broken nose and "the body of a wrestler" (238), she resembles an old man, "even perhaps that old lurking rapist she had so often warned me of" (240). This powerful figure—a "massive, ruthless combatant" (242)—pummels Vera, whose hair she "pulled out by the handfuls" (243). The girl wonders if her guardian "has never been herself at all but someone else" (240). Perhaps not as graphic as the birthday transformation scene, the novel is nonetheless filled with such nondiabolical grotesquery.

Similarly, *Darconville's Cat,* while not essentially grotesque, contains one of the most vivid contemporaneous diabolical figures by the name of Dr. Abel Crucifer, professor emeritus at Harvard, who lives on the top floor of Adam's House, where he shows his blasphemy through an "antique prie-dieu" holding a "chamberpot."[16] Author of *Christianity and the Ages Which It Darkened,* Crucifer has an unnatural physical appearance. He is an Egyptian eunuch with "a foul odor" (469), the voice of a woman, globoidal contours, and "eyes . . . lit by the fires of hell" (547). At one point, "Crucifer drew himself up like a bat, his ears almost growing points" (655). His associations with the devil are equally explicit. On page 414 we learn that "this Crucifer was the organizer of every last deviltry"; on page 467 he says, " 'I saw *through* God' "; on page 545 he embodies "a depth of actual evil"; on page 569 he asks, " *'When are you going to learn that Satan isn't a metaphor?'* " Misogyny, the foremost of Crucifer's perverse views, is expressed through his vast antifeminine library, his Unholy Litany, and his discourse on Hate. This sophistry so impresses protagonist Alaric Darconville—suffering from unrequited love—that Darconville, after becoming comatose, temporarily accepts the role of devil's disciple, directing a Malediction! against Isabel Rawsthorne, accepting Crucifer's pronouncement, " 'You are me!' " (653) with jade ring and pistol before going on a Journey to the Underworld that restores the ill man's sanity and independence.

Although examples of grotesquery without diabolism and vice versa may be found in our and other literatures, the connection made between the two by Kayser most often holds true. This is especially noticeable in American literature, where Flannery O'Connor and John Hawkes are anything but asymptomatic, as two outside examples, one modern and one postmodern, which also combine the bizarre and the satanic, demonstrate.

Feature editor Willie Shrike (a carnivorous bird that impales its prey on thorns and barbed wire) enacts the Antichrist during Nathanael West's *Miss Lonelyhearts* (1933). The novel begins with his blasphemous prayer ("Help me, Miss L, help me, help me. / In saecula saeculorum. Amen."), proceeds through additional sacrilegious utterances (" 'The church is our only hope, the First Church of Christ Dentist, where He is worshipped as Preventer of Decay' "), and concludes soon after "The gospel according to Shrike."[17] Meanwhile, as a cynical joke machine, he taunts colleague Miss Lonelyhearts, "the son of a Baptist minister" (3) and the bearer of "a Christ complex" (13). Much strangeness stems from the latter's psychosis—spiking the ivory Christ, mutilating the lamb, tormenting the old man—but much also derives from external reality. The letters written to him by Sick-of-it-all, Desperate, Harold S., Broad Shoulders, and other victims originate there. There, too, physical deformity seems commonplace: Desperate has no nose, yet wants boyfriends; the "ragged woman" has "an enormous goiter," yet salvages "a love story magazine" (39). Epitomizing these unfortunates, Peter Doyle, inadvertent cause of Miss Lonelyheart's grotesque death, wears "a box-shaped shoe with a four-inch sole" (44) and looks even odder, for "His eyes failed to balance; his mouth was not under his nose; his forehead was square and bony; and his round chin was like a forehead in miniature" (45). The "little cripple," whose movements remind the narrator of "a partially destroyed insect" (44), later plays "dog." Human beings take on vegetal, as well as bestial characteristics, and so nipples become roses (then hats) and nerves become "small blue flowers" (57). Often objects acquire life—an obelisk may "spout a load of granite seed" (19) and "a battered horn" can grunt "with pain" (30) —while people often acquire inanimate characteristics: The "fat cheeks" of Goldsmith resemble "twin rolls of smooth pink toilet paper" (25); Faye Doyle is a "tent, hair-covered and veined" (26); and Miss Lonelyhearts feels "like an empty bottle" (50). In this absurd world, Shrike, the impotent Antichrist, prevails.

William Gaddis makes Recktall Brown of *The Recognitions* (1955) more grotesque than earlier devils. Compared to a "wart hog" and a "soft toad,"[18] he possesses thick fingers, uneven teeth, misshapen ears, and heavy glasses. Some talk about Goethe and Mephistopheles transpires shortly before Brown falls dead in his overheated quarters wearing medieval armor. This talk has significance, since the Faust legend dominates *The Recognitions*, where the antagonist owns a black poodle, and where the hero, Wyatt Gwyon, strikes "a bargain" (362) with him to forge paintings. However, Gaddis's Satan also descends from the American confidence man/devil tradition, which includes Hawthorne, Melville, Twain, and Faulkner.[19] Recktall Brown, like the title character of *The Great God Brown*, is a tycoon, though far corrupter than the unimaginative O'Neill character. The fortune he amasses on defective, overpriced commodities—cleaning fluid, chalk toothpaste, breakfast cereal, and so forth—purchases vulgar diamond and gold jewelry. A cigar-smoking Philistine, he debases art, for not only does he sell corrupt portraits, but also plans to start " 'a novel factory, a sort of assembly line of writers, each one with his own especial little job. Mass production, he said, and tailored to the public taste' " (243).

The international society of Recktall Brown is as abnormal as Hawthorne's Salem or West's New York. Almost all the individuals inhabiting *The Recognitions* are grotesque. At one typical party, we meet a wide spectrum: the childless couple, ghost writer, literary agent, Village artist, devout Catholic, obsessed poet, onanistic critic, practical joker, flamboyant homosexual, befuddled old man, drug addict, would-be playwright, and those comically named Charles Dickens, Buster Brown, and Adeline Thing. Their aberrant behavior is often manifested. Thus, Ed Feasley, the practical joker, and Otto Pivner, the would-be playwright, steal an amputated leg, while Esme, the drug addict, succumbs to a " 'staphylococcic infection' " after " 'kissing Saint-Peter-in-the-Boat' " (953), and Stanley, the devout Catholic, expires when his organ music causes an Italian church to collapse. Most events affecting the Gwyon family also seem bizarre. The father, Reverend Gwyon, ritually sacrifices a Barbary ape. Later, he is crucified and the ashes are sent to Spain, where the son, Wyatt, eats them as bread. The latter had already joined Frank Sinisterra in a counterfeit mummy scheme which had necessitated abducting the corpse of a cross-eyed virgin scheduled for canonization until the corpse of the Gwyon mother, Camilla, was mistakenly substituted.

The little girl's decayed body sits between the two men with "hands clasped one over the other on the sunken basin of the pelvis, above the wide separation of the lower limbs, and the head, tilted forward slightly, the surface of the face unbroken by a nose, the eyes sunken, the jaw dropped" (812). Only love can counter such grotesquery, the hero must learn.

Grotesque figures, objects, and situations are perfectly compatible with the fragmented/decentralized universe previously discussed, since the nature of the grotesque mirrors the nature of the disjointed, both being estranged, incoherent, incongruous. Bizarre characters, epitomized by the devil or principle of chaos, thrive in what Hawkes terms "our godless actuality," "our absurd condition," for they too confirm the world as madhouse. Fittingly this nightmare transpires on imaginary or mental landscapes, though often these bear striking similarities to what many still consider rational.

CHAPTER 6

Imaginary Landscapes

The majority of American landscapes prior to World War II possessed that "air of reality" or "solidity of specification" Henry James considered the novel's "supreme virtue."[1] Sometime fabulist Eudora Welty has defended this view more cogently than any other contemporary native writer:

[T]he novel from the start has been bound up in the local, the "real," the present, the ordinary day-to-day of human experience. . . .
Besides furnishing a plausible abode for the novel's world of feeling, place has a good deal to do with making the characters real, that is, themselves, and keeping them so. . . .
Place in fiction is the named, identified, concrete, exact and exacting, and therefore credible, gathering spot of all that has been felt, is about to be experienced, in the novel's progress.[2]

Conversely, John Barth, having already said, " 'France is shaped like a tea pot, and Italy is shaped like a boot. . . . But the idea . . . that they'll never be shaped like anything else . . . can get you after a while, ' "[3] regarded fictional location more mental than physical:

The very notion of place, or "setting," realistically evoked as a main ingredient of fiction, is no doubt as suspect at this hour of the art as are the conventions of realistic characterization or linear plot as practiced by our literary great-grandparents. . . .
In his recent book *Invisible Cities,* Italo Calvino—one of the most appealing of the "postmodernists"—imagines a Marco Polo who describes for a weary Kublai Khan a great many fantastical, no doubt imaginary cities; at one point the Khan observes that perhaps all these invisible cities are variations of Venice: that Marco Polo has never left home.[4]

It would be easy to attribute the source of post-1950 antirealistic settings to surrealistic works like Alfred Jarry's *King Ubu* (1896), where the action occurs within a "timeless and spaceless" geography involving Warsaw, Moscow, the Ukraine, Lithuania, Livonia, Elsinore, Spain and France, or Guillaume Apollinaire's *The Breasts of Tiresias*

(1917), where "present-day Zanzibar" does not remotely resemble the island off the east coast of Africa. However, long before the surrealists, Western literature had incorporated imaginary landscapes, as *The Divine Comedy, The Tempest*, and *Gulliver's Travels* illustrate. This was true also of American fiction, despite Henry James and the realists, which had long employed fantastic settings, actual locations bearing fictitious names, and, finally, real places with real names that nevertheless seemed bizarre. All three types of imaginary landscapes —the fantastic (e.g., Soulsville of *The Free-Lance Pallbearers*), the disguised (e.g., Quinsyburg-Farmville, Virginia of *Darconville's Cat*), and the actual (e.g., Africa of *Alphabetical Africa*) have burgeoned since 1950, for, according to Alain Robbe-Grillet, verisimilitude is no longer at issue. When Vonnegut treated Trafalmadore, Ilium-Schenectady, New York and Manhattan during *Slaughter-House Five*, he unconsciously demonstrated that the three types could coexist in a single work.

Among contemporary antirealists, William S. Burroughs has created the most vivid fantastic settings, and among them, the ones called *Cities of the Red Night* (1981) are especially memorable. Tamaghis, Ba'dan, Yass-Waddah, Waghdas, Naufana, and Ghadis "were located in an area roughly corresponding to the Gobi Desert, a hundred thousand years ago."[5] Their system was initially stable, with "inhabitants divided into an elite minority known as the Transmigrants and a majority known as the Receptacles" (154). When some old Transmigrant died, Receptacle parents copulated before him, causing his spirit to enter the female's womb. Hardier Transmigrants sought hanging, strangulation, and orgasmic drugs because these supposedly ensured "successful transfer." Then came artificial insemination, and, worse, the "portentous event" of a fallen meteor and its concomitant Red Night. The resulting mutants, who possessed "altered hair and skin color," eventually outnumbered the black natives. One, the White Tigress, conquered Yass-Waddah, "reducing the male inhabitants to slaves, consorts, and courtiers" (155). Other cities developed new means of transmigration, but rather than supermen for space exploration, the product was "ravening idiot vampires." Ultimately, "the cities were abandoned and the survivors fled in all directions, carrying the plagues" (157). Also taken were books filled with "flagrant falsifications," which Mayan priests later owned.

Since Burroughs's landscapes are as fantastical as Marco Polo's—perhaps "a god dreamed Yass-Waddah" (329)—they recur during the fictive present through drug-/viral-related nightmare/fever. Thus, Audrey Carsons (alias Clem Snide) and the boys "arrive at Ba'dan around midnight local time" (266), and, after arming themselves, proceed to "a vast casbah . . . that contains the largest per capita criminal population ever seen anywhere" (267). Here, The Hanging Fathers, "one of the most powerful organizations" controlled by the Council of the Selected (269), materialize, as does their occupation, for the visitors find suspended bodies at the Stretch Nest leather bar, the O.K. Corral (the Earps/Doc Holliday), and at the amusement park. A character named Dimitri lectures them about Ba'dan, using slides and film. They learn that it " 'is the oldest spaceport on planet Earth' " (274); that " 'adjacent to the spaceport is an international and intergalactic zone known as Portland' " (277); and that besides the Casbah, Ba'dan has another vicious area, Fun City, " 'occupying a plateau on the north side' " (279). Across the river stands rival spaceport Yass-Waddah, " 'a matriarchy ruled by a hereditary empress' " (283).

Book 1 gives these and the other red night cities, which dominate book 2 and book 3, a more or less verifiable international context involving people and places from the Near and Far East, North, Central, and South America, Europe and Africa to prepare us for the subsequent melding of real and unreal locations, ancient and modern eras, conscious and unconscious states. Consequently, Tamaghis contains "bits and pieces of many cities" and its "worn blue cobblestones" resemble "the outskirts of Edinburg" (234). The Double G bar of 1860 New York is juxtaposed to the Double G bar of this mythical environment, while "the smouldering ruins of Yass-Waddah and Manhattan" appear together during a high school play, preparing the way for the novel's final apocalyptic vision: "I remember a dream of my childhood. I am in a beautiful garden. As I reach out to touch the flowers they wither under my hands. A nightmare feeling of foreboding and desolation comes over me as a great mushroom-shaped cloud darkens the earth. A few may get through the gate in time. Like Spain, I am bound to the past" (332).

In a 1978 interview, Coleman Dowell explained Tasmania, Ohio, the disguised locus of his novel, *Mrs. October Was Here* (1974):

I invented Tasmania, Ohio, in *Mrs. October*. I went into the Army from Columbus and I had family in Cleveland; that's about all I know of Ohio. Somebody said, "Why do you hate Columbus so much?" How could I hate Columbus, I don't know Columbus! That whole thing in *Mrs. October* was because of Columbia, the gem of the ocean, and what Christopher Columbus means to America. It could have been any city with a similar aura. But Ohio is the home of presidents and *Mrs. October* is a very political book. I think that it is a radical book. It hates everything and that's surely radical. But if Tasmania were a real city and a major character in the book, then I had better know the city. If I were going to write about New York the way Nelson Algren writes about Chicago, it would have to be absolutely accurate. If you're writing about cooking or about building a chair, you had better know the materials.[6]

Dowell, who bore no knowledge of Columbus or Ohio, chose this location as model for "invented" Tasmania strictly on symbolic grounds. Unlike Algren's "absolutely accurate" Chicago, his antirealistic setting "could have been any city with a similar aura." Indeed, he dissociates Tasmania from Columbus during the FOREWARD, which calls the latter more "mean-spirited" and larger. The revolution fomented by Mrs. Septimus October may begin with "[s]lum clearance-banishment of The Wolves to Columbus."[7] Links between Tasmania, Ohio—a mythical village "[s]omewhere, out beyond the limits of the twentieth century" (1)—and Tasmania, Australia—an actual island dividing Indian Ocean and Tasman Sea—are tenuous too:

Of rivers, as noted, there are two: the Tasman . . . and the Demon. . . . In passing, it should be speculated that Demon could be a shortening of Van Dieman ['s Land], which could have been the original name of Tasmania, as in the case of the island off Australia. (2)

It is Tasmania's slum and borgo and is called The Wolf. (There is an Australian marsupial, a carnivore, named the Tasman or Tasmanian Wolf; perhaps this is the derivation.) (4)

The four sectional headings of *Mrs. October Was Here*—"*Tasmania*," "*Tasmania—Now and Then*," "*Tasmania—Now*," "*Tasmania, Then*"—emphasize setting. They are framed by FORWARD and AFTERWORD that invoke a man who mysteriously polishes brass plaques "like the empty, atavistic gestures of some animals" (5), giving the novel its circular structure.

The FOREWORD, which terminates with Dowell's handmade map

(compare the Yoknapatawpha County sketch affixed inside *The Portable Faulkner* cover), is insistent about cartography. Although the town "has appeared on American maps only since the Revolution" (1), a French traveler drew one during 1753. Now early "hand-colored samples" may be found, curiously enough, in Paris, Dresden, Madrid, as well as at the Tasmania Museum and Library. To detect this "outpost"—surrounded by mountains and bordered by rivers—on a current map, you must "turn the map so that the line separating Indiana and Ohio runs parallel to your mouth. With this image, think of a beast crouching upon the map, drinking from Lake Erie at Cleveland—a firewater drinker. Its forepaws rest upon Toledo, its hindfeet—the animal is in bas-relief—lightly touch Springfield. That little round hold, or anus, is Columbus" (4).

Like the town and the Demon River, the streets have symbolic names: for example, Splendor, Marvel, Rue Flambeau, and Powhatan. "Inconvenient; Ohioan; American," X-shaped Tasmania contains the usual private/public, commercial/residential establishments, a "normalcy" justifying the epithet, TASMANIA, THE HEART CITY, OHIO. Before Mrs. October's activities, which ended with her immolation, bigotry, xenophobia, "sexual repression and adultery" existed here, but afterward the transformed village lost its prejudice, poverty, and rudeness. These days "[e]veryone has about the same amount of income and the average age will soon be eighteen" (5). So much for revolution in Dowell's tragicomic satire!

Donald Barthelme called one of his most celebrated stories "Paraguay," yet the first-person narrator says, "This Paraguay is not the Paraguay that exists on our maps. It is not found to be on the continent, South America; it is not a political subdivision of that continent, with a population of 2,161,000 and a capital city named Asunción. This Paraguay exists elsewhere."[8] Even more imaginary than disguised Columbus (i.e., Tasmania), an Ohio town near Indiana, Lake Erie, Cleveland, Toledo, and Springfield, Barthelme's ostensibly Spanish landscape must be approached over Asian terrain—Burji La, Sekbachan, Malik Mar, Deosai Plains, and Sari Sangar Pass—or so his initial paragraph that concludes "Ahead was Paraguay" implies and his initial footnote that cites *A Summer Ride Through Western Tibet* by Jane E. Duncan affirms. Later, the last sentence also underscores this absurd geography: "We began the descent (into? out of?) Paraguay" (27).

After the initial paragraph/footnote, fourteen short, titled sections focusing on one "silver" city and parodying conventional travel literature, follow. Temperature affects male and female movement differently, intercourse occurring at "66, 67, 68, 69 degrees" (21). "Heavy yellow drops like pancake batter fall from its sky," while shedded skin, described as "[t]hin discarded shells" or "disposable plastic gloves," appear "in the street" (22) and "in the green official receptacles" (23). Silence, which may be purchased from "the larger stores . . . in paper sacks like cement," may be gotten "in the form of white noise" too. Lives have been saved by "[a]nechoic chambers placed randomly about the city" (24), whose girdless layout owes much to "the lost-horse principle." There, "anything not smooth is valuable," " '[c]reative misunderstanding is crucial,' " and "[r]hathymia is the preferred mode" of self-presentation. There, where "[e]veryone . . . has the same fingerprints" (25) and all remain accountable, crimes are punished arbitrarily. A free, if complex, sex life involves such "technical refinements" as " 'impalement,' " " 'dimidiation' " and " 'quartering.' " Because of "[m]icrominiaturization," matter becomes "smaller and smaller" in larger and larger spaces, while a new, inaccurate physics "based on the golden section . . . enjoys enormous prestige." What the narrator reveals concerning the "field of red snow" (26) behind Paraguay's great wall probably defines the entire tale for most readers: "It seemed to proclaim itself a mystery, but one there was no point in solving—an ongoing low-grade mystery" (27).

There are recurrent negative allusions to the arts as practiced in the Barthelmean dystopia: for instance, one character plays "a tiny sonata of Bibblemann's"; nobody wants the prize for "the best pastiche of the emotions" (21); comedy is never performed, but consists solely of rules given to the audience and supervised by an arbiter; "softening of language" transpires so "[i]mprecise sentences" may "lessen the strain of close tolerances" (24). That "[t]he problems of [pictorial] art" (22) derive from mass production and mass consumption the section headed *Rationalization* makes clear:

Rationalization produces simpler circuits and, therefore, a saving in hardware. Each artist's product is translated into a statement in symbolic logic.

The statement is then "minimized" by various clever methods. The simpler statement is translated back into the design of a simpler circuit. Foamed by a number of techniques, the art is then run through heavy steel rollers. Flip-flop switches control its further development. Sheet art is generally dried in smoke and is dark brown in color. Bulk art is air-dried, and changes color in particular historical epochs.

Quality-controlled, artistic products go "from central art dumps to regional art dumps, and from there into the lifestreams of cities," where "[e]ach citizen is given as much art as his system can tolerate" (23). Our own analogous systems have virtually unlimited tolerance for travel guides and sketches, Barthelme suggests. This parodic tone, *Mrs. October Was Here*'s satiric tone, and the *Cities of the Red Night*'s prophetic tone demonstrate how flexibly landscapes like Paraguay, Tasmania, and Ba'dan can be employed.

All three are located with reference to the real world, for Ba'dan lies in the Gobi Desert, Tasmania in Ohio, and Paraguay in western Tibet. Yet, simultaneously, these heterocosms function outside that world: Ba'dan flourished "a hundred thousand years ago"; Tasmania is "[s]omewhere, out beyond the limits of the twentieth century"; and "Paraguay exists elsewhere." By juxtaposing the real and the unreal, events pertaining to the latter—apocalypse during *The Cities of the Red Night*, revolution during *Mrs. October Was Here*, conformity during "Paraguay"—tacitly presage future events on earth. Whether the dominant setting has a fantastic, a disguised, or an actual name, what appears in such urban locales may be equally imaginary, since Dowell's revolution, Burroughs's Hanging Fathers, and Barthelme's red snow all defy verisimilitude.

Jorge Luis Borges and Vladimir Nabokov, who exerted considerable influence on contemporary antirealism, were grand masters of fabulous settings, as "Tlön, Uqbar, Orbis Tertius," *Pale Fire*, and *Ada* prove. The Borges story differs from *Cities of the Red Night*, *Mrs. October Was Here*, "Paraguay," and most postwar work in treating locations that are only make-believe, or so we feel until Princess Faucigny Lucinge receives her mysterious compass, "the first intrusion of this fantastic world into the world of reality."[9]

Narrator Borges first heard about Uqbar when his friend Cesares dined with him several years ago. They soon uncovered a discrepancy between two copies of *The Anglo-American Cyclopaedia*, volume 46, for one contained 917 pages and the other 921, though both were *Encyclopaedia Britannica* tenth edition reprints. The four discrepant pages in the second constituted the vague article devoted to Uqbar previously alluded to by Cesares. However, they could not find the items listed under bibliography, nor did the National Library indicate anybody had ever visited such a place.

Part 2 begins with recollections of Herbert Ashe, an English acquaintance suffering "from unreality" while alive. When Ashe died in 1937, he left "a book in large octavo" (6) that Borges discovered. This 1001-page tome disclosed no publication data, but possessed the title, *A First Encyclopaedia of Tlön. Vol. 11 Hlaer to Jangr.*, and the inscription, *Orbis Tertius*. Now Borges held "a vast methodical fragment of an unknown planet's entire history" (7), even if questions remained about missing volumes and their authorship.

Claiming Tlön is cosmic rather than chaotic, he proceeds to discuss its "concept of the universe," which perceives the world as "successive and temporal, not spatial." Thus, "impersonal verbs, modified by monosyllabic suffixes (or prefixes) with an adverbial value" (8) have replaced nouns in the southern hemisphere, while in the northern hemisphere "the prime unit" has become "the monosyllabic adjective." Other disciplines serve psychology, and "monism or complete idealism invalidates all science" (9). Even though Tlönians consider "metaphysics . . . a branch of fantastic literature" (10), philosophies, like nouns, paradoxically proliferate, producing many schools, including sophistic materialism. One "common sense" refutation of the last now insists "All men, in the vertiginous moment of coitus, are the same man. All men who repeat a line from Shakespeare *are* William Shakespeare." Twofold geometry there comprises "the visual and the tactile," the second, resembling ours, "subordinated to the first" (12) because visual geometry tells us knowledge has but a single, eternal subject. This belief directly affects "literary practices" on Tlön and such practices indirectly echo contemporary critical theories on earth:

> In literary practices the idea of a single subject is also all-powerful. It is uncommon for books to be signed. The concept of plagiarism does not exist; it has been established that all works are the creation of one author, who is atemporal and anonymous. . .

Their books are also different. Works of fiction contain a single plot, with all its imaginable permutations. . . . A book which does not contain its counterbook is considered incomplete. (13)

Ostensibly, Borges, the narrator, concludes his account by analyzing secondary objects *(hrönir)* and so fulfills a plan Borges, the author, had outlined in 1936: "'Tlön, Uqbar, Orbis Tertius" would "describe accurately a false country with its geography, its history, its religion, its language, its literature, its music, its government, its mathematical and philosophical controversies," and so forth.[10] Actually, however, the story, published during 1940, even then contained the crucial postdated *Postscript (1947)*.

This section amplifies much besides Princess Faucigny Lucinge's compass and additional Tlönian incursions into reality. Here we learn about the 1941 letter elucidating Tlön, whose history began in seventeenth-century Lucerne or London, where "[a] secret and benevolent society . . . arose to invent a country." Country became planet after one affiliate contacted an ascetic American millionaire ("freethinker," "fatalist," "defender of slavery") eager to show "nonexistent God that mortal man was capable of conceiving a world." By 1944 300 collaborators had produced the forty-volume *First Encyclopedia of Tlön*, humanity's "vastest undertaking," which formed the basis of the more elaborate *Orbis Tertius* (15). About 1944 these volumes surfaced in Memphis and soon multiplied because "any symmetry with a semblance of order—dialectical materialism, anti-Semitism, Nazism— was sufficient to entrance the minds of men. How could one do other than submit to Tlön, . . . an orderly planet?" (17). Our world has disintegrated ever since. "English and French and mere Spanish will disappear" and no doubt Tlön will one day dominate all. Meanwhile, impervious Borges continues "revising . . . an uncertain Quevedian translation (which I do not intend to publish) of Browne's *Urn Burial*" (18).

His North American peer, in *Speak, Memory: An Autobiography Revisited,* alludes to "Nova Zembla . . . where 'Nabokov's River' is named after my ancestor,"[11] the great-grandfather who had explored and mapped this area. Reference books confirm the existence of Novaya Zemlya—a 35,000-square-mile nuclear test site—as two large Arctic Ocean islands belonging to the Soviet Union. During *Pale Fire* (1962), in which that "distant northern land"[12] becomes the major location,

Nabokov, like Burroughs, Dowell, Barthelme, and Borges, establishes the illusion of geographical veracity by citing actual places. For instance, the regicide Jakob Gradus travels to Copenhagen, Paris, Geneva, Nice, Paris, and New York.

However, as we have seen in other antirealistic works, the world of fact merely serves the world of fancy, and so Nabokov, through *Pale Fire's* mad narrator, asserts " 'reality' is neither the subject nor the object of true art which creates its own special reality having nothing to do with the average 'reality' perceived by the communal eye" (130). This "special reality" involves the conversion of authentic Novaya Zemlya into fabulous Zembla, a "wild, misty, almost legendary" landscape (255) ruled by Dr. Charles Kinbote no less dictatorially than Faulkner—Yoknapatawpha's "sole owner and proprietor"—freely inventing language, literature, history, religion, topography, inhabitants, manners, and so forth.

Unlike "Tlön, Uqbar, Orbis Tertius," where the fabricated language is discussed at length but few illustrations occur, *Pale Fire* incorporates a wide range of Zemblan usages. Often we get isolated terms—for example, *grados* = tree; *grunter* = mountain farmer; *carpula* = hangover; *shargar* = puny ghost—and less frequently, whole sentences such as the saying *belwif ivurkumpf wid snew ebanumf* (A beautiful woman should be like a compass rose of ivory with four parts of ebony) and Kinbote's accented translation from Goethe: *Ret wóren ok spóz on nátt vt vétt? / Éto est vótchez ut míd ik détt.*[13]

Whereas the "atemporal and anonymous" literature in "Tlön, Uqbar, Orbis Tertius" was characterized by "fantasy" and "ideal objects," it remains firmly Western in *Pale Fire*, whose humorous epigraph quotes the *Life of Samuel Johnson* and whose professorial narrator alludes to several Occidental writers. His compatriot "Conmal, the great translator of Shakespeare" (75–76) and other poets, recurs. Before him, we learn, "no English author was available in Zemblan except Jane de Faun" (286). Western also is this heterocosm's "brand of Protestantism . . . related to the 'higher' churches of the Anglican Communion" (224), even though New Wye lacks the particular denomination fanatical Kinbote worships. Conversely, Tlön seems altogether secular because its wealthy patron required " 'The work will make no pact with the imposter Jesus Christ' " (15).

The twin hemispheres of the Borges planet are topographically vague, while the physical configurations of the Nabokov nation are presented in detail. Thus, when King Charles Xavier (the narrator) fled revolution through "[t]he Bera Range, a two-hundred-mile-long chain of rugged mountains, not quite reaching the northern end of the Zemblan peninsula" (137), he traveled among specific places like Mandevil Forest, Bregberg Pass, Mt. Glitterntin, and Rippleson Caves. Both he and Zembla bear strong Russian ties and so conduct there is markedly "human," as opposed to the strange customs contrived by the Tlönian conspirators.

The story of 1940 and the novel of 1962 resemble each other to the extent that their narrators become historians and their historians become protagonists in fictions involving alternate worlds. History for sane Borges focuses on the evolution of a secret document, but for insane Kinbote, it focuses on the revelation of a secret life. The latter claims that he is Charles the Beloved, "last king of Zembla" (75); that his grandfather was Thurgus the Third, his father, King Alfin, his mother, Queen Blanda; that he once loved Oleg, Duke of Rahl; that he divided his time subsequently between university and regiment; that he married, then exiled Disa, Duchess of Payne; that he refused to abdicate during the Zemblan Revolution and survived many adventures; that, finally, he parachuted into the United States from a chartered airplane. Literary like Borges, Kinbote, whose name may anagrammatically signify Botkin or the "American scholar of Russian descent" cited by the *Index* (306), ends up revising another man's work too.

If the distant past of *Pale Fire* unfolds on a fanciful version of an actual landscape, the recent past is associated with disguised settings —Wordsmith College = Cornell University; New Wye = Ithaca, New York; Appalachia = New York State—all realistically located in New England, U.S.A. Things seem plausible where Kinbote rented the Dulwich Road house of Judge Hugh Warren Goldsworth and had the Shades for neighbors and Professors Emerald, Nattochdag, and Pnin for colleagues. However, repeated allusions to Arcady undermine such verisimilitude: for example, "Personally I have not known any lunatics; but have heard of several amusing cases in New Wye ('Even in Arcady am I,' says Dementia, chained to her gray column)" (237). Identification with the mountainous region of ancient Greece symbolizing pastoral innocence mythicizes the American town. Here,

Kinbote creates a legend almost as weird as those attributed to the original Arcadia.

His Foreword is dated *Oct. 19, 1959, Cedarn, Utana,* the setting of the fictive present, "where I am trying to coordinate these notes" (235) at a motor lodge log cabin near some noisy campers. He chose this location because John and Sybil Shade had rented there, but later he finds it "dry and drear" (183). The ghost town called Cedarn varies from Zembla and New Wye by being impossibly situated: that is, in Utana (Utah/Montana) along the Idoming (Idaho/Wyoming) border. Thus, the creative act transpires amid a never-never West.

Reviewing *Ada or Ardor: A Family Chronicle* (1969) for the *New Yorker,* realist John Updike criticized such fabulous places: "I confess to a prejudice: fiction is earthbound, and while in decency the names of small towns and middling cities must be faked, metropolises and nations are unique and should be given their own names or none. I did not even like it when Nabokov, in *Pale Fire,* gave New York State the preempted appellation of Appalachia."[14] *Ada,* which juxtaposes the planet Terra (Earth) and the planet Antiterra or Demonia (Antiearth), reverses the usual science fiction procedure, making the "real" world irreal and the irreal world "real." A five-part, 589-page *tour de force* about incestuous love, it is undoubtedly the most elaborate treatment of imaginary landscapes among modern/postmodern texts. It is also an eycyclopedic novel and that may explain why putter-inner Nabokov seems to scorn leaver-outer Borges under the anagram Osberg as a "Spanish writer of pretentious fairy tales and mystico-allegoric anecdotes, highly esteemed by short-shift thesialists."[15]

Terra the Fair emerged during the nineteenth century through the mysterious L disaster. Afterward, radical spatial differences between the two worlds were purported, differences the principal narrator-protagonist Van Veen considers ludicrous: "Russia, instead of being a quaint synonym of Estoty, the American province extending, from the Arctic no longer vicious Circle to the United States proper, was on Terra the name of a country, transferred as if by some sleight of *land* across the ha-ha of a doubled ocean to the opposite hemisphere where it sprawled over all of today's Tartary, from Kurland to the Kuriles!" (17–18). Besides this terrestrial division of Abraham Milton's/Milton Abraham's Judeo-Christian Amerussia "into its com-

ponents," there arose an "even more preposterous discrepancy" regarding time "not only because the history of each part of the amal-
gam did not quite match the history of each counterpart in its discrete
condition, but because a gap of up to a hundred years one way or
another existed between the two earths" (18).

Lifelong deliberations over the "problems of space and time, space
versus time, time-twisted space, space as time, time as space" (153)
culminate with *The Texture of Time*, where Van, who champions "Pure
Time, Perceptual Time, Tangible Time, Time free of content, context, and running commentary" (539), develops the concept Veen's
Time, which now rivals Bergson's Duration and Whitehead's Bright
Fringe. Meanwhile, "research in terrology (then a branch of psychia-
try)" (18) produces an unfinished dissertation, "Terra: Eremitic Reality or Collective Dream?" and earns him the Rattner Chair of
Philosophy at Kingston University, Mayne (Maine), attractive because
the Department of Terrapy was famous and the Kingston madhouse
was first-rate.

That Van Veen is crazy like Humbert Humbert and Charles Kinbote
seems confirmed by his philosophical novel *Letters from Terra*, since
this early work evolved out of "a passion for the insane" (338) and
owed much to "notes . . . on the 'transcendental delirium' of . . .
patients" (340). Through Van's heroine Theresa—the American
Roving Reporter and alien contact—he exposed the "sibling planet"
as no "paradise" and revealed Demonia as "much maligned." Unfortunately, information tended to be botched and thus the Union of
Soviet Socialist Republics became the "Sovereign Society of Solicitous
Republics" and Adolph Hitler became "Athaulf the Future" (341).

During an unauthorized film version of *Letters from Terra* later,
"Athaulf Hindler"/"Mittler" replaced "Athaulf the Future." Other
distorted material pertaining to twentieth-century terrestrial "wars
and revolutions" (580) appeared there too, yet director Victor Vitry,
who accurately dated World Wars I and II, emerged a better historian than the novelist because he used "old documentaries" instead
of "extrasensorial sources and manic dreams." Nevertheless, Van and
Ada, having seen "the film nine times, in seven different languages,"
regarded his "historical background absurdly farfetched" and almost
started "legal proceedings" against him (581). As the consequence of
Vitry's successful picture, "Demonian reality dwindled to a casual

illusion," for "Russian peasants and poets had not been transported to Estotiland, and the Barren Grounds, ages ago—they were dying, at this very moment, in the slave camps of Tartary. Even the governor of France was not Charlie Chose, the suave nephew of Lord Goal, but a bad-tempered French general" (582). The two hemispheres of Demonia or Antiterra are divided between Tartary (Baltic to Pacific) and "the Anglo-American coalition" (580). One province controlled by the latter, Estoty [16] (Arctic Circle to United States), is also called Amerussia, since its mixed population speaks English, Russian, and French, Nabokov's and Ada's principal languages.[17] Beyond that simple scheme, however, geography on Antiterra (the irreal world become "real") appears far more garbled than geography on Terra (the "real" world become irreal), as the following timetables charting "three great American transcontinental trains" demonstrate:

From Manhattan, via Mephisto, El Paso, Meksikansk and the Panama Chunnel, the dark-red New World Express reached Brazilia and Witch (or Viedma, founded by a Russian admiral). There it split into two parts, the eastern one continuing to Grant's Horn, and the western returning north through Valparaiso and Bogota. On alternate days the fabulous journey began in Yukonsk, a two-way section going to the Atlantic seaboard, while another, via California and Central America, roared into Uruguay. The dark-blue African Express began in London and reached the Cape by three different routes, through Nigero, Rodosia or Ephiopia. Finally, the brown Orient Express joined London to Ceylon and Sydney, via Turkey and several Chunnels. (345)

This passage contains international, verifiable versus nonverifiable, and distorted locations. All these recur throughout *Ada* to characterize Antiterra/Demonia.

Often nationalities and languages commingle, as when Van, who is both Russian and American, and who was born in Switzerland and educated in England, tells some "Gipsy politicians, or Calabrian laborers" to go away, using "Vulgar Latin, French, Canadian French, Russian, Yukonian Russian" (268–69). On another occasion, "Knowing how fond his sisters were of Russian fare and Russian floor shows," he "took them . . . to 'Ursus,' the best Franco-Estotian restaurant in Manhattan Major" (410). Van's beloved Ada eventually translates "Griboyedov into French and English, Baudelaire into English and Russian, and John Shade into Russian and French" (577).

Hundreds of authentic place-names, mostly drawn from the Occident, are also invoked, one page alone citing Mozambique, Manhattan, Geneva, Nice, Cuba, Florence, Rome, Capri, America, Lake Garda, Leman Lake. Like nationalities and languages, they frequently commingle to form hybrid settings: New Cheshire, U.S.A.; Ladoga, Mayne; Scoto-Scandinavia; Kaluga, Conn.; Lugano, Pa.; Moscow, Id. Other invented names echo recognizable locales—Canady (Canada), Manitobogon (Manitoba), Balticomore (Baltimore/Como), Bahamudas (Bahamas/Bermuda)—or designate totally fictitious sites —Lolita (in Texas), Centaur (in Arizona), Gamlet ("a half-Russian village"), Ardis *(Paradise)*, Eden National Park, Babylon College (in Nebraska), Valentine State. Laurie Clancy points out, with minor inaccuracies, that

These refracted realities extend to even such tiny details as the name of the ocean liner 'Queen Guinevere' instead of Queen Elizabeth, a "Chunnel" between France and England, and above all, to the names of writers and their works. . . . *Palace in Wonderland, Les Malheurs de Swann, Love Under the Lindens, Klara Mertvago, Chekhov's Four Sisters* (the extra one is a deaf nun), a poem called *The Waistline* ('a satire in free verse on Anglo American feeding habits') (p. 506), *What Daisy Knew* and *Alice in the Camera Obscura*. In addition there are various manglings of writers' names, such as Osberg (Borges), Lowden (the marriage of Lowell and Auden), Floeberg (Flaubert), Herr Masoch (presumably de Sade), a poet laureate named Robert Brown, Falkermann, and an obscure messenger named James Jones. There is even an artist variously named Paul J. Gigment and Pig Pigment.[18]

Understandably, the buried title *Van's Book* anagrammatically spells "Nabokov's," since the psyche of the author himself would appear to be the ultimate landscape here. That explains why the last four self-conscious paragraphs focus on the finished artifact, their initial sentences reading: "Ardis Hall—the Ardors and Arbors of Ardis—this is the leitmotiv rippling through *Ada*, . . ."; "In spite of the many intricacies of plot and psychology, the story proceeds at a spanking pace"; "The rest of Van's story turns frankly and colorfully upon his long love-affair with Ada"; "Not the least adornment of the chronicle is the delicacy of pictorial detail" (588–89). Some "imaginary gardens," then, lack "real toads," Marianne Moore!

John Hawkes, who shares the admiration virtually all subsequent antirealistic American writers feel for Vladimir Nabokov, remains our greatest living poet of fictional landscapes.[19] Though often remote, exotic, and vague, these are seldom fantastic because they arise from the actual world directly apprehended. He started *The Cannibal* after reading about a real cannibal in Bremen and *The Lime Twig* after reading about legalized gambling in England. Moreover, Hawkes had been to Germany before *The Cannibal;* Italy before *The Owl* and *The Goose on the Grave;* the American West before *The Beetle Leg;* Grenada, West Indies before *Second Skin;* France before *The Blood Oranges, Travesty, The Passion Artist, Virginie, Innocence in Extremis;* and Alaska before *Adventures in the Alaskan Skin Trade.* Drawn to Flannery O'Connor and Nathanael West's "improbable yet fictionally true" settings,[20] his landscapes combine familiarity and unfamiliarity.

Hawkes, the habitual traveler, whose childhood and adolescence was spent in Old Greenwich, Connecticut, New York City, Juneau, Alaska, and Poughkeepsie/Pawling, New York, likes "to write in beautiful, unexpected, totally new landscapes."[21] He equates detachment with travel:

There's a kind of renewal in a fresh landscape, a constant stimulation of the self and the perceptions, but also being in a new, unknown place is liberating. It allows me to focus more clearly on what I'm trying to do. The new landscape is analogous to the newness of what I'm trying to create. It's a way of achieving detachment. To be in a new world, a different world, an unfamiliar world makes the achievement of detachment easier.[22]

Earlier he had stated, "Detachment . . . is at the center of the novelist's experiment."[23]

These words echo Joyce's "The artist, like the God of the creation, remains within or behind or beyond or above his handiwork," and Eliot's "the only way of expressing emotion in the form of art is by finding an 'objective correlative.' " Subsequently, Bertolt Brecht systematized detachment, calling the result "alienation effect," which signified antipathy toward plot, experience, involvement, growth, linear development, and feeling. He argued, "A representation that alienates . . . allows us to recognize its subject, but at the same time makes it seem unfamiliar." For him, "A place need only have the credibility of a place glimpsed in a dream."[24] His locations reflect the

A-effect through spatial distancing, sometimes accompanied by temporal remoteness.

Similarly, Hawkes achieved detachment through spatial distancing when he chose Germany, Italy, the American West, Grenada, West Indies, France, and Alaska as fictional locations. The novelist, like the playwright, has also employed temporal remoteness, for *The Owl* evokes the Renaissance, *Virginie,* the eighteenth century, and *The Cannibal,* World War I.

Both writers merge character and locale, with *Mother Courage* dramatizing the protagonal mind and *The Passion Artist* representing "a conscious effort to create a landscape that is a version of the unconscious."[25] During the latter, "inner landscape had become externalized,"[26] the author's main character, an amateur psychologist, perceives. But perhaps only Hawkes among the contemporary fabulators who have expressionistically projected distorted mentalities on external reality enacts the collective unconscious, exploiting his own psychic life because it reveals the *general* ethos. With regard to *The Cannibal* (1949), he observed:

> This of course is a landscape of sexless apathy, and the phrase "ox's tongue black with ants" is the archetype of the world I care most about. This passage really doesn't suggest humour, and yet it's to me not very far from humour. It brings to my mind the Spanish picaresque writers, Quevedo say, and his work "The Buscon", in which just this kind of landscape, the decomposed, physical world is the setting for grotesque humour, in which all of our aspirations and our worst fears are somehow actualised.[27]

Hawkes, despite his juxtaposition of the two world wars in *The Cannibal* and his focus on the second in several other novels and stories, mythicizes rather than historicizes. He parodies, burlesques, and even travesties mytho-ritualistic elements drawn from contemporaneous, pagan, and Judeo-Christian sources, especially during the fiction published between 1949 and 1971. We have already seen how *The Beetle Leg,* which treats the Osiris and Fisher King legends, mocks the popular conception of the American West, achieving comedy through exaggerated figures and situations, and how *The Lime Twig,* which introduces the Circe and Icarus legends, mocks the crime thriller, making underworld events inordinately sensational and inexplicable. *The Cannibal,* where myth and history become synonymous, and *The Owl,* whose judgment supper celebrates death and therefore inverts the life-giving Eucharist and Messianic Fish Meal, are other early instances.

This tendency to mythicize climaxes in *Second Skin* (1964) and *The Blood Oranges* (1971). Nevertheless, like many Hawkes fictions, both disguised semitropical landscapes possess a verifiable origin. He called L'Anse aux Epines, "the most southerly tip" of Grenada, "our paradise spot and the terrain that gave off *Second Skin*." Another letter elaborated: "Incidentally, the swamp used to lie immediately behind the little crescent of beach below the 'great' house—the beach that used to have a small jetty and a few dangerous stinging trees at its edge. But I think they filled in the swamp when they put a bunch of hotel-cottages there." His next novel, *The Blood Oranges*, contains hidden solidity of specification, as well. According to Hawkes, "I began *The Blood Oranges* in Vence (near Nice) and worked on it for a few more months in Tolon, Greece, which you may know is down near Nauphplion (sp?) and Epidaurus (sp?) in the Peloponnessus (sp?), so the world of *The Blood Oranges* is mixed Mediterranean (sp?)," and "Yes, the Roman cistern in *Blood Oranges* was actually located in a small much-overlooked temple on a ridge above Epidaurus, where we spent many a lovely sunset being pleased and renewed."[28] Clearly, then, Grenada supplied the prototype of *Second Skin*'s "wandering island," while French and Greek locations were the models for *The Blood Orange*'s Illyria.

Skipper, the narrator of *Second Skin*, terms another island (Atlantic/ Gentle) "my mythic rock," echoing Hawkes, who referred to "my 'mythic' England, Germany, Italy, American west, tropical island, and so on."[29] Throughout the narrative, Caribbean wandering island (Grenada) opposes New England Atlantic island (Vinalhaven, Maine). *Second Skin* begins and ends with the wandering island (fictive present), which, except for sections two, three, eight, and nine, the author juxtaposes to the Atlantic island (fictive past). Their alternation is symbolic, Atlantic island connoting a northern setting and wandering island a southern one. Skipper's apparent escape from death-oriented Western society to the primitive, life-oriented wandering island parallels his previous odyssey across North America, the epitomization of civilized decadence. This odyssey had commenced on the West Coast and terminated on the East, carrying him ever deeper into Occidental darkness. Later he believes he has abandoned the tempest of reality or Atlantic Island for the tranquility of unreality or wandering island, a landscape that seems "quite invisible . . a mirage,"[30] and that evokes "romance," "pageant," and "pastoral." The recurrent phrase, "my time of no time," and the final words, "The sun in the evening. The moon at dawn. The still voice" (210) indicate he thinks time as well as space may be eluded.

Second Skin combines myths. For instance, in one chapter, The Golden Fleas, Hawkes inverts the Golden Fleece story and treats the Night of All Saints, while throughout the narrative we encounter allusions to the Trojan War, with Skipper becoming Menelaus/Priam/ Iphigenia and daughter Cassandra retaining her prophetic name. More importantly, the novel also travesties *The Tempest.* Skipper's wandering island in the West Indies reminds us of Prospero's uninhabited island in the Bermudas, both being geographically remote and psychologically fantastic. However, once shipwrecked there as Ariel (rather than Alonso), the ridiculous earthbound narrator caricatures his Shakespearean counterpart: "I was tossed up spent and half-naked on the invisible shore of our wandering island—old Ariel in sneakers, sprite surviving in bald-headed man of fair complexion" (162). Soon he acquires black disciples and metamorphoses from Ariel to Prospero, though he occupies Plantation House instead of a cell and practices artificial insemination instead of magic. For the original Prospero, controlling nature meant restraining sexual impulses and so this father supervised the courtship of Ferdinand and Miranda. But the modern parent, whose promiscuous daughter has committed suicide, shares pubescent Catalina Kate with a pal, while son-in-law Fernandez (homosexual) is dead and arch-enemy Miranda (fornicatress) is alive on the Atlantic Island.

Ostensibly utopian, the wandering island nonetheless contains the ominous swamp Hawkes's letter mentions, the swamp where Skipper vainly attempts to wrench an iguana off the back of Kate. Such primordial scenes implying paradise lost are so pervasive in his work that special attention must be paid them. Recurring over a thirty-year period, they begin with the bodies that defy burial at *The Cannibal* swamp and conclude with the tokens of decay and acts of violence at *The Passion Artist* marsh.

Two similar watery places bear the designation "Eden." One appears during "The Innocent Party" (1966):

"Can you imagine an ambulance in . . . The Garden of Eden. . . ."
"It's not paradise. . . ."
"You think it's not? Orchids, bougainvillea, acacia trees, all these doves and the swamp moss like frozen mist—lots of people would call it paradise."
"This place? . . . Look around you at desolation. No electricity, no water in the swimming pool, no telephone. . . ."
"Dust and weeds and rampant jungle and rotting mattresses in empty rooms. . . ."
"An inexpensive retreat amidst luxuriant growth, baby. What more do you want? It's beautiful."
"An abandoned motel on the edge of the universe. It smells of obsolescence and rank decay, it smells of the tears of uncouth strangers and the refuse of their sordid pleasures. It smells of death."[31]

Fifteen years before, Eden had materialized in *The Beetle Leg* too. There, forsaken town sites of unrecorded communities like Fat Chance, Reshuffle, and Dynamite lay under the river. Water is still treacherous, as Luke Lampson proves by hooking an infant corpse at the bottleneck. Eventually he comes upon a boat that has survived the disappearance of the great forks. It capsizes, but before doing so, strikes an empty house, whose windows have been closed and whose furnishings have been suspended. "The first man had died in Eden, they pronounced him dead," we learn, and then, Luke's father "found himself sitting in the middle of the washed-out garden's open hearth."[32]

If *Second Skin* owes a debt to *The Tempest*, *The Blood Oranges* owes one to *Twelfth Night*. Shakespearean Illyria becomes Hawkesian Illyria, which "doesn't exist unless you bring it into being."[33] We are told that "*The Blood Oranges* was in part based on my own feelings about *Twelfth Night*, and I wanted very much to strive for the ambience, atmosphere, harmony that exist in the play."[34] However, the answer to the epigraph drawn from Ford Madox Ford's *The Good Soldier*, "Is there then any terrestrial paradise . . .?" would be "No," because "even in the most paradisal of the worlds I've created the roses conceal deadly thorns."[35]

During *Twelfth Night* alignment (the Duke loves Olivia who loves disguised Viola who loves the Duke) and realignment (Olivia wins Sebastian, Viola the Duke) lead toward a quaternion, but during *The Blood Oranges*, where married Cyril pursues married Catherine, they generate a triad (past) and a dyad (present). Even Hawkes's use of Shakespeare's subplot is negative. The protagonist, a latter-day Sir

Toby by virtue of their "cakes and ale" philosophy, tells his friend Hugh that his wife Fiona calls him Malvolio and "says she loves her Malvolio best."[36] Yet whereas the play ends harmoniously with Sir Toby virile and Malvolio appeased, the novel, following *The Good Soldier*, ends disharmoniously, with Cyril impotent and Hugh dead. Hawkes dramatizes the conflict between Cyril/"lyric" (Eros) and Hugh (Thanatos), in part, through the symbolic settings that embody this mythical landscape. A wall of funeral cypresses separates and a clothesline connects the twin villas where the two married couples live. Both dwellings appear desolate, dilapidated, and old, but the one Hugh and Catherine occupy suggests "transient lives" and the one Cyril and Fiona share, "harmonious life." Surrounding these villas are positive aspects (golden glen, fruit trees, flowers) and negative aspects (crabgrass, dead gardens, gloomy pines, brambles, weeds, thorns). As the funeral cypresses represent death-oriented Hugh, the grape arbor represents life-oriented Cyril.

Upper and lower worlds reminiscent of those in *The Cannibal* also become juxtaposed. The upper world sanctuary at which Catherine convalesces has cheerful colors and "is antithetical to the brambles and broken tiles of the primitive landscape" below. Each week Cyril leaves the gloom and darkness of the funeral cypresses and coastal village for "the sudden light, peace, charm of this walled sanctuary" (5).

Hawkes poses lower world town and fortress against countryside and villas. Hugh's studio in town, characterized by "monastic gloom" and "thick walls," resembles a crude, dark, medieval cell. Accidental or intentional, his death occurs at an appropriate location, for the studio overlooking the black canal links him with the retarded natives. Words like polluted, fetid, pestilential, viscous and excremental emphasize the noxiousness of this "historically significant canal" (27), whose lethal atmosphere reflects the aboriginal savages once festering there.

Religious and military images keep past time before us. The seaside chapel on the "small timeless island" (230) contains a cross, and the medieval church beside the cemetery holds "all the effluvium of devotion and religious craftsmanship" (20). Here, in the dark, empty, barbarous, humorless, and cold environment, Fiona and Hugh steal a wooden arm, Catherine collapses, and Cyril looks at sketches showing Eros versus Thanatos. "[A]ncient violence" permeates the church, partly because "[t]he windows were cut through those deep walls as if for the arrows, lances, pikes and small cannon of sturdy peasants" (17).

Even more than studio, canal, and church, though, the fortress across the water serves to externalize puritanical Hugh's mind. When the quaternion faces this "gutted shape of history" joined by "wind and light and hands" (118), Cyril considers the hard, unhealthy, damp, treacherous fortress ominous. The chastity belt, which Hugh had had a premonition about and which they find here, becomes an analogue for him. Cyril, who prefers lyrical landscapes, ties such dismal places to his "secret self," his "regressive nature." Besides dramatizing the conflict between these two men/forces, then, the settings that constitute *The Blood Oranges*'s mythical geography make Hawkes's novel a psychic as well as a symbolic triumph.

This tendency to mythicize landscape is not uncommon among antirealists. Nor is another Hawkesian tendency, to project mental states—author's or character's—on physical surroundings, as *Cities of the Red Night* and *Ada* demonstrate. Like masters Nabokov and Borges, and their descendants Burroughs, Dowell, Barthelme, and others, Hawkes reflects a tradition that blends fantastic, disguised, and actual locations with international scope. Often reported by demented protagonists, such alternate worlds are defamiliarized through parody, burlesque, and travesty. They provide the geography where absurd questers make absurd quests.

CHAPTER 7

Absurd Quests

The journey has always been the main structural paradigm of Western narratives. When travel is undertaken to find or obtain something, we call the result "quest," familiar instances of which include masterpieces like *The Odyssey, The Divine Comedy* and *Pilgrim's Progress.* These quests, based upon stable values, depicted a rational universe. However, over the past 200 years, the old verities have eroded, and so the modern quest, though it retains various traditional aspects, has grown increasingly absurd to reflect nineteenth- and twentieth-century madness.

The Fisher King thus terminates an intermittent journey through Eliot's surrealistic *Waste Land* shoring "fragments . . . against my ruins" as Occidental civilization collapses. And, later, the epical journey of Faulkner's *As I Lay Dying* to bury Addie Bundren in Jefferson despite flood and fire betrays ulterior family motives epitomized by the false teeth and the duck-shaped woman Pa eventually acquires. Even more ridiculous are the journeys we get from Nathanael West, whose *The Dream Life of Balso Snell* begins when the protagonist enters the Trojan horse via its Anus Mirabilis, and whose *A Cool Million* bears the subtitle *The Dismantling of Lemuel Pitkin.*

To one extent or another, all these pre–World War II works parody the conventional quest motif, but none seems more comprehensive on this score than *The Great Gatsby* (1925), which unconsciously mirrors Otto Rank's *The Myth of the Birth of the Hero* (1910) and prefigures Joseph Campbell's *The Hero with a Thousand Faces* (1949). Rank had asserted:

> The hero is the child of most distinguished parents; usually the son of a king. . . . As a rule, he is surrendered to the water, in a box. He is then saved by animals, or by lowly people (shepherds) and is suckled by a female animal, or by a humble woman. After he has grown up, he finds his distinguished parents, in a highly versatile fashion; takes his revenge on his father, on the

one hand, is acknowledged on the other, and finally achieves rank and honors.[1]

Long before he wrote *The Great Gatsby*, Scott Fitzgerald experienced this venerable pattern, as the following statement during the 1936 *Esquire* piece "Author's House" indicates: " 'That is where I buried my first childish love of myself, my belief that I would never die like other people, and that I wasn't the son of my parents but a son of a king, a king who ruled the whole world.' "[2] No wonder both *The Great Gatsby* and its original opening chapter, the story "Absolution" (1924), invoke the hero myth. In "Absolution" Rudolph, feeling superior to an immigrant freight-agent father, will not believe they are related, so he exchanges their drab Dakota environment for fantasy land and becomes noble, romantic Blatchford Sarnemington. A similar transformation marks the novel when James Gatz evolves into Jay Gatsby:

His parents were shiftless and unsuccessful farm people—his imagination had never really accepted them as parents at all. The truth was that Jay Gatsby of West Egg, Long Island, sprang from his Platonic conception of himself. He was a son of God—a phrase which, if it means anything, means just that—and he must be about His Father's business, the service of a vast, vulgar, and meretricious beauty.[3]

Along with this new, more glamorous name, Gatz invents aristocratic ancestors and even an Oxford education. Yet, he does not obtain "rank and honors," for the notorious bootlegger dies ignominiously from bullet wounds. Travesty supplants parody as Dr. T. J. Eckleburg, the bodiless optometrist who advertises eyeglasses above the valley of ashes, emblemizes God, the Father, and Trimalchio, the vulgar and ostentatious multimillionaire in Petronius Arbiter's *Satyricon* who inspired the galley proof title, adumbrates Gatsby, His son.

Travestied too is the figure Joseph Campbell designates Wise Old Man or guide/teacher. Here, this protective personage becomes Dan Cody (compare Buffalo Bill), "a gray, florid man with a hard, empty face," personifying destiny to the "quick and extravagantly ambitious" young man. Because "the pioneer debauchee" (101) convinces him of the importance of money, reinforcing earlier influences like Franklin, Alger, and Hill, he pursues its embodiment, Daisy Fay, more *femme fatale* than Campbell's Queen Goddess. No sacred marriage will occur.

Beyond the threshold of adventure, his quest echoes romance or fairy tale as the pursuit of Daisy—"High in a white palace the king's daughter, the golden girl" (120)—is compared to "the following of a grail" (149). Characterized by tests and ordeals, this pursuit transpires on the dangerous dreamlike landscape *The Hero with a Thousand Faces* mentions. Fitzgerald's version is the faraway East, which, for storyteller Nick Carraway, held "a quality of distortion" (177), West Egg resembling "a night scene by El Greco" (178). Parties there and at the Plaza Hotel are thematically linked to the symbolic valley of ashes located between Long Island and Manhattan, where Myrtle's violent death triggers Gatsby's.

Meanwhile, identification with antiheroic Trimalchio supplies considerable absurdity. Many similarities between Roman buffoon and American bootlegger appear: both rise from rags to riches *sans* formal education; both amass enormous fortunes; and both throw extravagant parties attended by ingrates. The garish house, cream-colored car, and pink suit of the bootlegger are gauche; his attempts at formality, ridiculous. Still, since he was "predestined," has "extraordinary powers," and becomes transfigured—all heroic attributes —we must consider him much more than a clown.

Idealistic Gatsby allows our materialistic culture, represented by Cody, Tom, and Daisy, to divert him from transcendence. Neither virginal nor immortal, she constitutes a vampiric quest-object: "He knew that when he kissed this girl and forever wed his unutterable visions to her perishable breath, his mind would never romp again like the mind of God" (112). Thus, Gatsby, reflecting larger-than-life predecessors such as Captain Ahab and Mister Kurtz, fails to complete Campbell's monomyth, which consists of separation, initiation, and return. Before he can leave the fateful region with a boon or elixir for mankind, he, too, perishes.

Nevertheless, modern quests, if not contemporary ones, tend to retain ancient circularity. In *Moby-Dick, Heart of Darkness, The Great Gatsby,* and other novels where a sympathetic observer becomes the biographer of a symbolic hero, the *observer* returns, not merely because the tale must be told, but also because the more individuated, less static observer, having matured through contact with the hero, confirms survival. Therefore, average men like narrators Ishmael (schoolteacher), Marlow (sailor), and Nick (bond salesman) are the *real* protagonists of these works. Their message seems to be that heroism nowadays is destructive as well as inspirational.

Fitzgerald's parallel quester—"guide," "pathfinder," "settler" (4)— almost immediately telescopes his circular journey and plays ethical yardstick, wanting "the world to be in uniform and at a sort of moral attention forever" (2). Nick disapproves of Gatsby throughout the book, yet the latter is "worth the whole damn bunch put together" (154) because he had an "incorruptible dream" (155). Toward the end, there is "solidarity between Gatsby and me against them all" (166), which may imply that unified sensibility could still be achieved in Eliot's world of dissociation by blending old romantic and new realistic energies.

Compared to such pre–World War II journeys, whose circularity through return suggests traditional coherence amid latter-day chaos, the post–World War II quest is an abortive construct. That it is often self-conscious as well, texts like John Barth's *Giles Goat-Boy* (1966) and Gilbert Sorrentino's *Blue Pastoral* (1983) demonstrate.

No American writer since Eliot has been more aware of the quest motif than Barth. *The Friday Book* contains many allusions to this motif, some quite elaborate. For instance, during a 1966 lecture titled "Mystery and Tragedy: The Twin Motions of Ritual Heroism," he reproduces the "twenty-two prerequisites" of "mythic heroism" found in *The Hero* (1936) by Lord Raglan, prerequisites Campbell Tatham and others have applied to *Giles*. The author said at the University of Wisconsin's 1978 conference on "Myth and Modernism":

> My particular interest in classical mythology, as distinct from classical literature, is a tale quickly recounted. When my novel *The Sot-Weed Factor* appeared in 1960, several critics remarked that it showed the influence of Otto Rank and the comparative mythologists. I had not in fact read Rank and company; I quickly did, and found the critics to be correct. Indeed, as I wandered through Jung and Lord Raglan and Joseph Campbell and the rest —the way I'd once wandered through the Classics stacks—I became fairly obsessed by the detailed abstract pattern, the actuarial profile, of wandering heroes in the myths of the world's cultures. That cyclical model tyrannized my imagination.[4]

If *Giles Goat-Boy* was "a long comic orchestration of the abstract model,"[5] subsequent stories and novellas *(Lost in the Funhouse* [1968] and *Chimera* [1972]) also employed it.

Barth's Goat-Boy "fed on hero-tales"[6] much as Cervantes's knight-errant ingested "ill-contriv'd Romances," and the former meets "nearly all the prerequisites of herohood" recorded in "scores of hero-histories":

... the mystery of my parentage, about which it could be presumed only that I was the offspring of someone high in the administration; the irregularity of my birth, which had so seemed a threat to someone that an attempt had been made on my life; the consequent injury to my legs; the circumstances of my rescue, and my being raised by a foster parent in a foster-home, disguised as an animal and bearing a name not my own ... (108–9)

Furthermore, cognizance of the hero and his quest becomes apparent through the influence works like the Old Testament,[7] *The Divine Comedy,* and *Oedipus Rex* obviously exerted on *Giles.*

That this is a metafictional novel, both the autoreferential frame and the librarian who reads the book as Barth composes it (see p. 770) verify. Such reflexivity, when applied to mythic materials by perceptive writers, will, Robert Scholes contends, produce allegorical comedies:

Once so much is known *about* myths and archetypes, they can no longer be used innocently. Even their connection to the unconscious finally becomes attenuated as the mythic materials are used more consciously. All symbols become allegorical to the extent that we understand them. Thus the really perceptive writer is not merely conscious that he is using mythic materials: He is conscious that he is using them consciously. He *knows,* finally, that he is allegorizing. Such a writer, aware of the nature of categories, is not likely to believe that his own mythic lenses really capture the truth. Thus his use of myth will inevitably partake of the comic.[8]

A political allegory set during the cold war (Quiet Riot), *Giles Goat-Boy* presents the universe as university, substituting academic for historical terms: for example, Studentdom = Mankind; New Tammany College = America; Nikolay College = Russia; Siegfrieder College = Germany; Campus Riots I, II, and III = World Wars I, II, and III; Student Unionism = Socialism; the Bonifacists = the Germans; the Moishans = the Jews ("Chosen Class"); the Moishicaust = the Holocaust; the Frumentians = the Blacks. Consequently, the quest itself focuses on academic rituals that entail Candidate, Commencement, Finals, Pass/Fail, and Graduation. And since all this occurs within a Christian era, the Founder = God; the Founder's Scroll = the Bible; Old and New Syllabuses = Old and New Testaments; Enos Enoch = Jesus Christ; the Seminar-on-the-Hill = the Sermon on the Mount; the Twelve Trustees = the Twelve Disciples, and so forth. Some personal designations like GILES (Grand-Tutorial Ideal, Laboratory Eugenical Specimen), Spielman (minstrel), Eierkopf (egghead), Stoker (Dean o'Flunks or devil), and Virginia (virgin) are symbolic too.

Though Barth's academic context is satirical, a parodic tone dominates *Giles*. One self-contained instance concerns *The Tragedy of Taliped Decanus*, which covers sixty-six pages. Done in slangy heroic couplets, replete with strophes and antistrophes, it parodies *Oedipus Rex* while it satirizes institutional life. The two plays share a common plot, but the Barth imitation burlesques, even travesties the Sophocles original, as Taliped, whose name also signifies "swollen feet," represents Dean of Cadmus College rather than King of Thebes. Jocasta becomes nymphomaniacal wife Agenora; Tiresias becomes homosexual Proph-prof Gynander; and Laius becomes unpublished sire Labdakides.

Metamorphosed from Billy Bockfuss, the Kid, to George, the Undergraduate, Barth's protagonist watches this play empathetically, feeling indignation toward the maiming of infant Taliped, involvement over his identity search, and horror after the doomed man exclaims, "*I'm flunked forever!*" These passionate reactions occur because he, too, was betrayed, crippled, abandoned, and rescued. Just as foster parents raised Taliped, keeper Max and dam Mary raised George on a goat farm. Taliped married his mother, but George, who likewise possesses the Oedipus complex, tried unsuccessfully to seduce Lady Creamhair/Virginia Hector, who had borne him following her Immaculate Conception. George's father is a computer, so George cannot murder WESCAC the way Taliped murdered Labdakides at the Three-Tined Fork. Nevertheless, in good heroic fashion, offspring ultimately revolts against progenitor.

Surrogate father Maximilian Spielman unknowingly inspired this revolt through "the Spielman Proviso in WESCAC's Menu-program," which "called for a new Grand Tutor to change the AIM and give to contemporary West-Campus culture a fresh direction, a Revised New

Syllabus, as Enos Enoch had done in His term" (253). Like Christ, he will be falsely accused (of murder) and willingly executed (by shafting). Meanwhile, "the great Mathematical Psycho-Proctologist and former Minority Leader in the College Senate" (5), caricatures the Wise Old Man figure as " 'the best advisor any hero ever had' " (172), though the Jew insists " *'Self-knowledge . . . is always bad news'* " (85).

Donning "a long and splendid cape" (106), George answers the Campbellian call to adventure, the Barthian time to matriculate (buckhorn shophar), and sets "out a-tap down the hard highway" (106), soon joined by mentor Max and savior G. Herrold. His sole function was "to *do* the hero-assignment," but he meets Anastasia Stoker, "the white-smocked Siren," and realizes lust has been "the source and pattern of my ruin" (119). Forsaking Max and pursuing Anastasia, George makes the traditional descent to the hellish Power Plant/Furnace Room beneath Founder's Hill, where her husband Maurice, the devilish Dean o'Flunks, reigns. There, at a carnival party, he becomes bestial, even carousing near his drowned savior's bier. This descent, it should be noted, prefigures three others that involve the Belly of WESCAC, during which the still flawed hero, who purveys bad advice, will gradually exchange dualism for relativism to confront an incomprehensible world.

The threshold of adventure in *Giles Goat-Boy* is the debased Trial-by-Turnstile ritual. When George conquers this formidable obstacle, circumventing the Dean o'Flunks as "Opponent rather than Tempter," he becomes "a fully matriculated Candidate." However, the Goat-Boy bears "no ID-card" and must steal antagonist Harold Bray's "silk-dry mask" to clear Scrapegoat Grate. Now that he has vanquished both turnstile and grate—"a feat never before managed outside of legend" (337)—he receives the circular registration paper listing his "ASSIGN-MENT / *To Be Done at Once, In No Time*" on the verso side: "1) *Fix the Clock* 2) *End the Boundary Dispute* 3) *Overcome Your Infirmity* 4) *See Through Your Ladyship* 5) *Re-place the Founder's Scroll* 6) *Pass the Finals* 7) *Present Your ID-card, Appropriately Signed, to the Proper Authority*" (383). About these tasks, which occupy volume II, Raymond M. Old-erman says:

> "Initiation" begins for Campbell's hero with "The Road of Trials." George, continuing his comic pursuit of herohood, engages in seven tasks, each done twice and each round resulting in disaster, chaos and a lynching. After each

disastrous completion of the seven tasks, George makes a hopeful trip to the Belly of WESCAC, but only on the third trip does he complete his initiation, combining two of Campbell's steps—"The Meeting with the Goddess" and "Atonement with the Father."[9]

Both orphans, unorthodox hero had actually met unorthodox goddess much earlier, as we know. Their initial encounter revealed Anastasia in the role of Siren, directly or indirectly luring G. Herrold to his death, Croaker to his rape, and George to his disgrace. That she never loses sexual appeal is illustrated throughout the text, where, for instance, Stacey, the nurse, has sex with a married couple at the New Tammany Psych Clinic, then, later, causes the duel between Leonid and Greene. "[P]rotest she might, refuse never" (469), George thinks, blaming this promiscuity on lack of will rather than nymphomania. Her concern about him—" 'A Grand Tutor doesn't get drunk and make a public fool of himself!' " (191)—explains why the girl defects to "lustless" rival Bray. When George learns she was the daughter of "some luckless co-ed" instead of his sister, he calls Anastasia My Ladyship. Campbell's "[w]oman, in the picture language of mythology, represents the totality of what can be known. The hero is the one who comes to know";[10] but Barth's hero, even with a fluoroscope, cannot see through his Ladyship, soon admitting after orgasm, " 'I don't understand anything!' " Mystical marriage will transpire, nonetheless, though he remains single and she wed. "I and My Ladyship, all were one" (673), we discover during the final WESCAC episode, and, during the Posttape, we greet their son Giles Stoker. Therefore, love, as in other Barth, Gaddis, and Pynchon fictions, constitutes our *summum bonum*.

Antithetical to this is Harold Bray, the traditional antagonist who unites clown and devil. He had appeared at New Tammany College eight years before and had probably played diverse roles: "avant-garde poet," "psychotherapist," "entomologist," "explorer," "survival expert." If " 'A crazy-man. a fake. A mountebank' " (328), the "gifted imposter" was also "a genius," as "his poems, paintings, and scholarly articles" (329) proved. No wonder Bray subsequently convinces almost everybody that he embodies the "Grand-tutorial Ideal." Finally, George manages to drive Bray off, yet beforehand the magical fellow "changed color and physiognomy," "leaped over the reflecting pool," "walked up the vertical face of the Founder's Shaft" (692), and assumed many guises, including Max, Anastasia, G. Herrold, and George. This last transformation, which recurrent mask exchanges foreshadowed, indicates Bray really incarnates an alter ego. Indeed, the depiction of him as troll toward the end echoes George's question, "Was I not a troll after all . . .?" (44) toward the beginning. *The Hero with a Thousand Faces* tells us the quester "discovers and assimilates his opposite (his own unsuspected self),"[11] and that sums up precisely what happens here.

Though the protagonist visits home during *Giles Goat-Boy,* there is no return in the monomythic sense. Nor will humanity accept the lesson George learned, since the possibly spurious Posttape, where he recounts intervening events twelve years later, evinces a "hopeless, even nihilistical tone." Detained for the last time, the hero now reviews the futility of his mission, having taught none, alienated all. Except for Peter Greene and Anastasia Stoker, who believes Giles "will establish 'the New Curriculum' on every campus" (700). Meanwhile, their Grand Tutor knows that "we lose," that entropy must prevail. "Naked, blind, dishonored," he shall be cast out, "Passed, but not forgotten" (707–8).

As Barth told Joe David Bellamy, some of his readers, like most of George's students, ignored the boon or elixir provided by him:

What I did in the case of the Goat-boy novel was to try to abstract the patterns and then write a novel which would consciously, even self-consciously follow the patterns, parody the patterns, satirize the patterns that with good luck transcend the satire a little bit in order to say some of the serious things I had in mind to say. Otherwise it would be a farce, a great trifle—which, of course, some readers found it to be.[12]

"A farce, a great trifle" better describes *Blue Pastoral* (1983), published seventeen years after *Giles Goat-Boy.* Undoubtedly the most absurd American quest since *The Dream Life of Balso Snell,* this work is an episodic or picaresque novel lacking, for the most part, the criteria Joseph Campbell, Lord Raglan, Otto Rank, and other mythographers have set forth as the heroic model. Rather, *Blue Pastoral* uses the journey structure to parody à la *Mulligan Stew* (1979) several traditional and popular genres and styles with pronounced reflexivity.

"Blue" Serge Gavotte, another Wandering Jew, whose last name signifies "old French dance," begins the Great Quest when Mouth

King Dr. Ciccarelli tells him he must "travel the length and width and height of this . . . land . . . . *until* you come to that secret place wherein you will find the Perfect Musical Phrase."[13] Subsequently, we follow his magic wagon (see *Mother Courage*) from New York City to San Francisco along an often illogical route that "would look like a diagram out of *Tristram Shandy*" (240) but that also resembles the itinerary presented during the more or less realistic *The Sky Changes* (1966). At San Francisco, cart, rope, and piano plunge into the Bay, "[t]hen the Phrase climbed to Blue Serge's trembling ears."[14] Sorrentino concludes with its musical transcription and "S p l a s h" (315).

Dr. Vince Dubuque, the first of many narrative voices, who happens to be a "Dean of Funds and Meetings" and who happens to have a sexy "Private Assistant, Miss Clarke Grable," introduces the subject by giving us background information about the "unlikely hero." His beard is "ratty," his hair is "frizzy," his occupation is "plastic-lens tester" (1). The comic exploits he performed as peripatetic student were legendary before he married Helene Lundi and they begot Zimmerman. Blue demonstrated "the powerful and almost unbearable urge to be a musician" (3) at The University when he purchased "cheapo things," including tinwhistle, Jew's harp, and ocarina. The "real bad mouth infection" (44) that resulted explains why Dr. Ciccarelli soon appears.

Blue's wife and son are equally ridiculous. Far from Helen of Troy physically, Helene, whose dandruff-ridden hair keeps falling out, is a thirty-six-year-old Jewish housewife "on the plump side in the rear area" (16). Morally she leaves much to be desired too, since, after bawdy sex with her husband during chapter 18, she becomes insatiable, even accommodating "the gnarled and pasty-visaged cart-repairer" (104) while Blue waits. Their son, "little Zimmerman," departs on page 191 because he "was 'not pulling his weight' as a character," to surface again on page 296, "now, oddly enough, nineteen or twenty years old." Zim later tells "the whole incredible tale of his years-long search for his mother and father" (305).

Blue Pastoral, like *Giles Goat-Booy*, contains much academic satire, so the Gavottes encounter other pedagogues besides the ubiquitous Vince Dubuque on this "holie Quest for the perfect phrase of musick" (64). Prior to reaching The University (Illinois), they visit affiliate, Annex College (Indiana). Here, Dr. Weede Bone—"baggy flannels," "rim-

less specs," "stultifying pipes"—serves as rector. "[E]ngaged in finding cures for and preventive measures against the age-old oral afflictions that have beset mankind" (108), its lab is no less bizarre than
Jonathan Swift's grand Academy of Lagado. Technicians are busy
conducting freakish experiments to eliminate "citronella stains," to
succor fellatio "fever blisters," to produce "aggravated laryngitis."
The "most gifted scientist, his apron heavy with foundation loot," has
begun "the fourteenth year of his heartbreaking quest for the elixer
that will make all men sing with the voice of the gringo nightingale,
Pat Boone" (111). Lastly, Bone and guests see graduate students
"dulcifying dental floss donated by the leper colony," where "Humil-
ity and Compassion," as well as "Self-Abnegation," may be studied
(112).

At a faculty cocktail party, the Gavottes join the "catalogue of shits"
(113) spouting nonsensical non sequiturs; then, next day, Blue meets
Dr. Ryan Poncho, Musical Department chairman and Rotary Club
member, who plays the kazoo for him. Afterward, he suggests that
Blue "witness a memorial for Jacques-Paul Surreale" tomorrow while
Helene takes a "lonely, quiet road" (121). If the lab scene ended with
Bone's "flannels all abulge" (112), the kazoo scene ends with Poncho's
"trousers curiously tented" (122). Later, Helene, angry because Poncho prematurely ejaculated at their rendezvous, betrays chairman to
rector and rector swears chairman " 'will never get, no! nor will he
e'er present another plaque!' " (133). Later yet, Doc Dubuque ad-
mits, " '[W]e possess no "Phrase,' " then advises, " 'Pack up your
family and your crap and scud away.' " (178).

As in *Giles Goat-Boy*, however, the dominant tone seems to be
parodic rather than satiric. Barth mocked the heroic monomyth, but
Sorrentino, having already published *Mulligan Stew* and *Crystal Vision*,
once again derides diverse literary and subliterary genres. His focus
is the pastoral, a conventionalized poem about shepherds and rustic
life which "for some hidden reason has appealed to wild-eyed poets
down through all the ages" (86). Here, the title, with its adjective
"Blue," and the epigraph excerpted below from Michael Drayton
reveal the innovative strategy of the author:

The subject of Pastorals, as the language of it ought to be poor, silly, and of
the coursest Woofe in appearance. Nevertheless, the most High, the most
Noble Matters of the World may bee shadowed in them, and for certaine

sometimes are: but he who hath almost nothing Pastorall in his Pastorals, but the name (which is my Case) deales more plainly. . . .

Like Drayton's "Pastorals bold upon a new straine," Sorrentino's bucolic novel becomes self-evident when, for example, Rep. Harold "Hal" Glubit defends himself against the charge of sheep molestation. Besides sheep, flora recur during the narrative, where similar inversions often fill modes traditionally linked to the pastoral form: *blason,* eclogue, elegy, epic, georgic, idyll, and *pastourelle.* Therefore, instead of relating an encounter between knight and shepherdess, *Pastourelle: Dr. Poncho Tells of His Afternoon of Ecstasy* describes one between lech and whore. Consequent deflation may be measured by Poncho's confession, " 'Oh pepsi, twinkie, milky way,' . . . / 'I'm in your thing and oops, I've shot my wad!' ", and Helene's reaction, " 'Is this the type of hump / That scholars throw?' " (130).

Their exchange certainly reflects the Drayton criteria for pastoral language: "poor," "silly," "coursest Woofe." Throughout the text, such street slang mixes with archaic diction and verbal invention while Sorrentino celebrates words by parodying numerous contemporary and traditional written and spoken styles. Only *Darconville's Cat,* whose author also owes an incalculable debt to Joyce, rivals *Blue Pastoral* and *Mulligan Stew* as a post–World War II native linguistic experiment. That Sorrentino's gift is more exclusively comic than Theroux's may be deduced from the five scattered installments of *La Musique et les mauvaises herbes.* This play, which involves foreign students and professors at The University, revels in twisted English. Even the stage directions are hilarious:

> When Suzanne is returning from her dynamic rendezvous with Andre yesterday evening, Alice is waiting. What the else? She has been regarding a soap story on the "tubes," and she wishes to recount it to Suzanne. Suzanne has sleepy and wishes to couch herself and have a tropical dream on Andre, but she has to listen to the recital of Alice. What putrid! It is a duty of a young lady to listen when her pal of the chamber has a wish to speak. That is how a ball springs, no? (184)

Another token of the ludic impulse helps make *Blue Pastoral* the most absurd American quest since *Balso Snell.* More or less confined to a closed frame in *Giles Goat-Boy,* self-consciousness pervades the entire later work. Writers from *Mulligan Stew*—Dermot Trellis, Lorna Flambeaux, Horace Rosette, Antony Lamont—reappear amid much discussion of narrator, reader, characters, and story. During chapter

33, a voyage is arranged for Helene and Zimmerman, since, otherwise, we might think "their unexplained absence" stemmed from the author's inability to "handle simple fictional techniques" (147). Elsewhere, the narrator "cannot remember if he gave them a mattress" (269). One conversation between husband and wife implies an awareness of postmodern French criticism: " 'I suspect that the "text" is being "deconstructed" beneath our very feets!' Blue muttered. 'And here . . . I thought that we were in a Novel of Ideas . . . invested with a Desperate and Aching Significance and a Sadness filled with Smiles.' " After he tells her, " 'Being alive is like being in a novel,' " Helene "thought that she was *not* real, was not a flesh-and-blood character, but a glob of *écriture*" (192–93).

Indeed, Sorrentino's text does deconstruct, as "California! The End of the Quest," demonstrates. Illogical footnotes suddenly begin to emerge. On page 304, they number 3, 5, 6, 21, 30, 36, 37, 40, 43, though only 3, 7, 36, 40 (plus 44!) have referents and these are disconnected. There ensues excised/bracketed prose, leading toward the comment, *"Here the Ur-manuscript breaks off. The following fragment, arguably a variant version of an earlier, apocryphal manuscript, is in the Piscardi Library of the University"* (309). Progressively, grammar and punctuation deteriorate while the author becomes more and more intrusive, admitting, "I fear, like Blue, my comely hero, . . . that I may have lost my way, and cannot find nor thread nor rhyme nor reason in this subtly lavender display of schlock!", yet threatening, "You don't shut uppa you mout I make a fuckin list go on three hundred pages!" (312). He concludes with the protagonist's long stream-of-consciousness passage to convince us quest and novel are both mad. About the latter, John O'Brien observes:

> *Blue Pastoral* is not a pastoral that would be recognizable to Spenser, Shelley, or Wordsworth—except to the degree that they found words and lines lifted from their works. It is a book that wanders—as do its characters —, a book that keeps falling apart at its structural seams, a book in which its "author" has lost almost all control over his materials. It is excessive and overdone. It is just the book Sorrentino intended to write.[15]

Parody, which focuses on literary *form,* holds special appeal for self-conscious writers like Ssorrentino and Barth because of their preoc-

cupation with fictional *process*. It enables them to vivify genres grown
exhausted through usage; defamiliarized, the heroic quest in *Giles
Goat-Boy* and the eclogue and others in *Blue Pastoral* are renewed.
Though parody is not restricted to autoreferential productions, as
The Beetle Leg and *The Lime Twig* illustrate, most nonreflexive novels
imitate archetypal patterns less blatantly, less flamboyantly. Joseph
McElroy and Thomas Pynchon call *Hind's Kidnap* (1969) and *V.* (1963)
quests, but while each presents a son journeying toward a well-de-
fined, if ambivalent, goal, neither evokes many monomythic details.
Yet, despite greater realism of character, plot, and landscape than
evidenced by *Giles Goat-Boy* and *Blue Pastoral*, these other two inconclusive searches may also be considered absurd.

The pastoral concept gave Sorrentino an opportunity to mock
various interrelated poetic modes; for McElroy, however, it signifies
theme in the musical sense, as the subtitle of *Hind's Kidnap—A Pastoral on Familiar Airs—*implies. These well-known tunes or melodies
include the traditional town versus country opposition, with the action juxtaposed between New York City and vague rural locations.
Both contain displaced persons who embody the psychic imbalance
the guardian sought to avoid when he "designed a city-country coun-
terpoise for young Hind," since together they represented "the true
human whole."[16] Later, Hind spoke of converting " 'the guardian's
land' " into " 'a wildlife sanctuary,' " but was ignorant " 'of birds and
animals' " (146).

Home is an undertaker's East Side brownstone, where the protagonist now occupies the top floor apartment alone. He spends considerable time on the telephone—his link to the amorphous world—
and at the window—his link to the particularized neighborhood.
Through this window, he views the first of several heifers we will
meet, "longing for the field" (5) while "two shaggy-haired young
men" force the rented creature toward an ad studio (4). And through
this window, he hears the recurrent Church bells of The Good
Shepherd one block south.

Maps recur too, making the "grid city" (450) appear as complex as
Borges's labyrinth, Barth's funhouse, and McElroy's own iterative
"Jesus-puzzle portrait." Yet Hind, who records " 'Naked Voice' " tapes
for an "insatiable FM station" (120), navigates Manhattan/Brooklyn
Heights the way Bloom did Dublin, so we encounter numerous au-

thentic places during his excursions around town on foot or via car, bus, and subway. References to construction remind us the metropolitan area is changing and anticipate rural wife Sylvia's paraphrase of urban husband Hind's remark about their depersonalized future landscape: " 'I was by then of the city, which you said tonight looks less to be that old bag of dramatic dilemmas with its old geographical name, and more and more a less and less distinct coastal density marked by ever-rise edifices—seal-tight see-through solid-state tubeless dead-end-tubey vertical message units' " (255).

The opposed agrarian landscape of plants and animals materializes directly when Hind visits Sylvia and their daughter May near Mount Mary or his old pals Ash and Peg Sill near Laurel land. Indirectly, various allusions keep this environment omnipresent, among them the Art Courage Country Put-on, a travesty featuring " 'Norway spruce trees' " and " 'two giant two-girl sheep' " (155–56). During Courage's recitation, Dewey Wood tells Hind, " 'We are all of us trees' " (157), an observation which rings true because Hind knows several "friends (and associates)" that "were trees or possessed of tree connections" (451): besides *Wood*, they include Maddy *Beech*er, *Ivy* Bowles, Mr. Grune*wald*, the *Laurel*s, *Olive*r *Plane*, Larry *Poplar*, *Holly* Roebuck, and *Ash*ley Sill (emphasis added). The tree motif culminates toward the end, as Hind starts the guardian's *Life* with "This is a man . . . who thought himself a shepherd but found himself a tree" (533).

The *ostensible* surname Hind, like other names—Bean, Dove, Heather, Plante, Staghorn, and Sylvia (sylvan)—implies some natural phenomenon (female deer), while his *actual* surname Foster (to care for or cherish) suggests the shepherd guardian "Fossie" ultimately failed at being. Hind has been protective ever since participating in high school sports. A "city shepherd" now (10), he watches curbs, supervises seat belts, and still likes crippled girls. Predictably, McElroy's "guardian of trees" (212) substitute teaches when unreliable Plane becomes involved, then donates blood when cancerous Wood becomes hospitalized. He might well tell a third companion, " 'My talent . . . was to care rather than be cared for, to herd rather than be heard' " (71).

Another catcher in the rye, Jack Hind is especially concerned about children, saving them from real or imagined dangers throughout the novel. He once belonged to Brother, Incorporated, which aided underprivileged kids, and presently, as a member of Foster Parents, Incorporated, he sponsors The Unknown Child (512). We learn that the guardian read him *Grimm's Fairy Tales* and we realize that Hind, the chronic dreamer, has always felt comfortable about this special pastoral universe. At one point, a boy depressed over parental problems discusses his fairy tales with Jack "and their conversation evened into magic narrative communion" (489). The focus is "Hansel and Gretal" and "The Water of Life," though Eddy does mention the English folktale dominating *Hind's Kidnap:* " 'Like Jack and the Beanstalk, but I don't see how it fits you. . . . I like giants. You don't look so big as when I was a child. Some giants are good, some are bad' " (491). However, the protagonist, who stands 6'7″ on "size-fifteen feet," incarnates *both* giant (adult) and child (Jack). These roles get reinforced by other repeated "bean" images: " 'the giant string bean' " billboard of ten-year-old Sylvia and the "Magic Bean Bag" of four-year-old Hershey.

The good shepherd air reaches its climax when Hind, after a long hiatus, resumes his quest for the latter's kidnappers. Similar to Eddy and even Jack, Hershey Laurel had been victimized by dissension between mother and father, "displaced" and "unfit parents" (9) soon dead. Shirley had made love, while Sears was away, to a neighbor, whose wife and her sister-in-law were probably involved during the abduction. At any rate, the husband of this sister-in-law, one Dove, warns Hind shortly before the book closes, " 'Don't know what you think you are, a cop or welfare, but the kid stays with us, we're his parents now and he's happy with us' " (500).

Hind's quest is renewed because an old woman later identified as Miss Foster communicates this message: " 'If you're still trying to break the kidnap, visit the pier by the hospital' " (3). A sequence of clues follows, leading him from pier (Orientals) to Santos-Dumont Sisters (Maddy) to golf course (Ash) to Fieldstone Hotel Health Club (Dewey) to university (Oliver) to island (Sylvia). During these odysseys, he expresses typical postwar paranoia about a possible conspiracy involving the clue-bearers. Postwar absurdity becomes obvious too when Hind takes seriously several fantastic clues like the one gained from Dewey Wood at the Country Put-on—"Confucius was the Orientals who led to Maddy and precipitated the deepening search. And the giveaway was chlorophyll: for *Phil*, the druggist, chewed green Clorets chewing gum" (157). He does indeed enter "a new and necessary range, terrain, field, plot, tract . . . where nothing could follow" (106), a range reflecting two ubiquitous mazes, the aforementioned Jesus-puzzle portrait and the guardian's "annual summer treasure hunt" (163).

The opening section, *Faith, or the First Condition,* concludes with the visit Hind pays Sylvia. There ensue II, and then C. About his tripartite structure, McElroy said:

> *Hind's Kidnap,* which I like for its traditional mythic narrative force but which I grant is the most artificial of my books, is a contrast in formalities. On the one hand, the mass of material that is gathered into the book is rigidly organized into three parts, the first and third being mirror images of each other. On the other hand, the titles of the three sections suggest that each section is part of an independent sequence which is going on. The novel is rigidly formal about something which can be only partially known, so the independent parts are seen as parts of systems which no doubt interpenetrate. But you can only have intuitions of this.[17]

Sylvia addresses the second part—an internal monologue resembling a dramatic monologue—to Jack while he sleeps. Besides exposition about his guardian and their marriage, the monologue reveals her secret life much as the Molly Bloom and Adddie Bundren soliloquies do. Ironically, obsessed amateur detective Hind knows nothing of Sylvia's previous sexual experiences with Mitchell Staghorn or the Gypsy Woman, and little of Sylvia's current affair with John Plante. Nor does he suspect what she terms "my mystery . . . that Daddy waited in . . . every may I ever wanted" (320), including him. This blindness toward individuals Hind loves will be exploited during C, where past erotic intrigues between Oliver Plane and Cassia Meaning and between the guardian and his mother surface. No wonder he adopts " 'the new theory . . . called Infra-Structural Non-Depth Perspective' " (379), though wife and lame mistress Laura Rosenblum (her advocate) both believe perspective exists. The latter had stated: " 'You say it's all background—us too—there is no foreground, we are part of a flat design. Maybe you want to disappear into your background. But I see myself *against* mine' " (235).

Altruistic Hind, grown so selfish through the renewed quest he even forgot the birthday of daughter May, leaves Sylvia convinced he must stop using people like Laura as means rather than ends. Then, perhaps, the family will be reunited, his goal when the Old Woman's note arrived. If section 1 treated the kidnap, its mirror image, section 3, treats the "dekidnap," an equally absurd process reversing the original sequence: "from Oliver to Dewey to Ash to Maddy . . . from the university to FHHC to the golf course to S-D Sisters to the pier" (347). Hind, "[h]aving seen people as leads," must now "turn the leads back into people" (513). However, "nearly everyone he met had eager information" (404) and therefore he gets enmeshed in the kidnap once again. Sylvia finally succumbs too, for the last words are hers: " 'Don't end it' " (534).

The Old Woman, who might be considered a perverse Wise Old Man figure, inspired both the renewal of and the reversion to the endless search, reversion by supplying new evidence concerning Hershey Laurel's present life in New York City. Simultaneously, C tells us much about Miss Foster: that she was a cousin of the guardian through marriage; that she loved him, they battled over the Hind adoption, and he rejected her; that she still resents those near the guardian, particularly this "son." The latter slowly realizes "[s]he had seemed, and for months had perhaps tried, to catch his mind in one notion in order to keep it from seeing another notion perilously close to it" (396). "One notion" implies child Hershey; "another notion," child Jack.

We should pronounce the title *Hind's Kidnap* rather than *Hind's Kidnap* or *Hind's* **Kidnap,** since *kidnap* defines both what Hind possessed and what possessed Hind. Clues for this abound. The guardian—such a snobbish and puristic amateur philologist he abhors words like "O.K."—regrets not having written about the possessive case. Hind shares his linguistic bent, even his genitive obsession, at one point "explaining the difference between the 'of' after 'talent' and the 'of' after 'free' " (184). Earlier, in a dream, the guardian had cautioned him when he mentioned " 'my wife,' " " 'The *wife of Hind:* with an event as active as "wife" be sure not to confuse object of preposition with possessive' " (134). Accordingly, if "Hind's kidnap" becomes "the kidnap of Hind," the possessor (subject) becomes the possessed (object).

Jack feels especially protective toward small boys because he was also victimized by parents, though he remains ignorant of this until he learns during the dekidnap that his nameless mother had betrayed

Frank Hind with John Foster much as Shirley Laurel had betrayed Sears with Ken Love. Then, following their fatal autogyro accident, father-cum-guardian had adopted the orphan, calling him John, but not Foster. Abducted by adoption, Hind, the Christlike good shepherd of uncertain paternity, later projects vague doubts about his origin—doubts Sylvia detects—onto counterpart Hershey Laurel, reminding her, " '[H]e has been lost (mislaid, taken away). He doesn't know who he is' " (146). Thus, Hind's conscious quest for Hershey's past becomes an unconscious pursuit of self-identity, which explains why they share "bean" imagery and why Hind claims to "have persevered in being a unilateral colaurel" (500). Meanwhile, other fathers and sons besides Fossie/Jack and Sears/Hershey emerge—Maddy/Eddy, Mr. Amondson/Christy, Mr. Morales/Siggofreddo, Elder/Oliver "Daddy"/Herbie (adopted)—suggesting the archetypal conflict posing male progenitor against male progeny.

Throughout most of the novel, John Foster appears godlike. His own father had been a scientist and his " 'ancestral home' " had been Harvard. There was even some " 'familial tie between . . . Boston and New York Fosters and the Fosters of Stephen fame' " (436). While alive, many women had loved this charming Renaissance man, who would never ride the subway, for he had enjoyed "education, mind, force, looks, money" (86); after death, people admired him as "Botanist, adviser, Independent, sportsman, idealist" (101). Fossie, the liberal conservative humanist, had been devoted to Burke, Gibbon, and Johnson, but had also read Ariosto, Shakespeare, and others. And Fossie, the art practitioner-connoisseur, though only less preoccupied with Dürer than linguistics, had "preferred the decorous fitnesses and limpidities of the Italians of that day" (202).

Sylvia had asked sleeping Jack, " '[W]hy will you not investigate your guardian?' "—that " 'charming, pathetic, handsome, stuffy' " prig (330). Yet, thirty-six pages further, Jack still considers him "extraordinary . . . a giant." The dekidnap progresses, however, and by page 471 he wonders if the guardian were just "an ineffectual dilettante." Besides using women, avoiding permanent relationships—even with faithful Thea Dover—Hind's unacknowledged father had been meddlesome, dogmatic, and hypocritical. Fossie exemplified his own truism, " 'you can turn away from your real nature' " (81), then founded the College Advisory Service so he could preach something he had never practiced. From him, the son also assimilates "You finish what you embark" (501), but the posthumous files of the father, who had composed a "belated and unfinished paper" about two unfinished Dürer treatises (494), reveal "nothing was complete, much was begun" (529). Consequently, look-alike Hind, "the inadequate re-enactor" (534), must continue his absurd quest, as Sylvia no doubt understands.

Another inadequate re-enactor, appropriately named Herbert *Stencil*, resumes during middle age an even more absurd quest, begun by and perhaps fatal to ex-music hall entertainer Stencil, Sr., known as "Soft-shoe Sidney" among fellow Foreign Office agents. Stencil, Jr., fears Valletta, where "[t]he Father died under unknown circumstances in 1919 while investigating the June Disturbances in Malta,"[18] and so does not arrive there until the final chapter of Pynchon's novel. An Epilogue with this date follows, emphasizing the hold old Stencil and the past have on young Stencil and the present. It was then the former envisioned " 'nothing but a dead end for myself, and . . . for my society' " (460–61), and encountered "V."—now Veronica Manganese—the last time before he drowned. Besides correspondence, his legacy to Herbert included manuscript books, journals, and an unofficial log. The latter memorized one passage marked Florence, April, 1899, which read, " 'There is more behind and inside V. than any of us had suspected. Not who, but what: what is she. God grant that I may never be called upon to write the answer, either here or in any official report' " (53).

Between 1901—the year of his birth and of Queen Victoria's death—and 1945, Stencil, Jr., "the world adventurer" (like Stencil, Sr.), had been "croupier," "plantation foreman," "bordello manager," and civil servant. That he still lacks definition is obvious when Pynchon's *"quick-change artist"* alludes to "himself in the third person. . . . only one among a repertoire of identities" (62). This dramatic flair produces an unreliable raconteur who embellishes yarns, causing them to become "Stencilized."

Since "the century's child" was "motherless," Tony Tanner has tentatively suggested his search may be for both a natural and a historical mother. However, the motive remains doubtful throughout as " 'part of the quarry,' " though another explanation seems more plausible regarding an individual suffering from " 'borderline metabolism.' " Slothful before 1945, afterward Stencil conducted "a conscious campaign to do without sleep" (54) because "he didn't know which he was most afraid of, V. or sleep. Or whether they were two versions of the same thing" (346). The "grim, joyless" chase at least represents action in our inert, death-oriented, entropic world. Thus Stencil's greatest fear involves its termination:

> Finding her: what then? Only that what love there was to Stencil had become directed entirely inward, toward this acquired sense of animateness. Having found this he could hardly release it, it was too dear. To sustain it he had to hunt V.; but if he should find her, where else would there be to go but back into half-consciousness? He tried not to think, therefore, about any end to the search. Approach and avoid. (55)

A possessed clown already scattered with V. "all over the western world" (389), Stencil must consequently end the book—not the quest—pursuing "one Mme. Viola, oneiromancer and hypnotist" to Stockholm (451).

Six women (or a protean Victoria Wrenn), who appear on the international scene between 1898 and 1956, embody the concept "V." After Victoria Wrenn, they are chronologically: nameless lesbian, Veronica Manganese, Vera Meroving, Bad Priest (transvestite), and Mme. Viola. The recurrent ivory comb shaped as "five crucified. . . . soldiers of the British Army" (167), which Victoria first owns, would seem to epitomize V.'s nature. About this, Frederick R. Karl writes: "Behind both Justine and V. is a long tradition of women in literature, described by Mario Praz in *The Romantic Agony:* merciless women, deeply sadistic and often masochistic, whose appeal is their ability to convey pain and suffering as sexual substitutes."[19]

Herbert Stencil fantasizes V., seeing her nearly everywhere—Spain, Crete, Corfu, Asia Minor, Rotterdam, the Roman Campagna (364)—while Thomas Pynchon makes her "magic initial" textually omnipresent through nouns like Valletta, Vatican, Venezuela, Venus, Veronica (rat), Vesuvius, Vheissu, Victoria (Queen), Vogelsang, and Vogt. Vheissu (code name?) emerges as the most significant among these, Valletta notwithstanding. Antarctic explorer Captain Hugh Godolphin says, " 'If Eden was the creation of God, God only knows what evil created Vheissu. The skin which had wrinkled through my nightmares was all there had ever been. Vheissu itself, a gaudy dream. Of what the Antarctic in this world is closest to: a dream of annihilation' " (206). His remote, volcanic dystopia now serves some mysteriously directed cabal, for the barbarous inhabitants " 'are . . . blasting the Antarctic ice with dynamite, preparing to enter a subterranean network of natural tunnels' " the English have detected (197). Years later, Stencil believes that the Vheissu plot included Victoria Wrenn and that the V. concept remains inseparable from an "ultimate Plot":

Truthfully he didn't know what sex V. might be, nor even what genus and species. To go along assuming that Victoria the girl tourist and Veronica the sewer rat were one and the same V. was not at all to bring up any metempsychosis: only to affirm that his quarry fitted in with The Big One, the century's master cabal, in the same way Victoria had with the Vheissu plot and Veronica with the new rat-order. If she was a historical fact then she continued active today and at the moment, because the ultimate Plot Which Has No Name was as yet unrealized, though V. might be no more a she than a sailing vessel or a nation. (226)

This "ultimate Plot Which Has No Name" may be "leveled against the animate world" to establish "here . . . a colony of the Kingdom of Death" (411), entailing Armageddon and apocalypse. If Stencil seeks personal identity through V., as does Hind through Hershey, the question posed by him prior to leaving for Stockholm must be answered affirmatively: " 'Is it really his own extermination he's after?' " (451). Thus, the fear of sleep, the need for movement.

V. emblemizes conspiracy "against the animate world," for in one role (Vera Meroving) she possessed an artificial eye, and in another (Bad Priest) she further acquired an artificial foot, hair, and teeth. Stencil daydreams about her "now, at age seventy-six," as the complete mechanical woman, composed of "plastic," "photoelectric cells," "electrodes," "copper wire," "Solenoid relays," "servo-actuators," "nylon," "hydraulic fluid," "platinum," "butyrate," "polyethylene," and so forth (411).

The Queen Goddess's existence, where the animate resembles the inanimate and vice versa reminds us of Nathanael West's *A Cool Million or, The Dismantling of Lemuel Pitkin* (1934). Its two-part show ("animate" and "inanimate") features "a gigantic hemorrhoid that was lit from within by electric lights," creating "the effect of throbbing pain." But while West concentrates on deception—"Paper had been made to look like wood . . . glass like paper"[20]—Pynchon stresses extinction.

Nowhere is this presented more graphically than during the chapter titled *V. in love*. There, young Mélanie l'Heuremaudit ("Mlle. Jarretière"), who had been molested by Germanic "Papa," portrays the heroine in the ballet *L'Enlèvement des Vierges Chinoises*, which utilizes automata as handmaidens. She grows sexually aroused dreaming about a lay figure that comes alive and winds her up. Soon patroness lady V. appears among several perverts and calls Mélanie " 'Une fétiche.' " Their lesbian affair, based on voyeurism, requires mirrors and signifies death: "Dead at last, they would be one with the inanimate universe and with each other. Love-play until then thus becomes an impersonation of the inanimate, a transvestism not between sexes but between quick and dead; human and fetish" (410). Subsequently, the suicidal girl is impaled on stage when she abandons her metal chastity belt.

Stencil oscillates between the international world of V. and the American world of Benny *Profane* and The Whole *Sick* Crew. Soft and fat, half Catholic and half Jewish, Profane functions as self-styled schlemiel, " 'somebody who lies back and takes it from objects, like any passive woman' " (288). He fears disassembly, yet cohabits with Rachel Owlglass, the "true windup woman" (200), occupying a world "of objects coveted or valued"—even erotically—, where he "couldn't breathe" (18). His temporary job at Anthroresearch Associates is no more fortuitous, since there Profane must guard SHROUD, the "synthetic human," and SHOCK, the "marvelous maniken." If seventy-six-year-old V. represents dehumanized man, these two Frankensteinian monsters represent anthropomorphized objects. Such an interchange between animate and inanimate spells uniform inertness or entropic death.

Tanner claims "The illusory purposiveness of Stencil's travels, and the manifest purposelessness of Profane's meanderings, both serve to illuminate the condition of movement bereft of all significance except the elemental one of postponing inanimateness."[21] Because the American nonquester shuttles "up and down the east coast" (10), "back and forth underneath 42nd Street" (27), and to-and-fro "on the Staten Island ferry" (371), Pynchon calls him "*human yo-yo*" (1). That yo-yoing symbolizes *a state of mind* (344) as well as futile motion becomes clear when we are told the Whole Sick Crew, which experiences rather than lives and talks rather than creates, regards this activity its favorite pastime. Like Profane an associate of the "Raoul-Slab-Melvin Triumverate," atheistic *Pig* Bodine, the AWOL sailor who spends his time brawling, drinking, and fornicating, epitomizes their lifestyle. Our universe seems equally meaningless to the omniscient author: "If you look from the side at a planet swinging round in its orbit, split the sun with a mirror and imagine a string, it all looks like a yo-yo. The point furthest from the sun is called aphelion. The point furthest from the yo-yo hand is called, by analogy, apocheir" (45).

Directed action can be nihilistic too. Accordingly, *Mondaugen's story* (chapter 9) and *Confessions of Fausto Maijstral* (chapter 11) encapsulate man's inhumanity toward man during the twentieth century, "[a] street we are put at the wrong end of, for reasons best known to the agents who put us there" (324). The first treats Sudwestafrika (1922), where "a tiny European Conclave or League of Nations" constituted Foppl's Siege Party—characterized by sexual perversion—"while political chaos howled outside" (235). Throughout this siege, Herr Foppl attempts to relive the Great Rebellion of 1904–07, when his hero General Lothar von Trotha, an expert at "suppressing pigmented populations," had killed some 60,000 Hereros, Hottentots, and Berg-Damaras (244–45). The second treats the bombing raids on Malta (1942–1943). Though the grisly atrocities perpetuated with erotic pleasure against the black population of Sudwestafrika are absent, chapter 11 also stresses dehumanization: "Decadence, decadence. What is it? Only a clear movement toward death or, preferably, non-humanity. As Fausto II and III, like their island, became more inanimate, they moved closer to the time when like any dead leaf or fragment of metal they'd be finally subject to the laws of physics" (321). V. was present during both wars—Vera Meroving in 1922, the Bad Priest in 1942–1943. Still haunting " 'this century's streets,' " Herbert Stencil must seek her elsewhere.

Giles Goat-Boy, Blue Pastoral, Hind's Kidnap, and *V.* are by no means the only contemporary antirealistic American novels that employ the quest. Many other absurd journeys come immediately to mind: for example, Barthelme's *The Dead Father,* Coover's *The Public Burning,* Ellison's *Invisible Man,* Gaddis's *The Recognitions,* Hawkes's *Second Skin,* Mailer's *Why Are We in Vietnam?,* Nabokov's *Lolita,* and Reed's *The*

Free-Lance Pallbearers. Of the four discussed here, *Giles Goat-Boy* alone renders the heroic monomyth in scrupulous detail, while *Blue Pastoral, Hind's Kidnap,* and *V.* reproduce aspects. All parody this motif, self-conscious *Giles Goat-Boy* and *Blue Pastoral* explicitly; semirealistic *Hind's Kidnap* and *V.* implicitly.

However absurd, *The Great Gatsby* remains a plausible story, but these later antirealistic fictions, which echo modern models like *The Dream Life of Balso Snell* and *A Cool Million,* often violate verisimilitude. This is less obvious during *Hind's Kidnap* and *V.* than during *Giles Goat-Boy* and *Blue Pastoral,* though the first two contain implausible phenomena such as the dekidnap and the Bad Priest.

Whether to change WESCAC'S AIM or to locate musical phrase, kidnapped child, mysterious female, the quests under consideration share *ostensible* goals. Additionally, three—*Giles Goat-Boy, Hind's Kidnap,* and *V.*—offer a *real* goal—self-identity—, for George Giles, Jack Hind, and Herbert Stencil are orphaned sons who cannot understand themselves without understanding their fathers. Similar to Jay Gatsby, they must travel alien landscapes, sometimes as detectives (Hind/Stencil) fathoming mazes (metropolis/history). His Wise Old Man figure (Dan Cody) reappears, more ridiculous than ever: Maximilian Spielman (Mathematical Psycho-Proctologist), Dr. Ciccarelli (Mouth King), the Old Woman (jilted lover), and Sidney Stencil (foreign agent). So too does his Queen Goddess (Daisy Buchanan), more promiscuous than ever: Anastasia Stoker, Helen Gavotte, Sylvia Hind, and *V.* Gatsby returned through Nick, the message-bearer, but now there can be no return, no message, since the search has become inconclusive. Instead, we have conspiracy, paranoia, entropy, nightmare, and apocalypse.

The Future as Death

Part 3 also consists of four sections: chapter 8 "Fictitious History"; chapter 9 "Conspiracy and Paranoia"; chapter 10 "Entropy"; and chapter 11 "Nightmare and Apocalypse."

"Fictitious History" is a term coined by John Barth in *The Friday Book* to describe the blend of fact and fancy dominating works like *The Sot-Weed Factor*, a 1960 novel which greatly embellishes a 1708 poem, and *Letters*, a 1979 novel which deals with "false documents, falsified documents, forged and doctored letters, mislaid and misdirected letters and the like." This predilection for spurious writing explains why supposedly real yet actually fraudulent accounts—The Privie Journall and A Secret Historie—recur during these books. Both present the antirealistic view of history as unreliable intrigue, though the earlier emphasizes plots and counterplots and the latter, "Reenactment, or Recycling, or Revolution." Fictitious history well defines the other works paired in chapter 8. Because they employ autobiography and treat military situations, Norman Mailer's nonfiction novel *Armies of the Night* and Kurt Vonnegut, Jr.'s, science fiction novel *Slaughter-House Five* are linked. Their authors, who merge subjective reaction and objective documentation, would probably agree that the novelist is a better historian than the journalist. Finally, Robert Coover's *The Public Burning* and E. L. Doctorow's *The Book of Daniel* are linked too because of a joint focus on the Rosenberg case, the first fictionalizing the execution and the second its aftermath. Impressively researched, the two texts also blend fact and fancy, but with major differences, for the antirealistic *The Public Burning*, which regards history as ritual, becomes an extravagant satire, while *The Book of Daniel*, which regards history as record, becomes an ironic memoir.

The plots and counterplots that permeate fictitious history closely relate to another crucial motif: conspiracy and paranoia. Through a comparative analysis of Joseph Heller's *Catch-22* and Ken Kesey's *One*

Flew Over the Cuckoo's Nest, various conspiratorial institutions are exposed, including the international cartel of *Catch-22* and the Combine of *One Flew Over the Cuckoo's Nest.* Yossarian and Broom (alien outsiders) learn from Orr and McMurphy (renegade insiders). All four embody Eros in a world ruled by Thanatos, whose representatives embrace institutional types such as Colonel Cathcart (military) and Big Nurse (matriarchy). Though the Life Force may win temporary personal victories, conspiratorial death, associated with inanimateness and inertness—here in symbolic hospital environments—will prevail. Only paranoia, which William Burroughs and Thomas Pynchon likewise consider positive, can help. Conspiracy during *Naked Lunch* is general (medicine, business, politics) and during *The Crying of Lot 49,* specific (Tristero), while both authors elsewhere suggest that a gigantic extraterrestrial plot motivates human history. Sex, drugs, and so forth control their characters, who wander about entropic landscapes lacking affection/protection.

Inanimateness and inertness characterize these landscapes, since entropy, whether thermodynamic (heat loss) or informational (noise), constitutes a parallel path toward imminent death. After reviewing the dual phenomena abstractly, chapter 10 examines how they function in "Entropy" and other Pynchon texts. Next, William Gaddis as the creator of three impressive entropic novels—*The Recognitions, J R,* and *Carpenter's Gothic*—becomes central. The last, compared with *The Crying of Lot 49,* receives extended treatment, emphasizing internal and external instability, compositional fragmentation and coherence, disinformation and conspiracy, appearance and reality, clutter and clatter. Many antirealists—Gaddis and Pynchon among them—have been scatalogical, a fact that leads to Norman O. Brown and the homology of feces/sex/death. This homology is effectively dramatized by Ishmael Reed during *The Free-Lance Pallbearers,* where Armageddon and apocalypse are manifested.

Native apocalypses—both private sacrifice and group cataclysm—conclude chapter 11. Contemporary fictions such as Robert Stone's *A Hall of Mirrors* and Robert Coover's *The Origin of the Brunists* illustrate the relativistic nature these catastrophes exhibit. Other contemporary fictions—for example, Joseph Heller's *Catch-22* and Susan Sontag's *Death Kit*—contain nightmare material reflecting apocalyptic states. Ralph Ellison's *Invisible Man,* which is filled with dreams and dream-

like moments, brings nightmare, Armageddon, and apocalypse together, though the circumstance that the first-person narrator, a
latter-day Ishmael, survives to tell his story, makes this masterwork
more hopeful than most other catastrophic antirealistic confronta-
tions/revelations.

CHAPTER 8

Fictitious History

In *The Friday Book* piece entitled "Historical Fiction, Fictitious History, and the Chesapeake Bay Blue Crabs, or, About Aboutness," which was first delivered to the Dorchester County Historical Society, then published by the Washington *Post,* John Barth discusses several kinds of historical writing. The historiographer "reconstructs the political, social-economic, and cultural past" as objectively as possible.[1] More subjective, yet dependent on documents too, the historical novelist dramatizes "not only what happened, but what it might have felt like to be a live human being experiencing that history in that place" (188). And, last, "your flat-out, big-time, big-money book-of-the monthers . . . move in on a culture or a subject and 'work it up' like a real-estate developer" (189).

Barth's own "more or less 'historical' fiction[s]," *The Sot-Weed Factor* (1960) and *Letters* (1979), are radically different from these approaches:

. . . for both I did a respectable amount of homework on the historical periods involved. But it was a novelist's homework, not a historian's, and novelists are the opposite of icebergs: Eight-ninths of what I once knew about this region's history, and have since forgotten, is in plain view on the surface of those two novels, where it serves its fictive purposes without making the author any sort of authority. Since *The Sot-Weed Factor* isn't finally "about" Colonial Maryland at all, any more than LETTERS is really "about" the burning of Washington in 1814 or the burning of Cambridge in 1967, I'm already uncertain which of their historical details are real and which I dreamed up. (180–81)

A creator of "fictitious history," Barth concludes with three rules: *"Fiction about history almost never becomes part of the history of fiction"; "The literature that finally matters in any culture is almost never principally about that culture"; "Whatever else it is about, great literature is almost always also about itself"* (190–91).

Barth did not have many facts to consider when he chose the

historical Ebenezer Cooke as protagonist for *The Sot-Weed Factor,* which bears the title of Cooke's best-known poem. During 1662 Thomas Manning sold Andrew Cooke, from St. Giles-in-the-Fields, Middlesex, England, 500 acres of land called Malden, located on the Chesapeake Bay and the Choptanck River, Dorchester County, Maryland, an estate that eventually doubled in size and became Cooke Poynt. Three years later, Andrew Cooke II married Anne Bowyer, who bore him two children, Anna and Ebenezer. Through the bookseller Benjamin Bragg at the Raven in Pater-Noster Row, the latter published *The Sot-weed Factor: Or, a Voyage to Maryland* (1708). Cooke's "Satyr" employing "Burlesque Verse" depicted "The Laws, Government, Courts and Constitutions of the Country; and also the buildings, Feasts, Frolicks, Entertainments and Drunken Humours of the Inhabitants of that Part of *America.*" Though personal observations permeate the text, it yields little autobiographical data. However, external sources show Andrew Cooke II bequeathing Cooke Poynt to Ebenezer and Anna in 1711 and in 1717 brother and sister selling their shares. Soon Henry Lowe II, descendant of another St. Giles family, appointed Ebenezer Cooke Gent as his deputy, but after 1722 Cooke can be traced only by way of subsequent literary works, the most important being the 1730 sequel *Sotweed Redivivus.*[2]

While he maintains an erratic factual substructure, Barth manipulates the sketchy information available on his subject's life. Ebenezer and Anna are made twins because, twinned himself, this motif obsesses their author (see *The Sot-Weed Factor,* part 3, chapter 2, and *The Friday Book,* pp. 1–3). Nothing is certain about the formal education of Cooke, the man, whose poems and activities point toward legal training, but the fictional character matriculates at Cambridge and studies the liberal arts. Barth admitted, "Since no one knows when the historical Ebenezer Cooke died or where he's buried, it was my privilege to close the novel with a dippy epitaph, which I have the disillusioned old poet compose."[3] According to Alan Holder, changes were often conceived for thematic reasons:

> To heighten the effect of inexhaustible colonial energies being channeled into devious plots, Barth has taken some liberties with the historical records as these appear in the *Archives of Maryland.* He has either altered the facts or linked them together in the shape of a plot. So, for example, he has Burlingame attribute to Claiborne an accusation against a colonial official that was

actually made by a woman. . . . What emerges from these alterations of and additions to items in the *Archives* is the conception of history as intrigue, the sense of historical events as the products of plots and counterplots.[4]

The juxtaposition of fact and fancy in *The Sot-Weed Factor* may be illustrated through the title poem's supposed evolution. When still innocent, The Laureate plans his *Marylandiad*, which will relate " 'the heroic founding of that province!' "[5] This panegyric becomes the satirical *Sot-Weed Factor* after he discovers " 'that province' " contains only " 'scoundrels and perverts, hovels and brothels, corruption and poltroonery!' " (493). The novel includes passages from the *Marylandiad* and *The Sot-Weed Factor*. Ostensibly, both were written by the fictitious Ebenezer Cooke, but indeed the first belongs to Barth and the second to his colonial predecessor. Realizing that Samuel Butler had influenced the latter, Barth also uses Hudibrastic verse (octosyllabic couplets), a form discussed during part 2, chapter 26. The inauthentic *Marylandiad* commences:

> *Let* Ocean *roar his damn'dest Gale;*
> *Our Planks shan't leak; our Masts shan't fail.*
> *With great* Poseidon *at our Side*
> *He seemeth neither wild nor wide.* (184)

And the authentic *Sot-Weed Factor:*

> *Condemn'd by Fate, to wayward Curse,*
> *Of Friends unkind, and empty Purse,*
> *Plagues worse than fill'd* Pandoras Box,
> *I took my Leave of* Albions Rocks,
> *With heavy Heart, concern'd that I*
> *Was forc'd my native Soil to fly,*
> *And the old World must bid Good-b'ye.* (494)

The 1960 novel took several episodes from the 1708 poem. For instance, near the beginning of part 2, chapter 29, Barth's protagonist awakes in a corncrib to find his clothes missing, which is precisely what had happened to Cooke's first-person narrator, ll. 438–45. Later, the "jolly female crew . . . deep engaged at Lanterloo" of the poem, l. 544ff., reappears as the three surly women playing cards during part 2, chapter 31, of the novel, where the few insults exchanged by the Cooke characters multiply to cover six pages. And, finally, among the several misadventures the poetic sot-weed factor and his fictional descendant share are those involving a benighted provincial court system.

Yet there exists no precedent in the poem for the novel's preoccupation with history. Barth's Cooke voices historical deceptiveness when he exclaims to Charles Calvert (actually Henry Burlingame): " 'Ne're have I encountered such a string of plots, cabals, murthers, and machinations in life or literature as this history you relate me!' " (102). That history is problematical too may be surmised from the summary Barth provides of part 3, chapter 18: "*The Poet Wonders Whether the Course of Human History is a Progress, a Drama, a Retrogression, a Cycle, an Undulation, a Vortex, a Right- or Left-Handed Spiral, a Mere Continuum, or What Have You. Certain Evidence Is Brought Forward, but of an Ambiguous and Inconclusive Nature*" (734). During both *The Sot-Weed Factor* and *Letters,* history metaphorically becomes the legendary *Ouida* bird who flew "in ever diminishing circles until at the end he disappeared into his own fundament" (737).

The brief fourth part of Barth's "lengthy history" begins by examining "the rival claims of Fact and Fancy." Here, he offers "three blue-chip replies" to the charge he has "played . . . fast and loose with Clio": (1) "we all invent our pasts"; (2) she "was already a scarred and crafty trollop when the Author found her"; and (3) "the most engaging company imaginable" have violated this "strumpet" (805). However, an artist may ignore claims involving substance more safely than ones involving form. From the dramatic point of view, *The Sot-Weed Factor* is over and only anticlimax or denouement remains; but from the historical point of view, "there is . . . much more—all grounded on meager fact and solid fancy." Barth hopes the Reader will "indulge some pandering to Curiosity at Form's expense" (806) as he recounts what happened subsequently.

Perhaps the unreliability of history can best be appreciated through two supposedly real yet actually fraudulent *Sot-Weed* documents that will recur in *Letters,* the first ascribed to a nonhistorical figure and the second to a national hero who despise each other: "The Privie Journall of Sir Henry Burlingame" and "A Secret Historie of the Voiage Up the Bay of Chesapeake From Jamestowne in Virginia Undertaken in the yeer of Our Lord 1608 by C^{apt} J^{no} Smith, & Faithfullie Set Down in Its Severall Parts By the Same."

About his ancestor's work, Henry Burlingame III informs Ebene-

zer Cooke, " '[T]he title's mine. . . . As you can see, the journal is a
fragment, but the journey it describes is writ in John Smith's *Generall
Historie*. 'Twas in January of 1607, the first winter of the colony, and
they traveled up the Chickahominy River to find the town of Powhatan, Emperor of the Indians' " (161). "The Privie Journall," a fictitious document, travesties *The Generall Historie*, a genuine document
(unlike the above-mentioned "Secret Historie"). From the latter, Barth
quotes the famous intercession scene, which scholars consider spurious:

> Being ready with their clubs, to beate out his braines, Pocahontas, the
> Kings dearest daughter, when no entreaty could prevaile, got his head in her
> armes, and laid her owne upon his to save him from death; whereat the
> Emperour was contented he should live to make him hatchets, and her bells,
> beads, and copper; for they thought him as well of all occupations as them-
> selves. (162)

"The Privie Journall" has two portions in *The Sot-Weed Factor*. During the earlier one (part 2, chapter 6), Sir Henry Burlingame depicts
Captain John Smith as an ignorant, selfish coward. He is obsessed by
sex, fancying "him selfe a Master of Venereall Arts," and boasting "to
have known carnallie every kind of Woman on Earth, in all of Are-
tines positions" (162–63). Smith saves them from the Indians through
his pornographic cards and compass, and soon the pair meets lecherous Powhatan and Powhatan's sixteen-year-old daughter. After
feasting, gluttonous Smith shows the "Emperour" the compass, and
Pocahontas, with whom he has exchanged "amourous glances," some
dirty drawings. Additional food and drink are consumed, then, as in
The Generall Historie, she intercedes on behalf of the endangered
captain. Her name, signifying *"smallnesse and impenetrabilitie"* (168),
describes her genitalia, which many warriors have essayed unsuccessfully. Should now "affianc'd" Smith fail to devirginize Pocahontas at
their "carnall joust . . . set for sunup" (169), he and Burlingame must
die. The action grows more grotesque during the later portion of
"The Privie Journall" (part 3, chapter 21). That night Smith secures
an eggplant, and shocks his companion, whose narrative temporarily
breaks off, by preparing it "in the strangest manner" (792). When
Burlingame continues, the captain is heading awkwardly toward "the
publick square," where, within a circle of savages, naked and bound

Pocahontas lies waiting. "She did swoone dead away" (794) before Smith's penis, usually "a modest endowment" (793), but presently eleven inches long and three inches wide. He penetrates her, gives Powhatan the eggplant recipe, and the Englishmen depart. On the way to Jamestowne, Burlingame attacks what will become the published chronicle: "Moreover, he made so bold as to shew me a written account of his salvation by Pocahontas, the wch he meant to include in his lying *Historie:* this version made no mention whatever of his scurrilous deflowring of the Princesse, but merelie imply'd, she was overcome by his manlie bearing & comlie face!" An entry of March 1608 adds, "He shuns her as much as possible, albeit in her absence, and in his *Historie,* he makes the finest speaches in her praise" (795).

Clearly, Barth's Captain John Smith and Sir Henry Burlingame are both unreal, though one was a national hero and one is a nonhistorical figure. They function as reciprocal antagonists in fraudulent counterdocuments created by the pseudohistorian Barth for the pseudohistory *The Sot-Weed Factor.* Like the Cooke material, these documents reveal an erratic factual substructure evident throughout the Powhatan/Pocahontas episode. That Smith scholars question the original story only makes the fictitiousness of history more convincing.

"A Secret Historie" treats Burlingame even worse than "The Privie Journall" treats Smith. "[P]robably meant as the initial draft of part of the author's well-known *Generall Historie of Virginia*" (276), the first begins almost immediately after the second terminates. It contains three sequences—Accomack (part 2, chapter 15), *Limbo Straits* (part 2, chapter 25), and the *Ahatchwhoops* (part 3, chapter 7)—during each of which the captain outsmarts the "Liverpooler." Two composite portraits emerge. Whereas Smith is virile, resourceful, and wise, Burlingame is impotent, stupid, envious, ill-humored, fat, crude, and cowardly. The former fears the latter's subversiveness. In sequence no. 1 "he meant to noyse the truth about my egg-plant receipt all over Jamestowne, and London as well" (280); in sequence no. 2 he "looses no opening to sowe the seedes of discontent & faction" (400); and in sequence no. 3 he "had done all in his power to thwart me & my explorations" (604). We are not surprised, then, that Smith ultimately abandons Burlingame, or that a concluding couplet explains the title of his "Secret Historie": *"When one must needs Campanions leave for dead, / 'Tis well the tale thereof were left unread"* (611).

Barth's predilection for spurious writing did not fade with the 1960 publication of *The Sot-Weed Factor*, as "Historical Fiction, Fictitious History,"—originally presented during 1979—attests. He told the Dorchester County Historical Society, "Fictitious history is something that my LETTERS novel *is* more or less about: false documents, falsified documents, forged and doctored letters, mislaid and misdirected letters and the like, in the history of History."[6] A memorable instance involves the postscript to the epistle A. B. Cook VI dated "Wednesday, 17 Sept. 1969," where "H. B." (Henry Burlingame VII) advises "J. B." (John Barth), "[E]xcept that it is now genuinely posthumous, this letter, like its author, is a fraud. So too are the *'lettres posthumes'* of A. B. Cook IV: forgeries by his eponymous descendant. . . . The man who died at Fort McHenry was not my father."[7]

"The Author" of *Letters* claims to have borrowed the "Tragic View" and the "Anniversary View" of history from former protagonists Todd Andrews *(The Floating Opera)* and Jacob Horner *(The End of the Road)*, respectively. These interact with a third view, "Reenactment," giving both *Letters* and its spinoff *Chimera* their unique historical perspective. After the publication of *Letters*, John Barth apprised interviewer Charlie Reilly, "I became increasingly aware that the book's true subject, stated simply, would be Reenactment, or Recycling, or Revolution—the last in a metaphorical sense rather than a political sense." However, for him, reenactment must entail more than repetition à la Kurt Vonnegut's "trademark" figure Kilgore Trout.[8]

That it may also involve what Barth has elsewhere called "transcension" (transcendence) is evident when we examine the "second cycle" of Jacob Horner's life dramatized in *Letters*. We meet him at the Remobilization Farm fifteen years after his *End of the Road* flight from Wicomico State Teacher's College, where he had taught Prescriptive Grammar and conducted an adulterous affair with Rennie Morgan. While forty-six-year-old Jake has done virtually nothing but become administrative assistant here since her fatal abortion, once-conventional husband Joe Morgan, who arrives on March 3, 1969, has lost several academic positions and now takes psychedelic drugs. Soon the two men are playing themselves in *Der Wiedertraum*, a therapeutic recapitulation of their original rivalry. The supporting cast includes figures reflecting earlier Barth works: Jeannine Mack as Rennie Morgan; Marsha Blank as Peggy Rankin; Monsieur Casteene as President Schott. Throughout this ordeal, Horner is haunted by Morgan's ultimatum "to Redream our story and Present . . . by 9/1/69 . . . Rennie Alive and Unadulterated" (739). The Doctor tells him " 'You have Made No Progress in eighteen years' " (99), but when Horner starts to love the ex-wife of old graduate school acquaintance Ambrose Mensch *(Lost in the Funhouse)*, "remobilization" occurs. He rescues addicted Marsha from Lily Dale, where Jerome Bray (compare Harold Bray in *Giles Goat-Boy*) was sexually abusive, then monitors "her withdrawal symptoms and her schedule of therapies" (576). Next he sends Todd Andrews seven self-directed letters, citing the "many years since I Wrote Anything to anyone" (739) and noting "I Wrestled him to an impasse" before Morgan committed suicide (744). His supreme action, marriage, adumbrates the match between Mensch and Lady Amherst, especially as Marsha, too, is pregnant, though by somebody else. Thus, while Morgan, Bray, and Andrews perish during *Letters*, Horner and Mensch experience transcension to life via Eros.

A. B. Cook VI, another doomed figure, resembles Jerome Bray to the extent that both are descendants rather than incarnations of people inhabiting prior books. The four 1812 letters from A. B. Cook IV to his unborn child, which summarize and extend the prose *Sot-Weed Factor*, and the eight 1969 letters from A. B. Cook VI to his son and others, which summarize and extend the 1812 letters, constitute a comprehensive, if fictitious, history of the Burlingame/Castine/Cook line, whose early genealogy on page 112 prefigures the Bray genealogy on page 641. A. B. Cook VI—possible imposter, forger, even plagiarist—identifies with dual author Ebenezer Cook-John Barth all through the *Letters* sequel: "The fact is, sir, my major literary effort over the past dozen years—that is to say, since I gave you my 'Sot-Weed Factor Redevivus' material as the basis for your novel—has been the planning of a poetical epic of this Border State. . . . It was to be entitled *Marylandiad*" (408). Like professional historians Lady Amherst and Joe Morgan, the "historical consultant" and self-appointed "poet laureate of Maryland" becomes obsessed with "the fateful Pattern of our history," in his case, the "endless canceling of Cooks by Burlingames, Burlingames by Cooks" (747). Reenactment also inspired the focus during *Letters* on the War of 1812. Barth's

> interest in the War of 1812 did not derive so much from a historical novelist's interest in past events as from the fact that, when it was going on, the war was frequently referred to as the "Second American Revolution." One thinks immediately of Marx's famous observation that important events in history tend to occur twice: the first time as tragedy, the second time as farce. In short, what I'm trying to say is that I looked around for a "history" to fit the theme, rather than a theme to coincide with the history.[9]

Paralleling *Letters,* the Reg Prinz film not only "reenacts and re-creates events and images from 'the books' " (383), but from the War of 1812, as the location reports Lady Amherst sends to the Author about *The Battle of Niagra, The Fort Erie Magazine Explosion, The Burning of Washington, [T]he Bombardment of Fort McHenry* and so forth reveal.

Revolutionary computer expert Jerome Bray threatens to recycle Barth before Barth can recycle him: "You think to make us a character in yet another piece of *literature!* You, 'sir'—now we have your number programmed into LILYVAC—will be a character in our *18 14* (a.k.a. *R.N.*): the world's 1st work of Numerature!" (527). Ironically, this demented fellow voiced his enemy's credo when he said two years previously: *"Art is as natural an artifice as Nature; the truth of fiction is that Fact is fantasy; the made-up story is a model of the world"* (33).

Novelists have always blended fact and fancy, sometimes giving their fictional works a factual basis, as in Dickens's *Hard Times,* where we experience nineteenth-century industrial conditions. Less often the process has been reversed so that an essentially factual account is rendered through fictional means, as in Defoe's *A Journal of the Plague Year,* where we enter virulent London during 1665. Both methods characterize American literature. Melville's *Billy Budd,* based on records, and Crane's "The Open Boat," based on observations, represent the first—that is, fictional works with a factual basis—while Twain's memory book, *Life on the Mississippi,* and Hemingway's "absolutely true book," *Green Hills of Africa*, represent the second—that is, essentially factual accounts rendered through fictional means.

Though James Fenimore Cooper and others have contributed to the historical novel, and Nathaniel Hawthorne *(The Blithedale Romance)* and Ernest Hemingway *(The Sun Also Rises)* have contributed to the *roman à clef*, "in which actual persons and events are presented under the guise of fiction,"[10] Americans did not invent a genre of their own to express the interweaving of fact and fancy until the 1960s when Truman Capote coined the term "nonfiction novel" and Pete Hamill coined the term "new journalism." These terms merged and there appeared books like *In Cold Blood* (1965) and *The Electric Kool-Aid Acid Test* (1968).[11] Soon Norman Mailer became the chief exponent of the embryonic form, producing *Armies of the Night* (1968), *Miami and the Siege of Chicago* (1968), *Of a Fire on the Moon* (1970) and *The Executioner's Song* (1979). The last bears on its jacket the phrase "A True Life Novel."

The New Journalism, with an Anthology Edited by Tom Wolfe and E. W. Johnson (1973) "demonstrates how fictional techniques may be adapted by journalists to create the new form." Thus,

Historical sequencing is eschewed in favor of dramatic scenes; quotation is out and dialogue is in, some of it even invented. A context is constructed, so that people in a situation come to us with the thickness of background, status, behavioral patterns. The reporter must describe events as they unfold, and therefore needs a point of view, a voice.[12]

The long first book of *Armies of the Night*, which Mailer calls HISTORY AS A NOVEL: THE STEPS OF THE PENTAGON employs these techniques. He does not forego historical sequencing altogether, since its four parts take us chronologically from Thursday evening through Sunday, but this sequencing is dramatic. The context—a typical nonfiction novel crisis—was the October 1967 march on the Pentagon to protest the Vietnam War. After an old friend enlists reluctant Mailer's support, we get "a history of himself over four days, and therefore . . . history in the costume of a novel."[13] Tension builds, despite his discursiveness, as he turns up at the Hay-Adams hotel, the liberal party, the Ambassador Theater, the Department of Justice, the Lincoln Memorial, and the Pentagon parking lot. Book 1, part 3 ends with a climactic event—the arrest of Mailer—and the nearly 100 remaining pages (part 4) constitute the denouement. They show him in a police van, prison, and court; finally free, he returns full-circle to Washington, then New York. The Novelist had started out by quoting *Time* magazine, 27 October 1967 on his activities and by vowing we would now learn what really occurred, so the entire drama has been a voyage of discovery.

Armies of the Night contains several scenes, the most memorable of which occupies part 1, chapters 5 and 6. Arriving drunk at the Ambassador Theater from the liberal party, where Robert Lowell reiterated, " 'you are the best journalist in America,' " and he replied, " 'there are days when I think of myself as . . . the best writer' " (33), Mailer, who happily contemplates being "both speaker and master of ceremonies" tonight (41), "metamorphose[s] into the Beast" (42). He urinates on the floor, causes "a considerable stir in the orchestra," slaps the acting M.C.'s solar plexus, waits while despised Paul Goodman recites, reprimands Ed De Grazia, and takes the stage. There, without microphone, he addresses the audience, an obscene clown launching a "butcher boy attack" (54). When he fails to regain the M.C. job by popular acclaim, Mailer, keeping the chair anyway, introduces Dwight Macdonald and retreats to study aristocratic Lowell until the latter falls backward on his "much-regarded, much-protected brain" (55). Macdonald finishes a boring presentation, then Mailer introduces Lowell respectfully but vulgarly and envies Lowell's reception because Lowell "was loved and he was not." Now the situation is *mano a mano* (59), Dominguen vs. Manolete, as the brash Jewish writer follows the low-keyed Yankee poet to address the audience again. Still intoxicated, Mailer delivers a second round of loud, humorous obscenities, during which he becomes " 'Lyndon Johnson's little old *dwarf* alter ego' " (63) castigating the press. Back at the Hay-Adams after more boozing, he concludes: "[I]f this were a novel, Mailer would spend the rest of the night with a lady. But it is history, and so the Novelist is for once blissfully removed from any description of the hump-your-backs of sex" (66).

Goodman, Macdonald, and Lowell's "thickness of background, status, [and] behavioral patterns" had surfaced earlier (chapter 4). The poet would remain the most important character in *Armies of the Night* except for Mailer, the participant, whom Mailer, the narrator, also perceives from a third-person point of view. Lowell had been treated ambivalently. They were secret sharers, detesting "liberal academic parties," and, though "doomed to be revolutionaries . . . champions of one Left cause or another," both remained *grands conservateurs* (29). Yet Mailer had felt that the "most distinguished poet in America" (32) possessed an "unchristian talent for literary logrolling" (33). This ambivalence continues at the Ambassador, where his antipode is said to be a "disconcerting mixture of strength and weakness" (53)— mournful, delicate, spoiled, courageous, elegant, superior, diffident, modest, petulant, and so forth—which makes Lowell almost as complicated as Mailer.

But not quite, because Norman presents Norman in the guise of protean public protagonist. The Ambassador Theater offers an ideal setting to display "the frustrated actor" (65). Here, he can mimic Irish/Southern (Cassius Clay, LBJ) accents and assume diverse roles: Master of Ceremonies, the Beast, Prince of Bourbon, Tory, the Existentialist, minor poet, vaudeville clown, Dominguin, dwarf, demagogue, and, above all, the Novelist. (We encounter the Historian, General Mailer, the Participant, Left Conservative, and the Protagonist elsewhere, besides the many other parts recorded on page 153). A filmmaker too, he is the object of television and motion picture cameras during the march. This does not surprise Mailer, "for people had been regarding him by his public image since he was twenty-five years old. He had in fact learned to live in [its] sarcophagus" (16).

Mailer, the character, has cannibalized the private life of Mailer, the man. At forty-four, they have led the same stormy existence. Both attended Harvard, served in the army, published books, divorced three times, fathered six children, assaulted one wife and occupied jails. Their discontent with the reception of *Why Are We in Vietnam?* (1967) emerges,[14] as do their opinions. Left Conservatives, they appreciate America and its richly obscene speech, but detest totalitarianism/totalitarianese/technology/technologese. Mother love, small towns, and Paul Goodman fare badly too. Goodman, whose "dishmop prose" (115) offends the Mailers' "neo-Victorianism" by advocating the equal validity of "heterosexuality, homosexuality, and onanism" (36), leads the "middle-class, cancer-pushers and drug-gutted flower generation" (47). However, though this generation is "pill-ridden, electronically oriented, [and] chemically-grounded" (299), hippy villains are better than "corporation-land villains" (110).

Voices in *Armies of the Night* derive from the double-vision John

Dos Passos ascribed to *The Great Gatsby* and *The Last Tycoon,* the author of which Mailer invokes beside Hemingway and Wolfe. Part 2, chapter 1 (THE HISTORIAN) tells us that the "ambiguous" Pentagon march requires "a participant but not a vested partisan . . . a ludicrous figure with mock-heroic associations" (67). His "monumental disproportions" mirror the "monumental disproportions" of the event, yet, while "our comic hero" "should be an egotist . . . outrageously and often unhappily self-assertive," as "narrative vehicle" he must "command . . . detachment classic in severity" (68).

Mas'ud Zavarzadeh calls him "both 'generator' and 'reflector' of reported actions and emotions."[15] A "double-minded man" like Dos Passos's Fitzgerald, Mailer

let his "actant" Participating self interpret the data of American reality and his "actee" Scribal self acknowledge the untenability of his reading of reality. . . . By articulating his divided loyalties in the actant and actee, he transcends the limitations of his fictive vision, and mocks his own effort to view the actual through his fictive imagination. . . . The split self has its counterpart in the split nation—the book is full of references to the schizophrenia of America. . . . He draws a parallel between his [fourth] wife and America and implicitly acknowledges the realization that both elude his habitual and learned categories of knowing and connecting. . . . As a quest for the grand informing pattern of meaning behind the facade of chaotic reality, *Armies* is a failure, but as an enactment of the tension between "interpretive" frames of reference and the untamable flow of actualities, it is a great triumph.[16]

In book 2, THE NOVEL AS HISTORY: THE BATTLE OF THE PENTAGON, the Novelist hands the Historian his baton. Their "secret collaboration" on the nonfiction novel, which represents "the personification of a vision" metaphorically associated with "tower," "telescopes," "master builder," "lens grinder," and "microscope," dissolves when we approach the mass media world (245). After recounting the sociopolitical background of the march, Mailer cites several sources for its actualization: the *New York Times,* the *National Guardian,* the Washington *Free Press,* the *Washington Star,* and others. He finds "the journalistic information available from both sides is so incoherent, inaccurate, contradictory, malicious, even based on error that no accurate history is conceivable." But if this were otherwise, documents still could not supply "sufficient intimation," and, therefore, midway through book 2, Mailer abandons "historic inquiry" to write "a collective novel" of "strange lights and intuitive speculation." Fact and fancy are hardly the "comfortable opposites" his bipartite structure might suggest, yet "the instincts of the novelist" remain different from and superior to "the methods of history" (284).

The nonfiction novel is not the only prose genre that mixes fact and fancy. For instance, we also have the science fiction narrative, whose most notorious antirealistic practitioner William Burroughs appears intermittently throughout his own researched texts. Though quite different with regard to method and manner, Kurt Vonnegut, Jr., writes science fiction as well. The latter's finest achievement, *Slaughter-House Five* (1969), contains this observation apropos a radio talk show where "literary critics . . . discuss whether the novel was dead": "[A]uthors had to do what Norman Mailer did, which was to perform in public what he had written."[17] Via Robert, the Green Beret son of protagonist Billy Pilgrim, the Vietnam War plays a role, albeit small, here too.

Like *Armies of the Night*, *Slaughter-House Five* employs dual focus, however dissimilarly. Mailer the "actee" *versus* Mailer the "actant" gives way to Vonnegut the author *plus* Pilgrim the persona and thus the double-mindedness of the nonfiction novel is succeeded by the single-mindedness of the totalizing novel. If Mailer mocked himself as buffoon opposite, concluding no fair or dependable history of the march on the Pentagon could be written, Vonnegut and his counterpart clown agree that people are "the listless playthings of enormous forces" (164). Predictably, then, Manichean characters (e.g., good Derby/evil Lazzaro) replace ambiguous Lowell, while recurrent phrases signal nature's indifference to man *("Poo-tee-weet?")* and man's resignation to death ("So it goes").

The bipartite structure of *Armies of the Night* becomes the closed frame of *Slaughter-House Five*, where framework chapters 1 and 10 feature "old fart" Vonnegut and framed chapters 2 through 9 feature everyman Pilgrim. Contrary to Mailer, who equated autobiography and fiction, Vonnegut projects the factual world through personal history, past and present, though, again contrary to Mailer, "I've changed . . . the names." He begins, "All this happened, more or less. The war parts, anyway, are pretty much true" (1), and information follows concerning the evolution of the novel and its dedication; Vonnegut's current habits; his army experiences; his marriage and family; his education and jobs; his return to Dresden. Such data, along with the new material in chapter 10 and the various authorial intrusions during the framed sections, was prefigured by the central importance given to autobiography on the title page. There, Kurt Vonnegut, Jr. is "A FOURTH-GENERATION GERMAN-AMERICAN / NOW LIVING IN EASY CIRCUMSTANCES / ON CAPE COD / [AND SMOKING TOO MUCH], / WHO, AS AN AMERICAN INFANTRY SCOUT / *hors de combat,* / AS A PRISONER OF WAR, / WITNESSED THE FIRE-BOMBING / OF DRESDEN, GERMANY, / THE FLORENCE OF THE ELBE. / A LONG TIME AGO, / AND SURVIVED TO TELL THE TALE."

Reflecting nonfiction novel practice, *Slaughter-House Five* weds its private disclosures to facts about an extreme public situation. We learn, among other things, that the demolition of Dresden occurred on 13 February 1945; that 130,000 individuals were killed; that afterwards "Dresden was like the moon . . . nothing but minerals" (178). Documents were invoked: *Extraordinary Popular Delusions and the Madness of Crowds,* by Charles Mackay, LL.D.; *Dresden, History, Stage and Gallery,* by Mary Endell; and *The Destruction of Dresden,* by David Irving.

Both *Armies of the Night* and *Slaughter-House Five* refer to literature often, yet whereas in the first style is a moral index, in the second attitude prevails. Consequently, Vonnegut dislikes American traitor Howard W. Campbell, Jr., the Nazi war criminal who "had written many popular German plays and poems" (165), and Harvard history professor Bertram Copeland Rumfoord, the rich military superman who had produced twenty-six books, including the volume "about sex and strenuous athletics for men over sixty-five" (184). Kilgore Trout, on the other hand, "became Billy's favorite living author, and science fiction became the only sort of tales he could read" (101). His prose might be frightful, but "his ideas were good" (110). At the Pilgrim anniversary party attended by optometrists, this "friendless and despised" (111) "circulation man" (166) "alone was without glasses" (170). Billy comes across several unpopular Trout works as "window dressing" in a pornographic New York bookstore, and when he offers to purchase one, the clerk considers him perverted (204).

While nonfiction texts like *Armies of the Night* never leave our world, the marginally antirealistic *Slaughter-House Five* juxtaposes earthly locations (Ilium, Dresden, and others) and extraterrestrial Trafalmadore. Books here have "no beginning, no middle, no end, no sus-

pense, no moral, no causes, no effects" because the Trafalmadorians
"love . . . the depths of many marvelous moments seen all at one
time" (88). Thus, they will relegate their sole English specimen, Jac-
queline Susann's *Valley of the Dolls*—with its "ups and downs"—to a
museum (87).

Numerous differences exist between Earth and Trafalmadore, where
we encounter four-dimensional vision and five sexes, but none seems
more crucial than chronology versus simultaneity, for when distinctions regarding past, present, and future disappear, so too does
death. That Billy became "unstuck in time" (23) and got kidnapped
by the Trafalmadorians, who gave him as zoo mate actress Montana
Wildhack, is attributable to his archetypal role of divine fool. Both
"nonviolent mental patients," he and Eliot Rosewater met at the
"veterans' hospital near Lake Placid" after World War II (99), during
which Eliot had mistakenly "shot a fourteen-year-old fireman" and
Billy "had seen the greatest massacre in European history . . . the
fire-bombing of Dresden." These events made "life meaningless. . . .
So they were trying to re-invent themselves and their universe. Science fiction was a big help" (101). Reminiscent of Mailer's lens-
grinder, Billy, the optometrist, later prescribes "corrective lenses
for Earthling souls" (29), while Vonnegut, his shadow, reiterates
"Listen."

Trafalmadore is scarcely utopia, since it conducts wars and will
blow up the doomed cosmos, yet Trafalmadorians advise: " 'Ignore
the awful times, and concentrate on the good ones' " (117). This,
Billy, despite time-travel, cannot do. Connected to Ilium—the Latin
name of ancient Troy—on a planet always " 'engaged in senseless
slaughter' " (116), he has lived through Dresden, Hiroshima, Vietnam, genocide, and assassination. Such historical catastrophes mirror
the many private tragedies Billy experienced, as, for example, the
violent death of father, wife, friends, acquaintances, strangers, and
even himself. It is significant that the Trout book he wished to buy
was about Christ, because, Vonnegut tells us, the epigraph from a
"famous Christmas carol" also applies to Billy:

The cattle are lowing,
The Baby awakes.
But the little Lord Jesus
No crying he makes. (197)

Although Trafalmadore gives Vonnegut's science fiction a fantastic dimension Mailer's nonfiction lacks, *Slaughter-House Five* and *Armies of the Night* both employ the conventions of the traditional novel: first-/third-person voices, syntactic language, linear plots with exposition/action, believable characters, recognizable locations, familiar themes, and so forth. Thus, they observe verisimilitude or the appearance of actuality, which playwright Bertolt Brecht considered Aristotelian, dramatic, and illusionist, but which we know as realism.[18] However, since mimetic art, no less than nonmimetic art, is fictitious, it too mixes fact and fancy, albeit differently. Perhaps a brief comparative analysis of one realistic and one antirealistic text treating the same subject will elucidate these differences.

Like *The Sot-Weed Factor, Letters, Armies of the Night,* and *Slaughter-House Five, The Book of Daniel* (1971), by E. L. Doctorow, and *The Public Burning* (1977), by Robert Coover, are meticulously researched, depending for their knowledge of the Julius and Ethel Rosenberg case on public documents such as *Death House Letters.* If Doctorow is interested in what happened after the execution, Coover is interested in the execution itself. Background and trial receive fuller treatment during the more ambitious, 534-page *Public Burning,* where considerable additional data about Richard Nixon, Dwight Eisenhower, and others surface.

Both novels fictionalize certain facts: for instance, *The Book of Daniel* makes the younger Rosenberg son, Robert, a daughter, Susan, while nonrelated Selig and Sadie Mindish replace Ethel's brother and sister-in-law David and Ruth Greenglass; similarly, Nixon, whom *The Rosenberg File* (1984) mentions just once, not only becomes the protagonist of *The Public Burning,* but discovers numerous parallels between himself and the convicted couple. Whereas these and other changes are fictionally plausible in *The Book of Daniel,* they are often outlandish in the later work. We can accept Susan Lewin's madness and death even though Robert Meeropol remains alive and well, yet, when Mr. Nixon, the vice-president, tries to seduce Mrs. Rosenberg, the Sing Sing inmate, our willing suspension of disbelief vanishes.[19]

Doctorow introduces several actual people, among them Ronald Sukenick, Paul Robeson, and Norman Mailer. Each functions inside the novel as he does or did outside, with Sukenick teaching at Columbia, Robeson singing at Peekskill, and Mailer showing up at Pentagon Weekend. Conversely, the behavior of the actual people presented by Coover, who, unlike most Doctorow counterparts, all bear their own names, is frequently absurd.[20] The realist then tends to put disguised principal figures in more or less authentic situations, where they encounter actual people, but the antirealist reverses this, placing his undisguised, historically verifiable cast in more or less inauthentic situations, where they may encounter fabulous characters. Doctorow's first-person narrator, Daniel Lewin (i.e., Michael Rosenberg/Meeropol) therefore studies with the real Professor Ronald Sukenick, while Coover's first-person narrator, Richard Nixon, serves under the surreal Uncle Sam.

Throughout *The Book of Daniel,* Lewin composes his self-conscious dissertation that will become the novel we are reading. He calls it, "A Life Submitted in Partial Fulfillment of the Requirements for the Doctoral Degree in Social Biology, Gross Entomology, Women's Anatomy, Children's Cacophony, Arch Demonology, Eschatology, and Thermal Pollution."[21] This description, though facetious, suggests how much research the dissertation, like the novel, demanded. Just as author Doctorow focused on biographical facts, narrator Lewin focuses on historical facts. The graduate student's field of specialization is evidently modern Russian and American history, and so allusions to one or the other occur every few pages. During the section called TRUE HISTORY OF THE COLD WAR: A RAGA, he typically cites several sources: Bernard Baruch, George Kennan, Dean Acheson, John Foster Dulles, Henry Stimson, W. A. Williams (THE TRAGEDY OF AMERICAN DIPLOMACY), "Horowitz in THE FREE WORLD COLOSSUS quoting Blackett" (251), Winston Churchill, Eugene Varga, and Senator Vandenberg. "History, that pig, biting into the heart's secrets" (115) might be unreliable, but, nonetheless, it constitutes our chief human record. Consequently, Daniel can identify with his Biblical namesake, the Jewish prophet who interpreted dreams and experienced visions. The Old Testament Book of Daniel provides the initial epigraph and final passage of the Doctorow-Lewin version, which concludes: *"But thou, O Daniel, shut up the words, and seal the book, even to the time of the end"* (319).

In *The Public Burning,* narrator Nixon muses, "What was fact, what intent, what was framework, what was essence? Strange, the impact of History, the grip it had on us, yet it was nothing but words. Accidental accretions for the most part, leaving most of the story out."[22] He speculates further about this on his chapter 10 Pilgrimage to *The New York Times*. Despite their "effort to reconstruct with words and iconography each fleeting day in the hope of discovering some pattern, some coherence, some meaningful dialogue with time" (191), such publications contain "sequences but no causes, contiguities but no connections." "Design ironically revealing randomness. Arbitrariness as a principle, allowing us to laugh at the tragic" (190) defines one advertisement, while the famous *Times* crossword puzzle reflects "the structure of the newspaper and thus history itself" (206). Unlike Russia, whose imposed plot inspired the Rosenbergs to become " 'historical models or precedents' " (407), we remain patternless.

Americans are histrionic, if not historical, so drama constitutes Coover's controlling metaphor. Several chapters bear theatrical titles: A Little Morality Play for Our Generation, A Roman Scandal of Roaring Spectacle, High Noon, Singalong with the Pentagon Patriots, Introducing: The Sam Slick Show! The second INTERMEZZO is A Dramatic Dialogue by Ethel Rosenberg and Dwight Eisenhower; the third, A Last-Act Sing Sing Opera by Julius and Ethel Rosenberg. Finally, chapter 26 includes exchanges between Jack Benny/Dennis Day/Mary Livingston/Rochester, Edgar Bergen/Charlie McCarthy, and Groucho/Chico Marx.

Theater represents the main parallel uniting Nixon and Ethel. She had been an actress *(The Valiant)* and singer (Schola Cantorum) and he—a winner of "oratorical contests, debates, and extemporaneous speaking contests from grade school to law school" (294)—had been an actor *(Bird-in-Hand,* etc.) and writer ("skits and plays"). At one point, the latter says, "It was as though we'd all been given parts to play decades ago and were still acting them out on ever-widening stages. Tragic lover, young author, athlete, host, father, and businessman—I'd played them all and was playing them still" (361). Disguised behind a moustache as Thomas Greenleaf, amorous Nixon approaches imprisoned Ethel, who, looking "a little bit like Claudette Colbert" (433), will exclaim, " 'You could write the plays and I could act in them! I could even sing!' " (443).

Coover's public world is more histrionic, if possible, than his private world. During the trial, "the Rosenbergs and their lawyers were the only ones not rehearsed, and were in effect having to attempt amateur improvisation theater in the midst of a carefully rehearsed professional drama" (121). Then, for the double execution—"the biggest thing to hit Broadway since the invention of the electrical spectacular" (212)—Times Square was rebuilt to resemble the Sing Sing Death House. Meanwhile, the 3-D movie *House of Wax* runs at the Trans-Lux and Arthur Miller's *The Crucible* runs at the Martin Beck, two among many shows that appear during *The Public Burning*.[23] Another, the surrealistic Sam Slick Show which features dozens of entertainers from various fields (e.g., the Radio City Rockettes, Kate Smith, Sister Emma Fowler, Sir Winston Churchill, Fred Astaire and Ginger Rogers, Bob, Bing, and Dottie) transpires before the electrocutions. Irreal scenes from the Revolutionary War mock "the high drama of building a nation and taking over the world" (424). Later, as the Rosenbergs die, Cecil B. De Mille projects his documentary film about their orphaned sons on the Claridge Hotel "to augment the pathos" (511). Bobo Olson's fight with Paddy Young will follow.

Several allusions indicate that the Rosenberg executions are ritualistic. For example, in the PROLOGUE, Coover calls Times Square "an American holy place long associated with festivals of rebirth" (4), and in chapter 8, he regards "this place of feasts, spectacle, and magic . . . the ritual center of the Western World" (166). Julius and Ethel expire during a section titled "Freedom's Holy Light," where Ethel achieves apotheosis before "all the gleaming great of the nation—" (517). They include President Eisenhower, Vice-President Nixon, Attorney General Brownell, G-man Hoover, Senator McCarthy, Judge Kaufman, and Prosecutor Saypol.

These ritual slayings result from the tendency in *The Public Burning* to dramatize life through abstractions. When the conflict between democracy and communism becomes an allegorical battle involving Uncle Sam and the Phantom, historical ambiguity becomes mythical certainty. Thus, Nixon, the empathetic lawyer who sees through the case against the Rosenbergs, surrenders to Nixon, the ambitious politician who will succeed Eisenhower as Uncle Sam's Incarnation. Following the pattern that makes *Time* magazine "Mother Luce" (our "National Poet Laureate") and Betty Crocker "Holy Mother" (our

"Mistress of Ceremonies"), both enjoy abstract epithets, Eisenhower embodying "The Man of Destiny" and Nixon, "The Fighting Quaker." Their progenitor, replete with corn cob pipe and plug hat, is also Sam Slick, "the foxy, soft-spoken Yankee peddler and the forth-right, tall-talking, ring-tailed roarer from old Kaintuck,"[24] introduced by American humorist Thomas Chandler Haliburton in 1836.

While drama, ritual, and myth comprise the very fabric of *The Public Burning*, they dominate only one scene during *The Book of Daniel*, DISNEYLAND AT CHRISTMAS, which emerges as an isolated phenomenon presented logically through conventional prose. The womblike park contains "five major amusement areas": Frontierland, Tomorrowland, Fantasyland, Adventureland, and Main Street USA (301–302). Here, where customers may "participate in mythic rituals of the culture," rides are "impressively real—that is to say, technologically perfect and historically accurate," yet "the simulated plant and animal and geological surroundings are unreal" (302). Here, too, literature and history undergo "cartoon adaptation," making *Alice in Wonderland* "a sentimental compression" and piracy "a moving diorama" (304). This "symbolic manipulation" or "abbreviated shorthand culture for the masses" has right-wing political implications (305), according to narrator Lewin.

His technique of calling himself both "I" and "he" seems gimmicky, as do his scattered reflexive and unpunctuated paragraphs. Conversely, Coover balances the subjective view (Nixon) and the objective view (author) by juxtaposing first-person and omniscient chapters. Therefore, satire characterizes *The Public Burning*, but *The Book of Daniel*, though bitter, reads like a plaint. Even bitterer, Coover's text is also funny. For instance, he invokes the excremental vision associated with antirealism. During "Iron Butt Gets Smeared Again," Nixon steps in some horseturds that dirty him all over. And, during chapter 26, where the vice-president appears revealing " 'I AM A SCAMP' lipsticked on his butt" (469), the six anti-Rosenberg Supreme Court Justices wallow about "up to their thighs and elbows" in Republican elephant dung.

The settings of these two novels are actual places: for *The Book of Daniel*, New York City, Worcester, Washington, D.C., and Los Angeles; for *The Public Burning*, New York City, Washington, D.C., and Ossining. Yet the first group *remains* verisimilar, while the second grows bizarre. Figurative Times Square Disneyland for Coover is very different from literal Anaheim Disneyland for Doctorow:

[H]e and his Disney Imagineers have reserved a number of key corner locations for their own Mouse Factory specials: a rocking model of Steamboat Willie's tub, the Dwarfs' cottage, the belly of the whale, and an adults-only show of the girl centaurs from *Fantasia* with their nippleless breasts and oddly disquieting horse-rumps. . . . He has also built a scale model of Sing Sing prison, using all the little braying schoolboy truants from *Pinocchio* for the prisoners and an imaginative simulation, using life-size models with moving eyeballs, of Harry Gold's complicated fantasy love life. (281–82)

This is the other 3-D world into which a disoriented *House of Wax* viewer "gets swept along . . . like Vincent Price lurching about out of his wheelchair" (283–84). Through grotesque dreams and fantasies, such nightmarish public scenes are augmented at the private level by Coover's protagonist.

The Book of Daniel and *The Public Burning* have chronological organizations, however much they intersperse the past, with the former focused on 1967 occasions—MEMORIAL DAY (book 1); HALLOWEEN (book 2); STARFISH (book 3); CHRISTMAS (book 4)—and the latter on execution day, 19 June 1953—WEDNESDAY-THURSDAY (part 1); FRIDAY MORNING (part 2); FRIDAY AFTERNOON (part 3); FRIDAY NIGHT (part 4). As the single-day focus makes *The Public Burning* more dramatic than *The Book of Daniel*, so too PROLOGUE/EPILOGUE and three INTERMEZZO sections separating the four parts give it greater structural complexity. That complexity is reflected in the mixed genres Coover employs. Besides the theatrical forms previously mentioned, and many long lists, he includes material from letters, magazines, newspapers, poems, songs, speeches, transcripts, and so forth. Concomitantly, *The Public Burning* celebrates language, which becomes most vivid when Uncle Sam/Slick harangues:

"I am Sam Slick the Yankee Peddler—I can ride on a flash of lightnin', catch a thunderbolt in my fist, swaller niggers whole, raw or cooked, slip without a scratch down a honey locust, whup my weight in wildcats and redcoats, squeeze blood out of a turnip and cold cash out of a parson, and out-inscrutabullize the heathen Chinee—so whar's that Johnny Bull to stomp his hoof or quiver his hindquarters at *my* Proklymation?" (7)

During *The Book of Daniel*, Susan's attempted suicide, confinement, and death parallel the composition of her brother's thesis. And,

during *The Public Burning,* the Rosenbergs' last Supreme Court defeat, Times Square preparations and execution parallel Nixon's fre-
netic peregrinations, national disgrace, and rape. These double plots
are intertwined in both narratives, but whereas Doctorow ends plau-
sibly, with Daniel hiring prayer makers at the cemetery, then com-
pleting his tale, Coover remains fantastic. After Nixon returns home
from New York disheveled and dejected, Uncle Sam declares, " '*I
want* YOU!' " (530) and sodomizes him. The vice-president's consequent apotheosis—" '*I . . . I love you, Uncle Sam!*' " (534)—negatively
mirrors Ethel's earlier transcendence.

Six years before *The Public Burning* appeared, Philip Roth, whose
Our Gang (1971) would also feature Richard Nixon as narrator-protagonist, observed:

[T]he American writer in the middle of the 20th century has his hands full
in trying to understand, and then describe, and then make *credible* much of
the American reality. It stupifies, it sickens, it infuriates, and finally it is even
a kind of embarrassment to one's own meager imagination. The actuality is
continually outdoing our talents and the culture tosses up figures almost
daily that are the envy of any novelist. Who, for example, could have invented Charles Van Doren? Roy Cohn and David Schine? Sherman Adams
and Bernard Goldfine? Dwight David Eisenhower?[25]

The answer: Robert Coover and other subsequent antirealistic satirists.

Henry Burlingame told Ebenezer Cooke, " 'History, in short, is like
those waterholes I have heard of in the wilds of Africa: the most
various beasts may drink there side by side with equal nourish-
ment.' "[26] Our beasts present three separate categories: fictitious history *(The Sot-Weed Factor/Letters),* nonfiction novel *(Armies of the Night),*
and science fiction novel *(Slaughter-House Five);* and two separate
approaches, "realistic" *(The Book of Daniel)* versus antirealistic *(The
Public Burning).* To different degrees, their waterhole cannot be trusted
though objectively documented, since accurate history is inconceivable. Unique Barth, Mailer, Vonnegut, Doctorow, and Coover, who
represent various animals, drink individually, some becoming more
inebriated than others, but all proving that fact and fancy remain
inextricable and that such an intoxicant, which affects only imaginative creatures, separates imbibers called novelists from imbibers called

historians. These waterholes are dangerous as well as euphoric because they contain impurities—intrigue, deception, randomness—capable of making even authorial gods ill. The conspiracy or plots and counterplots responsible for this paranoia should convince us we have not left the wilds of Africa.

CHAPTER 9

Conspiracy and Paranoia

In *The Paranoid Style in American Politics and Other Essays*, Richard Hofstadter observes:

> The distinguishing thing about the paranoid style is not that its exponents see conspiracies or plots here and there in history, but that they regard a "vast" or "gigantic" conspiracy as *the motive force* in historical events. History *is* a conspiracy, set in motion by demonic forces of almost transcendent power. ... The paranoid spokesman sees the fate of this conspiracy in apocalyptic terms—he traffics in the birth and death of whole worlds, whole political orders, whole systems of human values.[1]

Several postwar antirealistic American novelists may be included among the exponents of Hofstadter's paranoid style: John Barth *(The Sot-Weed Factor, Giles Goat-Boy, Letters, Sabbatical)*, Coleman Dowell *(Mrs. October Was Here)*, Robert Coover *(The Public Burning)*, Stanley Elkin *(A Bad Man)*, Ralph Ellison *(Invisible Man)*, William Gaddis *(Carpenter's Gothic)*, John Hawkes *(The Lime Twig)*, Joseph McElroy *(Lookout Cartridge)*, Vladimir Nabokov *(Pale Fire)*, Gilbert Sorrentino *(Mulligan Stew)*, Robert Stone *(A Hall of Mirrors, Dog Soldiers, A Flag for Sunrise)*, and Kurt Vonnegut *(Cat's Cradle)*. To some, conspiracy is indeed "the *motive force* in historical events," while others "see ... plots here and there in history." Many invoke "demonic forces," "transcendent power," and "apocalyptic terms"; and all treat one or more public institutions representing crime, education, government, industry, law, medicine, the military, politics, psychology, race, religion, sex, and technology as conspiratorial.

Currently, our most complex literary paranoid spokesmen are William Burroughs and Thomas Pynchon, but before considering *Naked Lunch* and *The Crying of Lot 49*, we should glance at two less difficult texts by way of introduction: *Catch-22* (1955) and *One Flew Over the Cuckoo's Nest* (1962).

According to Raymond M. Olderman, these and other 1960s novels express "the fear that the power which rules us is really some inexplicable, abstract Conspiracy."[2] This conspiracy, originating in the evil nature of man in *Catch-22*, as chapter 39 "The Eternal City" (Rome/hell), makes clear, and in modern mechanization in *One Flew Over the Cuckoo's Nest*, as the designation "Combine" (combination/machine), suggests, assumes concrete institutional guises.

The military represents the immediate conspiratorial system of the Heller story. Its hierarchical structure becomes evident through the chapter headings that often affix rank to name and thus signal a rigid, officer-dominated, pecking order: "General Dreedle," "Colonel Cathcart," "Major Major Major Major," "Captain Black," "Lieutenant Scheisskopf," and "Corporal Whitcomb." Advancement within the hierarchy seems irrational; for example, Scheisskopf ("Shithead"), who progresses from lieutenant (chapter 8) to general (chapter 37), is an ROTC graduate obsessed by parades. The recurrent term for illogical logic, "catch-22," defines this absurd world, where victimizers like Black and Whitcomb plot against victims like Nately and the chaplain. Thus, Yossarian, the protagonist, asserts, " 'The enemy . . . is anybody who's going to get you killed, no matter which side he's on.' "[3]

As if echoing Dwight Eisenhower's warning about the military-industrial complex, Heller juxtaposes to the airforce system an international cartel that deals in foodstuffs. Mess officer Milo Minderbinder, director of this syndicate, wears business clothes. Professedly moral, but observably corrupt, he fights on the American *and* German sides under a "cost-plus-six agreement," claiming "an important victory for private enterprise . . . since the armies of both countries were socialized institutions" (250). The notes he leaves after other subversive acts echo the General Motors slogan: "What's good for M & M Enterprises is good for the country" (301, 426). Implicated in Milo's illegal transactions, Colonel Cathcart promises to assign his combat missions to somebody else.

Chief Broom calls the "inexplicable, abstract Conspiracy" behind *One Flew Over the Cuckoo's Nest* the "Combine." Dedicated to conformity, it is manifested principally through the mental hospital, a recurrent postwar antirealistic setting. This familiar microcosm, like Heller's airforce, has a hierarchical organization: doctors, nurses, attendants, and patients. The last, who include Acutes and Chronics

(Walkers, Wheelers, and Vegetables), follow a rigid daily routine imposed by Big Nurse. As in *Catch-22*, however, madness lay beneath her rational world of white and bright surfaces, so that here, too, the sane are actually insane and vice versa.

Big Nurse, or Miss Ratched (ratchet), whose appearance is synthetic ("enamel-and-plastic face")[4] and maternal ("nippled circles . . . swelled out and out," [305]), embodies both the Therapeutic Community and "the juggernaut of modern matriarchy" (68). The second, no less than the first, serves the Combine's purpose to keep men boys. Though an unmarried virgin, its principal "ball-cutter" precipitates the suicide of Billy Bibbit by playing his mother—an old friend and hospital colleague—after he sleeps with a girl. *One Flew Over the Cuckoo's Nest* and *Catch-22*, following an American literary tendency analyzed by Leslie Fiedler in *Love and Death in the American Novel* and reflected by Mark Twain in *Adventures of Huckleberry Finn*, where Huck flees disciplinary Miss Watson, contain much misogynistic matter. During *Catch-22*, Mrs. Daneeka's grief over the supposed demise of her spouse vanishes as the insurance money multiplies, and during *One Flew Over the Cuckoo's Nest*, Mrs. Harding seems to be a promiscuous castrator. These books celebrate the whore, since whores, unlike mothers and wives, make men feel potent. Having inherited the masculine worlds of Cooper, Melville, and Hemingway, Heller and Kesey anticipate the virulent antifeminism that characterizes postwar American writing. The most positive woman in *Catch-22* is an Italian servant, and in *One Flew Over the Cuckoo's Nest*, a Japanese nurse.

Behind the military-economic establishment of *Catch-22* and the psychiatric-matriarchal system of *One Flew Over the Cuckoo's Nest* lies the government. This institution, which encompasses both airforce and hospital, emerges elsewhere too. Throughout *Catch-22*, it behaves absurdly. We are told, for instance, how Major Major's father fares as a farmer: "The government paid him well for every bushel of alfalfa he did not grow. The more alfalfa he did not grow, the more money the government gave him, and he spent every penny he didn't earn on new land to increase the amount of alfalfa he did not produce" (82). Governmental machinations are more pervasive and more ominous during *One Flew Over the Cuckoo's Nest* because they reveal the dominant pastoral motif. Thus, the narrator includes much information regarding efforts to buy off his tribe's treaty and to replace their village with a hydroelectric dam. Papa, "a full-blood Columbia Indian—a chief" (11), whose name was Tee Ah Millatoona (The-Pine-That-Stand-Tallest-on-the Mountain), finally capitulated to the Combine: " 'It worked on him for years. He was big enough to fight it for a while. It wanted us to live in inspected houses. It wanted to take the falls. It was even in the tribe, and they worked on him. . . . Oh, the Combine's big—big. He fought it a long time till my mother made him too little to fight any more and he gave up' " (208).

Disparagingly called Broom, as counterpart third-person protagonist Yossarian becomes Yo-Yo, Kesey's narrator, like unmanned Papa, has taken the surname of his white mother (Bromden), thereby preparing us for the dimunition in size Big Nurse imposes on him. The fact that he is a half-breed and Yossarian, an Assyrian (Armenian?) connects them with other alien outsiders—Ishmael, Huck Finn, Jay Gatsby, and Joe Christmas—who learn both positive and negative lessons from renegade insiders—Ahab, Tom Sawyer, Dan Cody, and Joanna Burden.

One renegade insider, Yossarian's roommate Orr, whose name implies "alternative," acts deranged, but demonstrates know-how when installing "running water, wood-burning fireplace, cement floor" (17). Fake madness and real ingenuity—attributes of a survivor—enable him to escape to Sweden. Already among the few aware people Heller introduces, Yossarian becomes the perfect disciple. He, too, fears death, though obsessively: "Man was matter, that was Snowden's secret. Drop him out a window and he'll fall. Set fire to him and he'll burn. Bury him and he'll rot, like other kinds of garbage. The spirit gone, man is garbage. That was Snowden's secret. Ripeness was all" (429–30). This obsession derives from the life-force, manifested in the protagonist by frequent avowals of love for women and profound bitterness over man's inhumanity to man, particularly during "The Eternal City" sequence. As Eros, Yossarian opposes Thanatos, the mindless power propelling Olderman's "inexplicable, abstract conspiracy."

Both alien outsider and renegade insider are more fully developed in *One Flew Over the Cuckoo's Nest* than in *Catch-22*, yet Chief Broom —the "Vanishing American"—and R. P. McMurphy—the tall-tale braggart—remain archetypal. Like many autochthonous heroes, Mack is subversive: " 'Thirty-five years old. Never married. Distinguished

Service Cross in Korea, for leading an escape from a Communist prison camp. A dishonorable discharge, afterward, for insubordination. Followed by a history of street brawls and barroom fights and a series of arrests for Drunkenness, Assault and Battery, Disturbing the Peace, *repeated* gambling, and one arrest—for Rape' " (42). This official data, plus other information about McMurphy—that he has been a logger and a con man, that he spins yarns and sings songs, that his grin is devilish and his hair red, that he wears gaudy shorts and bears flashy tattoos—makes him the natural enemy of Big Nurse. Whereas *Catch-22* lacks conflict, with Orr merely confirming what fellow survivor Yossarian already knows, the clash between rebellious McMurphy and virginal Ratched for the Chief's soul, becomes quite dramatic. It ends when the alien outsider escapes and the renegade insider perishes. Since Big Nurse and Colonel Cathcart retain their control, the life-force, whether represented by love (Yossarian) or lust (McMurphy), can win only temporary, personal victories over conspiratorial death.

Heller keeps inanimateness and inertness before us through a ubiquitous "stuffed and sterilized mummy" (167) called the soldier in white. But while aircraft contribute to such dehumanization during *Catch-22*, they function more as engines of destruction than as agents of mechanization. Contrariwise, machinery during *One Flew Over the Cuckoo's Nest* becomes the Combine's principal instrument for reducing people to automata: "[T]he inside of the asylum is like the guts of a computer, all elements wired and connected. . . . Ratched is programmer, the inmates the programmed, the entire system the computer."[5] Chief Broom, an ex-electrician and electronics student, notes that Big Nurse runs her "precision-made machine" with "mechanical insect skill" (27). Surrounded by contraptions proliferating like surrealistic objects, he conjures up technological analogies (ward = factory) and struggles against "the fog machine." His narrative records many actual devices, the most ominous of which administers shock therapy. When this crucifixion fails to render the new Christlike McMurphy impuissant, Big Nurse orders him lobotomized.

Dangerous throughout post–Civil War American literature, machines have sometimes actually desexed men and women, as in *The Sun Also Rises,* where a plane destroys Jake's penis, and in *The Great Gatsby,* where a car destroys Myrtle's breast. To restore the vitality sapped by urbanized, industrialized culture, the American hero has often lighted out for the territory. Mack is no exception, since before his death he takes twelve inmate disciples on a regenerative fishing trip. At sea, these broken men come alive, catching fish, drinking beer, and enjoying wantonness. All return changed: "[T]hese weren't the same bunch of weak-knees from a nuthouse that they'd watched take their insults on the dock this morning" (242).

Of the two alien outsiders and two renegade insiders, only Mc-Murphy refuses to hide behind Hamletesque feigned madness, even though " 'the court ruled that I'm a psychopath' " (13). His disciple, Chief Broom, whose narration manifests periodic dementia, has enough caginess to play deaf and dumb. Giggly Orr ("crackpot," "freak," and "moron") also deceives the authorities. " 'He knew what he was doing every step of the way!' " (439) exclaims Yossarian, remembering how the goofy fellow would stuff both cheeks with crab apples and horse chestnuts. If paranoia may be defined as "chronic psychosis characterized by delusions of persecution," Heller's protagonist is certainly paranoid too, since "somebody was always hatching a plot to kill him" (19). Associates consider Yo-Yo crazy throughout *Catch-22*, and so he behaves, receiving the Distinguished Flying Cross while nude after the foolish heroism at Ferrara had cost several lives, and, after the horrendous experiences at Avignon, watching the burial of Snowden from a tree. Yossarian, Orr, Chief Broom, and McMurphy are all more or less unstable, but whereas the first three survive because they use their illness for self-preservation, the last, who insists upon his sanity and integrity, succumbs. Thus, postwar antirealists like Heller and Kesey echo Emily Dickinson when she wrote, "Much madness is divinest sense / To a discerning eye; / Much sense the starkest madness."

According to William Seward Burroughs, the paranoid is "a man in possession of all the facts."[6] These would presumably include the dangers posed by New York City, for the wary author named his apartment on the Bowery "the Bunker." Victor Bockris has described this abandoned YMCA locker room. Gymnasium above and furniture shop below, Burroughs's walkup was windowless. Access could be gained only by telephone through a locked front gate. He told

Bockris, " 'I have four doors between me and the outside and I have people down there in the daytime. It's pretty impregnable.' "[7] Burroughs hoarded an "arsenal of blackjacks, Japanese throwing stars and knives" (229) inside. When leaving, he carried tear gas and cane, both of which—plus blackjack—he supplied Bockris, who quotes him on a recently acquired property near Tallahassee: " 'My house in Florida presents itself as a shimmering mirage. . . . The front forms a wall with a heavy iron door and two barred windows. . . . From the two back corners of the house runs a wall eight feet to form a courtyard with an iron door at the far end. . . . And I have an indoor shooting range for my guests" (231–32, 34). When Burroughs adds that he killed a huge catfish with a .22 Magnum, we may recall that the Mexican police released him after he had slain his second wife, Joan Vollmer, during their drunken reenactment of "William Tell."

There is no reason to suppose inaccessible Thomas Pynchon behaves like accessible William Burroughs. Of the former, Thomas LeClair says: "Thomas Pynchon, age forty-four, has not been photographed since high school, has never been interviewed, cannot be located by his parents or agent, and had the comedian 'Professor' Irwin Corey accept his National Book Award for *Gravity's Rainbow* in 1973."[8] LeClair attributes the invisibility of Pynchon and other contemporary reclusive writers to artistic integrity, denying paranoia as motivation. Applied to a novelist more obsessed by this psychosis than any previous American writer, that disclaimer seems inadequate.

Paranoia explains why Burroughs and Pynchon, though poles apart artistically, share the Heller/Kesey fear of systems. Like the latter, "they regard a 'vast' or 'gigantic' conspiracy as *the motive force* in historical events." The "demonic forces" with "transcendent power" pushing our world toward apocalyptic annihilation represent Thanatos. Various institutions, including Heller's military-economic establishment and Kesey's psychiatric-matriarchal system, further the might of "some inexplicable, abstract Conspiracy." Still, there are differences between anarchical Burroughs and puritanical Pynchon. Burroughs, focuses on addiction, pits "host" against "parasite"; for Pynchon, the "preterite" embodies "us," and the "elect" embodies "them." The first attacks matriarchy more savagely than Kesey, while the second, following Heller, advocates love, yet degrades women too.

Finally, Pynchon employs a conventional style and Burroughs, the cut-up method and other techniques to subvert the word virus.

If the novels of Thomas Wolfe and Henry Miller may be considered single books, so may the works of William Burroughs, whose *Naked Lunch* (1959), *The Ticket That Exploded* (1962), *Nova Express* (1964), and *The Soft Machine* (1961, 1966)—replete with ubiquitous characters like William Lee, Mr. Bradly Mr. Martin, and Dr. Benway —constitute his early tetralogy. *Naked Lunch,* the most impressive of these, treats the relationship between victim and victimizer that runs all through conspiratorial fiction. Testifying at its obscenity trial in Boston, Allen Ginsberg cited Burroughs's phrase, "The Algebra of Need," to explain how diverse addictions were modeled on junk or heroin. Victimizers became victims themselves when they lusted after control over individuals trapped by drugs, homosexuality, money, and so forth.

Naked Lunch is a framework narrative, the fantastic past of the novel's action sandwiched between the realistic present, an introduction subtitled DEPOSITION: TESTIMONY CONCERNING A SICKNESS, and an appendix from *The British Journal of Addiction.* Both were written by Burroughs, whose personae narrate the framed story. Though problematic because of pronominal shifts, everything but the last section of the framed story would appear to be projected through William Lee, a surname derived, perhaps, from the author's paternal grandmother, Laura Lee Burroughs. The last section, or ATROPHIED PREFACE,—as ironically positioned as the Appendix in *The Sound and the Fury*—records the voice, "I, William Seward." Thus, the present, nonaddicted writer, Burroughs/Seward, presides over the nightmare of his past addicted self, Lee The Agent.

During the ATROPHIED PREFACE, he tells us, "I do not presume to impose 'story' 'plot' 'continuity.'" However, *Naked Lunch* does contain a discernible, if shadowy, action. Like other surrealistic texts, the framed story substitutes spatial for temporal organization. It begins in New York City, then proceeds like *On the Road* across the United States to Mexico. There, actual locations become imaginary, and we find ourselves touring Freeland and Interzone (compare *Gravity's Rainbow*). Coming full circle, the book returns to New York. Meanwhile, Lee, who steps forward only intermittently throughout the middle sections, experiences a therapeutic odyssey. He has been engaged by Islam Inc. to secure the services of Dr. Benway, director at the Reconditioning Center. This mission commences with him fleeing a "narcotics dick," continues with him performing or observing various destructive rituals, and ends with him killing two City Narcotics Squad members and taking "the junk cure." Consequently, the curve of the action, which reflects Burroughs's own rehabilitation, seems positive.

Yet *Naked Lunch* is anything but sanguine, as several remarks made during the ATROPHIED PREFACE indicate. Soon after we are told about the junk cure, we learn, "And Lee back to sex and pain and time and Yage."[9] There follows a kaleidoscopic account of nefarious events past and present, private and public, real and unreal, rendered via Seward, the "recording instrument" possessing a "word horde" that spills "off the page in all directions" (229). On the lonely American continent, where politicians support capital punishment, "[t]he black wind sock of death undulates over the land, feeling, smelling for the crime of separate life" (223–24). Thanatos rules the whole world, since "[t]he Planet drifts to random insect doom. . . . / Thermodynamics has won at a crawl. . . . Orgone balked at the post. . . . Christ bled. . . . Time ran out. . . ." (224). Furthermore, the subsequent reference to the Mayan Codices, a conspiracy treated at length by *The Soft Machine,* suggests that this death wish is timeless as well as placeless. Opposing it, stands the author, with the "principle occupation" of "patrolling" (221). His "How-To-Book," his "Revelation and Prophecy," offers urgent advice: "Gentle reader, we see God through our assholes in the flash bulb of orgasm. . . . Through these orifices transmute your body. . . . The way OUT is the way IN." (229).

" 'Death was their Culture Hero,' " William Seward's "Old Lady" (233) says about the Mayans, though her statement applies equally well to other manifestations of the demonic plot against human life. In *Naked Lunch,* such manifestations include medicine, big business, and politics.

Ominous physicians pervade the novel. We meet, for example, Doc Browbeck, " 'retired abortionist and junk pusher' " (29); Doctor "Fingers Schafer," "the Lobotomy Kid" (103); Doc Scranton, " 'a good old boy' " (126); and the host of "Dr. Berger's Mental Health Hour" (136). Most sinister, self-styled " '*pure* scientist' " Dr. Benway becomes the arch-villain in *Naked Lunch.* He practices sadistic quackery assisted by Violet, the baboon and " 'only woman I ever cared a damn about' " (30). Benway once "performed an appendectomy with a rusty sardine can' " and " 'removed a uterine tumor with [his] teeth' " (60). Addicted to narcotics and pederasty, he was " 'drummed out of the industry' " for drinking a patient's ether (31). William Lee has not seen Benway "since his precipitate departure from Annexia, where his assignment had been T.D.—Total Demoralization." Now, as director of the Freeland Reconditioning Center, he coordinates "symbol systems" and supervises "interrogation, brainwashing and control" (21), using drugs, hypnosis, and sexual humiliation to achieve " 'automatic obedience.' " He claims that Latahs (compulsive imitators) " 'have no feelings. . . . [j]ust reflexes' " (140), which describes him too, for the doctor displays "cold and intense, predatory and impersonal eyes" (189) and a "flat and lifeless" voice (191). Appropriately, his first love is cancer.

When an electronic brain goes berserk and releases the subjects from the Reconditioning Center, Benway accepts the Islam offer carried by Lee. The objectives of this Arab conspiracy remain obscure, so we must base our assumptions on the activities of its representatives. Besides A. J., "the notorious Merchant of Sex" (144) adept at cover stories, and Salvador Hassan O'Leary, "the After Birth Tycoon" adept at aliases, they include "Clem and Jody, the Ergot Brothers, who decimated the Republic of Hassan with poison wheat, Autopsy Ahmed, and Hepatitis Hal, the fruit and vegetable broker" (145). A. J. "is an agent . . . but for whom or for what no one has ever been able to discover" (146), while Clem and Jody masquerade "as Russian agents whose sole function is to represent the U. S. in an unpopular light" (158). We learn that "A. J. is agitating for the destruction of Israel" and that "Clem and Jody . . . are interested in the destruction of Near East oil fields to boost the value of their Venezuelan holdings" (160). Ancestor of Milo Minderbinder, the even more treacherous Salvador Hassan O'Leary operates internationally through "an inexplicable, shifting web of subsidiaries, front companies" (156). His dealings, like those of other Islam schemers, are illegal: "He opened a sex shop in Yokohama, pushed junk in Beirut, pimped in Panama. . . . He prospered and proliferated, flooding the world with cut medicines and cheap counterfeit goods of every variety" (157–58).

Just as the military conspired with the economic *(Catch-22)* and the psychiatric with the matriarchal *(One Flew Over the Cuckoo's Nest),* and all four institutions were related to government, during *Naked Lunch* medicine, big business, and politics comprise a vague cabal. Therefore, Dr. Benway accepts the Islam offer and Salvador Hassan O'Leary dances "the Liquefactionist Jig." The Liquefactionists, sadomasochistic perverts who support a program involving "the eventual merging of everyone into One Man by a process of protoplasmic absorption" (146), number among Interzone's three conspiratorial political parties, its rivals being the Senders and the Divisionists. "These top Senders are the most dangerous and evil men in the world." Ultimately, they will substitute telepathic control for biocontrol and then a single Sender might rule the earth (162–64). More moderate, homosexual Divisionists "grow exact replicas of themselves in embryo jelly"; unless this practice stops, "there will be only one replica of one sex on the planet" (164).

"Anti-Liquefactionist, Anti-Divisionist, and above all Anti-Sender" define the Factualists, the single constructive Interzone party. It opposes replication—"an attempt to circumvent process and change"—and telepathy when "such knowledge" is used "to control, coerce, debase, exploit or annihilate . . . individuality" (167). *"Sending,"* we discover, *"can never be a means to anything but more sending, Like Junk,"* and The Sender embodies The Human Virus, whose symptoms consist of "Poverty, hatred, war, police-criminals, bureaucracy, insanity" (168–69). Fortunately, asserts Factualist William Lee, *"The Human Virus can now be isolated and treated"* (169).

That will be his task throughout the tetralogy. As Inspector J. Lee, Nova Police, he must face Mr. Bradly Mr. Martin (alias The Ugly Spirit and Mr. & Mrs. D), the Nova Mob leader who had appeared briefly during *Naked Lunch.* Their conflict assumes mythological proportions, according to Burroughs: " 'The world is not my home, you understand. I am primarily concerned with the question of survival—with Nova conspiracies, Nova criminals, and Nova police. A new mythology is possible in the Space Age, where we will again have heroes and villains, as regards intentions toward this planet. I feel that the future of writing is in space, not time—' "[10] The Nova Conspiracy, which interpenetrates *The Ticket That Exploded, Nova Express,* and *The Soft Machine,* seems less nebulous than the interrelated institutions of *Naked Lunch*. Its adherents are equally colorful: Sammy The Butcher, Green Tony, Iron Claws, The Brown Artist, Jack Blue Note, Limestone John, Izzy the Push, Hamburger Mary, Paddy the Sting, The Subliminal Kid, and The Blue Dinosaur. These criminals have brought vices and diseases from other planets, but their blockade, involving word and image, has been broken. They wish to achieve nova or disintegration here by creating and aggravating conflicts through alien life forms. Since Burroughs views the body physical and the body politic analogously, the antipodal Nova Police resemble apomorphine, the substance that cured him of junk addiction and now attacks parasite invasion. Once again, the author, identifying reflexively with the narrator, becomes his own hero:

"The purpose of my writing is to expose and arrest Nova Criminals. In *Naked Lunch, Soft Machine* and *Nova Express* I show who they are and what they are doing and what they will do if they are not arrested. Minutes to go. Souls rotten from their orgasm drugs, flesh shuddering from their nova ovens, prisoners of the earth to *come out*. With your help we can occupy the Reality Studio and retake their universe of Fear death and Monopoly—
(Signed) INSPECTOR J. LEE, NOVA POLICE"[11]

During *Catch-22* and *One Flew Over the Cuckoo's Nest*, psychosis is necessary for self-preservation. Unbalanced Orr, Yossarian, Broom, and McMurphy fit the Burroughs definition of the paranoid because they possess "all the facts." Said facts disclose a demonic, death-driven conspiracy, vast and gigantic, whose institutional agencies devise intrigues against humanity. As Burroughs lived among weapons at the Bunker, so too must Heller/Kesey characters protect themselves: Orr by goofiness, Yossarian by nudity, Broom by deaf-mutism. Thus, private craziness, which consists of taking the public menace personally, may be manipulated to ensure survival.

Reclusive Thomas Pynchon investigates conspiracy, paranoia, and the relationship between the two more deeply than any other native novelist. As we already know, Stencil, the protagonist of *V.*, posits some inexplicable, abstract Conspiracy. Stencil's master cabal, the Plot Which Has No Name, reappears ten years later in *Gravity's Rainbow* (1973). References are made there to "the Firm," "the Bulkharin conspiracy," "the Father-conspiracy," the "teletype plot," the "Masonic plot," the " 'chemical cartel,' " the "*Rocket-cartel*," "the international light-bulb cartel," "the Meat Cartel," and others. Pervasive also are the juxtaposed allusions to paranoia like "Proverbs for Paranoids" and "Paranoid Systems of History." Among these allusions, we encounter three definitions suggesting how complex this subject is for Pynchon. Paranoia signifies "the onset, the leading edge, of the discovery that *everything is connected.*"[12] It has a positive and a negative pole: "creative paranoia"[13] and "anti-paranoia." The first " 'means developing at least as thorough a We-system as a They-system' " (638), while the second means "nothing is connected to anything, a condition not many of us can bear for long" (434).

An article entitled "Pynchon's Paranoid History," which concentrates on *Gravity's Rainbow,* methodically elucidates such matters. Scott Sanders, the author, says:

A mind that preserves Puritan expectations after the Puritan God has been discredited will naturally seek another hypothesis that explains life as the product of remote control, that situates the individual within a plot whose furthest reaches he cannot fathom, that renders the creation legible once again. Paranoia offers the ideally suited hypothesis that the world is organized into a conspiracy, governed by shadowy figures whose powers approach omniscience and omnipotence, and whose manipulations of history may be detected in every chance gesture of their servants. It substitutes for the divine plan a demonic one.[14]

Now identified with William Pynchon, treasurer of the Massachusetts Bay Colony, the Pyncheon family in *The House of the Seven Gables,* and additional New England Puritans, contemporary Thomas may well have the mentality Sanders describes. The latter shows this through several Puritan-Pynchon analogues: faith = paranoia; God's plan = cosmic conspiracy; God's will = Gravity; election = membership in the Firm; preterition = exclusion from conspiracy; typology = multiple narrative patterns; grace = remote control; theism/atheism = binary vision; depravity of man = decadence of history; personal salvation = paranoid self-reference; Last Judgement = the Zero (188). Pynchon tells us during *Gravity's Rainbow* that Tyrone Slothrop, whose ancestry matches his own, possesses the "Puritan reflex of seeking other orders behind the visible, also known as paranoia" (188). But though the hero reveals a conspiratorial imagination, he has actually been the victim of schemes involving scientist Laszlo Jamf, Pavlovian Edward Pointsman, and various operators. Slothrop is not alone, since Pirate Prentice, Roger Mexico, Greta Erdmann, Franz Pökler, and Messrs. Silvernail, Tchitcherine, Enzian, and Pointsman himself are paranoiac with some justification. Sanders traces "the recurrent imagery of external manipulation" (182) and discusses "a global industrial cartel" as the conspiracy "behind the Rocket's evolution" (183). Yet even the Firm remains subject to technology, technology to matter, and matter to thermodynamics, so "[t]he planetary mission, the incalculable plot . . . is a movement toward death," in which "Gravity becomes the paranoid God" (184–85). This "entropic tide" cannot be verified, and therefore the author's binary worldview poses paranoia (connectedness) against antiparanoia (disconnectedness). Because order, however sinister, seems preferable to disorder, Pynchon protagonists are less terrified by conspiracy than chaos. The Puritan dichotomy of elect (saved) and preterite (passed over) functions anew throughout Gravity's Rainbow, where those who drop from plots lose their identity. Finally, Sanders claims that "Metaphor—the projection of analogies and correspondences—is the key feature of Pynchon's style," for the artist, like the paranoid, "must project meanings out of sheer terror of meaninglessness" (187).

Published between V. and Gravity's Rainbow, The Crying of Lot 49 (1966) represents his most condensed comment on the binary worldview. It transpires during an unspecified summer and employs spatial organization. Reminiscent of Naked Lunch, the book travels from town to town, real and fanciful—Kinneret-Among-the-Pines (chapter 1); San Narciso (chapters 2, 3, 4); the Bay Area/Kinneret (chapter 5); San Narciso (chapter 6)—and from establishment to establishment, some private, but most public, that also recur. This repetitive, circular structure well suits the second long Pynchon search, which will be as inconclusive as V.'s because the heroine never gains "the central truth itself."[15]

Psychologically, twenty-eight-year-old Oedipa quests after love in a world almost devoid of women and adequate males. Her personal Kinneret relationships occupy the first chapter. There we find husband Wendell "Mucho" Maas, ex-lover Pierce Inverarity, psychotherapist Dr. Hilarius, and family lawyer Roseman. The last two are paranoiac, flirtatious Roseman about Perry Mason and Benwayesque Hilarius, who worked "on experimentally induced insanity" (102) at Buchenwald, about Israeli pursuers. Too thin-skinned for a used car salesman, Mucho becomes a disc jockey, able to commit statutory rape, yet unable to communicate with Oedipa. He will grow more and more irrational, eventually taking LSD, recounting NADA (National Automobile Dealers' Association) nightmares, and losing his identity.

Of greater importance, the material concerning Pierce Inverarity frames chapter 1. It begins when Oedipa returns "home from a Tupperware party" to learn that Pierce has died and that she is executrix of the real estate mogul's will. This triggers thoughts about their affair, "ended a year before Mucho married her" (6). It terminates immediately after juxtaposing a fairy tale by the Grimm brothers ("Rapunzel") and a painting by Remedios Varo ("Bordando el Manto Terrestre"). Both depict maidens imprisoned in towers trying to contact the world via tiny windows. Because they symbolize the plight of Oedipa, trapped "from outside and for no reason at all," she had wept over them. Chapter 1 asks, "If the tower is everywhere and the knight of deliverance [i.e., Pierce] no proof against its magic, what else?" (11). The answer could be Tristero, which, she later thinks, might "bring to an end her encapsulation" (28).

Pynchon's lonely protagonist turns to co-executor Metzger during chapter 2. They play Strip Botticelli at the Echo Courts motel while drunkenly watching, amid zany interruptions, a film that the still good-looking attorney starred in as Baby Igor. She experiences orgasm and becomes his companion, but subsequently "my one extramarital fella . . . eloped with a depraved 15-year-old" (114). The mechanical farewell note does not mention their intimacy.

Throughout her peregrinations, Oedipa encounters several other men, whose names, like Dr. Hilarius and Mucho Maas, resurrect the Whole Sick Crew. These largely unattached, self-involved, eccentric males dominate *The Crying of Lot 49* more completely than treacherous women do in *V*. Theirs is a world without love, where childless Oedipa reveals affective deprivation when she comforts an old sailor: "She was overcome all at once by a need to touch him. . . . She felt wetness against her breast and saw that he was crying again. . . . She let go of him for a moment, reluctant as if he were her own child" (93–94). In this wasteland, maternalism, which infantile Metzger (Baby Igor) had mocked, claiming, " 'My mother . . . was really out to kasher me, boy, like a piece of beef on the sink, she wanted me drained and white' " (16), faces rejection here, too, since the old sailor calls Oedipa " 'Bitch.' " She will grow physically and mentally ill, suffering severe toothaches and malignant dreams. "Your gynecologist has no test for what she was pregnant with" (131), we read toward the end, as paranoia and conspiracy have supplanted love and conception.

But though *The Crying of Lot 49* evidences credible psychological underpinning, the characters are more symbolical than representational, so Oedipa becomes a contemporary Everywoman/private eye seeking "connection" and wanting to "right wrongs." Her creative paranoia, realized at the group level by the Peter Pinguid Society and The Tristero (We-systems) that oppose communism and the Thurn and Taxis (They-systems), appears even before she discovers the initial conspiratorial clue on Mucho's envelope or The Scope's latrine wall, whose WASTE symbol inspires her question, *"Shall I project a world?"* (34). Thus, San Narciso makes Oedipa aware of "outward patterns" with "a hieroglyphic sense of concealed meaning, of an intent to communicate" and "she and the Chevy seemed parked at the centre of an odd, religious instant" (13). This recurs during the Echo Courts tryst when Oedipa wonders if Baby Igor were "part of . . . an elaborate, seduction plot" and detects "some promise of hierophany" (18).

The history of Tristero ("a pseudo-Italianate variant on *triste*," signifying "wretched, depraved" [75]) is as labyrinthine as Borges's projections. Simplified, the organization was founded during the sixteenth century by Hernando Joaquin de Tristero y Calavera (El Desheredado, The Disinherited), whose followers wore black and whose iconography included muted post horn and dead badger. Hernando "began a sub rosa campaign of obstruction, terror and depredation along the Thurn and Taxis mail routes" (120), the latter being the official postal service of the Low Countries. Its monopoly ended in the eighteenth century when Tristero may have "staged the entire French Revolution" (124). But soon Hernando's system experienced a schism and most adherents immigrated to America (1849–1850), where they "fought the Pony Express and Wells, Fargo, either as outlaws in black, or disguised as Indians." Called WASTE, Tristero now serves "those of unorthodox sexual persuasion" (80) and other California deviants.

Conspiratorial clues abound for Oedipa between chapters 3 and 6, multiplying unbelievably throughout the San Francisco sequence, where, after The Greek Way episode, she "spent the rest of the night finding the image of the Trystero post horn" (86). It materializes in Chinatown, in Golden State Park, in a restaurant off Twenty-fourth, in a laundromat near Fillmore, on the beach, on the bus, on the plane. Oedipa comes across several grotesques who bear the telltale image: "Decorating each alienation, each species of withdrawal, as cufflink, decal, aimless doodling, there was somehow always the post horn." And yet, according to Pynchon, the investigator may be unreliable: "She grew so to expect it that perhaps she did not see it quite as often as she later was to remember seeing it" (91).

The Crying of Lot 49 proposes four alternatives, two involving conspiracy, and two, paranoia: (1) either Tristero exists, or (2) Oedipa hallucinates the organization, or (3) Inverarity has mounted a plot against her, or (4) Oedipa imagines he did.

At one point, she wishes the subversive WASTE (WE AWAIT SILENT TRISTERO'S EMPIRE) system were fantasy—the "result of . . . several wounds, needs, dark doubles"—but she had noticed postmen, mailbox, stamps, and cancellations (98). Neither inexplicable nor abstract, this counterforce coexists with actual institutions like the John Birch Society and Cosa Nostra. Destructive events ensue: Zapf's Used Books burns down, Dr. Hilarius goes mad, Mucho takes LSD, and Metzger flees.

Oedipa learns about this conspiracy from numerous sources, among which postage stamps and textual editions predominate. Philatelist Genghis Cohen helps her examine The Tristero forgeries of the Inverarity stamp collection throughout the novel, and, at the end, she awaits their crying or sale under the designation lot 49. When Oedipa visits the Tank Theatre—also owned by Pierce—Richard Wharfinger's seventeenth-century *The Courier's Tragedy* is running. The script contains several suspicious references, so she tracks down its model in *Jacobean Revenge Plays* (Zapf's Used Books). One text leads to another: *Plays of Ford, Webster, Tourneur and Wharfinger* (The Lectern Press), a pornographic Vatican edition of *The Courier's Tragedy* and Blobb's *Peregrinations* (Bortz's library).

Stamp collection and Tank Theatre are not the sole contacts between The Tristero and Pierce Inverarity. Besides real estate holdings in Arizona, Texas, New York, Florida, and Delaware, his interests near San Narcisco, where he was a founding father, encompass the Galactronics Division of Yoyodyne, Fangoso Lagoons, Osteolysis, Inc., Hogan's Seraglio, Vesperhaven House, Zapf's Used Books, Tremaine's surplus store, among others. Oedipa asks:

It's unavoidable, isn't it? Every access route to the Tristero could be traced also back to the Inverarity estate. Even Emory Bortz . . . taught now at San Narcisco College, heavily endowed by the dead man.
Meaning what? That Bortz, along with Metzger, Cohen, Driblette, Koteks, the tattooed sailor in San Francisco, the w.a.s.t.e. carriers she'd seen—that all of them were Pierce Inverarity's men? (127–28)

Much evidence emerges for a personal plot against Oedipa Maas as the true conspiracy behind *The Crying of Lot 49*, rather than an organizational plot against the U. S. Mail, though this would entail "the forging of stamps and ancient books, constant surveillance of . . . movements, planting of post horn images . . . bribing of librarians, hiring of professional actors. . . ." Perhaps, her irrepressible ex-lover, who last year added the codicil naming Oedipa executrix, then imitated diverse dialects over the telephone—Slavic, comic-Negro, Pachuco, Gestapo, Lamont Cranston—has designed "some grandiose practical joke" (128). But why? To embarrass? To terrorize? To improve? Such a hoax is only one of many possible motives, however: "He might himself have discovered The Tristero, and encrypted that in the will. . . . Or he might even have tried to survive death" (134).

Just before *The Crying of Lot 49* closes, a long passage suggests "the legacy" Oedipa ("heiress") had gotten from Pierce "was America" (134). Its "squatters," "drifters," "walkers," and "voices" throughout this computerized land are as disinherited as The Tristero. They also wait, for "there would either be a transcendent meaning, or only the earth" (136). Should nothing exist "beyond the appearance of the legacy of America," Oedipa must become "alien, unfurrowed, assumed full circle into some paranoia" (137). Clearly this legacy is sick, for the post office portrait of Uncle Sam hanging above her bed shows "his eyes gleaming unhealthily, his sunken yellow cheeks most violently rouged." "I want you," the "finger pointing between her eyes" (7) indicates.

In contrast to the progressive view of history developed earlier, twentieth-century authors, who have experienced two world wars and other horrors of similar magnitude, view chronological advancement as regressive. The world is moving toward entropic inanimateness and inertia through nightmare and apocalypse. The forces representing Thanatos are demonic and so often extraterrestrial like Burroughs's Nova Mob and Pynchon's "They." These abstract servants of death assume concrete shapes on earth, becoming various systemic or institutional machines controlled by government. A few individuals inexplicably embodying Eros oppose what Stencil considers the nameless plot, but these individuals feign madness, often as paranoia, to protect themselves from external insanity recurrent hospitals keep before us. Like Hamlet, trying to survive under analogous circumstances, an antic disposition may help.

CHAPTER 10

Entropy

Though German physicist Rudolf Clausius had proclaimed the second law of thermodynamics during 1850 and American physicist Josiah Willard Gibbs had published *On the Equilibrium of Heterogeneous Substances* during 1876–1878, entropy was largely unknown to native writers until *The Education of Henry Adams* (1918) and *The Degradation of the Democratic Dogma* (1919), containing Adams's "A Letter to American Teachers of History," appeared. Dictionary definitions of the term include: "the ultimate state reached in the degradation of the matter and energy of the universe: state of inert uniformity of component elements: absence of form, pattern, hierarchy, or differentiation"; "the irreversible tendency of a system including the universe, toward increasing disorder and inertness; also, the final state predictable from this tendency."

T. S. Eliot, who reviewed *The Education of Henry Adams* for *The Atheneum,* and who borrowed from the book, soon issued the paradigmatic Anglo-American entropic masterwork. As such, *The Waste Land* (1922) exhibits barren terrain ("What are the roots that clutch, what branches grow / Out of this stony rubbish?"), nightmarish city ("A crowd flowed over London Bridge, so many, / I had not thought death had undone so many"), and telltale debris (". . . empty bottles, sandwich papers, / Silk handkerchiefs, cardboard boxes, cigarette ends"). Among the many novels *The Waste Land* influenced, *The Great Gatsby* (1925) remains the most renowned. There, America, once "a fresh green breast of the new world," has become between Long Island and Manhattan "a valley of ashes." However, Fitzgerald's antirealistic acquaintance Nathanael West—an Eliot devotee too—invoked entropy more self-consciously than any other *modern* American writer. During *Miss Lonelyhearts* (1933), the protagonist reflects: "Man has a tropism for order. . . . The physical world has a tropism for disorder, entropy. Man against Nature. . . . Every order has within it the germ of destruction. All order is doomed."[1]

Direct references to entropy increase after World War II, recurring throughout the fiction of Burroughs, Barth, Gaddis, and Pynchon, and in such texts as *Death Kit, The Free-Lance Pallbearers,* and *The Public Burning.* Though less explicit, perhaps, Donald Barthelme and John Hawkes have also created entropic works.

Postmodernists differ radically from modernists when combining a new concern about information with the old anxiety over thermodynamics. This new concern was inspired by Norbert Wiener, whose *The Human Use of Human Beings* (rev. ed. 1954) explained how the two are linked: "That information may be dissipated but not gained, is, as we have seen, the cybernetic form of the second law of thermodynamics."[2] If books like Hawkes's *The Beetle Leg* dramatize thermodynamic entropy and books like McElroy's *Lookout Cartridge* exploit informational entropy, the imaginative worlds of Thomas Pynchon and William Gaddis[3] incorporate both. We learn during *The Crying of Lot 49*

that there are two distinct kinds of this entropy. One having to do with heat-engines, the other to do with communication. The equation for one, back in the '30's, had looked very like the equation for the other. It was a coincidence. The two fields were entirely unconnected, except at one point: Maxwell's Demon. As the Demon sat and sorted his molecules into hot and cold, the system was said to lose entropy. But somehow the loss was offset by the information the Demon gained about what molecules were where.[4]

Six years earlier (1960), in the short story "Entropy," Pynchon had already merged thermodynamics (heat-death) and information (noise). This orderly exposition of disorder, which transpires at some Washington, D. C., apartment house during February 1957, juxtaposes four downstairs and four upstairs scenes. Downstairs Meatball Mulligan and his cronies have been holding a long "lease-breaking party,"[5] while upstairs Callisto and his girlfriend Aubade have been keeping an even longer vigil focused on the thirty-seven degrees Fahrenheit temperature outside, where the "false spring" has recently brought snow, wind, sun, and now rain. Meatball's apartment is vulnerable to intrusion, as friend Saul, three coeds, and five sailors intermittently crash the party. By contrast, Callisto and Aubade, who never exit, occupy a "hothouse jungle," replete with birds, plants, and "ecological balance." "Hermetically sealed," their apartment "was a tiny enclave of regularity in the city's chaos" (83).

Chaos aptly describes Meatball's open environment. Besides the pattern of haphazard intrusions, we find here drinking, smoking *(cannabis sativa)*, game playing, lusting, and fighting. However, noise represents the greatest discordance. Saul, whose wife has just left him after throwing *Handbook of Chemistry and Physics* out the window, tells Meatball they had battled over communication theory (89). Already " 'bugged at this idea of computers acting like people,' " Miriam " 'hit the roof' " when he suggested the reverse, a notion " 'crucial to communication, not to mention information theory' " (90). As Saul explains to Meatball: " 'Tell a girl: 'I love you.' No trouble with two-thirds of that, it's a closed circuit. Just you and she. But that nasty four-letter word in the middle, *that's* the one you have to look out for. Ambiguity. Redundance. Irrelevance, even. Leakage. All this is noise. Noise screws up your signal, makes for disorganization in the circuit' " (90–91).

Meatball's revel, like many Washington affairs, becomes polyglot as Sandor Rojas babbles Hungarian and others scream French words. The racket downstairs is mainly musical, though. For instance, the Duke di Angelis quartet "sat crouched over a 15-inch speaker which had been bolted into the top of a wastepaper basket, listening to 27 watts' worth of *The Heroes' Gate at Kiev*" (81). They once recorded *Songs of Outer Space*, but now rehearse jazz without instruments. Later, during the wild kitchen scene, "noise . . . reached a sustained ungodly crescendo" (96), so Meatball, having passively opposed disorder all along, decides "to try and keep his lease-breaking party from deteriorating into total chaos."

This downstairs din penetrates the "private time-warp" (97) upstairs, where it threatens fragile Aubade, whose French name means both "dawn song" and "charivari." Since "every calorie of her strength" is needed to maintain a "delicate balance" between signal and noise (92), she pits the harmonies of life (love, nature) against "the howling darkness of discordancy" (84) represented by Earl Bostic's alto. Callisto, echoing Norbert Wiener, calls that constant readjustment to aural anarchy " 'feedback' " (88).

His own obsession involves thermodynamic rather than informational entropy. As the spiritual heir of Henry Adams, the fifty-four-year-old Italian dictates a "radical reevaluation of everything he had learned" (87). The old knowledge acquired through physicists like

Clausius, Gibbs, and Boltzmann at Princeton, together with subsequent personal experiences and correspondences in literature (Sade, Temple Drake, *Nightwood*) and in music (Stravinsky's *L'Histoire du Soldat*), now makes the entropy metaphor culturally applicable; consequently, "American 'consumerism' " reveals "a similar tendency from the least to the most probable, from differentiation to sameness, from ordered individuality to a kind of chaos" (88).

While Callisto recounts his education, he, too, combats entropic forces, holding off the steady three-day temperature and warming a sick bird. These efforts, which were bound to fail, cease after the latter dies and Aubade smashes a window. Callisto's earlier apocalyptic omens will come true, for the story ends as they silently "wait . . . until the moment of equilibrium was reached, when 37 degrees Fahrenheit should prevail both outside and inside, and forever, and the hovering, curious dominant of their separate lives should resolve into a tonic of darkness and final absence of all motion" (98).

Twenty-four years after its original publication, Pynchon excoriated "Entropy." In his introduction to *Slow Learner* (1984), where five early pieces appear, he says the story committed the amateurish "procedural error" of making "characters and events" fit "a theme, symbol, or other abstract unifying agent" (12). Thus, not only do "the humans" seem "synthetic, insufficiently alive" and "the marital crisis . . . unconvincingly simplified" (13), but the narrative displays "overwriting," affected diction, and "phony data." Yet Pynchon's current "bleakness of heart" (12) concerning "Entropy" is due to intellectual as well as aesthetic faults. "Somber glee at any idea of mass destruction or decline" was "congenial" during the 50s, so he decided then that *The Human Use of Human Beings* and *The Education of Henry Adams* were "just the ticket." Such "shallowness" led him to choose "37 degrees Fahrenheit for an equilibrium point because 37 degrees Celsius is the temperature of the human body" (13). Even now, Pynchon confesses, people believe he knows more about entropy than he actually does: "Since I wrote this story I have kept trying to understand entropy, but my grasp becomes less sure the more I read. "I've been able to follow the *OED* definitions, and the way Isaac Asimov explains it, and even some of the math. But the qualities and quantities will not come together to form a unified notion in my head" (14).

Though Pynchon's underestimation of his early story and overestimation of his private ignorance are sincere, the three novels published between 1970 and 1984—a quarter century during which he continued to study thermodynamics—treat entropic ideas more comprehensively than any other American fiction. However, the introduction indicates that the present Pynchon regards these ideas "in connection with time" as among *several* "processes" leading toward death (15). According to Zbigniew Lewicki, *Gravity's Rainbow* (1973) had already expressed his new view, for there entropy takes its place beside "scientific-related notions" like "relativity, gravity, the Rocket, and technological control."[6]

V. (1963) contains no direct allusions to entropy, but even so the text is dominated by the concept. Here, inert uniformity occurs through objectification, a crucial phenomenon in grotesque and entropic literature.[7] The hair spray can in *The Crying of Lot 49*—"hissing malignantly," knowing direction, threatening lives, shattering glass—suggests that objectification persists during subsequent work. Nevertheless, as Anne Mangel demonstrates through "Maxwell's demon, entropy, information: *The Crying of Lot 49*,"[8] the 1966 novel stresses material adumbrated before *V.* This article is particularly valuable because it provides considerable scientific background. Aided by diagrams and equations, Ms. Mangel connects "Entropy" and *The Crying of Lot 49* with the notions of James Clerk Maxwell, Leo Szilard, Leon Brillouin, Ludwig Boltzmann, and Claude Shannon. Maxwell's demon, which "sorts molecules" to increase order and decrease disorder (195), becomes "a metaphor for Oedipa's experiences" (196), and so Pynchon's second book mentions "sorting and shuffling" at the outset. Like the demon, the protagonist, who desires order too, must "link occurrences ... in what seems ... a random system," yet "increasing confusion" counteracts the acquired information (197). Ultimately, she cannot "distinguish reality from fantasy-insanity," though her efforts make the young woman unique (200). Ms. Mangel discusses other matters related to communication theory also: how information is altered and lost during transmission (e.g., *The Courier's Tragedy*); how codes and signals destroy information; and how "probability constraints," "redundancy," and "waste in language" enter Pynchon's own "elaborate stories with their irrelevant details" (207). This "radically separates" him from the great moderns—Yeats, Eliot, Joyce—

since "[t]hinking of literature in terms of order, rather than disorder, they saw art as perhaps the last way to impose order on a chaotic world" (207).

"Entropy rears as a central preoccupation of our time," asserted William Gaddis in his 1981 article, "The Rush for Second Place."[9] True, and *The Crying of Lot 49* notwithstanding, nowhere is it more prevalent than during *J R* (1975), the most impressive single entropic text we possess. If Pynchon's "central preoccupation" began with a 1960 story, Gaddis's began with a 1955 novel. *The Recognitions*, like *V.*, lacks specific references to entropy; however, the many Eliot allusions, especially concerning *The Waste Land*, prefigure later thematic and technical developments. The author has admitted this:

Well, I think the whole idea had occured [*sic*] to me already in the first book. It too is fragmented, you have the constant threat of breakdown. And then in *JR* [*sic*] I tried really to get to it, but it's been on my mind for long—long before *JR* [*sic*]—ever since I read Wiener's *The Human Use of Human Beings*, where he discusses at length entropy and entropy in communication. The more complicated the message, the more chance for error, and so forth.[10]

There are several mentions of entropy in *J R*. Jack Gibbs, whose name echoes Josiah Willard Gibbs, tells co-protagonist Edward Bast, "—there's too God damned much leakage around here, can't compose anything with all this energy spilling you've got entropy everywhere."[11] Turning off a televised lecture earlier that claimed "Energy may be changed but not destroyed," he had informed his elementary school class

—knowledge has to be organized so it can be taught, and it has to be reduced to information so it can be organized. [. . .] In other words this leads you to assume that organization is an inherent property of the knowledge itself, and that disorder and chaos are simply irrelevant forces that threaten it from outside. In fact it's exactly the opposite. Order is simply a thin, perilous condition we try to impose on the basic reality of chaos. (20)

More profoundly innovative than any other post–World War II American novel, *J R* is an acoustical masterpiece. It jumbles largely disjointed, undifferentiated voices rendered by direct dialogue, television, dictaphone, radio, tape recorder, and, above all, telephone.

The text, then, embodies as well as presents an entropic system. The marriage of substance and manner is intentional:

> In *JR* [sic] the form is fragmented, shattered, because that's what the content is about too. It is about the total fragmentation and chaos, the total chaos which is the last step in entropy, when everything is settled and everything equals everything else. People sees chaos as a battle, but it is not that, it is when energy has finally reached this equilibrium. That's the end of the line. [. . .] What I wanted in *JR* [sic] was to have the style and what the book is about be the same thing.[12]

One trenchant study, Stephen H. Matanle's "Love and Strife in William Gaddis' *J R*,"[13] contends that both it and *The Recognitions* enact what the author has termed " 'the separating of things today without love.' " Three interrelated topics follow: "The Problem of Chaos"; "The Rule of Strife"; and "The Plurality of Discourse."

"The Problem of Chaos" treats Jack Gibbs, *J R*'s "preeminent authority on disorder" (106). Besides Gibb's classroom lecture, Matanle discusses the book Gibbs has been composing for more than ten years. Ironically, this " 'book about order and disorder' . . . exists only as a fragment," and will remain a fragment because distractions like the telephone keep plaguing the inert writer-teacher. Thus, "his 'social history' " becomes victimized by "what it diagnoses" (107).

Empedocles, to whom Gibbs often alludes, dominates the next section, wherein Matanle reminds us that Love and Strife alternately rule the philosopher's world and that "the function of Love is to unite, to make one out of many, and incidentally to cause rest," while "the function of Strife is to separate, to disperse things without apparent design, and incidentally to cause movement" (109). During *J R*, though, the latter reigns supreme, since Love has disappeared or degenerated, so Edward futilely pursues Stella and Jack clumsily rejects Amy. Here, "most of the marriages . . . end in divorce, and families are consequently divided" (110).

Gibbs's allusions to *On Nature* comprehend those passages which delineate a disunited world through body parts gone awry, one example being fragment 57: " '[M]any foreheads without necks sprang forth, and arms wandered unattached, bereft of shoulders, and eyes strayed about alone, needing brows.' " This grotesque vision of Empedocles permeates *J R*, for Gaddis presents its characters through "their hands, feet, elbows, knees, eyes, backs, shoulders" (110). Phys-

ical accidents recur, and individuals behave awkwardly. Even when
Jack and Amy make love, they resemble contortionists, as " 'her arms
came free, came up, her shoulders' struggle against his knee come
down and legs drawn tight in a twist away' " (112).

"The Plurality of Discourse," Matanle's third and last topic, ap-
prises us that *J R* contains numerous contending modes of speech
drawn from "social, economic, legal, political, scientific, literary" do-
mains (112). The instrumentalist attitude toward language over-
powers the referential view and therefore "correspondence between
sign and referent" vanishes (113). Instead, we get double-talk. Bank
president and school principal Whiteback, who is the worst offender,
explains, "—[w]e know you didn't build it yourself it was, of course it
was the builder who ahm, who built it of course but the, since the
term of the mortgage is related to, dictated by . . ." (114). The telephone only aggravates matters for both characters and readers because telephonic conversations lack gestures, facial expressions, and
other orientative devices. Yet, as "visible perception in *J R* tends to
be unreliable" (116), these would not help much. People metonymi-
cally become "different styles of eyeglasses" in this "ocular chaos"
(117) governed by Strife.

Carpenter's Gothic (1985), the most recent Gaddis novel, also investigates "the separating of things today without love." Like *The Crying of
Lot 49*, it is short and contains a childless female protagonist surrounded by unsatisfactory males. Gaddis explores the reasons why
Elizabeth Booth chooses inferior types more fully than Pynchon does
those of Oedipa Maas, so *Carpenter's Gothic* evinces greater psychological depth than *The Crying of Lot 49*, just as *The Recognitions* surpasses
V. and *Gravity's Rainbow* on that score. At any rate, though her ex-vet
husband Paul and her hippy brother Billy appear to be opposites,
both are selfish and dishonest. And, while Paul (media consultant)
and lover McCandless (geologist) seem worlds apart too, these twin
failures share broken marriages and deranged minds. Liz's narcissis-
tic father—dead by suicide—becomes the archetypal figure behind
all three men, two of whom match Oedipa's spouse Mucho and
paramour Metzger.

Parallel copulation scenes well illustrate "the separating of things
today without love." During the first, which involves Liz and Paul,
human parts make mechanical contact—hand closing on breast, legs

easing between knees—and then Liz, worried about bruises, experiences shortness of breath. Paul discusses money matters: his disability benefits, her insurance claim, his companion suit. Meanwhile, the television screen reveals *Jane Eyre*, starring Orson Welles who will be blinded in a fire at Thornfield set by mad Mrs. Rochester. The second erotic episode, with McCandless, is almost pornographic. Starved for sex and talk, Liz speaks mainly of personal things and listens to McCandless speak mainly of impersonal things while they caress each other. Less troubled by the telephone calls that invade their intimacy than by the intimacy itself—"licensed as she was now to rummage through his life"[14]—McCandless grows distant. Upstairs he looks upon her "as though she were no one he'd ever seen" (163) and downstairs he calls her Mrs Booth. Later, after Liz accuses him of indirectly killing Billy and secretly desiring apocalpyse/Armageddon, but before she realizes the man has been institutionalized, he departs. A worse betrayal occurs subsequently when Paul starts to court his wife's best friend—another rich woman—immediately following her death. No wonder their love seat is frayed!

It does not surprise us either that Elizabeth Booth shares the mental and physical anguish of Oedipa Maas. Both experience bad dreams, and if the latter suffers from toothaches, the former must endure asthma and high blood pressure, aggravated by the heavy smoking and drinking husband and lover inflict. Often in *Carpenter's Gothic* Liz visits doctors, sometimes with reference to one of the many lawsuits pending throughout the narrative. Her ailments may explain the constant prevaricating and bathing she practices.

Even so, as moral center, Liz "—holds things together" (177). Gaddis's protagonist, like Pynchon's, needs order. His "redhaired former debutante" (255) tries to escape cultural chaos via external nature, which is viewed through dirty windows and on the pages of a natural history magazine and a bird book. However, the outside world, where lightning strikes the horse chestnut, seems no less unstable than the inside world. Tragicomic *Carpenter's Gothic* transpires during the Halloween season, whose macabre associations omnipresent leaves reinforce: "—[E]verything dying out there in the sun" (89). This also pertains to people, since those who perish besides Liz include brother Billy and the mugger Paul slays, Wayne Fickert, Senator Teakell, and others.

Like Jack Gibbs, Elizabeth Booth represents the frustrated author producing fragments. She confesses near the outset, "—[I]t was going to be a sort of novel but I haven't worked on it since we got here" (35). Consequent creative efforts are hobbled by dictionary definitions and telephone conversations. Liz tells McCandless, "—I think people write because things didn't come out the way they're supposed to be" (158), and, indeed, her messy manuscript treats "what it might all have been like if . . . father and mother had never met" (63). Despite violating his injunction against "—cheap . . . sentimental . . . vulgar" autobiographical work, Liz's goal is not "—to sell out" (159), but "to reorder" past "unlikelihoods" (247). Even this becomes compromised, though, when sexual fantasies about McCandless intervene. He, too, has written—-a *roman à clef*, the hero of which "—wants to rescue his life from chance" (137) and textbook/encyclopedia pieces on evolution. Obsessed with disorder, he spends much of *Carpenter's Gothic* filling trash bags. Estranged Mrs. McCandless may thus declare, "—[H]e didn't even really teach history no, no he wanted to change it, or to end it . . . to clean it up once and for all, like that room in there" (252). The implied connection between composition and coherence also affects Paul, who repeatedly tries "—to get the whole God damn thing together" (113) and who plans to write The Wayne Fickert Story. Reporter Doris Chin will contribute "—a final polish before we get into the movie" (201), the same cliché-ridden, bombastic Doris Chin mentioned earlier. Neither Paul nor McCandless nor Liz can ever achieve personal harmony through the written word, as sensational journalism for money, scientific articles for enlightenment, and romantic fiction for therapy hardly constitute the authentic art that eluded other Gaddis protagonists.

All three centers of consciousness—the prevaricator Liz, the publicist Paul, and the paranoid McCandless—supply disinformation during *Carpenter's Gothic*, which was also influenced by *The Human Use of Human Beings*. Related to the concept, "[t]he more complicated the message, the more chance for error," this disinformation affects several elaborate plots, not unlike other Gaddis and Pynchon novels. One involves the Vorakers estate/Grimes syndicate; one, Reverend Ude/Senator Teakell; and one, Lester/Cruikshank. McCandless claims these constitute a single conspiracy, but just as Paul may be wrong

about McCandless's criminality, McCandless may be wrong about
Paul's complicity, since both are unbalanced.

The focal emblem of the appearance versus reality motif is architectural. In contrast to peripatetic *Lot 49* and *J R, Carpenter's Gothic*
occurs exclusively at the "—beautiful old Victorian house . . . on the
Hudson" (33) the Booths have rented. Concerning his home, Mc-
Candless asserts:

—[I]t was built to be seen from outside [. . .] yes, they had style books, these
country architects and the carpenters it was all derivative wasn't it, those
grand Victorian mansions with their rooms and rooms and towering heights
and cupolas and the marvelous intricate ironwork. That whole inspiration of
medieval Gothic but these poor fellows didn't have it, the stonework and the
wrought iron. [. . .] a patchwork of conceits borrowings, deceptions. (227)

Here, the bigoted WASP hero Paul turns out to be a Jewish war victim,
and here the scientific thinker McCandless turns out to be a former
mental patient. Here, too, Liz's death, which the police regard as
murder, represents the last of many accidents scattered throughout
the text.

Like *The Recognitions* and *J R*, not to mention modern poetic sequences and postwar "poetic" fictions, *Carpenter's Gothic* is synecdochical, each part standing for the whole. Thus, the second chapter
contains virtually all the entropic elements we anticipate in a Gaddis
book. Though he has provided more narration and description than
during *J R*, dialogue—that instrument of linguistic noise—remains
his basic story-telling technique. The telephone, which rings constantly, competes against the radio, broadcasting such data as "thirty
five million Americans were functionally illiterate" (37), and the television, emitting such sounds as Mrs. Rochester's demoniac laugh.
The mail, with its bills, and the newspaper, with its "demand to be
read" (28), supplement these aural barrages.

Of course, waste accompanies noise. The living room holds so
much furniture "c'est comme un petit musée" (29), where individuals
trip over the coffee table. An envelope gets retrieved from the kitchen
refuse and money from beneath placemats. Spillage—milk, water,
ashes—and breakage—china dog, car, pipe—occur. Since the windows are dirty, fake flowers dusty, and draperies cobwebby, Madame
Socrate, who speaks no English while Spanish lessons play, must

continually clean. Likewise, the ubiquitous old man outside, carrying his dustpan as "an offering . . . toward an open garbage can . . . with ceremonial concern" (35). To little avail, however, for the clutter (and the clatter) increases.

Gaddis, opposing this chaos, fashions language that challenges the "—bad books and bad everything" characterizing our civilization, and that achieves coherence through recurrent images, such as love seat, chipped glass, mirror, sampler, moon, leaves, birds, and boys. He realizes McCandless's dictum, "—what's worth doing is worth doing well" (230); consequently, *Carpenter's Gothic* becomes the natural heir of *The Recognitions* and *J R*.

Thomas LeClair's "William Gaddis, *JR [sic]*, & The Art of Excess" implies a connection between debris and feces: "The apartment where Bast, Gibbs, and Eigen try to work is a rubbish heap of unused and unusable products. Garbage and excrement mark urban and suburban settings. Scenes take place in toilets: shit is found in Bast's piano, in J. R.'s *[sic]* speech ('holy shit'), and secretly spelled in JR *[sic]* Corporation logo."[15]

Pynchon, who took the epigraph for "Entropy" from notorious Henry Miller, was even more preoccupied with feces while composing *Gravity's Rainbow*. We find there a vessel called Toiletship, and episodes titled Shit 'N' Shinola, An Incident in the Transvestites' Toilet, and Listening to the Toilet. The most graphic such sequence involves Slothrop at the Roseland Ballroom, Roxbury, Massachusetts. He swoons when vomiting over an upstairs commode, so PLOP goes the dislodged mouth harp. Slothrop hesitates to follow because Red Malcolm, the black shoe-shine boy, might bugger him, but he finally plunges after the harp, "virgin asshole preserved." The "loathsome" bowl becomes fantastic, as, once inside, Slothrop identifies the excremental stains of Harvard acquaintances, survives a "shitstorm," traverses "waste regions," encounters homosexuals, and so forth. Here, he notices "shit nothing can flush away, mixed with hard-water minerals into a deliberate brown barnacling of his route, patterns thick with meaning, Burma-Shave signs of the toilet bowl world, icky and sticky, cryptic and glyptic."[16]

Many other contemporary antirealists—and some essentially real-

istic writers like Norman Mailer and Philip Roth—are also scatalogi-
cal: John Barth *(The Sot-Weed Factor),*[17] William Burroughs *(oeuvre),*
Robert Coover *(The Public Burning, Gerald's Party),* Coleman Dowell
(Mrs. October Was Here), Raymond Federman *(Double or Nothing),* John
Hawkes *(The Cannibal),* Vladimir Nabokov *(Ada),* Ishmael Reed *(The
Free-Lance Pallbearers),* and Kurt Vonnegut, Jr. *(Slaughter-House-Five).*
Allusions range from Billy Pilgrim's "excrement festival" to Harrison
Mack's "freeze-dried feces" to Naomi's "bottom." They usually have
a grotesque context, as when Dr. Benway expatiates on " 'the man
who taught his asshole to talk' " during *Naked Lunch.* This orifice
farted " 'out the words' " and even " 'started eating' " with " 'little
raspy incurving hooks,' " but the " 'one thing' " it " *'couldn't* do was
see.' "[18] Significantly, the word *dreck,* which Donald Barthelme substitutes for "detritus," means "trash," "junk," "garbage," *and* excrement.

These authors, sharing a derisive tone, illustrate that most satirists
are "what the world calls obscene."[19] Their psychologically valid homology of feces/sex/death (and sometimes money/language) is forti-
fied by various physical functions—belching, breaking wind, ejaculat-
ing, menstruating, spitting, sweating, urinating, vomiting—and
diseases. Burroughs told Bockris, "I've had a lifelong interest in
drugs and medicine and illness. Pharmacology was a lifelong hobby.
In fact, I took a year of medicine in Vienna."[20] Not unexpectedly,
then, he often invokes this homology, its dominant metaphor, hanging. Gregory Stephenson associates him with the Gnostics, for "[b]oth
view the material world as illusory, the body as the primary impediment to true being and identity, and escape from the body and the
world of the senses as man's paramount concern."[21]

If satire requires two elements, "wit or humor founded on fantasy
or a sense of the grotesque or absurd" and "an object of attack,"[22]
our irrealists—descended, in part, from Aristophanes, Rabelais, Cervantes, Swift, Fielding, Twain, and Joyce—certainly qualify, since
they are comic fabulators exploiting the deformed and the ridiculous
while assailing orthodox opinions and outworn conventions. Norman
O. Brown, during "The Excremental Vision" section of *Life Against
Death,* examines the argument which demonstrates how one predecessor, Jonathan Swift, displayed psychosexual infantilism through
coprophilia (love of feces), misogyny (hatred of women), misanthropy (hatred of mankind), mysophilia (love of dirt), and mysopho-

bia (fear of contamination). Unlike the traditional and psychoanalytic critics behind this argument, Brown is "not disturbed . . . that Swift had his individual version of the universal human neurosis"; "that his individual neurosis may have been abnormally acute"; and "that his abnormality may be inseparable from his art."[23] The Dean of St. Patrick's anticipated "the doctrine of anal erotism" and "the doctrine of sublimation" (192), involving feces as play, gift, property, and weapon. Anality provided him with the ultimate instrument to "assault . . . the pretensions, the pride, even the self-respect of mankind" (179). Though we are probably less sanguine about the misogyny, misanthropy, and other psychosexual infantilism in current American fiction, we, too, should appreciate the excremental vision because its tacit application by Barth, Burroughs, Coover, Pynchon, and Reed to the new entropic world has enriched the satiric mode.

Ishmael Reed, whom Pynchon mentions during *Gravity's Rainbow*, credits the antecedent native novelist most responsible for this: "I think the first fictional influence on me was Nathanael West's work, especially *The Dream Life of Balso Snell*, a piece I've read many times and still can't get over."[24] The 1931 fantasy, which transports the title character through the alimentary canal of the Trojan horse ("O Anus Mirabilis!"), enacts the theme, " 'Art is a sublime excrement.' " In one journal entry about diarists, Snell states: "They come to the paper with a constipation of ideas—eager, impatient. The white paper acts as a laxative. A diarrhea of words is the result."[25] Bukka Doopeyduk, an equally anti-heroic protagonist whose equally ignominious journey structures *The Free-Lance Pallbearers* (1967), also connects writing and defecating. Thus, the scholarly dean at Harry Sam College embodies both: "U2 and I shook hands and I left him to a paper he was preparing for an English literary quarterly, entitled: 'The Egyptian Dung Beetle in Kafka's metamorphosis.' " He had dropped to his knees and begun to push a light ball of excrement about the room by the tip of his nose. He wanted to add an element of experience to his paper."[26]

Reed's story contains even more scatalogical allusions than its model. They form two dominant interrelated patterns, prefigured in the Elias Canetti (from *Crowds and Power*) and Shirley Temple (after seeing *Night Games*) epigraphs. These begin, "The excrement, which is what remains of all this, is loaded with our whole blood guilt," and

"We felt so dirty after seeing it that we felt compelled to eat at Senor Picos, a popular Mexican restaurant." Subsequent food and feces images are coupled with images of disease and death, as protean Doopeyduk plays several roles: Nazarene apprentice, hospital orderly/psychiatric technician, Entropy Productions actor, and would-be religio-political tyrant.

Part 5, a surrealistic nightmare leading toward apocalypse/Armageddon, not only concludes *The Free-Lance Pallbearers*, but represents our most vivid dramatization of the feces/sex/death homology. Because Doopeyduk must always descend to reach HARRY SAM, who possesses some "weird ravaging illness" and one hoofed limb, "the great dictator, former Polish used-car salesman and barn burner" lives, metaphorically, in hell and the large intestine. His throne-room contains "a high toilet booth with a diamond-studded knob on its door of carved griffins and gargoyles. . . . surrounded on each side by seven smaller black and more austere little booths." Doopeyduk encounters various dignitaries wearing gas masks here: "the Chief of Screws, the Chief of the Nazarene Bishops, Nancy Spellman, the Chief Theoretician of the Party and the Chairman of the Joint Chiefs of Staff" (94). From a wheelchair, Sam the gangster, gourmet, and bigot, proclaims the philosophy, " '[w]hen they act up or give you some lip, bomb the fuken daylights out of um' " (98). To maintain control, he has devised " 'The Counter Insurgency Foundation,' " and now orders Doopeyduk, " 'Go down there in Soulsville and tell them IT'S GOIN' BE ALL RIGHT, BY AND BY IN THE SKY' " (99). That SAM is Uncle Sam, and ME, the USA, become clear through numerous references. Besides the allusion to Spellman, which pervades the book, we find during part 5 alone mention of the Princeton Institute of Advanced Studies, Rock Hudson, The Republican Club, Miles Davis, Ernest Hemingway, Rutherford B. Hayes, Roger Young, Betty Grable, *The Wall Street Journal*, Roy Rogers, Hershey bars, *Variety*, The University of Buffalo, Billy Eckstine, The Donna Reed Show, Gillette razor blades, and others.

HARRY SAM, like Coover's Uncle Sam, is a sodomite inhabiting the land of Richard Nixon. Even though he exudes foul order and "goo," representatives from religion, labor, and art practice anal (and oral) intercourse with him. Cipher X—MIT graduate, Entropy Productions manager—explains to former employee Bukka Doopeyduk,

" 'He and his washroom attendants control the museums so as long as they were forking over the bread I made them hoopla hoops. . . . they began selling them in the A&P' " (102–103). The corruption of Cipher X, Eclair Porkchop, and Mr. Nosetrouble, rather than the debasement of art, causes Doopeyduk to revolt. However, after subduing SAM and the toilet chain, he must flee the gnomes seated in those seven stalls behind the Great Commode.

Sexual perversion, like excrement, is inseparable from death and decay. For instance, prior to the confrontation with ME's dictator and his sodomitic slaves, Doopeyduk experiences

the slime of tiny animals squashed underfoot and rats dashed across my shoestrings. Wispy spider webs brushed against my face as I pushed on—my ankles moving through sludge—until I came nearer to the gasps and snorts echoing through the dank old house steeped in mildew. When I came to the middle landing an awful stench attacked my brain that smelled of the very putrescence of mass graves. I took a handkerchief and held it to my nose as I ran through the passageways and past propped-up human skeletons in chains. I finally came to a door. . . . I broke it open and saw on the tiled floor men in grotesque pretzel-shaped poses. It was a kind of underground cockfight. (101–102)

The entropic Black Bay linking this setting on SAM's island to the mainland and Soulsville illustrates how civilization has polluted nature. Near the end of part 4, we learn that during "the bad old days the sea was saturated with chemicals" produced by "cereal factories" (89). These, and a "puslike substance" expelled from the huge mouths of four RUTHERFORD BIRCHARD HAYES statues ever since the sick ruler occupied his motel john thirty years before, have spawned bizarre life forms: "[L]ong serpentine tentacles oscillated in the bay and what appeared to be white arms reached from beneath its surface. The silhouettes of peculiar-shaped animals leaped into the air—sometimes many feet high" (88). Presently, Doopeyduk must negotiate the Black Bay via battleship, but later he will swim across twice, thanks to a magical fluid.

After the protagonist escapes over the water in part 5, we see him at the Soulsville auditorium shouting, " 'LADIES AND GENTLEMEN, SAM'S EATING YOUR CHILDREN' " (107). Outside, he exhorts the crowd, "who now believed my discovery of sheer evil," " 'UP TO SAM'S' " (109), and everyone swims the seven miles back. Armageddon accompanies apocalypse when they tear "the Swiss guards to pieces" (110) and find

SAM watching the worldwide destruction of his forces on television. While the crowd defeats the gnomes, their "ailing leader" squirms through the Great Commode, leaving "blotches of fresh dung" (112). Reed's protagonist pursues, and, helped by lightning, drowns him. Then, he imagines, "NOW I WAS DA ONE. NOW NOT ONLY WOULD I BE THE NAZARENE BISHOP WHICH WAS AFTER ALL PEANUTS, BUT I WAS GOING TO RUN THE WHOLE KIT AND KABOODLE. ME DICTATOR OF BUKKA DOOPEYDUK." However, this fantasy soon passes, for "[t]he next-in-rank on the Civil Service list was being sworn in." Betrayed—Nose-trouble "administering the oath"; Cipher "pointing an accusing finger" (113)—he is hung by meathooks at the Emperor Franz Joseph Park, where selfish parents berate their son. The Free-Lance Pall-bearers finally arrive, yet cannot release Doopeyduk because a "great ball of manure" (115) bars the way. That the excrement U2 Polyglot began pushing around easily has grown from "a light ball" (4) to "a giant ball" (36) to a "great ball" reinforces the entropic proliferation of noxious wastes in Black Bay. Nevertheless, "my old professor" (36) remains unaware and unconcerned, since Reed's satire concludes right after "he dropped the greenish-brown envelope containing the manuscript into the mail" and "sat down to contemplate his next paper" (116).

The dictionary definitions of entropy are worth repeating since they describe the future according to post–World War II antirealistic American fiction: "the ultimate state reached in the degradation of the matter and energy of the universe: state of inert uniformity of component elements: absence of form, pattern, hierarchy, or differentiation"; "the irreversible tendency of a system including the universe, toward increasing disorder and inertness; also the final state predictable from this tendency." This happens initially through thermodynamics (heat loss), coupled later by communication theory (noise)—a wasteful world often rendered through the scatalogical psycho-literary homology involving sex/feces/death. The entropic motif of "disorder and inertness"—so well summarized in Eliot's title, *The Waste Land*—is more or less inseparable from previous topics: "Fragmentation/Decentralization," "The Grotesque," "Fictitious History," and "Conspiracy and Paranoia." When the universe as madhouse becomes the future as death, our worst nightmares, culminating in apocalypse, will have been realized.

CHAPTER 11

Nightmare and Apocalypse

During the prologue of *Camino Real* (1953), Don Quixote advises Sancho Panza, " 'Yes, I'll sleep and dream for a while against the wall of this town.' " Tennessee Williams's modern drama thus invokes the dream-vision, which, until the publication of August Strindberg's *A Dream Play* (1901), had been the conventional way to render dreamscapes. It dominated the Middle Ages with poems like *The Divine Comedy*, and it subsequently structured prose works like *Pilgrim's Progress*, *Looking Backward*, and *A Connecticut Yankee in King Arthur's Court*. Different though they are, these texts begin similarly: for example, Dante confesses, "I cannot well remember in my mind / How I came thither, so was I immersed / In sleep, when the true way I left behind," and Bunyan explains, "As I walked through the wilderness of this world, I lighted on a certain place where was a Den, and I laid me down in that place to sleep: and as I slept I dreamed."

Since actuality always introduces and sometimes concludes such experiences, they resemble the framework narrative, an old structure adopted later by ghost story, tall tale, and, as we saw in part 1, the metafictional novel. What Walter Blair notes about Southwestern humor also applies to the dream-vision: "[i]ncongruity between realism—discoverable in the framework wherein the scene and the narrator are realistically portrayed, and fantasy, which enters into the enclosed narrative."[1] *A Dream Play* abolishes this incongruity when it drops the realistic framework and includes only the enclosed fantasy. That the drama strives to eliminate the rational treatment of irrational phenomena characteristic of previous literary dreams, while maintaining the traditional notion of a single consciousness, as well, is evident from Strindberg's prefatory note:

> In this dream play as in his earlier dream plays *To Damascus*, the author has tried to imitate the disconnected but apparently logical form of a dream. Everything can happen; everything is possible and likely. Time and space do

not exist; on an insignificant basis of reality the imagination spins and weaves new patterns: a blending of memories, experiences, free inventions, absurdities, and improvisations. The characters split, double, redouble, evaporate, condense, scatter, and converge. But one consciousness remains above all of them: the dreamer's.

Having inherited the Strindbergian idea of the *entire* work as dream and its form dream image, the surrealists, who produced painting, poetry, fiction, and drama, flourished during the first half of this century. Their obsession with the irrational and the unconscious influenced *The Waste Land*, *Ulysses*, and *Finnegans Wake*, where Joyce employed dream logic and dream language. Like theoretician André Breton, Franco-American disciple Anaïs Nin was committed to depth psychology. She said in 1968:

> The conventional novel depicted character as a unity, already formed, while psychoanalysis studying the unconscious revealed the opposite, that character was fluctuating, relative, mutable, and asymmetrically developed, unevenly matured, with areas of rationality and areas of irrationality. I wanted to reveal not the fatality of character but its mysteries. . . . That is why I focused on dreams.[2]

Not only did postwar antirealistic American writers inherit her foreign tradition, but also a native tradition running from Poe through Hawthorne and Twain to Nathanael West and Djuna Barnes. Dreams occupy such books as *Ada*, *Death Kit*, *The Free-Lance Pallbearers*, and *A Hall of Mirrors*. Often they become nightmares, even echoing Twain's Satan when he said in *The Mysterious Stranger*, " '[T]here is no God, no universe, no human race, no earthly life, no heaven, no hell. It is all a Dream—a grotesque and foolish dream.' "

"Grotesque and foolish" dreams, dreamlike moments, and hallucinations flood John Hawkes's nightmarish canon. For example, during *The Lime Twig* (1961), the "worst dream, and best" of protagonist Michael Banks, concerns the racehorse Rock Castle, "which was itself the flesh of all violent dreams."[3] At the public lavatory, three eunuchs form "the triangle of his dreams" (94); at the widow's parlor, his orgy has dreamlike qualities. Nor do the nightmares of Monica and the hallucinations of wife Margaret, whose "own worst dream was one day to find him gone" (33), exhaust this irrational world. Their boarder Hencher functions as dreamer—"a man must take possession of a place if it is to be a home for the waiting out of dreams" (27)—*and* dream-detector too—"Behind each silent face was the dream" (26). Fittingly, then, the book unfolds in the interval between twilight and dawn. Thick beats Margaret and Sybilline seduces Michael during these hours; destiny for Hencher revolves around 3:00-4:00 A.M. when his mother died, his feeling over "home" grows acute, and his skull gets crushed; at 3:00 A.M. Annie visits Michael, and at about 4:00 A.M. Cowles killed the proctor.

Though not to the extent of surrealism, with which Hawkes has resisted identification,[4] Strindbergian techniques do appear. "Everything is possible" describes the arrival of the girl next door at the widow's parlor, just as the statement "The characters split, double . . . converge" describes the metamorphosis of Hencher into Cowles/constable, and the merging of the child-adult Margaret and the adult-child Monica during chapter 6. Time and space are not abrogated in *The Lime Twig*, but simultaneity results as Margaret's beating at the Roost alternates with Michael's orgy at the widow's parlor. Chapter 6 announces "It was 4 A.M.," then works backward to Thick's symbolic rape and forward to Larry's real rape; chapter 7 announces 'It was 2 A.M.," then reports Michael's sexual exploits and concern for Monica. 6 begins later than 7, yet the beating and the orgy represent two actions in different places transpiring concurrently.

Like Anaïs Nin, John Hawkes explores the unconscious. Infantile wishes and sexual anxieties abound. These and other distorted phenomena liberated from the authorial psyche suggest nightmare with its violence and bizarre humor. However, unlike Nin, Hawkes emphasizes the internconnectedness between public and private worlds. Public happenings reflect private desires: When Michael stops Rock Castle, "his own worst dream," the Golden Bowl also terminates. Michael's sacrificial atonement during the race, which was motivated by betrayal of Margaret and which was effected by death beneath "the silver horse," constitutes an apocalyptic event. Therefore, *The Lime Twig* merges dream/nightmare/apocalypse, a homology *Invisible Man* had extended nine years earlier to include Armageddon. The "three cardinal features" Ernest Jones examines in *On the Nightmare* —"agonizing dread," "suffocating sense of oppression," and "conviction of helpless paralysis"[5]—define both worlds.

William Burroughs creates self-contained nightmares too. He keeps a "dream diary" and expands "interesting or important" dreams into scenes that may appear "almost verbatim" as fiction: "The opening chapter of *Cities of the Red Night* . . . was . . . a dream . . . I had about a cholera epidemic. . . . And then the story *They Do Not Always Remember*, which appeared in *Exterminator*, was also a dream."[6]

Unlike Hawkes/Burroughs, many of whose books *are* nightmares, other antirealists, while treating similar aberrant material, set off their dream-scenes. Two particularly effective ones come to mind. Chapter 39 of Joseph Heller's *Catch-22* (1955), "The External City," deals with wartime Rome, a dark, dank, desolate, destroyed landscape. To protagonist Yossarian, arriving at and departing from this hellish wasteland via airplanes, "[n]othing warped seemed bizarre any more in his strange, distorted surroundings. The tops of sheer buildings slanted in weird, surrealistic perspective and the street seemed tilted."[7] He soon discovers "grotesque debris," for "[m]olars and broken incisors lay scattered everywhere" (406). Individuals seem as eerie as the environment. They include a "cadaverous" man "with a star-shaped scar in his cheek and a glossy mutilated depression the size of an egg in one temple," and a young woman "with her whole face disfigured by a God-awful pink and piebald burn" (407). Cruelty toward the helpless—children, women, old people, animals—is rampant: "On the other side of the intersection, a man was beating a dog with a stick like the man who was beating the horse with a whip in Raskolnikov's dream," and "At the next corner a man was beating a small boy brutally in the midst of an immobile crowd of adult spectators who made no effort to intervene" (405). Heller's nightmare concludes when Aarfy rapes innocent Michaela and throws her out the window. After Yossarian sees "the broken corpse" and reproaches him, the police arrest Yossarian and apologize to Aarfy.

During another impressive dream-scene, the last segment of Susan Sontag's *Death Kit* (1967), her self-destructive protagonist asks himself, "Is this place Diddy's nightmare? Or the resolution of his nightmare?"[8] That question remains unresolved, but the events leading toward it form one of the most ghastly journeys ever undertaken in American literature. They commence as Diddy leads his blind wife into a railroad tunnel where he may have committed murder earlier when their train stalled. Like Yossarian's Rome, this hellhole is dark, dank, and desolate, the perfect setting for the *déjà vu* sequence which follows. First, the murdered trackman reappears; then, as he behaves insolently again, Diddy again slays him with a crowbar. Afterwards, amid "brain juices and blood" (291), husband and wife repeat "the supplementary act" of love (289). While she sleeps securely, he nakedly enters the world inside the tunnel, "a long, wide, damp gallery" (292). Darkness gives way to light, coldness to heat. Here, Diddy reads "quotations and mottos . . . all relating loosely to the theme of death" (295). Next he discovers "a storage place for surplus bodies . . . of both sexes and all ages" (298–99), and later, having traversed "still more rooms" (302), he locates "the second grand crypt" (304), whose corpses stand upright and whose descriptive details are more ghoulish than anything conceived by Poe or Hawkes. Specialized smaller rooms containing children, firemen, priests, Civil War veterans, sports figures, and workers follow. Yet, rather than making the protagonist "physically uncomfortable," "this charnel house . . . is curiously soothing" (309). The nightmare and the book end with "More rooms. Diddy walks on, looking for his death. Diddy has made his final chart; drawn up his last map. Diddy has perceived the inventory of the world" (312). About Ms. Sontag's American necropolis, Frederick R. Karl observes, "Minimalism meets apocalypse."[9]

Because of films like *Apocalypse Now* and studies like *The Late Great Planet Earth*, even nonreligious Americans are becoming familiar with the term "apocalypse." It derives from "apokalypsis," a Greek word meaning "revelation," and defines certain Judeo-Christian works (The Book of Daniel; The Revelation of Saint John the Divine) that disclose God's eternal design, though, as Mircea Eliade points out, the "apocalyptic syndrome" pervades other traditions too. R. W. B. Lewis has listed the ten biblical stages:

(1) periodic natural disturbances, earthquakes and the like; (2) the advent and the turbulent reign of the Antichrist or the false Christ or false prophet (sometimes called the period of the Great Tribulation); (3) the second coming of Christ and (4) the resultant cosmic warfare (Armageddon) that brings in (5) the millennium—that is, from the Latin, the period of one thousand years, the epoch of the Messianic Kingdom upon earth; thereafter, (6) the gradual degeneration of human and physical nature, the last and worst apostasy (or falling away from God), featured by (7) the second and briefer "loosening of Satan"; (8) an ultimate catastrophe, the end of the world by

fire; (9) the Last Judgement; and (10) the appearance of the new heaven and earth.[10]

Among Western literatures, American literature, whose historical background emphasizes beginning anew, is the most consistently and pervasively apocalyptic.[11] Such early writings as John Cotton's sermons, Edward Johnson's *Wonder-Working Providence*, Michael Wigglesworth's *The Day of Doom*, Increase Mather's *The Necessity of Reformation*, Jonathan Edwards's "Notes on the Apocalypse," and Joseph Morgan's *The History of the Kingdom of Basaruah* launched this tradition. Nineteenth-century authors cited for apocalyptic ideas and images include Charles Brockden Brown, James Fenimore Cooper, Edgar Allan Poe, Nathaniel Hawthorne, Herman Melville, and Mark Twain. Of their fictions, *Moby-Dick* (1851) and *A Connecticut Yankee in King Arthur's Court* (1889) are the best examples because these novels more fully than other contemporaneous texts enact the religious apocalypse, albeit in the unorthodox, secular ways congenial to the modern imagination.

The positive apocalypse of Melville and the ambiguous apocalypse of Twain become the negative apocalypses of modern literature. W. B. Yeats's "The Second Coming" illustrates the later need to invert such phenomena. As in orthodox apocalypses, there are natural disturbances: "Things fall apart; the centre cannot hold." Predictably, "some revelation is at hand," and the millennium too, after "twenty centuries of stony sleep." Yet, instead of the Messiah, our "Second Coming" brings a nightmarish "rough beast." Robert Frost and T. S. Eliot share this inversion. Frost's "Fire and Ice" begins, "Some say the world will end in fire, / Some say in ice/," and Eliot's "The Hollow Men" concludes, "This is the way the world ends / Not with a bang but a whimper."

Native postwar apocalypses take two forms. On the one hand, we get the private sacrifice *(The Lime Twig)*, derived from the crucifixion of Christ, and, on the other, the group cataclysm *(Cities of the Red Night)*, derived from the destruction of Babylon. Faulkner's *Light in August* (1932) and West's *Day of the Locust* (1939) prefigure this division. Reminiscent of Billy Budd, Joe Christmas functions as scapegoat in *Light in August*. His executioner is a National Guard captain/American legion member. Bigot and super patriot, Percy Grimm shoots, then castrates symbolic Christmas. The latter, another Billy Budd—who, "ascending" to be hung, "took the full rose of dawn"—becomes apotheosized: "Upon that black blast the man seemed to rise soaring into their memories forever and ever." *The Day of the Locust* demonstrates that the more ordinary and secular group catastrophe transpires publicly too. West dramatizes his apocalypse during a Kahn's Persian Palace Theatre world premiere, where thousands of people have gathered. The ensuing riot, which accentuates sexual violation, was foretold by a prophetic painting artist-protagonist Tod Hackett had titled "The Burning of Los Angeles."

Like the expiation involving Michael Banks, our contemporary apocalypses focused on the individual tend to reflect their Christian origin. We would expect this from Roman Catholic Flannery O'Connor's *oeuvre*, where moments of grace are legion. Thus, in "A Good Man Is Hard to Find," the talkative grandmother makes contact with the outcast Misfit just before he fires, and, afterwards, we visualize "her face smiling up at the cloudless sky." And in "Greenleaf," when the potent bull gores hypocritical Mrs. May, "she had the look of a person whose sight has been suddenly restored but who finds the light unbearable."[12] Less expected is the Christian imagery that appears during antirealistic fictions as profane as *The Lime Twig* by authors as irreverent as John Hawkes. For example, Gaddis's *The Recognitions* terminates disastrously Easter Sunday inside the church at Fenestrula. There, organist Stanley, tragic counterpart of protagonist Wyatt, plays his composition despite admonitions from an Italian priest. When the building collapses and he dies, Gaddis comments, "Everything moved, and even falling, soared in atonement."[13] A more graphic and poignant Sabbath transcendence accompanies the Times Square electrocution of Ethel Rosenberg during *The Public Burning*. Coover commemorates this: "Her body, sizzling and popping like firecrackers, lights up with the force of the current, casting a flickering radiance on all those around her, and so she burns—and burns—and burns—as though held aloft by her own incandescent will and haloed about by all the gleaming great of the nation—".[14] One literal crucifixion occurs among postwar American novels in *Mrs. October Was Here*, whose title character selects it over hanging and then sketches a cross replete with PATIBULUM, STIPES, SEDILE, SUPPENDANEUM, and the legend NAILS THROUGH WRISTS—NOT PALMS.

Capturing the absurdity of contemporary apocalypses, Dowell includes suggestions regarding how to stage his spectacle: The crucifix could be "built on a revolving turntable" or the crowd could be lowered from helicopter ropes "round and round the agonizing figure." Finally, TV camera and commentator are chosen because these enable everybody both to participate and to observe.[15] The more commonplace symbolic crucifixion is typified by the shafting of Maximilian Spielman atop Founder's Hill as *Giles Goat-Boy* climaxes. Another spectacle, this Barthian event features "martial music," "strolling vendors," and newspaper headlines. Soon Max appears amid drum rolls, "[b]ent under the weight of a block-and-tackle rig" rather than a crucifix. They strap him onto the shaft and Max slowly ascends toward its flaming tip, where he gloriously combusts, showering "upon us all, gentle ashes."[16]

Group cataclysms, which contain fewer religious associations, also transpire at either real or unreal locations. Two representative apocalyptic novels from the early 1970s treat authentic geography. Walker Percy's *Love in the Ruins*, whose subtitle concludes *Near the End of the World*, focuses on survivor Thomas More occupying Louisiana while blacks have made Boston, Chicago, Detroit, Los Angeles, and Washington city-states. Thomas Pynchon's *Gravity's Rainbow* closes when the Blicero-Gottfried 00000 Rocket, portending nuclear devastation, plunges "nearly a mile per second" toward "this old theatre" (the Los Angeles Orpheus on Melrose?).[17] More exotic mass disasters mark *Cat's Cradle*, *The Soft Machine*, and *The Free-Lance Pallbearers*, for their unreal settings—San Lorenzo, Slotless City, Soulsville—become ravaged through *"ice-nine,"* "the Sex Enemy," and "manure." All five books are to a greater or lesser extent science fictions.

Because they treat the group cataclysm so elaborately and vividly, *The Origin of the Brunists* (1966) by Robert Coover and *A Hall of Mirrors* (1967) by Robert Stone deserve special consideration. The first takes place in fabulous West Condon and the second in factual New Orleans, but both employ multiple third-person perspectives, the first more elaborately than the second. Whereas narrative focus shifts during *A Hall of Mirrors* among three figures—Rheinhardt, Geraldine, and Morgan Rainey—whose lives interrelate, *The Origin of the Brunists* encompasses an entire town, moving montagelike from one resident to another even within chapters. The two novels, nevertheless, share discernible protagonists who function as professional communicators. Justin "Tiger" Miller of Coover's tale is a journalist, and Rheinhardt of Stone's story, a radio personality. Cynical anti-heroes, they survive, while their innocent sweethearts, Marcella and Geraldine, become victimized martyrs.

Fascistic Matthew J. Bingamon, who owns station wusa (where Rheinhardt works), organizes his patriotic revival at New Orleans's Sport Palace during *A Hall of Mirrors*. The guest list includes power structure representatives from the military services, politics, religion, and so forth. These bigots hate Negroes, Jews, Communists, hippies, and sexual deviants. They listen to songs like "Rally Round the Flag Boys" and "Leaning on the Everlasting Arm," and watch events like the shooting contest between The Sacramento Kid and Sidewinder Bates. Speeches are delivered, one by imposter Farley the Sailor, which poses " 'this small embattled band of Christians' " against " 'the face of Darkness Outside,' "[18] and one by Rheinhardt, self-styled " 'master of escape . . . master of disguise' " (147), which begins " 'Let us consider the American Way' " (366). Violence directed toward the enemy boomerangs, as in *The Day of the Locust:* "There were people fighting in the stands" (369). Injured Admiral Bofslar declares, " 'We're under attack. All sides. No quarter asked. None given. Armageddon' " (371). However, despite a mad Wobbly's abortive assassination attempt, no real confrontation can develop because Bingamon hired the blacks to provoke the whites. Farley kills this "Evil King" (326) and is accompanied on his crime spree and flight by cosurvivor Rheinhardt.[19] Bearing the name of Ellison's prototypical con artist, Stone's anti-hero symbolizes " 'the New Man' " (398).

The Origin of the Brunists, where such words as "Second Coming," "Apocalyptic," and "Antichrist" appear, treats the group cataclysm even more explicitly. Except for the epilogue, all six sections of the Coover text bear an epigraph denoted "Revelation to John." A disastrous mine explosion occurs in West Condon and afterward a religious cult grows up around Giovanni Bruno, who believes he alone was saved to proclaim the end of the world. Through opportunistic newspaper owner Tiger Miller, this cult receives national attention and support. The conflict between cult and community, between Brunists and Christians, reaches its climax one Sunday at the Mount of Redemption. A carnival atmosphere prevails: ticket booth, refreshment stands, bingo game, numbers game. When rain starts to fall, the cult members go wild—"people leaped up in the air as though trying to fly, ran about, rolled in the mud"[20]—and some helpless individuals die, including Marcella. Otherwise, mocks Coover, there were "only broken heads, collapsed lungs, bruised bellies, crushed spines . . . minor statistics."[21] Miller is brutalized, but, like Rheinhardt, he lives to leave town (with Happy Bottom, the blasphemous Whore of Babylon resurrected). Armageddon has confirmed what we previously suspected, that Brunists and Christians are both dangerous fanatics.

A Hall of Mirrors and The Origin of the Brunists typify modern apocalyptic fictions. They dramatize "warfare," yet the forces involved do not stand for allegorical "good" and "evil" since the two factions behave savagely, even toward themselves. No millennium, no Messiah here; rather, mere survivors, some moral, some immoral. As Yeats lamented in "The Second Coming," "The best lack all conviction, while the worst / Are full of passionate intensity."

Many American novels preoccupied with dreams also contain cataclysmic endings to suggest that Armageddon may be our ultimate collective nightmare. Nowhere is the homology uniting dream/nightmare/Armageddon/apocalypse more effectively presented than during Ralph Ellison's Invisible Man (1952).

This work takes his nameless black protagonist on a quest for self-identity from South to North, from boyhood to manhood, from fool (student) to sage (writer) via several initiatory embroilments comprised of battle royal, Golden Day calamity, job hunt, Liberty Paints incident, factory hospital stay, eviction-riot, cast-iron bank episode, Ras conflict, Clifton murder, and Rinehart sequence. Throughout these, "dream," "dreams," "dreamer," "dreaming," and "dreamed" recur. More significant, though, are the references to being awake or being asleep. They prepare us for the twilight state between wakefulness and sleep that attracted Hawthorne, Poe, Hawkes, and Djuna Barnes. The question posed by Keats's "Ode to a Nightingale," "Do I wake or sleep?" elicits an answer from the "invisible" first-person narrator: "It was a state neither of dreaming nor of waking, but somewhere in between, in which I was caught like Trueblood's jaybird that yellow jackets had paralyzed in every part but his eyes."[22] Accordingly, Jonathan Baumbach remarks:

> *Invisible Man* takes place, for the most part, in the uncharted spaces between the conscious and the unconscious, in the semilit darkness where nightmare verges on reality and the external world has all the aspects of a disturbing dream. . . . A sleepwalker in a world never real enough for him to believe in, the hero experiences a succession of awakenings, only to find himself participating in still another level of nightmare.[23]

Because this paralytic condition encompasses now sleep (darkness, "illusionment"), now wakefulness (light, enlightenment), Ellison's style—unjustly criticized for inconsistency—juxtaposes realism and surrealism. Therefore, we repeatedly find words like "real," "reality," "unreal," "unreality," and "surreal," too.

Five literal dreams appear in *Invisible Man*. One "recurring nightmare" belongs to the "beautiful girl" of the prologue who functions as the protagonist's equivalent when she dreams about her face "becoming a formless mass" (6), and one belongs to the black sharecropper of chapter 2 who dreams about the guilt and punishment attendant upon sexual relations with a white woman while actually, if involuntarily, seducing his own daughter. The three other dreams spring from the protagonist himself. Number two (chapter 1) "was a dream I was to remember and dream again for many years." It involves "my grandfather" and Dr. Bledsoe's later letter stating "Keep This Nigger-Boy Running" (33). Both the first or marijuna dream (prologue) and the third or coal cellar dream (just before the epilogue) occur underground and frame the narrative. That they are italicized stresses their importance. Of the first, Fritz Gysin writes:

> The peculiar form of this dream is largely determined by the fact that it combines several functions: A rapid descent into the dreamer's subconsciousness, which takes him to the origins of his existence, is connected with a slower but generally accelerating ascent, in which he is confronted with his mythical past; furthermore, the dream anticipates certain impulses of the plot and at the same time reproduces some significant experiences of the dreamer's former life aboveground.[24]

In the third dream, the protagonist is "the prisoner of a group consisting of Jack and old Emerson and Bledsoe and Norton and Ras and the school superintendent and a number of others." These men, who "had run me," castrate him, then query, " 'How does it feel to be free of one's illusions?' " With reference to his testicles dangling beneath a bridge, he replies, " '[T]here's your universe, and that drip-drop upon the water you hear is all the history you've made, and all you're going to make' " (556–58).

Ironically, the real world seems even more nightmarish than this dream world. Several episodes leading toward the final apocalypse are surrealistic. Among them, chapter 11, the factory hospital stay, is most bizarre. We move from the black and white imagery of chapter 10 to white imagery befitting a medical center staffed by Caucasians. Ellison's hero, having injured his head at the paint factory, experiences disorientation in its hospital. During the episode, he wavers between consciousness and unconsciousness, between wakefulness and sleep—that "helpless paralysis" Ernest Jones attributes to nightmare. He can neither cry out nor rise up; hallucinations occur; sights and sounds become distorted. Grotesquery prevails: "A pair of eyes peered down through lenses as thick as the bottom of a Coca-Cola bottle, eyes protruding, luminous and veined, like an old biology specimen preserved in alcohol" (230). A disembodied voice explains: " 'The machine will produce the results of a pre-frontal lobotomy. . . . and the result is as complete a change of personality as you'll find. . . . society will suffer no traumata on his account' " (231). Another shock treatment follows (compare *One Flew Over the Cuckoo's Nest*), then a series of increasingly absurd questions: " 'WHAT . . . IS . . . YOUR . . . NAME? / WHO . . . ARE . . . YOU? / WHAT IS YOUR MOTHER'S NAME? / WHO WAS BUCKEYE THE RABBIT? / BOY, WHO WAS BRER RABBIT?' " (234–36). When the protagonist fails to answer, he is pronounced cured and leaves the hospital "in the grip of some alien personality" but "no longer afraid" (243).

This and other episodes contribute to what Zbigniew Lewicki considers unique about the Ellison text:

Invisible Man thus stands alone in American literature as a novel which presents the cyclic apocalypse. The book develops through a series of cyclic sub-structures, all of which possess characteristic apocalyptic features. The life of the unnamed narrator uncoils not as a continuity, but in semi-independent phases, which all end in a symbolic death. The hero is then "reborn" and begins a new cycle.[25]

The culmination of this cycle and the final apocalypse of *Invisible Man* occupies chapter 25. It contains four sections. The first focuses on the protagonist's activities with Dupre and Scofield, and his simultaneous conversion to the people and alienation from the Brotherhood; the second focuses on his encounter with Ras the Exhorter/Destroyer; the third on the skirmishes between the latter and the police; and the fourth on the protagonist, immobile in the coal cellar, and his castration fantasy, which caps the dream pattern that gives the chapter such a nightmarish atmosphere. The first three sections cohere through the running motif, introduced previously, as the discombobulated hero heads for the Brotherhood clutching the briefcase given him after the battle royal.

Armageddon during segment one, where the protagonist hears " 'Time's flying / Souls dying / The coming of the Lord / Draweth niiiigh!' " (541), involves Harlem blacks versus establishment whites, whom "white-helmeted policemen" (539) represent. Here, amid chaotic sights and sounds, there are several grimly funny looting scenes like the four men pushing a safe or the "huge woman" atop "a Borden's milk wagon . . . drinking beer" (532). This abuse of property is epitomized when Dupre, Scofield, and others burn down their tenement. The protagonist, wounded earlier and a lifesaver later, assists them, since he has become *engaged*, knowing, despite rumors, that "The Committee had planned it. And I had helped, had been a tool" (541). Segment one ends on the following grotesque note: " 'I ran as in a dream. . . . Ahead of me the body hung, white, naked, and horribly feminine from a lamppost. . . . I had turned some nightmarish somersault. . . . and now there was another and another, seven. . . . They were mannequins—'Dummies!' " (543).

Sections 2 and 3 also invoke Armageddon, though with different warriors. During 2, the protagonist meets Ras "upon a great black horse. . . . in the costume of an Abyssinian chieftan" (544). After the black nationalist attacks, shouting, " 'Betrayer!' " (545), the protagonist, who feels "a certain new sense of self" (544), claims the Brotherhood planned this "race riot" and is using Ras "to do their work" (545). Then the black nationalist yells, " 'Hang him!' " and the protagonist flings back the spear, which rips "through both cheeks" (547) of his opponent. Eventually, he is saved from Ras's followers and the police by a broken water main.

Segment 3 commences when the protagonist overhears a conversation detailing the battle that had occurred " 'over on Lenox about two hours ago' " between Ras and the mounted police. This is rendered comically in terms of cowboys and knights. Ras, with " 'a big black hoss and a fur cap and some kind of old lion skin' " (549), had charged, bearing spiked shield and spear, but, driven off through gunfire, " 'him and that hoss shot up the street leaping like Heigho, the goddam Silver!' " (552). Soon the protagonist, also in flight, falls down an open manhole.

Here, during section 4, he creates light by burning the contents of the now-battered briefcase—"my high-school diploma," "the anonymous letter" (555), and so forth—all symbolic of the past. Revelation produces outrage, so the protagonist throws a tantrum before that "state neither of dreaming nor of waking" (556) yields the castration dream.

Aware at last, Ellison's invisible man, like Melville's Ishmael or Fitzgerald's Nick, who also participate in absurd quests, will tell his story, and thus lead himself and us toward fuller understanding. This postwar masterpiece has a more positive conclusion than most antirealistic apocalypses. Even so, it is presented as question rather than assertion: "Who knows but that, on the lower frequencies, I speak for you?" (568).

Coda

Though many postwar antirealistic American fictions include much from the eleven interrelated patterns explored in *Alternate Worlds*, no single text incorporates everything that has been discussed. Nevertheless, let us postulate, by way of summation, such a hypothetical, all-inclusive work.

Like *Invisible Man*, it would have to treat the dream/nightmare/Armageddon/apocalypse cluster, yet unlike Ellison's novel, it could be self-contained nightmare (Hawkes, Burroughs) rather than nightmarish receptacle for dreams. This hypothetical work might treat the group cataclysm, as do *Invisible Man* and other narratives derived from the destruction of Babylon, or the private sacrifice, as do *The Lime Twig* and other narratives derived from the crucifixion of Christ. If the more secular group cataclysm were chosen, the contending forces need not be racial, but political, or religious. Nor need their conflict—whether realistically located—end on a positive note, with the protagonist (writer) offering us humanistic alternatives *(Invisible Man)*, for, most often, we get cynical survivors who view relative good and evil opportunistically, two instances being Rheinhardt (radio personality) in *A Hall of Mirrors* and Miller (journalist) in *The Origin of the Brunists.*

If Armageddon and apocalypse represent the improbable bang in Eliot's famous line about how the world will end, entropy represents the probable whimper. Our hypothetical work, on the one hand, then, would have to show life becoming inert through entropic processes involving thermodynamics and cybernetics. As the world grows colder and colder and communication grows rarer and rarer, waste and noise proliferate, with excrement/sex/death forming a homology comparable to dream/nightmare/Armageddon/apocalypse. Consequently, order gives way to disorder, animateness to inanimateness. Whether entropy—the ultimate "scientific" catastrophe (Frost's ice) —precipitates, accompanies, or displaces apocalypse—the ultimate "metaphysical" catastrophe (Frost's fire)—the first, because it lacks the energy of the second, wherein forces, however ambivalent, clash, must be the more horrendous.

On the other hand, our hypothetical work should also have to treat conspiracy, the third avenue toward annihilation in postwar antirealistic American writing. This phenomenon may operate nationally, internationally, even extraterrestrially, and it affects all institutions, whose victims can defend themselves only through self-protective paranoia, which, when posed against a logical but mad universe, seems sane. The few preterites embodying the life-force are individuated enough to become protagonal characters, while their plentiful and powerful persecutors remain types that unconsciously yet successfully abet entropic sameness and apocalyptic havoc. These death-driven conspirators have dominated history, an unreliable record of intrigue characterized by fact and fancy, plot and counterplot, nonfictitious and fictitious documentation, and myth and ritual.

A world about to destruct through apocalypse, entropy, and conspiracy is absurd, as any all-inclusive postwar antirealistc American fiction would demonstrate. Thus, most questers, who are fundamentally fools, fulfill only in part the monomyth embodying heroic odysseys: dubious parentage, call to adventure, Wise Old Man, descent into hell, and mystical marriage. While these involve departure and initiation, the third prinicpal component—return—may often be absent, for this fiction does not usually give doomed humanity hopeful signals. Indeed, the once affirmative journey with a goal has become at best inconclusive. Defamiliarized by parody, it now recalls the mock epic. Questers making journeys during our hypothetical text must traverse landscapes stranger than themselves. No longer merely perilous or dreamlike, the terrain seems questionable—perhaps a figment of the author's imagination. Fabulous locations mingle with real or disguised places to illustrate how the actual and the fanciful fuse, as might the conscious and the unconscious. Not unexpectedly, these landscapes can produce hybrid nationalities and languages. The malformed and estranged creatures who occupy such improbable locales frequently share grotesque objects and situations; some are even demonic, since, after all, theirs is a mad world.

The most obvious symptom of this madness appears in omnipresent disjointedness. Forecasting the new apocalypse, Yeats wrote, "The center gives / Things fall apart"—precisely what happens during *The Waste Land* and related antirealistic American works when metamorphosis or the evolution of one character to another and androgyny or the superimposition of one sex on another happen. Human and artistic fragmentation take diverse additional forms, but not without resistance from artists whose conservative bent counteracts discord through techniques like montage and collage. Conversely, the radical imagination, which fears coherence because of its hierarchical implications, enlists these and more extreme devices to ensure a fractured reality. Conservatives and radicals alike have also employed Dos Passos's mixed focus, whose third-person voice shifts, sometimes calculatedly, sometimes randomly, among several fictional personages. Multiple perspectives produce multiple plots, so that decentralized characterization and decentralized structure become inextricable. Though it is possible to emphasize an absurd heroic protagonist while alternating narrative attention, even a hypothetical book would not view fragmentation both conservatively and radically.

Nor could it be both a maximalist and a minimalist novel, but, because antirealistic texts, as opposed to realistic ones, perpetuate the "Learned Wit" tradition, probably our all-inclusive effort would celebrate language through amplification. Within this context of abstruse

knowledge, either satire or parody could dominate, though rarely
function alone. Playfulness, which appears throughout most antirealistic texts besides the encyclopedic novel, might extend from actual
games-become-aesthetic-strategies to experiments treating syntax,
punctuation, typography, and graphics during narratives blending
several genres and styles. These are among the hallmarks defining
what many call "metafiction" or "the story of writing" rather than
"the writing of story." According to Robert Alter, "the continuous
acrobatic display of artifice in a self-conscious novel is an enlivening
demonstration of human order against a background of chaos and
darkness," yet he soon adds that autoreferential books paradoxically
represent "a long meditation on death" too.[26] Obviously, our new
authorial gods contrive alternate worlds as darkly humorous as the
one created by Faulkner's "cosmic joker."

James W. Tuttleton and John Kuehl

Tuttleton: The historic task of literature, namely to hold a mirror up to nature, to represent life realistically, with the premium on verisimilitude, has been commended by artists and critics at least since Aristotle first commented on mimesis in the *Poetics*. I find it disturbing that the contemporary postmodern antirealists have abandoned this task. What accounts for their bias against realism in fiction?

Kuehl: It has to do with the notion that reality is unknowable and that those who propose otherwise, namely the realists, are actually illusionist writers. They create the illusion that reality exists through verisimilitude, the fourth wall of an Ibsen play. Coleridge's "willing suspension of disbelief" presents no problem to the average person because he or she automatically suspends disbelief when he or she sees a play or a movie or whatever, but it is a problem for the antirealists, who feel that disbelief should not be suspended.

T: I find the metafictionists—who introduce themselves, by name, into their fiction—rather self-indulgent, if not egotistical. Does this use of the writer's personal identity, his personal voice, have a special literary value?

K: The metafictionists are authors who impose self-consciousness on literature and appear in their own books by initials or anagrams. They may talk about the writing process in terms of the book they are actually writing. For example, in *Giles Goat-Boy* there is a woman reading *Giles* on the very page where we encounter her. But I wouldn't say that the revelation of "personal identity" or "personal voice" is necessarily self-indulgent, since the metafictionists see themselves as fictional characters. Besides, more typically, these writers use the third person because, to create comedy, there must be distance. In novelists like John Hawkes, who do not introduce themselves directly, there may also be a preoccupation with the story of writing rather than the writing of story. He often employs the first person or a combination of first- and third-person voices. His self-conscious storytellers include Zizendorf of *The Cannibal*, Skipper of *Second Skin*, and Cyril of *The Blood Oranges*. Like authorial self-consciousness, narratorial self-consciousness is more central to them than experiential life. The egotism you sense probably comes from the fact that most metafictional writers are authoritarian; they have replaced the God of the Bible in what Nathanael West termed "our godless actuality." Their microcosmic creations are similar to the macrocosm except that they substitute a world of words for a world of phenomena. Barth says he doesn't think God is a bad author for a realist, but realism is rather boring. Another godlike novelist is John Hawkes, who claims that he controls everything in his books, and is, therefore, a very formal artist. He eschews automatic writing as in the surrealists and rejects the notion of organic growth as in the novels of Mark Twain.

T: At the very least, the metafictionists are "excessive," wouldn't you agree?

K: This stems from the inclusiveness of maximalist or gigantic fiction —the encyclopedic novel. Thomas LeClair praises books like William Gaddis's *J R* because, according to him, Gaddis is trying to render a whole society, a whole culture characterized by excess.

T: I see this as the "fallacy of imitative form," although one does get in some maximalist novels, supercharged with excess, a great deal of represented human experience.

K: Such books are exceedingly repetitious. They seem to be hostile at times toward the reader by subjecting him or her to a vast body of arcane knowledge.

T: Yes, the maximalist incorporates into his novel massive erudition, learning, and fact—usually in the service of so-called Menippean satire.

K: Alexander Theroux's *Darconville's Cat* has one passage written backwards in Latin. The reader is taxed with long lists in this kind of fiction, most notably those created by Gilbert Sorrentino. But lists appear elsewhere too. Even though they are defended by Sorrentino and William Gass, the reader tends to skip them.

T: So there is a risk these writers run of losing our attention?

K: No doubt. I have talked about *J R* to many literary people who can't read through the entire book. The first time I tried I got to page 150 and I had to give up. The next time I marked my own transitions, since they're not provided by the author. Incidentally, Coleman Dowell discovered he couldn't read Gaddis's first novel, *The Recognitions,* even though it has a more developed plot than *J R,* which is really an auditory achievement.

T: In *The Recognitions* and Thomas Pynchon's *Gravity's Rainbow* we have instances of learned wit. What is the aesthetic function of the display of encyclopedic knowledge about specific subjects like forgery or rocketry?

K: Comic writers are sensitive to the learned wit tradition that embraces *Gargantua and Pantagruel* and *Tristram Shandy.* Rabelais and Sterne fashioned complete universes and that is what the maximalists seek. Now these universes, following the American example of *Moby-Dick,* are international geographically and intellectually. Their creators tend to be academics who teach creative writing. As such, they are more aware of the history of ideas and literary history than ordinary authors. Whereas American writers before World War II were often involved in the experiential world through journalism (e.g., Stephen Crane, Frank Norris, Theodore Dreiser, Ernest Hemingway), the later group possesses the M.A. and a university appointment. Still, their excessiveness celebrates the largeness of life. This *joie de vivre* is markedly different from the bare texts offered us by Donald Barthelme and other minimalists.

T: What is the purpose of stripping down the narrative to slight, minimalist form?

K: To get the poetic essence, perhaps. It would be impossible for bawdy comic writers celebrating language and literature to practice the art of innuendo, undertone, nuance. But both maximalism and minimalism are as old as literature itself. *Don Quixote,* a massive novel at the beginning of our Western tradition, is full of erudition. By the same token, we have always had a minimalist impulse too. In prose fiction, Flaubert tried to eliminate every word that was not precise. I've called minimalists and maximalists "leaver-outers" and "putter-inners," after Thomas Wolfe. When responding to Scott Fitzgerald, whom he regarded as a "leaver-outer," Wolfe argued that there have also been great "putter-inners" like himself. If the foremost contemporary "putter-inner" is William Gaddis, surely the foremost contemporary "leaver-outer" is Donald Barthelme, who displays his wares not only in short stories but in spare novels such as *The Dead Father* and *Snow White*. However, if we are to trust the recent *Mississippi Review* critics (Winter 1985), minimalism is more nearly aligned with realistic than antirealistic writing. For instance, thinking of writers like Raymond Carver and Bobbie Ann Mason, Joe David Bellamy uses the term "minimalist/realist," and Raymond Federman refers to "a kind of realist revival." Even so, in the theatre since the 1950s, we have had several absurd one-act plays from nonrealistic Beckett, Ionesco, Adamov, Pinter and Genet. Sometimes a maximalist will pay tribute to minimalism, as demonstrated by Barth's piece in the *New York Times Book Review*.

T: Joyce wanted to get all narrative reduced into the single sentence or the single word. In Beckett we have the impulse to reduce even the single word to mere "breath" (in the play of that name). Blanchot advances the idea of a literature in which language disappears into itself. Do we have in the minimalist novel the impulse toward the disappearance of language itself and then the disappearance of the novel into utter silence?

K: Only in Beckett, the father of contemporary minimalism. No one else is so extreme, not even Barthelme, who calls excess verbiage "filling" or "stuffing." Such antirealists are hardly typical minimalists, though, since minimalism, we are told, is preoccupied with rendering surface reality.

T: Don't maximalist books often mix genres and styles with varying tones of parody and satire that result in defamiliarization?

K: Sorrentino's *Blue Pastoral* parodies a whole range of genres and styles traditionally associated with the pastoral, and at the same time, satirizes the academic world. This is not new if we think, for example, of the mock epic during the eighteenth century and before. Defamiliarization, or taking the familiar and giving it an unfamiliar aura may also be associated with romanticism, particularly the *Lyrical Ballads* preface. So there's nothing really experimental about defamiliarization. Rather, we have a question of degree, for this recent body of literature is crowded with works that parody, burlesque, or travesty various genres and styles. Besides Sorrentino's *Blue Pastoral* and *Mulligan Stew*, a notable instance is *Darconville's Cat*, which mocks a whole range of literary genres and styles. To find an immediate precedent for such work, we need only remember *Ulysses* and *Finnegans Wake*.

T: What's the advantage of shattering the boundaries of a genre and merging it with others? Do the metafictionists want merely to call attention to the artifice of art or is there some other purpose?

K: Certainly they want to call attention to the artifice of art. But also, when you cross styles, you destroy the illusion that literature represents the real. Anything hierarchical, anything signifying order is inimical to the antirealists. For example, the hierarchy of forms Northrop Frye dicusses in *Anatomy of Criticism*, which stands for an ongoing way of rendering reality. In effect, the antirealists are telling us that there is no reason for not mixing poetry and prose, sonnets and epics, because nothing can oppose it.

T: This bears upon the issue of the ludic impulse, whose practitioners take liberties with not only the formal characteristics of genres but with syntax, punctuation, the alphabet, typography, and so forth. How successful, do you think, is this kind of play?

K: Sometimes highly successful if you are able to tolerate it. Walter Abish's *Alphabetical Africa* uses a seldom-seen form that would attract only those drawn to ingenuity and manipulation. Abish writes the first chapter solely with words beginning with "A," then adds "B," "C," and others in subsequent chapters until he reaches the full alphabet, at which point he proceeds backwards and takes the letters away one by one in chapter after chapter. Game-playing is central to this kind of fiction because the world is perceived as verbal rather than phenomenal.

T: Abish's playing with the lipogram calls attention to the writer as the constructor of games, puzzles, and enigmas in his work. And he very often introduces himself, so that we have a literature that is self-conscious, with the processes of fiction elevated to the status of theme. Although Tzvetan Todorov affirms that "not only is all fiction fiction about fiction, but all fiction about fiction is . . . fiction about life," does this kind of life have any great interest or significance for the reader who is not a writer? What is the value for the nonwriter of learning, via fiction, how fiction is written?

K: Fiction about fiction is fiction about life in the sense that fiction is an aspect of life, an aspect of attraction to the metafictionists' audience of literary people with like minds, rather than humanity at large. Consequently, few books emerging from this movement have become popular. Barth's more or less realistic *Floating Opera* and *End of the Road* sold quite well, but the later tomes like *Letters*—his supreme metafictional achievement—have been remaindered. Few academics have read *Giles Goat-Boy* despite the fact that it is an academic novel with an academic appeal. Contemporary antirealists, whether reflexive or non-reflexive, will always have a small audience, Gaddis being a case in point.

T: Writers preoccupied with game-playing and the creation of wholly self-contained artifacts seem to be extensions of the art-for-art's sake movement. But I wonder, given the types of experience narrated, whether they aren't also extensions of the decadent movement lately arrived in America.

K: Well, it's interesting that so many of their techniques were inspired by surrealism and dadaism—for example, the proliferation of objects or the loss of bodily parts as during *V.*, which consequently becomes grotesque and nightmarish. Another French "school" related to dadaism, deconstruction has also affected books like *Giles Goat-Boy* and *Blue Pastoral*. The gusto over havoc shown by Barth and Sorrentino here is surely decadent, while their celebration of language and literature is reminiscent of the art-for-art's sake credo.

T: Is the resurgence of the framework narrative another aspect of the ludic impulse?

K: Yes, that and the antirealistic fondness for manipulating genres. By juxtaposing frame and framed story, the author may impart meaning. The framed story was frequently a dream in older literature, with the protagonist falling asleep during the opening frame. His dream would occupy the framed story, but, then, at the closure, the character woke up and reality reappeared. In the tall tale, reality is juxtaposed to extravagant events, the frame being realistic and the framed story fabulous. The frameworks of Barth and Nabokov cause calculated confusion, as they throw the certainty of the framed story into doubt. *Lolita*'s framework represents the world after Humbert Humbert dies. The opening frame, narrated by a psychologist, one John Ray, judges him, while the closing frame, narrated later by author Vladimir Nabokov, judges Ray. Barth's frameworks are even more ambiguous, casting greater doubt on the story than the story itself does. If we read *Giles Goat-Boy* without the frame, it would be far less confusing. Many critics feel that closure destroys this novel, since it undermines whatever Barth was trying to communicate. There is a pervasive use of frames in antirealistic writing, which varies depending on the fictional content. Sometimes these remain open as when books like *Mulligan Stew* begin with a frame that is never closed, but most often the frame forms double brackets. However the frame operates, the sharp differences between it, or present reality, and the framed story, or past fantasy, make this convention irresistible to our antirealists. Through the art of juxtaposition, which is both modern and postmodern, rather than nineteenth-century transition, they present their material.

T: Understandably writers depicting a fragmented world would choose juxtaposition over transition.

K: Yes. Those who regard reality as broken and nightmarish have usually been influenced by *The Waste Land*. If the author happens to be conservative like Eliot, he or she will seek coherence. Thus, Coleman Dowell and William Gaddis use collage and montage to restore order. In the case of individuals like William Burroughs and Thomas Pynchon, who fear systems and who believe that ultimate evil comes from institutional life, the goal is to break down hierarchical coherence through devices such as Burroughs' cut-up method.

T: Does the unity attained by collage and montage imitate external reality? Or does it derive from imagination only, as manifested in the artwork?

K: Collage and montage are the products of the imagination *and* the artwork. Eliot invokes these aesthetic strategies to counter chaos, but later his solution was a matter of religious belief. Yet even when that becomes apparent as during *The Four Quartets*, the work itself remains strictly modern. Talking about space in terms of time and time in terms of space would have been impossible without the new physics.

T: A corollary of fragmentation is what you call decentralization. Dos Passos, for example, disperses attention across a host of characters. In his case, the technique manifests the collectivist thinking of the socialist Left, to which he was drawn. But does the postmodern decentralized novel have any other purpose? Is it also an attack on the value of political individualism?

K: Dos Passos construes decentralization as a way of dramatizing the insignificance of the person and the significance of the group. He is a complicated figure who would not necessarily agree that he was leftist, at least not throughout his entire career as a writer. Also, one or two characters emerge as more central than the others (e.g., Jimmy Herf and Ellen Thatcher of *Manhattan Transfer*). They are Dos Passos's vestigial version of the protagonist or hero. He, himself, along with Faulkner, served as a model for post–World War II antirealism because he wrote antiprotagonal fiction. Whether the technique was collectivist or not, decentralization eliminated the hero, who became scattered among several people. Characterological metamorphosis, which occurs in *The Waste Land* and other American poetic sequences, if not in Dos Passos, achieved the same end. Decentralization reflects fragmentation. The world has fractured and so too the hero, who once presupposed unity but now no longer exists. Obviously decentralized characterization accompanies decentralized form.

T: About the use of multiple perspectives. In the realistic novel, the focus is usually on a central character as the site of significant experience and, if noble, the embodiment of authorial values. But where there are multiple perspectives, isn't there an attack on the adequacy of the single individual's view of the world? Isn't there a relativist ideology of perception that subverts the idea of certitude?

K: To the antirealistic writer, the single protagonist betokens an illusionist world which never existed. By presenting numerous perspectives, as Robert Stone does in *A Hall of Mirrors*, the author challenges the restricted viewpoint of one individual. Therefore, antirealists introduce few clear-cut heroes or villains in the Shakespearean sense. Instead, there are many voices, many shades of grey. The relativism of *U.S.A.* and *The Sound and the Fury* is antithetical to the certitude of *Tom Jones* and *Great Expectations*.

T: When it comes to relativism, surely the creator of *Giles Goat-Boy* stands out.

K: Yet he doesn't write in fragments held together by collage or montage. Rather, Barth remains a traditional storyteller whose books descend from *The Ocean of Story* and *The Thousand and One Nights*. As a post–World War II metafictionist, he is not content with plots *per se*, but he loves to toy with them. And since he views history as plot versus counterplot anyway, he often poses plot against plot against plot.

T: As in *Giles*, which you have termed an absurd quest.

K: Well, Barth both ridicules and admires quest literature, with which he is familiar through Lord Raglan, Joseph Campbell, and other mythographers. Our Western tradition is full of questers. They are special figures who represent the life-force and they usually return from their journeys not only wiser but with an elixir for us, according to Campbell. If a modern book like *The Great Gatsby* parodies the heroic monomyth, a postmodern book like *Giles Goat-Boy* travesties it. The most notable difference between the two is that, in the latter, everything finally deconstructs. No moral yardstick, no Nick Carraway survives to tell us about the successful completion of his quest; rather, everything becomes uncertain because of the frame. Once admired, the truth-seeker is now a fool.

T: If all quests are absurd in postmodern writing, are these authors counselling passivity, quiescence, the futility of action?

K: I don't think that they are *advocating* quiescence. Most of them merely try to capture the contemporary reality lying beneath phenomena, and so they could be considered "actualists" or "superrealists" who, despite different aesthetic credos, discern a world no less vivid than the one we perceive through our eyes. "Counselling" is a word that every antirealist would reject, since it connotes "teacher" or "moralist."

T: The traditional view of the function of art has been to please and to teach, in fact to teach by means of aesthetic pleasure. But many antirealists, notably Barth, seem self-confessed ethical nihilists—a fact I find disturbing. Even if these writers deny an ethical intention, do they inadvertently teach us? Is there a lesson communicated in this fiction, or ought we to take some of them at their own word and accept it as nondidactic? Could a distinction be made between anti-ethical parodists like Barth, Federman, Nabokov, Sorrentino, and Sukenick as game-players with nothing to teach, and moralists like Burroughs, Coover, Gaddis, Pynchon, and Theroux, who, in various ways, are satirists?

K: Although "teach" is a word all antirealists would reject, there are those more interested in satire than in parody. Both groups play games, but unlike the writers absorbed by reflexivity, Burroughs, Coover, Gaddis, Hawkes, and Theroux have a great deal to say—albeit indirectly—about the moral implications of present chaos and insanity. Such authors treat grotesque characters in a nightmarish world. Though Hawkes is often parodic, *The Beetle Leg* and *The Lime Twig* mocking the western and the crime thriller, he also focuses on the horror of the First and Second World Wars. But even more than the word "counselling," the word "teach" would disturb him, for he is dedicated to eliminating plot, character, and theme, the last of which becomes "concern." Neither Hawkes nor his peers believe that people should follow rigid ethical standards. Antirealists are not much involved with ethics or metaphysics. They focus instead on creating finely wrought artifacts. Beyond this, objective reality, so-called, appears hopelessly terrifying.

T: But don't the bizarre settings, the imaginary landscapes in this fiction, imply a hatred of the real world, the objective world, and a desire to escape from it?

K: Since there's not much belief in the objective world, there really is no need to see places as essentially real. They are commonly fictionalized in much the way Poe fictionalized foreign locations. Hawkes is very proud of the fact that he wrote *The Lime Twig* without having visited London or its environs and that these locations impressed even the English. Whether landscapes are real or imaginary, there is blurring between the fantastic and the actual to the point where the fantastic may be projected as actual and the actual may be projected as fantastic. Therefore, we get a story like Donald Barthelme's "Paraguay." He includes some statistics about this South American country that sound true, but it is entered and exited from geographically impossible areas. Paraguay, which "exists elsewhere," has become a state of mind. The most impressive post–World War II novel with respect to imaginary landscapes has to be Nabokov's *Ada,* treating Terra, Antiterra or Demonia, Amerussia, and so forth. This big book probably constitutes the most complex rendition of setting since *Gulliver's Travels.* Like Paraguay, its places have a mental rather than an objective reality. Even Ithaca, New York, the setting of *Pale Fire,* while it possesses recognizable details, is as imaginary as those Western states Nabokov blends: Utana or Utah/Montana, Idoming or Idaho/Wyoming. Liberties taken with geographical spots are matched by liberties taken with historical figures to demonstrate how illusive our world is.

T: You see these writers, then, as essentially solipsistic?

K: Absolutely. Private vision represents the only trustworthy instrument we have. Though godlike, metafictionists such as Nabokov, who appears in his own work, do not withdraw to pare their fingernails in the Joycean fashion.

T: Are these solipsistic human gods romantic enough to regard man as potentially perfectible if institutions that deform character and produce violence should be kept from corrupting him?

K: Burroughs, Pynchon, Coover, and others blame institutions for much of the evil in our lives. The first two feel that extraterrestrial forces control such institutions.

T: So the institutions by which American society is organized and by which we live our lives—institutions like the government, the army, the law, the economic structure, the church, the university —are part of an oppressive system? They don't embody and express important values, but form, as Emerson put it in "Self-Reliance," the conspiracy of society against the manhood of every one of its members?

K: Antirealistic writing is profoundly American, for native writers have always distrusted institutions, though conspiracy and paranoia seem more prevalent now than ever before. Authority does not always sit well with the citizens of a republic.

T: In the case of Emerson, there is a moral intention in the criticism of institutions: they can be improved by means of the improvement of the individual. Do you find, in the criticism of American institutions in postmodern antirealism a constructive intention: to improve the institutional character of American life? Or are these authors simply anti-institutional?

K: There is definitely no intention to improve them. That is viewed as hopeless. We are living at a time when the possibilities of reform, of correction, have long since passed. Institutions are dangerous and they get worse day by day. Consequently, Yossarian, the protagonist of *Catch-22*, must flee from the military-industrial complex to another country. Since *Huckleberry Finn*, flight has been one way of coping with intolerable situations.

T: If there is an impulse to flee life as structured by institutions, American or otherwise, would you say the antirealists are alienated from Western civilization? If so, do they hanker after a primitivist mode of life?

K: Whereas previous native writers, including the expatriates of the 1920s felt at home in Europe, the antirealists mistrust any place dominated by the failed white race. It has committed genocide on Pynchon's African and Ellison's American blacks. Burroughs and Hawkes treat primitive civilizations like those in *Cities of the Red Night* and *Second Skin*, with Hawkes frequently juxtaposing Anglo-Saxons and Mediterraneans. Unlike Burroughs and Pynchon, he presents primitive societies as barbaric, our ancestors. He is not romantic about the Illyrians of *The Blood Oranges*, who speak only two phrases: *croak peonie* and *crespi fagag*. However, most antirealists idealize blackness at the expense of whiteness or the irrational over the rational.

T: Speaking of a specific institution, the family, Daniel Hoffman remarks that "[t]here are no parents in the tales of Edgar Poe, nary a Mum nor a Dad." I note the same thing in postmodern antirealistic fiction—little of love relationships leading to marriage, children, and involvements of a complex social kind.

K: One of the most amazing things about the writers of this movement is that in their private lives there is a kind of stability and coherence we would associate with ordinary middle-class people who believe in the family. John Hawkes has been a husband and a father for many years, but dissociates himself, the man, from himself as the writer. Writing is something separate that comes from his imagination. Certainly in Hawkes's fiction marriage doesn't work and children are abused by adults and adults by children. If we look at Barth's early work, *The End of the Road* and *The Floating*

Opera, we find marriage failing through adultery. Relations between the sexes in *The Sot-Weed Factor* and *Giles Goat-Boy* continue to be unsatisfactory. Not until we get the later books like *Letters,* where the marriage of Lady Amherst and Ambrose Mensch is celebrated, and *Sabbatical,* where Fenwick and Susan Turner's boat trip becomes a romantic odyssey, does family life appear positive to Barth. But even if we exclude misogynistic William Burroughs, who accidentally killed his own wife, we would have to say that for the most part marriage and children are either nonexistent or negative in post–World War II antirealistic American fiction.

T: What about mothers?

K: Few emerge. Sometimes we get a woman like Madame Snow in *The Cannibal* who has produced a child, but she and another mother, Eva Laubenstein in *The Passion Artist,* lead revolts against men. Most women remain childless and seem to be anything but motherly. They are not creators, not nurturers, and certainly not housewives. All the roles and functions traditionally associated with motherhood have vanished and women have become whores, vampires, *femmes fatales,* throughout this body of essentially male writing.

T: Does it treat children somewhat differently?

K: Yes. These "chauvinistic" authors defend children. For example, there is Coleman Dowell, whose books are protective toward the young, as well as toward animals, for both groups are helpless in our evil adult world. During *The Recognitions,* Gaddis's protagonist Wyatt Gwyon lives with a mad father and a puritanical aunt. Adults regularly victimize children and childlike adults, *The Lime Twig* being one instance.

T: How about a child such as Lolita?

K: To a very large extent, her mother shaped Lolita's life.

T: And was quickly killed off.

K: She could be considered a prepubescent *femme fatale,* since children also abuse adults in antirealistic tales. During Hawkes's *The Goose on the Grave,* a child pushes an old man off a cliff, and during *Second Skin,* daughter Cassandra indirectly ruins father Skipper. Though Hawkes denies the culpability of children, this motif recurs in his fiction.

T: Let's turn from the institution of the family to political institutions. In *A Hall of Mirrors*, Robert Stone, if not an entirely experimental author, is certainly a political one. Are antirealistic novels assimilable to a party politics—say Democrat or Republican? Does this postmodern writing imply conservative, liberal, or any particular ideology? Does it have a preference for a socialist order of institutions like the Soviet Union?

K: Because antirealistic fiction seems so rebellious and revolutionary, you would think more of the contributors would be committed to the Left. However, their primary role as professional writer is even more elite than their secondary role as college professor, since anyone who considers himself a god because he can create art is far from liberal. A fundamental aberration, a fundamental inconsistency lurks here: Those appearing to be democratic are really autocratic—the well-known pitfall of both teachers and artists. In a sense, though, the metafictionists are collectivists too; they carry forward the group's literary tradition. People like Sorrentino do not feel merely godlike in the Barthean sense, but extensions of a long Eliotic authorial line, so that it's perfectly logical for them to borrow other writers' characters, use other writers' words, or rewrite other writers' books. Such individuals form a plagiaristic community furthering the triumph of language and literature as opposed to the failed tradition of philosophy, and religion.

T: What about organized politics?

K: Seldom invoked, two notable exceptions being *A Hall of Mirrors* and *The Public Burning*. In the first, fanaticism—whether from the Left or the Right—is condemned. Stone's liberal protagonist, who works for Mr. Bingamon, head of the rightest elite, perceives him as dangerous, demagogic, fascistic, dictatorial. Although Rheinhardt understands what the older man represents, he's an opportunistic self-server receiving a large salary as Bingamon's radio voice. Cynicism marks *The Public Burning* by Robert Coover too. There, the satirical novelist makes Richard Nixon another opportunist and the reactionary establishment another oligarchy. Still, Coover is more relative than Stone, since neither Nixon nor the Rosenbergs are all bad or all good.

T: Much of this appears anarchistic to me.

K: William Burroughs, the only figure I treat who might be considered an anarchist, exhibits paranoia about systemic organizations. Chaos characterizes Pynchon also, but he has never been as extreme as Burroughs. A descendent of *The House of the Seven Gables* family, Pynchon inherited New England Calvinism with its doctrine of the elect, which he inverts, championing the preterites. Burroughs's style lacks coherence and order, while Pynchon preserves subjects, verbs, objects, paragraphs, chapters, and so forth. Grammatically, then, the first denotes anarchy and the second, reason, albeit compromised.

T: Speaking of anarchy, I am perturbed by the recurrent image of the world as an insane asylum and man as a creature of drives and instincts, the id and the unconscious. Does this account for the antirealistic free associational method, full of non-sequitur thinking and of oneiric horror?

K: The insane asylum metaphor recurs in many works—for example, the hospitals of *The Cannibal, Catch-22,* and *One Flew Over the Cuckoo's Nest.* Indeed, such settings become central to many contemporary writers, most of whom would deny using free associational techniques. This, too, derives from the authoritarian stance of the artist, his tacit insistence that he is God, that he created the world. We are not dealing with expressionistic authors whose characters have their own thoughts, but, instead, authors whose controls have set universal parameters. Free associational techniques reflecting surrealism would lessen authorial dominance.

T: I cannot take seriously the idea of insane or psychotic characters embodying an appropriate defense of the self against the insanity of the world. Is this just a black comic device? Or do the antirealists actually believe, with R. D. Laing, that lunacy is a viable response to the world?

K: The use of insane narrators by Nabokov, Hawkes, and others could be considered "black comedy," since here rational writers are manipulating irrational characters. However, sometimes the notion "lunacy as a sane response to the world" has been sanctioned by novelists like Heller and Kesey.

T: So Humbert Humbert's childhood love of Annabel was not "real"?

K: Nabokov often mocks his crazy narrators and protagonists. Thus, he gives us Charles Kinbote/V. Botkin of *Pale Fire,* who regards himself as the last king of Zembla, but is only a homosexual paranoid. If Humbert Humbert dwells on Poe's "kingdom by the sea," Van Veen, one of *Ada*'s narrators, views childhood and its geographical location as utopian. Vladimir Nabokov, the sophisticated fictionist, knows better, knows that these mental landscapes are distorted. The perception of childhood as being a paradisaic state does not necessarily represent the author.

T: Since Nabokov and the rest are free to invent antiworlds different from our own, why mock the utopian vision? If they don't like reality and want to play God, surely they could do better than Antiterra or Tralfamadore. Is it in the nature of postmodern antirealistic fiction that utopias can no longer be created, but only dystopias?

K: Science fiction often lets us escape to a more or less utopian environment, yet these writers, some of whom have been influenced by science fiction, introduce extraterrestrial places even worse than the earth. Such places might be considered dystopian.

T: We get, then, a curious situation: There is a contempt for reality, but accompanying it is an alternate world, created by the artist, equally contemptible. Doesn't this express a pessimism so profound as to be nihilistic?

K: Paradoxically, in the creation of their heterocosms, antirealistic artists seldom fashion a universe superior to the universe of the gods they replace, making them more cosmic jokers than Faulkner's Old Testament Jehovah. The substitute world contains as much irrationality and immorality as the real one.

T: On Antiterra and Tralfamadore, human history is twisted. How does it fare on earth, according to the antirealists?

K: Well, American history as a motif appears in Barth's *The Sot-Weed Factor* and *Letters*, in Hawkes's *The Beetle Leg* and *Second Skin*, and in Coover's *The Public Burning*, but such books tend to be mythical rather than historical, satirical rather than lyrical. Antirealistic fiction rarely penetrates our national surface as Fitzgerald did through the image of Columbus in "May Day" and the Dutch sailors in *The Great Gatsby*.

T: Do these fabulators ever suggest that experience, chronologically viewed, has significance, or that history has a *telos*, is moving toward some purposeful ending? Or has history become meaningless, and, I suppose, the attempts to understand it merely an illusion to be parodied?

K: History signifies deception, the private property of those who interpret it. To create order and intelligibility, historians overlook the plots, counterplots, false documents, intrigues, and misleading data constituting the written record. Meanwhile, native post–World War II antirealists challenge the idea of progress, that you begin somewhere and end somewhere else, as in the Bible. For them, there is no earthly cause and effect to explain historical and biographical phenomena. Individuals like Jean d'Arc, Napoleon, and Bismarck are unimportant, the "great man" theory discredited.

T: I can find no ethical or aesthetic justification for introducing into a work of fiction the names of real historical people and putting them into compromising situations and having them say and do ridiculous things that the documents of history will not confirm.

K: This is a way not only of deflating sacred figures, but of questioning whether anyone can be truthfully recreated. If the historical portrait must necessarily be false, the artistic imagination may do what it wishes with its model.

T: I wonder whether the concept of entropy, the perceived degeneration toward which all is said to be tending, isn't just the last thematic peg for these pessimists to hang their despair on.

K: Not every antirealistic writer deals with entropy, but enough do so that you could say it has become a key philosophical view among them. William Gaddis is very aware of the entropic process in all three of his novels. Thomas Pynchon too, though in the introduction to *Slow Learner* he denies it. Barth and many other contemporary American writers, following the example of T. S. Eliot and Nathanael West, know about and sometimes employ this degenerative process. Like history, human life moves backward toward a darker age rather than forward to a millennium. The earth gets colder, yet—although entropy stemming from the second law of thermodynamics (popularly called "heat loss") is a recurrent theme in postmodern fiction—Norbert Wiener's information theory has probably been more influential because he extends entropic proliferation of waste into linguistics, where it becomes noise. Only during this historical period could an acoustical fiction such as *J R* or *Crystal Vision* be written. *Carpenter's Gothic,* while not acoustical, shows communication breaking down through incessant telephone calls, postal junk, television shows, radio broadcasts, and so forth. The violation of language—a pervasive Western motif from Flaubert to Pound—fascinates novelists like Gaddis, an expert, incidentally, at rendering jargon and double-talk.

T: Isn't there also a disturbing preoccupation with excrement in this literature?

K: Yes. Abhorrence of the human body leading toward misanthropy and abhorrence of the female gender leading toward misogyny explain why antirealism has grown so scatalogical. Some authors —for instance, Gaddis—focus less on excrement than others— for instance, Burroughs—though J R's repeated exclamation "Holy shit!" signals the presence of excrement in Gaddis's fiction too. Both treat its concomitant, disease, with Burroughs, a former medical student, again ahead of his experimental contemporaries. We have come a long way since *The Waste Land,* where innocuous detritus such as "empty bottles" and "cigarette ends" mar the landscape. Now dung, reminiscent of Henry Miller's excremental vision, is commonplace, three instances being Slothrop at the Roseland Ballroom *(Gravity's Rainbow),* the talking asshole *(Naked Lunch),* and the "great ball of manure" *(The Free-Lance Pallbearers).* This obsession over feces as the epitomization of waste is particularly bitter because here the satirist, reflecting a tradition that equates the body physical and the body politic, risks, with Jonathan Swift, the danger of appearing mad.

T: The very idea of entropy, whether founded on the second law of thermodynamics or information theory, constitutes a scientific explanation of life. Are these writers naturalists in the older nineteenth-century sense, yet, unlike the naturalists of that era, writing antirealistically?

K: They are determinists, but not naturalists concerned with cause and effect due to heredity and environment, as propounded by Zola or Dreiser. Social conditions that naturalistic leftists like Upton Sinclair thought could be improved remain unredeemable for them. Determinism in their case centers on the physical laws of the universe and how they govern our destiny. Thus, it's not surprising that Burroughs and Pynchon are familiar with the scientific attitude. Both view an earth controlled by extraterrestrial beings who misguide, confuse, and destroy us.

T: At the same time, the author creates a world of his own, and so becomes superior to the forces affecting his characters.

K: You're quite right. There is a contradiction here. By introducing such forces, he acknowledges a reality outside of himself even while playing God. Then, godlike, the author indifferently records what horrors lie beneath this reality's placid surface.

T: Do any antirealists believe in God or the devil? In original sin or the inevitable fallen condition of humanity? Or is the grotesque and demonic simply the nature of man's being?

K: With the exception of Catholic Flannery O'Connor and Alexander Theroux, these writers are not obvious believers. Secular Hawkes says throughout his letters to religious O'Connor that he shapes diabolical characters as an artistic strategy. She found this hard to accept because her devil is real. Yet Hawkes also comes from the Christian tradition and so employs Christian symbolism like his recurrent Eden. Such places appear to be paradisiac, but are actually the reverse. Though not every antirealist has Gaddis's or Pynchon's understanding of Calvinism, many attack Christianity for its puritanism and negativism. Armageddon and apocalypse often conclude their stories, which seem Manichean since our world is a battleground between light and darkness, good and evil, the life-force and the death-force.

T: Without God or devil, whence arises the sense of evil in such sinister places? Does the demonic merely imply basic human nature? Or do social maladjustments and personal psychopathology produce evil?

K: For Pynchon and Burroughs, evil ultimately lies beyond us. There are conspiratorial forces on other planets whose representatives, "They" or "Them," control human destiny and pervert human institutions. We become victims of self-indulgence, of sex and drugs, according to Burroughs. Apomorphine, which he took for his addiction, functions as a policeman, while the body resembles a continent where viral wars occur. Meantime John Hawkes considers humanity to be irrational and atavistic. Because of entropic processes, Gaddis's world steadily regresses too.

T: If this is a godless universe, a universe in which even the devil as a theological presence has been banished, then the image of man that emerges does not imply a humanistic, much less a religious, vision.

K: Correct. Most antirealists are neither supernaturalists nor naturalists. If the modern writers were humanists, who, forsaking God, at least believed in man, the antirealists eliminate both. You enter a violent nightmare existence when you desert God and His association with order. Should man—except perhaps as artist—disintegrate too, no criteria remain by which most people can live.

T: Is the cynicism, the nihilism, the decadence of this literature a tribute to the No! in Thunder tradition of Poe, Melville, and Hawthorne, celebrated in Harry Levin's *The Power of Blackness?* Or is it a reaction to specific historical events of the twentieth century, like the world wars, the Holocaust, the nuclear bomb?

K: These writers perceive the twentieth century as being the most treacherous one of all. Two world wars, the Holocaust, the nuclear bomb, and so forth have caused the despair and pessimism you mention. There were prefigurations of this attitude earlier in the century. Eliot's *The Waste Land,* an international poem like much contemporary antirealistic fiction, anticipates postmodernism technically and thematically. His influence on subsequent novelists has been even greater than that exerted by Nabokov or Borges. *The Waste Land* was a dead end for American poets, but not for Burroughs, Dowell, and Gaddis.

T: One difference between Eliot and these antirealists is his oscillations between contemporaneity and antiquity, which define skeptical pessimism and nihilism as perennial features of human life and not unique to the twentieth century. "The Hollow Men" are recurrent phenomena for him, whereas later fabulators seem to accord our time a special horror.

K: Eliot never disavowed history. Though the past is influenced by the present as much as the present is influenced by the past, he envisions an orderly succession of explicable events.

T: His contemporaries realized that the image of man projected by *The Waste Land* was intolerable. In 1930, just eight years after the poem appeared, Archibald MacLeish said the task of writers would be to create an image of man in which we could again believe. Is this notion ridiculous to the antirealists?

K: Eliot, who eventually rejected the humanistic tradition, opposed humanistic critics like Irving Babbitt. As a supernaturalist, he considered humanity to be flawed. Only Flannery O'Connor and Alexander Theroux among later antirealistic American novelists are concerned about such issues, since their peers believe neither in god nor in man.

T: Then there is no evidence of human perfectibility such as Emerson envisioned?

K: Definitely not. More often, the reverse.

T: No epiphanies, no intersection of the human with the divine, the temporal with the eternal?

K: Only O'Connor has such moments, but, then, "grace" for her now occurs through confrontation with the devil. Otherwise, characters who experience transcendence are considered deluded by their makers.

T: They never etherialize or spiritualize sex so that love becomes redemptive? Doesn't Humbert Humbert convert the sexual impulse into pure love? Or is he just a nympholept?

K: Nabokov's mad protagonists generally pursue something beyond themselves, here the *femme fatale* Lolita, who later inspired Isabel Rawsthorne of *Darconville's Cat*.

T: Aren't Isabel, with her co-ed triviality, and the actual girl Lolita, with her gum-chewing and teeny-bopper slang, inferior to the transcendental ideal they embody for their enflamed lovers?

K: From Don Quixote and Dulcinea to Ebenezer Cooke and Joan Toast, stories told by male intellectuals have explored the relation between educated upper-class heroes and uneducated lower-class heroines.

T: We're talking about the disappointment of the transcendental idealist at the hands of the female muse. Is this why the antirealists, most of whom are middle-class white men, degrade women characters so abominably?

K: Misogyny runs all through twentieth-century American literature. Still, some contemporary figures have the capacity to love, Wyatt Gwyon of *The Recognitions* and Roger Mexico of *Gravity's Rainbow* being notable instances. Generally, however, love occurs in postmodern texts no more often than in their immediate predecessors like *The Waste Land*, *Nightwood*, and *Miss Lonelyhearts*. For example, Oedipa Maas encounters a series of impotent men during *The Crying of Lot 49*, and several others destroy Elizabeth Booth in *Carpenter's Gothic*. Both novels have rare female protagonists.

T: I find the treatment of sexuality in such fiction appalling.

K: Sexuality is seen as an animal function. Subject to disease and perversion, the body (microcosm), mirroring the body politic (macrocosm), is also corrupt. Hence Burroughs's, Pynchon's, and Coover's excremental vision that identifies feces with death. When survival becomes the issue, the life-force or lust replaces romantic and spiritual love. Nowhere does this appear more pervasively than in the fiction of John Hawkes, whose dominant "concern" continues to be the war between Eros and Thanatos. For the antirealists, this conflict represents Armageddon, during which death triumphs.

T: His contemporaries often end the world—personal or universal —with a bang, as *Invisible Man*, *A Hall of Mirrors*, *Cat's Cradle*, and *Gravity's Rainbow* show.

K: Well, apocalypse takes two forms, involving a sacrificial individual on the one hand, and, on the other, the annihilation of degenerate society.

T: Do these, like conventional tragedy, have the cathartic effect of confirming or reaffirming traditional values?

K: No, sacrificial individuals tend to be mad in antirealistic fiction. There is Mrs. October of *Mrs. October Was Here*, an idealistic revolutionary who furthers her own crucifixion by designing the cruciform. Rather than being redemptive, the private sacrifice seems both perverse and futile. Even Faulkner's *Light in August*, where Percy Grimm castrates Joe Christmas, has an apotheosis, but current apocalypses, whether private or public, do not. Ambiguity marks the public catastrophe too, since whole societies deconstruct without a clear-cut moral purpose. In them, the destroyers resemble the destroyed, the new society the old. Thus, revelation is mocked, privately and publicly.

T: The conclusion of *Invisible Man* strikes me as more optimistic than most other antirealistic apocalypses. Although the epilogue only poses a series of questions, leaving the matter of politics and racial relations somewhat suspended, the novel affirms liberal democracy and the capacity of the races to coexist harmoniously.

K: Very different from *The Recognitions*, where the church at Fenestrula, by crumbling, kills a devout musician.

T: And *Gravity's Rainbow,* where Blicero's rocket will demolish the world. Does such plotting express full-blown nihilism? Or are these writers merely Jeremiahs warning of destruction so that we will mend our ways?

K: These writers see life and death in a struggle, with death the inevitable victor, a struggle wherein indifferent processes beyond good and evil appear. No attempt at reform is made because postmodern nihilists do not preach and their audience cannot change.

T: Writers who generalize a despairing worldview from science are, to me, unwisely premature. Physicists know so little. Henry Adams, in *The Education,* went on and on about how physics had destroyed life's meaning. The discovery of atoms and molecules, and their oddity of movement, led him positively to bewail the "supersensual chaos" underlying matter and therefore the instability and meaninglessness of all life. Recently the Heisenberg principle has been put to the same use. Some writers are always looking for laboratory confirmation that, as Adams put it, "Chaos is the law of nature; order is the dream of man." If science cannot prove the existence of God, let it at least prove the truth of nihilism.

K: Entropy is introduced by Henry Adams and dramatized by T. S. Eliot, but it doesn't become a conviction among fictionists until the post–World War II period. They emphasize imminent death through entropic processes, irrational creatures, and evil planets.

T: Yet you've called this movement "comic." Does it ever employ a traditional humor that affirms life? Or is it always black?

K: The great tradition of comedy from Roman plays through Victorian novels, the tradition associated with realism which has always exposed human folly by presenting the battle between the sexes and among social classes, is absent from contemporary antirealistic writing. Instead, we get the countertradition of black or grotesque humor, as modern American writers like Barnes, Faulkner, West, and postmodern American writers like Hawkes, O'Connor, and

Ellison illustrate. However, our contemporary metafictional authors, who follow Rabelais, Sterne, and Fielding rather than de Sade, Lautréamont, and Céline, celebrate hedonism with bawdy laughter and so could be considered somewhat "positive." Positive too are their parodies, burlesques, and travesties of older forms, since these indicate a love of language and literature.

T: I must confess that the antirealists' love of language appears suspect to me. In the intellectual universe inhabited by them, the word, the signifier, has become separated from its signified, its reference to the real world. Consequently, language loses the historic function of disclosing a nonlinguistic world. An artist may glorify language at the expense of the referential function, but because language refers to something outside even when pretending otherwise, the authentic hermeneutic task is activated: the search for understanding and truth. Recently, Joseph Brodsky remarked that he thought world leaders ought to read literature, since, nowadays, only literature is redemptive. But to anyone from Arnold onward claiming this, I ask, Who is writing the literature and what does it represent? About antirealistic writing we must know the implication, the truth-value—social, moral, ideological —of the form offered to determine whether the solipsist self-involvement, the nightmare horrors, the entropic despair, the violent comedies, and the ambiguous apocalypses are indeed ultimately valuable. If antirealism lacks life-affirmation and spiritual enlargement, it is too narrow, don't you agree?

K: Grave dangers arise from postulating the triumph of the death force. This may not be dishonest, but, rather, self-defeating. Such literature requires us to appreciate form because content matters very little. Accordingly, antirealism reflects other twentieth-century movements where form dominates content. For example, French structuralism and deconstruction emphasize form while they often exclude moral values. A levelling occurs thereby so that Philip Roth may become the equal of Joseph Conrad—both merely produce discourse—and the distinctions between popular and great literature are blurred.

T: The line from Nietzsche through Derrida, which subverts Western metaphysics, logic, causation, order, and authority, errs when postulating a linguistic universe alone, a world merely of texts.

There is for me, and most men, I think, an objective reality and a history that can be understood, though perhaps not fully. The values implicit in our liberal democratic institutions, in our Judeo-Christian religious thought, in our idea of university education, in our family structure, codify meaning and define goals that people may work toward. These institutions provide a rational direction unaccounted for by contemporary antirealists, who fail to express normative human experience. Their fiction may exhibit technical interest, but technique alone is questionable if it resembles John Cage's musical "rest" or a white-on-white canvas.

K: As intellectuals, as academics, the antirealists often lose sight of ordinary humanity. That's why they will never have a wide audience.

T: Most of them are men. Don't women find antirealism attractive?

K: During the twentieth century, many experimental female writers here, in England, and on the Continent have appeared. Among them, we find Dorothy Richardson, Gertrude Stein, Virginia Woolf, Djuna Barnes, Anaïs Nin, and Marguerite Young. Their descendants, like Susan Sontag, Joyce Carol Oates, Christine Brooke-Rose, and Gabrielle Burton continue this tradition. That experimentation was and is feminine as well as masculine Ellen Friedman and Miriam Fuchs demonstrate in their collection of essays about innovative female writers. However, not all female experimentalists consider antirealism, with its paranoia, entropy, and apocalypse, congenial. Nor have many achieved the stature of Barth, Burroughs, Gaddis, Ellison, Hawkes, and Pynchon.

T: Perhaps there are fewer female antirealists because the feminist movement has enlisted women writers in a campaign of social transformation, and because a literature intending to transform society must be more accessible and didactic.

K: Exactly. When psychic energy gets drawn off that way, no time remains for play, and antirealism is characterized by games. Although there are black antirealists such as Ralph Ellison and Ishmael Reed, they also represent minority voices in a realistic tradition of black liberationists that includes Richard Wright and James Baldwin.

T: If indeed women and black authors—those with a social agenda —regard the stakes too high for literary game-playing; if post-

modern antirealism seems distrustful of reality and self-preoccu-
pied; if this constitutes a literature where, as Wallace Stevens said,
"The gaiety of language is our seigneur," does it not suggest an
aesthetic hedonism?

K: Though the metafictional writers among the antirealists, writers
like Nabokov, Barth, and Sorrentino, may be aesthetic hedonists,
surely those who focus on the grotesque, the conspiratorial, the
entropic, and the apocalyptic are engaged thematically. Both game-
players and non–game-players belong to a school so large and so
distinctive that several major authors and several major texts inevitably materialize. No one attains the stature of Faulkner or
Joyce, except perhaps Nabokov, but Barth, Burroughs, Gaddis,
Hawkes, and Pynchon occupy the next rung. Meanwhile, other
antirealists have published extraordinary books: for example, Barthelme's *The Dead Father,* Coover's *The Public Burning,* Dowell's
Island People, Ellison's *Invisible Man,* Heller's *Catch-22,* O'Connor's
A Good Man Is Hard to Find, Sorrentino's *Mulligan Stew,* Theroux's
Darconville's Cat, and Young's *Miss MacIntosh, My Darling.*

T: My own view may be less generous, but let me play the prophet,
always a risky business. Since people read literature, Kenneth
Burke argues, as "equipment for living," the darkness and pessimism (however relieved from time to time by sick comedy) is likely
to sink much of this writing so low that its experimental techniques will not rescue it. Of the figures you mentioned, only
Ellison, Gaddis, and Pynchon strike me as likely to endure. I
disagree about John Hawkes, a writer's writer whose works are
too limited.

K: His early fiction—*The Cannibal, The Beetle Lag, The Lime Twig,* and
Second Skin—far surpass what Hawkes published later.

T: Novels like *The Cannibal* and *Second Skin* give me a chill, without
any compensatory enjoyment of language. Through obligation, I
look at many such stories, which were probably more pleasurable
to write than to read.

K: But Hawkes's style is brilliant, his tone, uncanny. He calls himself
an optimistic comic writer, though we might question this because
even *Second Skin* displays a negative dimension. Do you really
believe that nihilistic or pessimistic novels are destined not to be
read?

T: Rather, not to be valued highly as literary monuments of the human spirit. They never affirm life, an essential test for me.

K: Gaddis does, despite our institutions.

T: I agree with your praise of him. Still, in the long view, he and the rest must be judged against Hawthorne, Melville, James, Hemingway, Joyce, Faulkner, Dickens, Tolstoy, and other masters.

K: Often I read nineteenth-century novels just for enjoyment. Hardy is blackly deterministic, yet he embraces ordinary human values. You could be right. Without these, their pessimism will hurt the postmodern antirealists. They may end up being appreciated only by fellow professionals, the fate of Pound in *The Cantos,* Joyce in *Finnegans Wake,* and many "obscure" modern writers.

T: Evidently, we would both support Julian Symons, who contends in *The Making of the New* that there's a point beyond which experimentation with unreadable language produces diminishing returns. The extremity of much recent fiction, with its negations, may eventually appear to our descendants as peculiar as the optimistic transcendental literature of Emerson appears to us. If the earlier transcendentalists deny evil, the later antirealists deny good. This pendulum swing toward utter negation falsifies, for me, the actual balance of human qualities, of human motivations, of human experience.

K: Then Burroughs, Pynchon, and company are not prophets?

T: Let's hope their vision of the apocalypse is faulty. I'm advocating rationality and judgment, however difficult to attain in our imperfect world.

K: Charles Lamb's identification between sanity and genius?

T: We go to literature precisely for the genius of the eminently sane, for the writer as exemplary figure, for what a Shakespeare, a Dickens, a Dostoyevski, or a Tolstoy communicates about truth. But the antirealists have disavowed the artist's historic role: to voice profound thought and deep feeling through forms that illuminate complex modes of being in the world. My view is rather like that of Gerald Graff in "The Politics of Anti-Realism," who remarks that antirealistic writers' attempts to overturn consciousness of the objective world, ordinary language, and the canons of representational realism will inevitably lead to their social marginality, will insure their own unimportance to readers. Once writers start refusing attention to the social needs of art, society ceases to pay any attention to them. In *City Life*, Barthelme presents Tolstoy as a museum figure, a gigantic statue dwarfing every other author, so that it seems pointless to compete with him. But need every contemporary writer see himself as a pygmy? Tolstoy was great in part because he expressed a wisdom based on true perceptions of human experience and a celebratory vision that found a basis for life-affirmation. Lacking that, much contemporary work seems self-indulgent to me and must inevitably perish.

K: Yet I find creative excellence in many antirealistic books, self-indulgent or not, though I agree that philosophical nihilism and aesthetic positivism do not bode well for human or literary immortality.

Notes

Introduction: The American Roots of Contemporary Antirealism

1. Barth, incidentally, is not the first antirealist to be taken with the tales of Scheherazade. But Poe terminates Barth's favorite collection in his story "The Thousand-and-Second Tale of Scheherazade" (1845), where the hapless Scheherazade brings about her own death by inventing a fabulous land that is in fact filled with nineteenth-century American marvels like the electrotype, the telegraph, the daguerrotype, etc. The King is skeptical at her narrative of all of these ingenuities but becomes positively enraged at the imposition on his credulity when Scheherazade describes a form of womanly beauty which "consists altogether in the protuberance of the region which lies not very far below the small of the back.—Perfection of loveliness, they say, is in the direct ratio of this hump." Refusing to believe in any such fantastic land where female beauty is determined by the size of the bustle, he has her executed. Cf. *Complete Works of Edgar Allan Poe,* ed. James A. Harrison (New York: de Fau, 1902), 6–7: 101. Hereafter all quotations of Poe will cite this "Virginia Edition."

2. Alexander Theroux, "Theroux Metaphrastes," *Three Wogs* (Boston: Godine, 1972), 27.

3. William Gass, "Tropes of the Text," *Habitations of the Word* (New York: Simon, 1985), 141; Gerald Graff, "The Politics of Anti-Realism," in *The Salmagundi Reader,* ed. Robert Boyers and Peggy Boyers (Bloomington, Ind.: Indiana Univ. Press, 1983), 397; Frank Kermode, "Novels: Recognition and Deception," *Critical Inquiry* 1 (1974): 112; Leo Bersani, *A Future for Astyanax: Character and Desire in Literature* (New York: Little, 1976), 56.

4. Jacques Lacan, *Ecrits,* trans. Alan Sheridan. (New York: Norton, 1977), 150.

5. Paul de Man, *Allegories of Reading* (New Haven: Yale Univ. Press, 1979), 106.

6. Richard Chase, *The American Novel and Its Tradition* (Garden City, N.Y.: Anchor, 1957), 12–13.

7. Michael Davitt Bell, *The Development of American Romance: The Sacrifice of Relation* (Chicago: Univ. of Chicago Press, 1980), xiii.

8. William Dean Howells, "Novel-Writing and Novel-Reading," ed. William Gibson (New York: The New York Public Library, 1958), 24.

9. Rather differently, naturalists posit the self as a composite of the effects of forces like race, class, nationality, religion, politics, and so forth. But since naturalistic determinism is for the novelist untenable on theoretical grounds, most so-called naturalists like Dreiser, Norris, and Crane allow room for accidental or freely willed actions.

10. Henry James, *Literary Criticism: Essays on Literature, American Writers, English Writers*, ed. Leon Edel (New York: The Library of America, 1984), 55.

11. Henry James, "Anthony Trollope," *The Future of the Novel*, ed. Leon Edel (New York: Vintage, 1956), 236.

12. John Enck, "John Hawkes: An Interview," *Wisconsin Studies in Contemporary Literature* 6 (1965): 149.

13. Wallace Stevens, *The Necessary Angel: Essays on Reality and the Imagination* (New York: Vintage, 1965), 175.

14. Allen Tate, "The Angelic Imagination," in *The Recognition of Edgar Allan Poe: Selected Criticism Since 1829*, ed. Eric W. Carlson (Ann Arbor: Univ. of Michigan Press, 1966), 241–42.

15. Daniel Hoffman, *Poe Poe Poe Poe Poe Poe Poe* (Garden City, N.Y.: Anchor, 1973), 206–7.

16. Quoted in Frank Baldanza, *Mark Twain: An Introduction and an Interpretation* (New York: Barnes, 1961), 12.

17. Quoted in Jay Martin, *Harvests of Change: American Literature, 1865–1914* (Englewood Cliffs, N.J.: Prentice, 1967), 222–23.

18. Walter Blair, *Native American Humor* (San Francisco: Chandler, 1960), 45–47.

19. Cf. Kuhlmann's *Knave, Fool, and Genius: The Confidence Man as He Appears in Nineteenth-Century American Fiction* (Chapel Hill: Univ. of North Carolina Press, 1973); Lindberg's *The Confidence Man in American Literature* (New York: Oxford Univ. Press, 1982); and Wadlington's *The Confidence Game in American Literature* (Princeton: Princeton Univ. Press, 1975).

20. Herman Melville, *The Confidence Man: His Masquerade*, ed. Hershel Parker (New York: Norton, 1971), 58.

21. Peter J. Bellis, "Melville's Confidence Man: An Uncharitable Interpretation," *American Literature* 59 (December 1987): 563.

22. Oliver Wendell Holmes, *The Guardian Angel* (Boston: Houghton, 1894), 22–23.

23. John Ward Ostrom, ed., *The Letters of Edgar Allan Poe* (New York: Gordian, 1966), 1: 57–58.

24. Nathaniel Hawthorne, "Young Goodman Brown," *Nathaniel Hawthorne's Tales*, ed. James McIntosh (New York: Norton, 1987), 74–75.

25. Ralph Waldo Emerson, "The Divinity School Address," *Selections from Ralph Waldo Emerson*, ed. Stephen Whicher (Boston: Houghton, 1960), 103.

26. "Never Bet the Devil Your Head," *Complete Works of Edgar Allan Poe*, 4–5: 213–26.

27. Mark Twain, *Letters from the Earth*, ed. Bernard De Voto (New York: Harper, 1974), 32–33.

28. William Gaddis, "The Art of Fiction," *Paris Review* 105 (Winter 1987): 64.

29. Wallace Stevens, "Esthetique du Mal," *Poems by Wallace Stevens*, ed. Samuel French Morse (New York: Vintage, 1959), 120.

30. Allen Tate, "Our Cousin, Mr. Poe," *The Man of Letters in the Modern World* (New York: Meridian, 1955), 140.

31. "The Man That Was Used Up," *Complete Works of Edgar Allan Poe*, 3: 272.

32. "The Facts in the Case of M. Valdemar," *Complete Works of Edgar Allan Poe*, 6–7: 166.

33. Hoffman, 162.

34. *Mark Twain's Notebook*, ed. Albert Bigelow Paine (New York: Harper, 1935), 170.

35. Albert Bigelow Paine, *Mark Twain: A Biography* (New York: Harper, 1923), 3: 1238.

36. "The Poet," *Selections from Ralph Waldo Emerson*, 227.

37. *Nature, Selections from Ralph Waldo Emerson*, 53.

38. Oliver Wendell Holmes, *Elsie Venner: A Romance of Destiny* (New York: NAL, 1961), xii–xiii.

39. Stephen Crane, "The Monster," *The Red Badge of Courage and Other Writings*, ed. Richard Chase (Boston: Houghton, 1960), 355.

40. Melville, *The Confidence Man*, 7.

41. Ibid., 193.

42. Cf. Joseph Blotner and Frederick Gwynn, eds. *Faulkner in the University* (New York: Random, 1965), 274.

43. Alfred Bendixen, ed. *The Whole Family* (New York: Ungar, 1986), l–li.

44. Mark Twain, *The Mysterious Stranger*, in *The Portable Mark Twain*, ed. Bernard De Voto (New York: Viking, 1951), 743. My italics.

45. *Eureka, Complete Works of Edgar Allan Poe*, 16: 292.

46. Quoted in Michael McKeon, *The Origins of the English Novel, 1600–1740* (Baltimore: Hopkins, 1987), 12.

47. Susanna Haswell Rowson, *Charlotte. A Tale of Truth.* (Philadelphia, 1793), 1: 46–48.

48. Susanna Rowson, *The Inquisitor* (Philadelphia, 1793), 152–54.

49. *Eureka, Complete Works of Edgar Allan Poe*, 16: 315.

50. Allen Tate, *The Forlorn Demon* (Chicago: Regnery, 1953), 63.

51. Hoffman, 176.

52. *Complete Works of Edgar Allan Poe*, 2: 269–95.

53. *Chaucer's Major Poetry*, ed. Albert C. Baugh (Englewood Cliffs, N.J.: Prentice-Hall, 1963), 351.

54. George Eliot, *Adam Bede* (Boston: Houghton, 1908), 1: 253.

55. James, *Literary Criticism*, 1343; *The Future of the Novel*, 232; cf. René Wellek, *Concepts of Criticism* (New Haven: Yale Univ. Press, 1963), 249.

56. Herman Melville, *Moby-Dick; or The Whale*, ed. Charles Feidelson, Jr. (Indianapolis: Bobbs, 1964), 160–61.

57. Melville, *The Confidence Man*, 205.

58. Nathaniel Hawthorne, *The Scarlet Letter and Other Tales of the Puritans*, ed. Harry Levin (Boston: Houghton, 1960), 258.

59. Ibid., 6.

60. Ibid., 36, 37, 40.

61. Hawthorne, "Wakefield," *Nathaniel Hawthorne's Tales*, 75–76.

62. Quoted in Arlin Turner, *Nathaniel Hawthorne: An Introduction and an Interpretation* (New York: Holt, 1961), 68.

63. *The Journals and Miscellaneous Notebooks of Ralph Waldo Emerson*, ed. Ralph Orth and Alfred E. Ferguson (Cambridge: Harvard Univ. Press, 1971), 9: 405.

64. Henry James, *The Portrait of a Lady*, ed. Leon Edel (Boston: Houghton, 1963), 94.

65. Henry James, *The Bostonians* (New York: Modern Library, 1956), 5.

66. John E. Tilford, Jr., "James the Old Intruder," *Modern Fiction Studies* 4 (1958): 157–64.

67. William Dean Howells, *Indian Summer*, ed. William M. Gibson (New York: Dutton, 1958), 195.

68. Mark Twain, *Adventures of Huckleberry Finn*, ed. Henry Nash Smith (Boston: Houghton, 1958), 3.

69. Mark Twain, *Pudd'nhead Wilson* (New York: Collier, 1922), 207–9, 211, 295.

70. Mrs. E. D. E. N. Southworth, *Cruel as the Grave* (Philadelphia: Peterson, 1871), 208.

71. Mrs. E. D. E. N. Southworth, *The Family Doom* (New York: Lupton, 1897), 350.

72. Ernest Hemingway, *The Torrents of Spring* (New York: Scribner's, 1972), 89.

73. William Faulkner, *Mosquitoes: A Novel* (New York: Liveright, 1927), 145.

74. Dwight Thomas and David K. Jackson, *The Poe Log: A Documentary Life of Edgar Allan Poe, 1809–1849* (Boston: Hall, 1987), 290, 336.

75. "Berenice," *The Complete Works of Edgar Allan Poe*, 2: 19.

76. Gass, 150.

77. "X-ing a Paragrab," *Complete Works of Edgar Allan Poe*, 6–7: 236.

78. Mark Twain, *A Connecticut Yankee in King Arthur's Court* (New York: Washington Square, 1948), 206.

79. "The Murders in the Rue Morgue," *Complete Works of Edgar Allan Poe*, 4–5: 147–48.

80. Hoffman, 146.

81. Henry James, "The Figure in the Carpet," *Eight Tales from the Major Phase,* ed. Morton Dauwen Zabel (New York: Norton, 1958), 151–52, 155.

82. "The Unparalleled Adventures of One Hans Pfaall," *Complete Works of Edgar Allan Poe,* 2: 53.

83. *Narrative of A. Gordon Pym, Complete Works of Edgar Allan Poe,* 3: 2.

84. Ibid., 2–3, 243.

85. Hugh Henry Brackenridge, *Modern Chivalry* (New Haven: College and University Press, 1965), 19, 25, 29, 58, 262.

86. *Narrative of A. Gordon Pym, Complete Works of Edgar Allan Poe,* 3: 242.

87. Melville, *Moby-Dick,* xviii–xix.

88. James Fenimore Cooper, *The Chainbearer* (New York: Appleton, 1883), vii.

89. Quoted in Henry Nash Smith, *Mark Twain's Fable of Progress: Political and Economic Ideas in a Connecticut Yankee* (New Brunswick, N.J.: Rutgers Univ. Press, 1964), 41.

90. Henry James, *The Art of the Novel: Critical Prefaces by Henry James,* ed. R. P. Blackmur (New York: Scribner's 1934), 10.

91. "Sherwood Anderson on Winesburg, Ohio," in *Winesburg, Ohio: Text and Criticism,* ed. John H. Ferres (New York: Viking, 1966), 19.

92. Herman Melville, "Preface," *Mardi and a Voyage Thither,* ed. Harrison Hayford, Hershel Parker, and G. Thomas Tanselle (Evanston, Ill.: Northwestern Univ. Press, 1970), xvii.

93. Hawthorne, *The Scarlet Letter and Other Tales of the Puritans,* 38.

94. Karl Mannheim, *Ideology and Utopia: An Introduction to the Sociology of Knowledge* (New York: Harcourt, Brace, 1949), 185, 179, 192. Quoted in Jay Martin, *Harvests of Change: American Literature,* 1865–1914 (Englewood Cliffs, N.J.: Prentice-Hall, 1967), 218–19.

95. "The System of Dr. Tarr and Prof. Fether, *Complete Works of Edgar Allan Poe,* 6–7: 53–55, 57–58.

96. Quoted in Kenneth Silverman, *The Life and Times of Cotton Mather* (New York: Columbia Univ. Press, 1985), 88; Thomas Paine, "The American Crisis," in *The American Tradition in Literature,* ed. George Perkins et al. (New York: Random, 1985), p. 167.

97. "Self-Reliance," *Selections from Ralph Waldo Emerson,* 149.

98. "The Imp of the Perverse," *Complete Works of Edgar Allan Poe,* 6–7: 145–46, 150.

99. Melville, *Moby-Dick,* 302–3.

100. *Eureka, Complete Works of Edgar Allan Poe,* 16: 260.

101. "The Power of Words," *Complete Works of Edgar Allan Poe,* 6–7: 143.

102. Martin, 213–14.

103. Charles Nordhoff, *The Communist Societies of the United States: From Personal Visit and Observation: Including Detailed Accounts of the Economists, Zoarites, Shakers, the Amana, Oneida, Bethel, Aurora, Icarian, and Other Existing Societies, Their Religious Creeds, Social Practices, Numbers, Industries and Present Condition* (New York: Harper, 1875), 349.

104. "Earth's Holocaust," *Nathaniel Hawthorne's Tales*, 158–59.

105. Martin, 213–14.

106. Twain, *A Connecticut Yankee in King Arthur's Court*, 257–58.

107. David Ketterer, "Epoch-Eclipse and Apocalypse: Special 'Effects' in *A Connecticut Yankee*," in *A Connecticut Yankee in King Arthur's Court*, ed. Allison R. Ensor (New York: Norton, 1982), 426, 433–34.

108. Tate, "The Angelic Imagination: Poe As God," *The Forlorn Demon*, 60.

109. "The Fall of the House of Usher," *Complete Works of Edgar Allan Poe*, 3: 286.

110. Poe, "The Colloquy of Monos and Una," *Complete Works of Edgar Allan Poe*, 4–5: 204–5.

111. The Conversation of Eiros and Charmion," *Complete Works of Edgar Allan Poe*, 4–5: 8.

112. *Eureka, Complete Works of Edgar Allan Poe*, 16: 185–86. On Poe's apocalyptic sense, see David H. Hirsch, "The Pit and the Apocalypse," *Sewanee Review* 74 (1968): 632–52.

113. Hoffman, 170.

114. "The Transcendentalist," *Selections from Ralph Waldo Emerson*, 195.

115. *Nature, Selections from Ralph Waldo Emerson*, 40.

116. Henry Adams, *The Education of Henry Adams* (Boston: Houghton, 1961), 451.

117. Wallace Stevens, "The Relations between Poetry and Painting," *The Necessary Angel* (New York: Vintage, 1951), 170–71.

118. Quoted in Arthur M. Saltzman's *The Fiction of William Gass* (Carbondale: Southern Illinois Univ. Press, 1986), 3–4. Not all postmodern antirealists, it must be said, fit Sukenick's nihilistic portrait of the contemporary artist. In fact, the ardent Catholicism of Alexander Theroux is nowhere more evident than in his defense of "the God/Artist equation" as the means by which "the writer concelebrates creation" or "re-extend[s] the script of creation." Cf. "Theroux Metaphrastes," 12.

119. Quoted in Tate, "The Angelic Imagination: Poe As God," *The Forlorn Demon*, 77.

1. Reflexivity

1. Patricia Waugh, *Metafiction: The Theory and Practice of Self-Conscious Fiction* (London: Methuen, 1984), 2. Subsequent references will be cited parenthetically in the text.

2. Raymond Federman, "Fiction Today or the Pursuit of Non-Knowledge" in *Surfiction: Fiction Now and Tomorrow*, ed. Raymond Federman (Chicago: Swallow, 1981), 309.

3. Coleman Dowell, *White on Black on White* (Woodstock, Vt.: Countryman, 1983), 200.

4. Robert Coover, *Pricksongs & Descants* (1969; rpt. New York: Plume-NAL, 1970), 20. Subsequent references will be cited parenthetically in the text.

5. Alfred Appel, Jr., ed., *The Annotated Lolita* (New York: McGraw, 1970). All quotations from the Foreword appear on pp. 5–8 of this edition, while all quotations from "Vladimir Nabokov on a book entitled *Lolita*" appear on pp. 313–19. Other references will be cited parenthetically in the text. In " 'Combinational Delight': The Uses of the Story within a Story in *Pale Fire*," *The Journal of Narrative Technique* 17, no. 1 (Winter 1987): 83–90, Peggy Ward Corn writes: "*Pale Fire* [is] a Russian doll work which does not rely on a container-contained relationship between its parts. In that novel, John Shade's poem is accompanied but not framed by Charles Kinbote's Commentary." Obviously, I disagree.

6. Vladimir Nabokov, *Pale Fire* (New York: Putnam's, 1962), 58. Subsequent references will be cited parenthetically in the text.

7. Vladimir Nabokov, *Speak, Memory: An Autobiography Revisited* (1966; rpt. New York: Capricorn-Putnam's, 1970), 52, 193.

8. Gilbert Sorrentino, *Mulligan Stew* (New York: Grove, 1979), 28. Subsequent references will be cited parenthetically in the text. Nabokov is referred to repeatedly in *Imaginative Qualities of Actual Things*, where "Bart's wife is Lolita."

9. Gilbert Sorrentino, *Something Said* (San Francisco: North Point, 1984), 200–201, 265.

10. John O'Brien, "An Interview with Gilbert Sorrentino," *Review of Contemporary Fiction* 1, no. 1 (Spring 1981): 25.

11. It should also be noted that the reflexive *Crystal Vision* (1981), though published two years after *Mulligan Stew* (1979), was actually written three years earlier (1976).

12. John O'Brien, "Every Man His Voice," *Review of Contemporary Fiction* 1, no. 1 (Spring 1981): 66. Intertextuality is also the subject of Leon S. Roudiez's article "The Reality Changes," on pp. 132–42 of this same Gilbert Sorrentino number. His remarks on *Splendide-Hôtel* are particularly interesting.

13. Flann O'Brien, *At Swim-Two-Birds* (1939; rpt. Harmondsworth, England: Penguin, 1967), 33. O'Brien went on to say:

Characters should be interchangeable as between one book and another. The entire corpus of existing literature should be regarded as a limbo from which discerning authors could draw their characters as required, creating only when they failed to find a suitable existing puppet. The modern novel should be largely a work of reference. Most authors spend their time saying what has been said before—usually said much better.

14. Sorrentino, *Something Said*, 263. Sorrentino's debt to *Finnegans Wake*, *At Swim-Two-Birds*, and other literary works becomes abundantly clear in *The Review of Contemporary Fiction* 1, no. 1 (Spring 1981).

15. John Barth, *The Friday Book: Essays and Other Nonfiction* (New York: Putnam's, 1984), xx. Subsequent references will be cited parenthetically in the text.

16. John Barth, *Chimera* (1972; rpt. New York: Fawcett Crest, 1973), 49. Subsequent references will be cited parenthetically in the text.

17. John Barth, *Giles Goat-Boy or, The Revised New Syllabus* (Garden City, N.Y.: Doubleday 1966), ix. Subsequent references will be cited parenthetically in the text.

18. Frederick R. Karl says in *American Fictions 1940/1980* (New York: Harper, 1983) that "Barth began *Giles* in June of 1960, more research than writing, abandoned it for another novel, called *The Seeker,* or *The Amateur;* then returned to *Giles* in early 1962 and continued, with some starts and stops, until the end of 1965" (288).

19. James L. McDonald, "Barth's Syllabus: The Frame of *Giles Goat-Boy,*" *Critique* 13, no. 3 (1972): 7.

20. John Barth, "Hawkes and Barth Talk About Fiction," *New York Times Book Review,* 1 April 1979, 7.

21. John Barth, *The Floating Opera* (New York: Avon, 1956), 269.

22. John Barth, *The End of the Road* (1958; rpt. New York: Avon, 1960), 60.

23. Barth, *The Friday Book,* 191.

24. John O. Stark, *The Literature of Exhaustion: Borges, Nabokov & Barth* (Durham, N.C.: Duke Univ. Press, 1974), 133.

25. John Barth, *Sabbatical: A Romance* (1982; rpt. New York: Penguin, 1983), 71.

26. John Barth, *Lost in the Funhouse: Fiction for Print, Tape, Live Voice* (1968; rpt. New York: Bantam, 1969), viii.

27. In *Letters* (New York: Putnam's, 1979), Ambrose Mensch writes:

In fact I was once briefly lost in a funhouse, at age twelve or thirteen, and included the anecdote in section I of this Amateur manuscript. But it happened in Asbury Park, New Jersey, not Ocean City, Maryland. . . . I don't know how to feel about our friend's rendering, by far the most extravagant liberty that he's taken with what I gave him. . . . In that version, the ride to 'Ocean City,' seen omnisciently through young A's sensibility, is all covert dramatic irony and dark insinuation. . . . The action proceeds between these suppressed bourgeois-domestic hang-ups, scandals, and volatilities in the foreground and, in the background, implications of the larger bourgeois violence of World War II. (168–69)

28. John Barth, *Letters* (New York: Putnam's, 1979), 653. Subsequent references will be cited parenthetically in the text.

29. Thomas R. Edwards, "A Novel of Correspondences," *New York Times Book Review,* 30 September 1979, 32.

30. The term "defamiliarization," which recurs in this chapter, is discussed by Victor Shklovsky in *Russian Formalist Criticism: Four Essays,* ed. Lee T. Lemon and Marion J. Reis (Lincoln: Univ. of Nebraska Press, 1965), where his two essays, "Art as Technique" and "Sterne's *Tristram Shandy:* Stylistic

Commentary," illuminate his famous concept. For example, on p. 12, he says: "The purpose of art is to impart the sensation of things as they are perceived and not as they are known. The technique of art is to make objects 'unfamiliar,' to make forms difficult, to increase the difficulty and length of perception is an aesthetic end in itself and must be prolonged. *Art is a way of experiencing the artfulness of an object; the object is not important.*"

2. The Ludic Impulse

1. These three statements appear among the fourteen epigraphs Peter Hutchinson includes in *Games Authors Play* (London: Methuen, 1983).

2. Gerald Clarke, "The Art of Fiction L: Gore Vidal" (an interview), *Paris Review* no. 59 (1974): 139, 143.

3. John Barth, *The Friday Book: Essays and Other Nonfiction* (New York: Putnam's, 1984), 132.

4. Alexander Theroux, "Theroux Metaphrastes: An Essay on Literature," appended to *Three Wogs* (Boston: Godine, 1975), 27.

5. Robert Detweiler, "Games and Play in Modern American Fiction," *Contemporary Literature* 17, no. 1 (Winter 1976): 48–49, includes the following three categories: (1) "playful or whimsical fiction, writing that is based on exuberance and exaggeration, that appears spontaneous and casually composed (even though it is not), that is usually funny, and that does not portray a particular game, or play a game with the reader"; (2) "fiction in which particular games are portrayed and indeed usually form the foundation of a plot, characterization, or imagery. Very often these games are sports. . . . Otherwise, the games depicted are contests of some sort that have a traditional formal structure or an easily identifiable game configuration"; (3) "fiction in which or through which the author plays a game with the reader, either by presenting the story in some cryptic form as a puzzle to be solved or as an inside joke in which the reader understands that he is asked to share in the fun of a *roman à clef* or a similar combination of history and fantasy or a revision of an older narrative."

Robert Alter, *Partial Magic: The Novel as a Self-Conscious Genre* (Berkeley: Univ. of California Press, 1975), 182, cautions the reader of such writing: "If the self-conscious novel tends on one side to excessive cerebrality, . . . it tends on the other side to an unchecked playfulness that may become self-indulgent."

6. Vladimir Nabokov, *Speak Memory: An Autobiography Revisited* (New York: Capricorn-Putnam's, 1970), 290.

7. Vladimir Nabokov, Foreword to the American edition of *The Defense* (New York: Putnam's, 1964), 8, 9.

8. Mary McCarthy, "A Bolt from the Blue," *New Republic* 146 (4 June 1962): 23.

9. Robert Coover, *The Universal Baseball Association, Inc., J. Henry Waugh,*

Prop. (New York: NAL, 1968), 156. Subsequent references will be cited parenthetically in the text.

10. For Burroughs's linguistic experiments, see chapter 4, "Fragmentation/Decentralization."

11. Donald Barthelme, *City Life* (New York: Farrar, 1970), 107.

12. Ronald Sukenick, *Long Talking Bad Conditions Blues* (New York: Fiction Collective, 1979), 114.

13. Gilbert Sorrentino, *Splendide-Hôtel* (1973; rpt. Elmwood Park, Ill.: Dalkey, 1984), 13. Subsequent references will be cited parenthetically in the text.

14. On pp. 60–61 of his unpublished study, "The Fiction of Gilbert Sorrentino," John O'Brien writes:

The letter "F." This section begins with: "Well, why speak of children's games?" . . . So, in the process of talking "about" games, Sorrentino in this chapter is also creating a game by seeing what objects, names, and themes he can work into the chapter which is "about" games and is itself a game.

The section concludes with a list of more than one hundred "games," and appropriately a number of them are children's games, some rather easily identifiable as such: Ringaleevio, Red Rover, and Giant Steps. Others, however, are names of literary works and figures. . . . And there are card games and terms from baseball (Baltimore Chop and Texas Leaguer). "Mae West" appears in the list, perhaps because, on the previous page, Sorrentino talks about actors always playing roles, even in their private lives, so that what may appear as insanity is just another adopted act—or game. Further, she is part of the chapter's game of seeing how materials from the chapter itself can be worked into the list.

15. Jerome Klinkowitz, "Walter Abish: An Interview," *Fiction International* no. 4/5 (1975): 96. Subsequent references will be cited parenthetically in the text. Metafictionist Abish also told Klinkowitz, "In my writing I try to strip language of its power to create verisimilitude."

16. William Gass, *Habitations of the Word* (New York: Simon, 1985), 150.

17. L. Moholy-Nagy, "Literature," in *The Avant-Garde Tradition in Literature,* ed. Richard Kostelanetz (Buffalo, N.Y.: Prometheus, 1982), 95.

18. Raymond Federman, *Double or Nothing* (Chicago: Swallow, 1971), O. Subsequent references will be cited parenthetically in the text.

19. Richard Kostelanetz, "New Fiction in America," in *Surfiction: Fiction Now and Tomorrow,* ed. Raymond Federman (Chicago: Swallow, 1981), 96.

20. Gass, *Habitations of the Word,* 158.

21. Kostelanetz in Federman, *Surfiction,* 96.

22. For the plot of this novel, see chapter 1, "Reflexivity."

23. Gilbert Sorrentino, *Mulligan Stew* (New York: Grove, 1979), 414. Subsequent references will be cited parenthetically in the text.

24. Gilbert Sorrentino, *Something Said* (San Francisco: North Point, 1984), 198.

25. Max Eilenberg, "A Marvellous Gift: Gilbert Sorrentino's Fiction," *Review of Contemporary Fiction* 1, no. 1 (Spring 1981): 92–93. Here, Eilenberg says:

With a title and a progress typical of the Jacobean masque (e.g. "The Golden Age Restored"), the story is of a baseball player's return to form, and the restoration thereby of harmony and hope to a Brooklyn both contemporary and fantastic, crowded with representative figures: book editors, concrete poets, Guggenheim fellows, young tycoons, Eddy Beshary (back from *Steelwork*), the Marquis de Sade, and James Joyce, whose gnomic utterances are lifted from the obscurity of the Wake. . . . As a masque it owes much to the exuberantly coarse energy of Jonson's "The Gypsies Metamorphosed"; and as a Walpurgisnacht it's the first triumphantly worthy response/homage to the "Circe" episode in *Ulysses*. It is fitting, therefore, that it should be Joyce who at the end offers up the prayer of thanks for a joyful resolution to Fungo's crisis, in words that cryptically evoke the achievement of *Mulligan Stew:* "Loud *[sic]*, heap miseries upon us yet entwine our arts with laughters low!"

26. Hugh Kenner, "II. The Traffic in Words," *Harpers* 258, no. 1549 (June 1979): 90.
27. John O'Brien, "An Interview with Gilbert Sorrentino," *Review of Contemporary Fiction* 1, no. 1 (Spring 1981): 19–20. On pp. 78–79 of this issue, O'Brien discusses the evolution of Sorrentino's lists from *Steelwork* to *Mulligan Stew*.
28. Ibid., 20.
29. Alexander Theroux, *Darconville's Cat* (Garden City, N.Y.: Doubleday, 1981), 571. Subsequent references will be cited parenthetically in the text.
30. Evidently, this monograph and its author were invented by Theroux, though the other figures mentioned in the note on p. 234 are historically verifiable. The excerpts from *The Shakeing of the Sheets*, which appear on pp. 8, 13, 20, 25, and 31 of "Theroux Metaphrastes," parody Elizabethan style. These passages may be compared to Sorrentino's travesty of Shakespeare, in LIKE BLOWING FLOWER STILLED, *Mulligan Stew*, pp. 389–99.
31. Eilenberg, "A Marvellous Gift," 91.
32. Patricia Waugh, *Metafiction: The Theory and Practice of Self-Conscious Fiction* (London: Methuen, 1984), 65.
33. Alfred Appel, Jr., *The Annotated* LOLITA (New York: McGraw, 1970), xxvii.
34. Ibid., liii and lxv.
35. Robert Coover, *Pricksongs & Descants* (1969; rpt. New York: Plume-NAL, 1970), 42.
36. To some extent, *Heartbreak Hotel* by Gabrielle Burton (New York: Scribner's, 1986), which mentions *Snow White*, is a parody of the Barthelme text.
37. Donald Barthelme, *Snow White* (1967; rpt. New York: Bantam, 1968), 82–83. Subsequent references will be cited parenthetically in the text.
38. Lois Gordon, *Donald Barthelme* (Boston: Twayne, 1981), 75.
39. Gerald Graff, *Literature Against Itself* (Chicago: Univ. of Chicago Press, 1979), 227.
40. John Hawkes, *The Lime Twig* (New York: New Directions, 1961), 155. Subsequent references will be cited parenthetically in the text.

41. In his December 29, 1985 *New York Times* review of *Gerald's Party* (New York: Linden-Simon, 1986), Charles Newman indirectly acknowledged its parodic tone:

> By the time Pardew finally fingers the murderer, the initial crime seems the least of the horrors that have been perpetrated. It is a measure of Mr. Coover's relentlessness that we have been inured, like his characters, to *any* criminal behavior, and the culprit is not only "unlikely," but you have to reread the book to find out where he came in. The point being of course that the solution to the crime is the most inconsequential and arbitrary part of the mystery, that guilt, accountability and justice are mere literary conventions projected by the stupefied reader.

42. On p. 72 of *The Friday Book,* John Barth calls *The Sot-Weed Factor* and *Giles Goat-Boy* "novels which imitate the form of the Novel, by an author who imitates the role of Author." Both parody popular and serious forms, as chapter 7, "Absurd Quests" and 8, "Fictitious History" demonstrate.

43. John Hawkes, *The Beetle Leg* (New York: New Directions, 1951), 66. Subsequent references will be cited parenthetically in the text.

44. C. Hugh Holman, *A Handbook to Literature,* 4th ed. (Indianapolis: Bobbs, 1981), 319.

3. Maximalism versus Minimalism

1. Edmund Wilson, ed., *The Crack-Up* (New York: New Directions, 1956), 314. Stanley Elkin, remembering this " 'famous exchange between Fitzgerald and Thomas Wolfe,' " said, " 'My editor at Random House, Joe Fox, used to tell me, "Stanley, less is more." . . . I had to fight him tooth and nail in the better restaurants to maintain excess because I don't believe that less is more. I believe that *more* is more. I believe less is less, fat fat, thin thin and enough is enough.' " See *Anything Can Happen: Interviews with Contemporary American Novelists,* ed. Tom LeClair and Larry McCaffery (Urbana: Univ. of Illinois Press, 1983), 109.

2. John Barth, "A Few Words About Minimalism," *New York Times Book Review,* 28 December 1986, section 7: 2ff. Exactly one week before, John Rockwell's "The Death and Life of Minimalism" had appeared in the *Times* on p. 29.

3. Donald Barthelme, *Snow White* (1967; rpt. New York: Bantam, 1968), 96–98.

4. Donald Barthelme, *The Dead Father* (New York: Farrar, 1975), 20. Subsequent references will be cited parenthetically in the text.

5. See John Leverence, "Gaddis Anagnorisis," in *In Recognition of William Gaddis,* ed. John Kuehl and Steven Moore (Syracuse, N.Y.: Syracuse Univ. Press, 1984), 33, where he says that Morris W. Croll "found loose baroque syntax to have three recurring elements: coordinating conjunctions, absolute constructions, and parentheses." "The syntax of Gaddis' prose style is marked

by the frequent appearance of these elements, as well as apposition, conjunctive adverbs and relative clauses, all appearing in compound-complex sentences," adds Leverence.

6. Alexander Theroux, "Theroux Metaphrastes: An Essay on Literature," appended to *Three Wogs* (Boston: Godine, 1975), 9, 2.

7. Ibid., 24.

8. Alexander Theroux, *Darconville's Cat* (Garden City, N.Y.: Doubleday, 1981), 662. For the plot of this novel, see chapter 2, "The Ludic Impulse."

9. Ibid., 232.

10. Steven Moore, "Alexander Theroux's *Darconville's Cat* and the Tradition of Learned Wit," *Contemporary Literature* 27, no. 2 (Summer 1986): 233–34.

11. C. Hugh Holman, *A Handbook to Literature*, 4th ed. (Indianapolis: Bobbs, 1981), 263.

12. Northrop Frye, *Anatomy of Criticism: Four Essays* (1957; rpt. Princeton: Princeton Univ Press, 1971), 309–12.

13. Edward Mendelson, ed., *Pynchon: A Collection of Critical Essays* (Englewood Cliffs, N.J.: Prentice, 1978), 9–10.

14. For the plots of these two novels, see chapter 4, "Fragmentation/Decentralization."

15. Steven Moore, "Parallel, Not Series: Thomas Pynchon and William Gaddis," *Pynchon Notes* 11 (February 1983): 6–26.

16. Steven Moore, *A Reader's Guide to William Gaddis's "The Recognitions"* (Lincoln: Univ. of Nebraska Press, 1982), 4. Subsequent references will be cited parenthetically in the text.

17. The titles Moore cites on pp. 54–58 disclose the author's preoccupations while composing *The Recognitions: Architecture, Mysticism and Myth; The Apocryphal New Testament; Fox's Book of Martyrs; Counterfeiting: Crime against the People; The Devil's Share; Encyclopaedia Britannica*, 14th ed., *Faust; A Tragedy; The Gentle Art of Faking; The Golden Bough; How to Win Friends and Influence People; The Divine Comedy; Lives and Opinions of Eminent Philosophers; Love in the Western World; Mithraism; Magic, Myth and Morals; A Study of Christian Origins; Mediaeval and Modern Saints and Miracles; Psychology and Alchemy; The Pilgrim Hymnal; The Physical Phenomena of Mysticism; Star Lore of All Ages; The Van Eycks and Their Followers; The White Goddess; A Historical Grammar of Poetic Myth; The Waning of the Middle Ages*. Subsequently, Moore published "Additional Sources for William Gaddis's ' 'The Recognitions,' " *American Notes & Queries* 22, no. 7/8 (March/April 1984): 111–15.

18. See Miriam Fuchs, " 'il miglior fabbro': Gaddis' Debt to T. S. Eliot," in *In Recognition of William Gaddis*, 92–105, where Eliot's influence on Gaddis is traced. It should be noted tangentially that most scholars discount a similar influence stemming from James Joyce, since Gaddis claims he has never read *Ulysses*.

19. Quoted by David Koenig, "The Writing of *The Recognitions*," in *In Recognition of William Gaddis*, 21.

20. William Gaddis, *The Recognitions* (1955; rpt. Cleveland: Meridian-World, 1962), 465.

21. Ibid., 372–73.

22. For further information on the relationship between Gaddis's novel and the Clementine *Recognitions*, see Peter William Koenig, "Recognizing Gaddis' *Recognitions*," *Contemporary Literature* 16 (Winter 1975): 61–72, and Elaine B. Safer, "The Allusive Mode, the Absurd and Black Humor in William Gaddis's *The Recognitions*," *Studies in American Humor* n.s. 1 (October 1982): 103–18.

23. Frederick R. Karl, *American Fictions 1940/1980* (New York: Harper, 1983), 384.

24. Willa Cather, "The Novel Démeublé" (1922), in *On Writing* (New York: Knopf, 1962), 41–42.

25. Ernest Hemingway, *Death in the Afternoon* (New York: Scribner's, 1932), 192.

26. Karl, *American Fictions*, 384. Now minimalism is viewed as a return to realism. For instance, John Barth's "A Few Words About Minimalism" emphasizes the "American short story"—"the kind of terse, oblique, realistic or hyperrealistic, slightly plotted, extrospective, cool-surfaced fiction associated in the last 5 or 10 years with such excellent writers as Frederick Barthelme, Ann Beattie, Raymond Carver, Bobbie Ann Mason, James Robison, Mary Robison and Tobias Wolff." This echoes the position taken by the contributors to Special Section on "Minimalist Fiction," *Mississippi Review* no. 40/41 (Winter 1985): 7–94.

27. Donald Barthelme, *The Dead Father* (New York: Farrar, 1975), 54. Subsequent references will be cited parenthetically in the text.

28. Betty Catherine Dobson Farmer, "Mythological, Biblical, and Literary Allusions in Donald Barthelme's *The Dead Father*," *The International Fiction Review* 6, no. 1 (Winter 1979): 40–41.

29. Cf., the chapter entitled "The Golden Fleas" in John Hawkes's *Second Skin* (New York: New Directions, 1964), 205–10.

30. For example, Jerzy Kosinski's 148-page *Steps* has 49 brief scenes, and Richard Brautigan's 182-page *Trout Fishing in America* has 47. Barthelme's own first novel, *Snow White*, is a 177-page text with 106 units.

31. Barth, "A Few Words About Minimalism," 2, 25.

32. John Rockwell, "The Death and Life of Minimalism," *The New York Times*, 21 December 1986, 29.

33. Thomas LeClair, "William Gaddis, *J R*, & the Art of Excess," *Modern Fiction Studies* 27, no. 4 (Winter 1981–1982): 587–600. Steven Moore, "Parallel, Not Series: Thomas Pynchon and William Gaddis," *Pynchon Notes* 11 (February 1983): 6–26, calls *J R* an encyclopedic novel despite the fact that it "[u]ses literary allusions sparingly." Richard Wagner's *Der Ring des Nibelungen* and Empedocles' doctrine of love and strife form the two most important aesthetic patterns there.

34. John Barth, *The Friday Book: Essays and Other Nonfiction* (New York: Putnam's, 1984), 191.

4. Fragmentation/Decentralization

1. See Raymond M. Olderman, *Beyond the Waste Land: The American Novel in the Nineteen-Sixties* (New Haven: Yale Univ. Press, 1972), where Eliot's impact on Ken Kesey, Stanley Elkin, John Barth, Joseph Heller, Thomas Pynchon, John Hawkes, Kurt Vonnegut, Jr., and Peter S. Beagle is discussed, and Miriam Fuchs, " 'Persistent Pattern and Significant Form': The Conceptual and Formal Impact of *The Waste Land* on Selected Anti-Realistic American Novels" (Ph.D. diss., New York University, 1979), which treats Djuna Barnes's *Nightwood*, Nathanael West's *Miss Lonelyhearts*, John Hawkes's *The Beetle Leg*, and William Gaddis's *The Recognitions*. Other contemporary antirealistic American writers who have alluded to and/or were influenced by Eliot include Donald Barthelme, William S. Burroughs, Coleman Dowell, Ralph Ellison, and Gilbert Sorrentino.

2. Miriam Fuchs, " 'il miglior fabbro': Gaddis' Debt to T. S. Eliot," in *In Recognition of William Gaddis*, ed. John Kuehl and Steven Moore (Syracuse, N.Y.: Syracuse Univ. Press, 1984), 92–105.

3. Stephen Matanle, "Love and Strife in William Gaddis's *J R*," in *In Recognition of William Gaddis*, 106–18, traces the influence of Empedocles on Gaddis's second novel. See, chapter 10, "Entropy."

4. Roger Shattuck, *The Banquet Years* (1958; rpt. New York: Knopf, 1968), 332–33.

5. Robert Langbaum, "New Modes of Characterization in *The Waste Land*," in *Eliot in His Time: Essays on the Occasion of the Fiftieth Anniversary of "The Waste Land*," ed. A. Walton Litz (Princeton: Princeton Univ. Press, 1973), 110.

6. See Stephen Martin, "A Comparative Study of Androgyny in Twentieth-Century Experimental Literature" (Ph.D. diss., New York University, 1984), which focuses, in part, on *Island People* and *The Waste Land*. Earlier, David Lodge had said on p. 229 of *The Modes of Modern Writing* (London: Arnold, 1977): "One of the most emotively powerful emblems of contradiction, one that affronts the most fundamental binary system of all, is the hermaphrodite; and it is not surprising that the characters of post-modernist fiction are often sexually ambivalent." Although gender changes à la Virginia Woolf's *Orlando* do not occur even among contemporary antirealistic American novels, a number of authors besides Dowell employ something like metamorphosis (i.e., changes of identity, etc.). They include Barth, Burroughs, Gaddis, Hawkes, Kosinski, and Pynchon. See Joseph Campbell, *The Hero with a Thousand Faces* (1949; rpt. Princeton: Princeton Univ. Press, 1972) for an excellent discussion of the bisexual god.

7. John Kuehl and Linda Kandel Kuehl, "An Interview with Coleman Dowell," *Contemporary Literature* 22, no. 3 (Summer 1981): 282.

8. Ibid., 278.

9. Coleman Dowell, *Island People* (New York: New Directions, 1976), 287. Subsequent references will be cited parenthetically in the text.

10. Coleman Dowell, *Too Much Flesh and Jabez* (New York: New Directions, 1977), 1. For an analysis of metamorphosis and androgyny in this novel, see John Kuehl and Linda Kandel Kuehl, "Miss Ethel and Mr. Dowell," *Review of Contemporary Fiction* 2, no. 3 (Fall 1982): 129–34.

11. See John O'Brien, "Interview with Coleman Dowell," *Review of Contemporary Fiction* 2, no. 3 (Fall 1982). On p. 93 Dowell told O'Brien with regard to this final scene: "The woman standing at the window, turning to smile at him, is: the stepmother; the mother; Beatrix; Miss Gold. Joining her in death, he joins/makes peace with his feminine side, as he has made peace with old age and death."

12. Stephen-Paul Martin, "Exorcism and Grace: A Study of Androgyny in *Island People*," *Review of Contemporary Fiction* 2, no. 3 (Fall 1982): 124. On p. 283 of the *Contemporary Literature* interview with the Kuehls, Dowell had said: "Well, the dust jacket shows the superimposition of the male and the female. Yes, I'm trying to make them merge in myself and other people. It would be nice if we didn't have this split, if they could be friends. The ideal thing is a perfect balance between the two in a personality because both the male and the female have wonderful strengths as well as weaknesses."

13. Kuehl interview, *Contemporary Literature*, 284.

14. William Burroughs, *Nova Express* (1964; rpt. *Three Novels*, New York: Grove, 1980), 103.

15. Philippe Mikriammos, "The Last European Interview," *Review of Contemporary Fiction* 4, no. 1 (Spring 1984): 14.

16. Gregory Stephenson, "The Gnostic Vision of William S. Burroughs," *Review of Contemporary Fiction* 4, no. 1 (Spring 1984): 42.

17. David Lodge discusses others in *The Modes of Modern Writing*. According to him, Ronald Sukenick's

98.6 illustrates the most obvious sign of discontinuity in contemporary fiction—the growing fashion for composing in very short sections, often only a paragraph in length, often quite disparate in content, the breaks between sections being sometimes further emphasized by capitalized headings (as in Richard Brautigan's *In Watermelon Sugar* [1968]), numbers (as in Robert Coover's "The Gingerbread Man") or typographical devices (like the arrows in Vonnegut's *Breakfast of Champions* [1973]). Vonnegut's later novels and all of Brautigan's are built up in this way, out of sections too short to be recognized as conventional chapters. . . .

Leonard Michaels has recently developed what is virtually a new genre: the cluster (it is precisely *not* a sequence) of short passages—stories, anecdotes, reflections, quotations, prose-poems, jokes—each with an individual title in large type. . . .

In the work of Donald Barthelme the principle of *non-sequitur* governs the relationships between sentences as well as between paragraphs. . . . One of Barthelme's favourite devices is to take a number of interrelated or contiguous characters, or consciousnesses or conversations, and scramble them together to produce an apparently random montage of bizarrely contrasting verbal fragments. (232, 234, 235)

See also chapter 2, "The Ludic Impulse."
18. William S. Burroughs and Brion Gysin, *The Third Mind* (1978; rpt. London: Calder, 1979), 29.
19. William S. Burroughs, *The Burroughs File* (San Francisco: City Lights, 1984), 151.
20. Burroughs and Gysin, *The Third Mind*, 95–96. The fold-in method is demonstrated on p. 34 of *The Burroughs File*.
21. Eric Mottram, *William Burroughs: The Algebra of Need* (London: Boyars, 1977), 177.
22. Ibid., 239. During THE KETREAT DIARIES section of *The Burroughs File*, p. 192, Burroughs wrote:

Here Thursday and Friday may be cut in with Monday, or the elaboration of a dream cut in with the dream itself in a grid of past present and future. Like the last words of Dutch Schultz. Some of Dutch's associations cannot be traced or even guessed at. Others quite clearly derive from the known events of his life. The *structure* is that a man is *seeing a film* composed of past present and future, dream and fantasy, a film which the reader cannot see directly but only infer through the words. This is the structure of these diaries.

23. Burroughs and Gysin, *The Third Mind*, 5–6. This destructive attitude may be compared to the positive attitude of Donald Barthelme as discussed and quoted in Jerome Klinkowitz, *Literary Disruptions: The Making of a Post-Contemporary American Fiction* (Urbana: Univ. of Illinois Press, 1975), 76:

In a new world, old values must be expressed in new form. For irrational, inconsecutive times, Barthelme's forms revive the values of imagination: the rescue is performed with the finest attentions to art. Not just a juggler of fragments, Barthelme is an assembler and constructor of objects. "The principle of collage," he told Richard Schickel, "is the central principle of all art in the twentieth century in all media." More recently, and with specific reference to fiction, Barthelme has said that "The point of collage is that unlike things are stuck together to make, in the best case, a new reality. This new reality, in the best case, may be or imply a comment on the other reality from which it came, and may also be much else. It's an *itself*, if it's successful."

24. Victor Bockris, *With William Burroughs: A Report from the Bunker* (New York: Seaver, 1981), 6.
25. Burroughs and Gysin, *The Third Mind*, 34.
26. Ibid., 96, 89.
27. As translated in Nicholas Zurbrugg, "The Last European Interview," *Review of Contemporary Fiction* 4, no. 1 (Spring 1984): 30.
28. Quoted by David Keonig, "The Writing of The Recognitions," in *In Recognition of William Gaddis*, 28.
29. Ibid., 30.

30. C. Hugh Holman, *A Handbook to Literature*, 4th ed. (Indianapolis: Bobbs, 1980), 277.

31. William Gaddis, *The Recognitions* (1955; rpt. Cleveland: Meridian-World, 1962), 328.

32. Ibid., 305.

33. Steven Moore, *A Reader's Guide to William Gaddis's "The Recognitions"* (Lincoln: Univ. of Nebraska Press, 1982), 41.

34. Frederick R. Karl, *American Fictions 1940/1980* (New York: Harper, 1983), 451.

35. See Douglas Fowler, *A Reader's Guide to "Gravity's Rainbow"* (Ann Arbor, Mich.: Ardis, 1980), 44–45.

36. Ibid., 47.

5. The Grotesque and the Devil

1. William Van O'Connor, *The Grotesque: An American Genre, and Other Essays* (Carbondale, Ill.: Southern Illinois Univ. Press, 1962), 3.

2. Fritz Gysin, *The Grotesque in American Negro Fiction* (Bern: Francke, 1975), 29, 30.

3. Sally Fitzgerald, ed., *The Habit of Being* (1979; rpt. New York: Vintage-Random, 1980), 291. Subsequent references will be cited parenthetically in the text.

4. See Sister Kathleen Feeley, S. S. N. D., *Flannery O'Connor: Voice of the Peacock* (New Brunswick, N.J.: Rutgers Univ. Press, 1972), 6–7. Here, Sister Feeley writes:

Her predilection for the unusual, the incongruous, the bizarre had early roots. In an essay on peacock-raising, she tells of her childhood addiction to malformed chickens. "I favored those with one green eye and one orange or with overlong necks and crooked combs. I wanted one with three legs or three wings but nothing in that line turned up." . . . Flannery once said that her reading of *The Humorous Short Stories of Edgar Allen [sic] Poe* first inspired her to think of a writing career. Certainly it could have prompted a convergence of her comic spirit and her penchant for the grotesque.

5. John Hawkes, *The Cannibal* (1949; rpt. New York: New Directions, 1962), 43. Subsequent references will be cited parenthetically in the text.

6. Flannery O'Connor, *Wise Blood* (1952; rpt. New York: Signet-NAL), 54. Subsequent references will be cited parenthetically in the text.

7. Wolfgang Kayser, *The Grotesque in Art and Literature*, trans. Ulrich Weisstein (1957; rpt. New York: McGraw, 1966), 188. Subsequent references will be cited parenthetically in the text.

8. This reminds us of *Les Chants de Maldoror* (1868–1870)—a work admired by Hawkes—where pronoun shifts indicate a similar confusion over identification-detachment. Like Bonaventura's night watchman, Maldoror wears the satanic mask; but unlike Bonaventura, Lautréamont vacillates be-

tween "I" and "he," alternately merging with, then separating from, his protagonist.

9. John Enck, "John Hawkes: An Interview," *Wisconsin Studies in Contemporary Literature* 6, no. 2 (Summer 1964): 150.

10. John Hawkes, "Flannery O'Connor's Devil," *Sewanee Review* 70 (Summer 1962): 396. Subsequent references will be cited parenthetically in the text. Steven Weisenberger applies the views expressed in this essay to Hawkes's later work, particularly *Travesty*, in "The Devil and John Hawkes," *Review of Contemporary Fiction* 3, no. 3 (Fall 1983): 155–63.

11. John Kuehl, *John Hawkes and the Craft of Conflict* (New Brunswick, N.J.: Rutgers Univ. Press, 1975), 162.

12. Flannery O'Connor, *Mystery and Manners*, ed. Sally and Robert Fitzgerald (New York: Farrar, 1970), 117–18.

13. See Gilbert H. Muller, *Nightmares and Visions: Flannery O'Connor and the Catholic Grotesque* (Athens, Ga.: Univ. of Georgia Press, 1972), 3–4. Here, Muller observes:

Like Bosch, Flannery O'Connor creates a landscape wherein life is already hellish, and where men are possessed by demons and devils who completely control their souls and who subject them to excruciating torment. Her own Millennium canvas, dominated by the unexpected and disconnected, the malformed and the estranged, projects what is perhaps the most consistently grotesque body of work in our time. What both Bosch and Miss O'Connor present, in a style that is pointed and precise, is a violation of the limits which have been laid down by God for man. Thus, for these two artists, the grotesque does not function gratuitously, but in order to reveal underlying and essentially theological concepts.

14. Flannery O'Connor, *The Complete Stories* (New York: Farrar, 1971), 276. Subsequent references will be cited parenthetically in the text.

15. Marguerite Young, *Miss MacIntosh, My Darling* (1965; New York: Harvest-Harcourt, 1979), 242. Subsequent references will be cited parenthetically in the next.

16. Alexander Theroux, *Darconville's Cat* (Garden City, N.Y.: Doubleday, 1981), 432. Subsequent references will be cited parenthetically in the text.

17. Nathanael West, *Miss Lonelyhearts* (1933; rpt. New York: New Directions, 1962), 1, 35, 54. Subsequent references will be cited parenthetically in the text.

18. William Gaddis, *The Recognitions* (1955; rpt. Cleveland: Meridian-World, 1962), 227, 245. Subsequent references will be cited parenthetically in the text.

19. See Peter W. Koenig, " 'Splinters from the Yew Tree': A Critical Study of William Gaddis' *The Recognitions*" (Ph.D. diss., New York University, 1971), 134–55.

6. Imaginary Landscapes

1. Henry James, *Selected Literary Criticism*, ed. Morris Shapira (New York: McGraw, 1965), 57.

2. Eudora Welty, "Place in Fiction," in *The Eye of the Story: Selected Essays and Reviews* (New York: Random, 1977), 117, 121, 122.

3. John J. Enck, "John Barth: An Interview," *Wisconsin Studies in Contemporary Literature* (Winter-Spring 1965): 8.

4. John Barth, *The Friday Book: Essays and Other Nonfiction* (New York: Putnam's, 1984), 128, 129.

5. William S. Burroughs, *Cities of the Red Night* (New York: Holt, 1981), 153. Subsequent references will be cited parenthetically in the text.

6. John O'Brien, "Interview with Coleman Dowell," *Review of Contemporary Fiction* 2, no. 3 (Fall 1982): 98.

7. Coleman Dowell, *Mrs. October Was Here* (New York: New Directions, 1974), 123. Subsequent references will be cited parenthetically in the text.

8. Donald Barthelme, *City Life* (New York: Farrar, 1970), 20. Subsequent references will be cited parenthetically in the text.

9. Jorge Luis Borges, *Labyrinths: Selected Stories & Other Writings*, ed. Donald A. Yates & James E. Irby (New York: New Directions, 1964), 16. Subsequent references will be cited parenthetically in the text.

10. Quoted in Ana Maria Barrenechea, *Borges: The Labyrinth Maker*, ed./trans. Robert Lima (New York: New York Univ. Press, 1965), 123.

11. Vladimir Nabokov, *Speak, Memory: An Autobiography Revisited* (Rev. 1966; rpt. New York: Putnam's, 1970), 52.

12. Vladimir Nabokov, *Pale Fire* (New York: Putnam's, 1962), 315. Subsequent references will be cited parenthetically in the text.

13. Imaginary tongues also appear in *Alphabetical Africa, The Blood Oranges, and The Dead Father*.

14. Quoted in Bobbie Ann Mason, *Nabokov's Garden: A Guide to ADA* (Ann Arbor, Mich.: Ardis, 1971), 11.

15. Vladimir Nabokov, *Ada or Ardor: A Family Chronicle* (New York: McGraw, 1969), 344. Subsequent references will be cited parenthetically in the text.

16. Washington Irving referred to Estotiland in *Voyages and Discoveries of the Companions of Columbus*, ed. James W. Tuttleton (Boston: Twayne, 1986), 257ff. He said that Venetian Antonio Zeno gave his brother Carlo some fisherman's account of "an island called Estotiland, about one thousand miles from Friseland." But though "the Island of Estotiland has been supposed by M. Malte-Brun to be Newfoundland; its partially civilized inhabitants the descendents of the Scandinavian colonists on Vinland; and the Latin books in the king's library to be the remains of the library of the Greenland Bishop who emigrated thither in 1121," Irving felt these deductions were unwar-

ranted. His assertion, "The whole story abounds with improbabilities," would have delighted Nabokov.

17. Like imaginary tongues, foreign languages are used frequently in contemporary antirealistic American fiction.

18. Laurie Clancy, *The Novels of Vladimir Nabokov* (New York: St. Martin's, 1984), 149–50.

19. For the following discussion of Hawkes's landscapes, I have drawn on my earlier study, *John Hawkes and the Craft of Conflict* (New Brunswick, N.J.: Rutgers Univ. Press, 1975).

20. John Hawkes, "Flannery O'Connor's Devil," *The Sewanee Review* 70 (Summer 1962): 399.

21. Eliotic internationality is typical of other postwar fabulators: Abish, Burroughs, Gaddis, Nabokov, Pynchon, and Theroux.

22. Kuehl, *John Hawkes and the Craft of Conflict*, 178.

23. John Hawkes, "Notes on the Wild Goose Chase," *The Massachusetts Review* 3 (Autumn 1962): 787.

24. John Willett, ed., *Brecht on Theatre* (New York: Hill, 1964), 192, 233. On p. 37 of this book, we get the famous table showing "certain changes of emphasis as between the dramatic and the epic theatre." If we substitute Realism for Dramatic Theatre and Antirealism for Epic Theatre, we have virtually all the criteria involving these two opposite fictional modes long before novelist-critics like Barth, Gass, and Sorrentino began to write.

25. Patrick O'Donnell, "Life and Art: An Interview with John Hawkes," *Review of Contemporary Fiction* 3, no. 3 (Fall 1983): 119.

26. John Hawkes, *The Passion Artist* (1979; rpt. New York: Colophon-Harper, 1981), 84.

27. John Hawkes, "The Landscape of the Imagination," unpublished transcript of a B.B.C. recording, November 2, 1966, 4–5.

28. Unpublished letters from John Hawkes to John Kuehl of 10 November 1972, 19 April 1973, 10 February 1972, and 22 February 1972, respectively.

29. John Enck, "John Hawkes: An Interview," *Wisconsin Studies in Contemporary Literature* 6, no. 2 (Summer 1964): 154.

30. John Hawkes, *Second Skin* (New York: New Directions, 1964), 109. Subsequent references will be cited parenthetically in the text.

31. John Hawkes, *The Innocent Party: Four Short Plays* (New York: New Directions, 1966), 62–63.

32. John Hawkes, *The Beetle Leg* (New York: New Directions, 1951), 140.

33. Robert Scholes, "A Conversation on *The Blood Oranges* Between John Hawkes and Robert Scholes," *Novel* 5, no. 3 (Spring 1972): 203.

34. Kuehl, *John Hawkes and the Craft of Conflict*, 171.

35. Scholes, "A Conversation on *The Blood Oranges*," 198.

36. John Hawkes, *The Blood Oranges* (New York: New Directions, 1971), 177. Subsequent references will be cited parenthetically in the text.

7. *Absurd Quests*

1. Otto Rank, *The Myth of the Birth of the Hero,* trans. Dr. F. Robbins and Dr. Smith Ely Jelliffe (1910; rpt. New York: Brunner, 1952), 61.
2. F. Scott Fitzgerald, *Afternoon of an Author: A Selection of Uncollected Stories and Essays,* ed. Arthur Mizener (Princeton: Princeton University Library, 1957), 185.
3. F. Scott Fitzgerald, *The Great Gatsby* (New York: Scribner's, 1925), 99. Subsequent references will be cited parenthetically in the text.
4. John Barth, "My Two Muses," in *The Friday Book: Essays and Other Nonfiction* (New York: Putnam's, 1984), 158.
5. Ibid., 159.
6. John Barth, *Giles Goat-Boy or, The Revised New Syllabus* (Garden City, N.Y.: Doubleday, 1966), 372. Subsequent references will be cited parenthetically in the text.
7. In a 1964 interview reprinted in *The Contemporary Writer,* ed. L. S. Dembo and Cyrena N. Pondrom (Madison: Univ. of Wisconsin Press, 1972), Barth told John J. Enck: "What I really wanted to write after *The Sot-Weed Factor* was a new Old Testament, a comic Old Testament. I guess that's what this new novel *Giles Goat-Boy* is going to be. A souped-up Bible."
8. Robert Scholes, *The Fabulators* (New York: Oxford Univ. Press, 1967), 171.
9. Raymond M. Olderman, *Beyond the Waste Land: A Study of the American Novel in the Nineteen-Sixties* (New Haven: Yale Univ. Press, 1973), 77–78.
10. Joseph Campbell, *The Hero with a Thousand Faces* (1949; rpt. Princeton: Princeton Univ. Press, 1972), 116.
11. Ibid., 108.
12. Joe David Bellamy, "Having it Both Ways," *New American Review* no. 15 (April 1972): 146.
13. Gilbert Sorrentino, *Blue Pastoral* (San Francisco: North Point, 1983), 9–10. Subsequent references will be cited parenthetically in the text.
14. According to John O'Brien's unpublished study, "The Fiction of Gilbert Sorrentino," pp. 131–32, "The Phrase is taken from a rather obscure Dinah Washington blues song of the late 1940s, 'I Sold My Heart to the Junkman,' an appropriate enough song for a book that is filled with 'junk' and in which the author—or whoever!—has indeed given himself to the junk of literature."
15. Ibid., 136.
16. Joseph McElroy, *Hind's Kidnap: A Pastoral on Familiar Airs* (New York: Harper, 1969), 365. Subsequent references will be cited parenthetically in the text.
17. *Interviews with Contemporary American Novelists,* ed. Tom LeClair and Larry McCaffery (Urbana: Univ. of Illinois Press, 1983), 240–41.

18. Thomas Pynchon, *V.* (Philadelphia: Lippincott, 1963), 52. Subsequent references will be cited parenthetically in the text.

19. Frederick R. Karl, *American Fictions 1940–1980* (New York: Harper, 1983), 304.

20. Nathanael West, *A Cool Million or, The Dismantling of Lemuel Pitkin* (1934; rpt. in *The Complete Works of Nathanael West* [New York: Farrar, 1957]), 239.

21. Tony Tanner, "V. and V-2," in *Pynchon: A Collection of Critical Essays*, ed. Edward Mendelson (Englewood Cliffs, N.J.: Prentice, 1978), 32.

8. Fictitious History

1. John Barth, "Historical Fiction, Fictitious History, and the Chesapeake Bay Blue Crabs, or, About Aboutness," in *The Friday Book: Essays and Other Nonfiction* (New York: Putnam's, 1984), 187. Subsequent references will be cited parenthetically in the text.

2. See Edward H. Cohen, *Ebenezer Cooke: The Sot-Weed Canon* (Athens, Ga.: Univ. of Georgia Press, 1975). See also Philip Diser, "The Historical Ebenezer Cooke," *Critique* 10, no. 3 (1968): 576–604.

3. Barth, *The Friday Book*, 250.

4. Alan Holder, " 'What Marvelous Plot . . . Was Afoot?' History in Barth's *The Sot-Weed Factor*," *American Quarterly* 20, no. 3 (Fall 1968): 599.

5. John Barth, *The Sot-Weed Factor* (1960; rpt. New York: Bantam, 1980), 83–84. Subsequent references will be cited parenthetically in the text.

6. Barth, *The Friday Book*, 181.

7. John Barth, *Letters* (New York: Putnam's, 1979), 752–53. Subsequent references will be cited parenthetically in the text.

8. Charlie Reilly, "An Interview with John Barth," *Contemporary Literature* 22, no. 1 (Winter 1981): 10. Barth had cited Mark Twain and William Faulkner as antecedent American exponents of "recycling characters from earlier fictions." Among contemporaries, he could have added to Vonnegut's name those of Burroughs, Nabokov, Pynchon, Roth, and Sorrentino.

9. Ibid.

10. C. Hugh Holman, *A Handbook to Literature*, 4th ed. (Indianapolis: Bobbs, 1981), 386.

11. In the Author's Note appended to *The Electric Kool-Aid Acid Test* (1968; rpt. New York: Bantam, 1969), Tom Wolfe says, "All the events, details and dialogue I have recorded are either what I saw and heard myself or were told to me by people who were there themselves or were recorded on tapes or film or in writing." Many other new journalists have used tapes, notably Oscar Lewis in *The Children of Sanchez* and *La Vida* and Andy Warhol in *a.* See "The Tape-Recorded Nonfiction Novel" in Frederick R. Karl, *American Fictions 1940/1980* (New York: Harper, 1983), 582–86, and "The Austere

Actuality: The Notational Nonfiction Novel" in Mas'ud Zavarzadeh, *The Mythopoeic Reality: The Postwar American Nonfiction Novel* (Urbana, Ill.: Univ. of Illinois Press, 1976), 177–221. John Barth *(Lost in the Funhouse)*, Ronald Sukenick, and especially William Burroughs are authors outside the nonfiction novel group who have also used the tape recorder in their works.

12. Karl, *American Fictions*, 562.

13. Norman Mailer, *Armies of the Night* (New York: NAL, 1968), 241. Subsequent references will be cited parenthetically in the text.

14. After mentioning that "Macdonald was in the process of reviewing Mailer's new novel *Why Are We In Vietnam?* for *The New Yorker*" on page 37, on page 62 Mailer gives us a long passage on the language motif central to it and *Armies of the Night:*

[H]e had kicked goodbye in his novel *Why Are We In Vietnam?* to the old literary corset of good taste, letting his sense of language play on obscenity as freely as it wished, so discovering that everything he knew about the American language (with its incommensurable resources) went flying in and out of the line of his prose with the happiest beating of wings—it was the first time his style seemed at once very American to him and very literary in the best way, at least as he saw the best way. But the reception of the book had been disappointing.

Obviously, William Burroughs, whose name appears in both books and at whose *Naked Lunch* trial Mailer had testified admiringly during 1965, influenced this style, helping to make *Why Are We in Vietnam?* the writer's most antirealistic achievement. Though the earlier novel alludes to Vietnam only twice, it seems much less ambiguous about the war situation than *Armies of the Night.* Alternate first- and third-person sections explore the American killer psyche through Texas fathers (corporation executive, undertaker) and sons. Their aggression blossoms on an Alaskan bear hunt which travesties the famous Faulknerian rite of passage. This violence, emblemized by obscene language and guns, is directed toward minority groups like Jews, blacks, and women as well as animals. That it has a homosexual basis à la Leslie Fiedler becomes evident in the relationship between the sons, narrator D. J. ("Disc Jockey to America") and his buddy Tex. The former's speech, resembling "stream-of-conch" and "private tape," conveys an excremental vision replete with entropic and even satanic implications. Here, too, we encounter the America Mailer would delineate as "a beauty with a leprous skin."

15. Zavarzadeh, *The Mythopoeic Reality*, 130.

16. Ibid., 156, 158, 161, 170, 171.

17. Kurt Vonnegut, Jr., *Slaughter-House Five* (1969; rpt. New York: Dell, 1971), 206. Subsequent references will be cited parenthetically in the text.

18. See "Imaginary Landscapes," chapter 6, n. 24.

19. Our credulity is also violated in Coover's subsequent novel, *Whatever Happened to Gloomy Gus of the Chicago Bears* (New York: Linden-Simon, 1987), where Nixon becomes a professional football player.

20. Cf., Norman Mailer and Jack Kennedy in Walter Abish's "The Istan-

bul Papers"; Ebenezer Cooke and Isaac Newton in John Barth's *The Sot-Weed Factor;* Robert Kennedy in Donald Barthelme's "Robert Kennedy Saved from Drowning"; and Nancy Spellman, Chief Nazarene Bishop, in Ishmael Reed's *The Free-Lance Pallbearers.* That E. L. Doctorow has also rendered actual people antirealistically is demonstrated by *Ragtime* (1975), where Henry Ford and J. Pierpont Morgan meet secretly, Sigmund Freud and Carl Jung visit Coney Island, Evelyn Nesbit and Emma Goldman are sexually attracted, and Harry Houdine meets Archduke Francis Ferdinand.

21. E. L. Doctorow, *The Book of Daniel* (1971; New York: Bantam, 1981). Subsequent references will be cited parenthetically in the text.

22. Robert Coover, *The Public Burning* (New York: Seaver-Viking, 1977), 136.

23. The recurrent motion picture *High Noon,* which gives its name to chapter 14, is especially interesting, since the melodramatic action of this and other westerns parody Eisenhower's struggle against communism.

24. Walter Blair, *Native American Humor* (1937; San Francisco: Chandler, 1960), 56.

25. Philip Roth, "Writing American Fiction," *Commentary* 31 (March 1961): 224.

26. Barth, *The Sot-Weed Factor,* 525.

9. Conspiracy and Paranoia

1. Richard Hofstadter, *The Paranoid Style in American Politics and Other Essays* (New York: Vintage, 1965), 29.

2. Raymond M. Olderman, *Beyond the Waste Land: The Americans Novel in the Nineteen-Sixties* (New Haven: Yale Univ. Press, 1972), 96.

3. Joseph Heller, *Catch-22* (1961; rpt. New York: Delta-Dell, 1973), 122. Subsequent references will be cited parenthetically in the text.

4. Ken Kesey, *One Flew Over the Cuckoo's Nest* (1962; rpt. New York: Viking, 1973). Subsequent references will be cited parenthetically in the text.

5. Frederick R. Karl, *American Fictions 1940/1980* (New York: Harper, 1983), 59.

6. Quoted in Eric Mottram, *William Burroughs: The Algebra of Need* (London: Boyars, 1977), 159.

7. Victor Bockris, *With William Burroughs: A Report from the Bunker* (New York: Seaver, 1981), 89–91. Subsequent references will be cited parenthetically in the text.

8. Thomas LeClair, "Missing Writers," *Horizon* (October 1981).

9. William S. Burroughs, *Naked Lunch* (1959; rpt. New York: Grove, 1966). Subsequent references will be cited parenthetically in the text.

10. Bockris, *With William Burroughs,* 2.

11. William Burroughs, *Nova Express* (1964; rpt. New York: Grove, 1980), 14.

12. Thomas Pynchon, *Gravity's Rainbow* (New York: Viking, 1973), 703. Subsequent references will be cited parenthetically in the text.

13. See Mark Richard Siegel, *Pynchon: Creative Paranoia in "Gravity's Rainbow"* (Port Washington, N.Y.: Kennikat, 1978).

14. Scott Sanders, "Pynchon's Paranoid History," *Twentieth Century Literature* 21, no. 2 (May 1975): 177–78. Subsequent references will be cited parenthetically in the text.

15. Thomas Pynchon, *The Crying of Lot 49* (1966; rpt. New York: Bantam, 1967), 69. Subsequent references will be cited parenthetically in the text.

10. Entropy

1. Nathanael West, *Miss Lonelyhearts* (1933; rpt. *The Complete Works of Nathanael West* [New York: Farrar, 1957]), 104.

2. Norbert Wiener, *The Human Use of Human Beings: Cybernetics and Society* (1950; rpt. Garden City, N.Y.: Anchor-Doubleday, 1954), 78.

3. See Steven Moore, " 'Parallel, Not Series': Thomas Pynchon and William Gaddis," *Pynchon Notes*, no. 11 (February 1983): 6–26. On a postcard dated 6 August 1982, Gaddis wrote to Moore: "I haven't read Pynchon enough to have an opinion either of his work or whether it might have been 'influenced' (perilous word) by mine, though I've understood he feels not & who's to know if he'd ever read mine before V *[sic]?*"

4. Pynchon is referring here to James Clerk Maxwell, the great Scottish physicist, whose *Treatise on Electricity and Magnetism* appeared in 1873. On p. 62 of *The Crying of Lot 49*, Stanley Koteks explains "Maxwell's Demon"—which recurs during *Gravity's Rainbow*—to Oedipa. Wiener (*The Human Use of Human Beings,* 28) had asserted: "A brilliant expression of the role of information in this respect is provided by Clerk Maxwell, in the form of the so-called 'Maxwell's demon.' " Later (30), he concluded: "Thus while the demon may temporarily reverse the usual direction of entropy, ultimately it too will wear down."

5. Thomas Pynchon, "Entropy" (1960; rpt. *Slow Learner,* Boston: Little, 1984), 81. Subsequent references will be cited parenthetically in the text.

6. Zbigniew Lewicki, *The Bang and the Whimper: Apocalypse and Entropy in American Literature* (Westport, Conn.: Greenwood, 1984), 94.

7. Objects frequently become animated in surrealistic works (Apollinaire's *The Breasts of Tiresias*) and proliferate in absurdist plays (Ionesco's *The Chairs*). About Gaddis's *The Recognitions,* Stephen-Paul Martin writes; "One of the motifs . . . involves the vulnerability of the characters to physical objects. Gaddis' people are repeatedly overwhelmed by the intrusion of external forces, and often seem to exist only as vehicles through which nonhuman energies can manifest themselves" ("Vulnerability and Aggression: Characters and Objects in *The Recognitions,*" *Review of Contemporary Fiction* 2, no. 2

[Summer 1982]: 45.) Objects clutter the 96th Street apartment of *J R* and the Victorian house of *Carpenter's Gothic*.

8. Anne Mangel, "Maxwell's demon, entropy, information: *The Crying of Lots 49*," *Triquarterly* no. 20 (Winter 1971): 194–208. Subsequent references will be cited parenthetically in the text.

9. William Gaddis, "The Rush for Second Place," *Harpers*, (April 1981): 35.

10. Quoted in Marie-Rose Logan and Tomasz Mirkowicz, "An Interview with William Gaddis," trans. Julita Wroniak, *Literatura na Swiecie* no. 1/ 150 (Warsaw, Poland, 1984): 178–89. See also Gaddis's comments on entropy in *The Paris Review* (Winter 1987) interview.

11. William Gaddis, *J R* (New York: Knopf, 1975), 287. Subsequent references will be cited parenthetically in the text.

12. Quoted in Logan and Mirkowicz, "An Interview with William Gaddis," 178–89.

13. Stephen H. Matanle, "Love and Strife in William Gaddis' *J R*," in *In Recognition of William Gaddis*, ed. John Kuehl and Steven Moore (Syracuse: Syracuse Univ. Press, 1984). Subsequent references will be cited parenthetically in the text. In the same collection of essays, Susan Strehle distinguishes between manner and matter. She poses successive or public time against durational or private time. Victimized by the former, the characters own broken clocks, grow forgetful, repeat themselves, and quote each other. The narrator, however, regards time as a fluid process and so abandons conventional linear storytelling, replacing clocks and calendars with seasonal and solar cycles. A paradox develops, for the book's unified manner conveys disjunctive matter. This interpretation, which draws on Bergson and Heidegger, reminds us of those who feel that Wyatt, protagonist of *The Recognitions*, gropes toward integration through love while the civilization around him crumbles.

14. William Gaddis, *Carpenter's Gothic* (New York: Sifton-Viking, 1985), 165. Subsequent references will be cited parenthetically in the text.

15. Thomas LeClair, "William Gaddis, *JR*, & the Art of Excess," *Modern Fiction Studies* 27 (Winter 1981): 596. Recktall Brown in *The Recognitions* and the flushing toilet in *Carpenter's Gothic* show Gaddis's ongoing treatment of the excremental motif.

16. Thomas Pynchon, *Gravity's Rainbow* (New York: Viking, 1973), 65. Douglas Fowler's book on this novel claims: "Our Western fears of death are connected with odors and decay, with shit; white porcelain, immaculate and 'eternal,' gives us the feeling that shit, so intimate and terrible a precursor of our own organic destiny, can be carried away out of sight *and with dignity:* shit itself is unbearable, so we erect a mausoleum-toilet to it in our homes in order for the death-substance we deposit therein to be outwardly disguised —after all, we do not bury a corpse under *glass* because we cannot bear to see what nature will do to it; shit is a precursor of death, and we hold death in such fear and awe that we must propitiate its powers with a noble white

monument, the American toilet." Earlier, Fowler had pointed out that masochistic General Ernest Pudding dies from eating Katje's excrement. See *A Reader's Guide to "Gravity's Rainbow"* (Ann Arbor, Mich.: Ardis, 1980), 245, 75.

17. See Eugene Korkowski, "The Excremental Vision of Barth's Todd Andrews," *Critique* 18, no. 2 (1976): 51–58.

18. William S. Burroughs, *Naked Lunch* (1959; New York: Grove, 1966), 132–33.

19. Northrop Frye, *Anatomy of Criticism* (Princeton: Princeton Univ. Press, 1957), 235.

20. Victor Bockris, *With William Burroughs: A Report from the Bunker* (New York: Seaver, 1981), 108.

21. Gregory Stephenson, "The Gnostic Vision of William S. Burroughs," *Review of Contemporary Fiction* 4, no. 1 (Spring 1984): 40.

22. Frye, *Anatomy of Criticism*, 224.

23. Norman O. Brown, *Life Against Death: The Psychoanalytical Meaning of History* (Middletown, Conn.: Wesleyan Univ. Press, 1959), 185. Subsequent references will be cited parenthetically in the text.

24. John O'Brien, ed., *Interviews with Black Writers* (New York: Liveright, 1973), 167.

25. West, *The Complete Works*, 14.

26. Ishmael Reed, *The Free-Lance Pallbearers* (1967; New York: Avon, 1977), 4. Subsequent references will be cited parenthetically in the text.

11. Nightmare and Apocalypse

1. Walter Blair, ed., *Native American Humor* (San Francisco: Chandler, 1960), 92.

2. Anaïs Nin, *The Future of the Novel* (1968; rpt. New York: Collier Macmillan, 1970), 123.

3. John Hawkes, *The Lime Twig* (New York: New Directions, 1961), 33. Subsequent references will be cited parenthetically in the text. See John C. Stubbs, "John Hawkes and the Dream-Work of *The Lime Twig* and *Second Skin*," *Literature and Psychology* 21, no. 3 (1971): 149–60. Chapter 2, "The Ludic Impulse," sketches the "plot" of this novel.

4. On p. 180 of "Interview," in John Kuehl, *John Hawkes and the Craft of Conflict* (New Brunswick, N.J.: Rutgers Univ. Press, 1975), Hawkes said: " 'I appreciate being identified with the surrealists, but at the same time resist that identification because I don't think it's very applicable. There's nothing merely murky or dreamlike about my fiction, and it's not a matter of unconscious flow or automatic writing. I'm interested in highly shaped and perfected works of art.' "

5. Ernest Jones, *On the Nightmare* (New York: Liveright, 1971), 74–75.

6. Victor Bockris, *With William Burroughs: A Report from the Bunker* (New

York: Seaver, 1981), 31–32. That *Cities of the Red Night* has a "final apocalyptic vision," we have seen in chapter 6, "Imaginary Landscapes." For Burroughs's preoccupation with dreams, see THE RETREAT DIARIES in *The Burroughs File* (San Francisco: City Lights, 1984), 189–208.

7. Joseph Heller, *Catch-22* (1955; New York: Delta-Dell, 1973), 402. Subsequent references will be cited parenthetically in the text. Minna Doskow's "The Night Journey in *Catch-22*," an excellent article, appears on pp. 491–500 of this critical edition. For the plot of the novel, see chapter 9, "Conspiracy and Paranoia."

8. Susan Sontag, *Death Kit* (New York: Delta-Dell, 1967), 310. Subsequent references will be cited parenthetically in the text.

9. Frederick R. Karl, *American Fictions 1940/1980* (New York: Harper, 1983), 405.

10. R. W. B. Lewis, *Trials of the Word* (New Haven: Yale Univ. Press, 1965), 196–97.

11. See, for example, Douglas Robinson, *American Apocalypses: The Image of the End of the World in American Literature* (Baltimore: Johns Hopkins Univ. Press, 1985). Robinson discusses Edwards, Emerson, Poe, Hawthorne, Melville Twain, Faulkner, West, Ellison, Barth, Coover, and Pynchon.

12. Flannery O'Connor, *The Complete Stories* (New York: Farrar, 1975), 132, 333.

13. William Gaddis, *The Recognitions* (1955; Cleveland: Meridian-World, 1962), 956.

14. Robert Coover, *The Public Burning* (New York: Seaver-Viking, 1977), 517.

15. Coleman Dowell, *Mrs. October Was Here* (New York: New Directions, 1974), 235, 236, 237, 238.

16. John Barth, *Giles Goat-Boy or, The Revised New Syllabus* (Garden City, N.Y.: Doubleday, 1966), 693, 696.

17. Thomas Pynchon, *Gravity's Rainbow* (New York: Viking, 1973), 760, 754.

18. Robert Stone, *A Hall of Mirrors* (Boston: Houghton, 1967), 334–35. Subsequent references will be cited parenthetically in the text.

19. See L. Hugh Moore, "The Undersea World of Robert Stone," *Critique* 11, no. 3 (1969): 43–56. Moore writes: "By images, metaphors, and direct references Stone connects his setting . . . with the bloody, brutal, cold undersea world and his characters with the denizens of this icy environment. Further, he uses the metaphor of evolution to develop the comparison. Since the world is getting colder, the survivors are those who can withstand the moral chill and prey upon the less hardy creatures, those who maintain anachronistically and non-adaptatively, the old values of pity, concern, mercy, responsibility and love" (43–44).

20. Robert Coover, *The Origin of the Brunists* (1966; New York: Seaver-Viking, 1978), 489.

21. Ibid., 526.

22. Ralph Ellison, *Invisible Man* (1952; rpt. New York: Vintage-Random, 1972), 556. Subsequent references will be cited parenthetically in the text.

23. Jonathan Baumbach, *The Landscape of Nightmare: Studies in the Contemporary American Novel* (New York: New York Univ. Press, 1965), 68–69, 82.

24. Fritz Gysin, *The Grotesque in American Negro Fiction* (Bern: Francke, 1975), 200–201.

25. Zbigniew Lewicki, *The Bang and the Whimper: Apocalypse and Entropy in American Literature* (Westport, Conn.: Greenwood, 1984), 48.

26. Robert Alter, *Partial Magic: The Novel as a Self-Conscious Genre* (Berkeley: Univ. of California Press, 1975), 235, 243.

Select Bibliography

Adams, Henry. *The Education of Henry Adams*. Boston: Houghton, 1961.

Alter, Robert. *Partial Magic: The Novel as a Self-Conscious Genre*. Berkeley: Univ. of California Press, 1975.

Appel, Alfred, Jr., ed. *The Annotated Lolita*. New York: McGraw, 1970.

Baldanza, Frank. *Mark Twain: An Introduction and an Interpretation*. New York: Barnes, 1961.

Barrenechea, Ana Maria. *Borges: The Labyrinth Maker*. Ed./trans. Robert Lima. New York: New York Univ. Press, 1965.

Barth, John. *Chimera*. New York: Fawcett-Crest, 1973.

———. *The End of the Road*. 1958. New York: Avon, 1960.

———. "A Few Words About Minimalism." *New York Times Book Review*, 28 December 1986, sec. 7: 2+.

———. *The Friday Book: Essays and Other Nonfiction*. New York: Putnam's, 1984.

———. *Giles Goat-Boy or, The Revised New Syllabus*. Garden City, N.Y.: Doubleday, 1966.

———. "Hawkes and Barth Talk About Fiction." *New York Times Book Review*, 1 April 1979, sec. 7: 7+.

———. *Letters*. New York: Putnam's, 1979.

———. *Lost in the Funhouse: Fiction for Print, Tape, Live Voice*. 1968. New York: Bantam, 1969.

———. *Sabbatical: A Romance*. New York: Penguin, 1983.

———. *The Sot-Weed Factor*. 1960. New York: Bantam, 1980.

Barthelme, Donald. *City Life*. New York: Farrar, 1970.

———. *The Dead Father*. New York: Farrar, 1975.

———. *Snow White*. 1967. New York: Bantam, 1968.

Baugh, Albert C. *Chaucer's Major Poetry*. Englewood Cliffs, N.J.: Prentice, 1963.

Baumbach, Jonathan. *The Landscape of Nightmare: Studies in the Contemporary Novel*. New York: New York Univ. Press, 1965.

Bell, Michael Davitt. *The Development of American Romance: The Sacrifice of Relation*. Chicago: Univ. of Chicago Press, 1980.

Bellamy, Joe David. "Having it Both Ways." *New American Review* no. 15 (April 1972): 134–50.

Bellis, Peter J. "Melville's Confidence Man: An Uncharitable Interpretation." *American Literature* 59 (1987): 548–69.

Bendixen, Alfred, ed. *The Whole Family*. New York: Ungar, 1986.

Blair, Walter. *Native American Humor*. 1937. San Francisco: Chandler, 1960.

Blotner, Joseph and Frederick Gwynn, eds., *Faulkner in the University*. New York: Random, 1965.

Bockris, Victor. *With William Burroughs: A Report from the Bunker*. New York: Seaver, 1981.

Borges, Jorge Luis. *Labyrinths: Selected Stories & Other Writings*. Ed. Donald A. Yates and James E. Irby. New York: New Directions, 1964.

Brecht, Bertolt. *Brecht on Theatre*. Ed./trans. John Willett. New York: Hill, 1964.

Burroughs, William S. *The Burroughs File*. San Francisco: City Lights, 1984.

———. *Cities of the Red Night*. New York: Holt, 1981.

———. *Naked Lunch*. 1959. New York: Grove, 1966.

———. *Nova Express*. 1964. In *Three Novels*. New York: Grove, 1980.

Burroughs, William S. and Brion Gysin. *The Third Mind*. 1978. London: Calder, 1979.

Burton, Gabrielle. *Heartbreak Hotel*. New York: Scribner's, 1986.

Campbell, Joseph. *The Hero with a Thousand Faces*. 1949. Princeton: Princeton Univ. Press, 1972.

Chase, Richard. *The American Novel and Its Tradition*. Garden City, N.Y.: Anchor, 1957.

Clarke, Gerald. "The Art of Fiction L: Gore Vidal" (an interview). *Paris Review* no. 59 (1974): 130–65.

Cohen, Edward H. *Ebenezer Cooke: The Sot-Weed Canon*. Athens, Ga.: Univ. of Georgia Press, 1975.

Cooper, James Fenimore. *The Chainbearer*. New York: Appleton, 1883.

Coover, Robert. *Gerald's Party*. New York: Linden-Simon, 1986.

———. *The Origin of the Brunists*. 1966. New York: Seaver-Viking, 1978.

———. *Pricksongs & Descants*. New York: Plume-NAL, 1970.

———. *The Public Burning*. New York: Seaver-Viking, 1977.

———. *The Universal Baseball Association, Inc. J. Henry Waugh, Prop.* New York: NAL, 1968.

———. *Whatever Happened to Gloomy Gus of the Chicago Bears*. New York: Linden-Simon, 1987.

Crane, Stephen. "The Monster." In *The Red Badge of Courage and Other Writings*. Ed. Richard Chase. Boston: Houghton, 1960.

Dembo, L. S. and Cyrena N. Pondrom, eds. *The Contemporary Writer*. Madison: Univ. of Wisconsin Press, 1972.

Detweiler, Robert. "Games and Play in Modern American Fiction." *Contemporary Literature* 17, no. 1 (Winter 1976): 44–62.

Diser, Philip. "The Historical Ebenezer Cooke." *Critique* 10, no. 3 (1968): 576–604.

Doctorow, E. L. *The Book of Daniel*. New York: Bantam, 1981.

Dowell, Coleman. *Island People*. New York: New Directions, 1976.

———. *Mrs. October Was Here*. New York: New Directions, 1974.

——. *Too Much Flesh and Jabez.* New York: New Directions, 1977.

——. *White on Black on White.* Woodstock, Vt.: Countryman, 1983.

Edwards, Thomas R. "A Novel of Correspondences." *New York Times Book Review*, 30 September 1979, sec. 7: 1 +.

Eilenberg, Max. "A Marvellous Gift: Gilbert Sorrentino's Fiction." *Review of Contemporary Fiction* 1, no. 1 (Spring 1981): 88–95.

Ellison, Ralph. *Invisible Man.* 1952. New York: Vintage-Random, 1972.

Emerson, Ralph Waldo. "The Divinity School Address." In *Selections from Ralph Waldo Emerson.* Ed. Stephen Whicher. Boston: Houghton, 1960.

——. *Nature.* In *Selections from Ralph Waldo Emerson.* Ed. Stephen Whicher. Boston: Houghton, 1960.

——. "The Poet." In *Selections from Ralph Waldo Emerson.* Ed. Stephen Whicher. Boston: Houghton, 1960.

Enck, John J. "John Barth: An Interview." *Wisconsin Studies in Contemporary Literature* (Winter–Spring 1965): 3–14.

——. "John Hawkes: An Interview." *Wisconsin Studies in Contemporary Literature* 6, no. 2 (Summer 1964): 141–54.

Farmer, Betty Catherine Dobson. "Mythological, Biblical, and Literary Allusions in Donald Barthelme's *The Dead Father.*" *The International Fiction Review* 6, no. 1 (Winter 1979): 40–48.

Faulkner, William. *Mosquitoes: A Novel.* New York: Liveright, 1927.

Federman, Raymond. *Double or Nothing.* Chicago: Swallow, 1971.

——. "Fiction Today or the Pursuit of Non-Knowledge." In *Surfiction: Fiction Now and Tomorrow.* Ed. Raymond Federman, 291–311. Chicago: Swallow, 1981.

Feeley, Kathleen Sister. *Flannery O'Connor: Voice of the Peacock.* New Brunswick, N.J.: Rutgers Univ. Press, 1972.

Ferres, John H., ed. "Sherwood Anderson on Winesburg, Ohio." *Winesburg, Ohio: Text and Criticism.* New York: Viking, 1966.

Fitzgerald, F. Scott. *Afternoon of an Author: A Selection of Uncollected Stories and Essays.* Ed. Arthur Mizener. Princeton: Princeton Univ. Library, 1957.

Fowler, Douglas. *A Reader's Guide to "Gravity's Rainbow."* Ann Arbor Mich.: Ardis, 1980.

Frye, Northrop. *Anatomy of Criticism: Four Essays.* Princeton: Princeton Univ. Press, 1971.

Fuchs, Miriam. "'il miglior fabbro': Gaddis' Debt to T. S. Eliot." In *In Recognition of William Gaddis.* Ed. John Kuehl and Steven Moore, 92–105. Syracuse, N.Y.: Syracuse Univ. Press, 1984.

Gaddis, William. "The Art of Fiction." *Paris Review* no. 105 (Winter 1987): 55–89.

——. *Carpenter's Gothic.* New York: Sifton-Viking, 1985.

——. *J R.* New York: Knopf, 1975.

——. *The Recognitions.* 1955. Cleveland: Meridian-World, 1962.

Gass, William. *Habitations of the Word.* New York: Simon, 1985.

Gordon, Lois. *Donald Barthelme.* Boston: Twayne, 1981.

Graff, Gerald. *Literature Against Itself.* Chicago: Univ. of Chicago Press, 1979.

Gysin, Fritz. *The Grotesque in American Negro Fiction.* Bern: Francke, 1975.

Harrison, James A. *The Complete Works of Edgar Allan Poe.* New York: de Fau, 1902.

Hawkes, John. *The Beetle Leg.* New York: New Directions, 1951.

———. *The Blood Oranges.* New York: New Directions, 1971.

———. *The Cannibal.* 1949. New York: New Directions, 1962.

———. "Flannery O'Connor's Devil." *Sewanee Review* 70 (Summer 1962): 395–407.

———. *The Innocent Party: Four Short Plays.* New York: New Directions, 1966.

———. *The Lime Twig.* New York: New Directions, 1961.

———. *The Passion Artist.* 1979. New York: Colophon-Harper, 1981.

———. *Second Skin.* Norfolk, Conn.: New Directions, 1964.

Hawthorne, Nathaniel. *The Scarlet Letter and Other Tales of the Puritans.* Ed. Harry Levin. Boston: Houghton, 1960.

———. "Young Goodman Brown." In *Nathaniel Hawthorne's Tales.* Ed. James McIntosh. New York: Norton, 1987.

Heller, Joseph. *Catch-22.* 1955. New York: Delta-Dell, 1973.

Hemingway, Ernest. *The Torrents of Spring.* New York: Scribner's, 1972.

Hoffman, Daniel. *Poe Poe Poe Poe Poe Poe Poe.* Garden City, N.Y.: Anchor, 1973.

Hofstadter, Richard. *The Paranoid Style in American Politics and Other Essays.* New York: Vintage, 1965.

Holder, Alan. " 'What Marvelous Plot . . . Was Afoot?' History in Barth's *The Sot-Weed Factor.*" *American Quarterly* 20, no. 3 (Fall 1968): 596–604.

Holman, C. Hugh. *A Handbook to Literature,* 4th ed. Indianapolis: Bobbs, 1981.

Holmes, Oliver Wendell. *Elsie Venner: A Romance of Destiny.* New York: NAL, 1961.

———. *The Guardian Angel.* Boston: Houghton, 1894.

Howells, William Dean. *Indian Summer.* Ed. William M. Gibson. New York: Dutton, 1958.

———. "Novel-Writing and Novel-Reading." Ed. William Gibson. New York: New York Public Library, 1958.

Hutchinson, Peter. *Games Authors Play.* London: Methuen, 1983.

Irving, Washington. *Voyages and Discoveries.* Ed. James W. Tuttleton. Boston: Twayne, 1986.

James, Henry. "Anthony Trollope." In *The Future of the Novel.* Ed. Leon Edel. New York: Vintage, 1956.

———. *The Art of the Novel: Critical Prefaces by Henry James.* Ed. R. P. Blackmur. New York: Scribner's, 1934.

———. *The Bostonians.* New York: Modern Library, 1956.

———. "The Figure in the Carpet." In *Eight Tales from the Major Phase.* Ed. Morton Dauwen Zabel. New York: Norton, 1958.

———. *Literary Criticism*. Ed. Leon Edel. New York: The Library of America, 1984.

———. *The Portrait of a Lady*. Ed. Leon Edel. Boston: Houghton, 1963.

———. *Selected Literary Criticism*. Ed. Morris Shapira. New York: McGraw, 1965.

Jones, Ernest. *On the Nightmare*. New York: Liveright, 1971.

Karl, Frederick R. *American Fictions 1940/1980*. New York: Harper, 1983.

Kayser, Wolfgang. *The Grotesque in Art and Literature*. Trans. Ulrich Weisstein. 1957. New York: McGraw, 1966.

Kenner, Hugh. "II. The Traffic in Words." *Harpers* 258, no. 1549 (June 1979): 83–84, 88–90.

Kesey, Ken. *One Flew Over the Cuckoo's Nest*. 1962. New York: Viking, 1973.

Ketterer, David. "Epoch-Eclipse and Apocalypse: Special 'Effects' in *A Connecticut Yankee*." In *A Connecticut Yankee in King Arthur's Court*. Ed. Allison R. Ensor, 417–34. New York: Norton, 1982.

Klinkowitz, Jerome. *Literary Disruptions: The Making of a Post-Contemporary American Fiction*. Urbana: Univ. of Illinois Press, 1975.

———. "Walter Abish: An Interview." *Fiction International* no. 415 (1975): 93–100.

Koenig, David. "The Writing of *The Recognitions*." In *In Recognition of William Gaddis*. Ed. John Kuehl and Steven Moore, 20–31. Syracuse, N.Y.: Syracuse Univ. Press, 1984.

Koenig, Peter W. "Recognizing Gaddis' *Recognitions*." *Contemporary Literature* 16 (Winter 1975): 61–72.

———. "Splinters from the Yew Tree." Diss. New York Univ. 1971.

Kostelanetz, Richard. "New Fiction in America." In *Surfiction: Fiction Now and Tomorrow*. Ed. Raymond Federman, 85–100. Chicago: Swallow, 1981.

Kuehl, John. *John Hawkes and the Craft of Fiction*. New Brunswick, N.J.: Rutgers Univ. Press, 1975.

Kuehl, John and Linda Kandel Kuehl. "An Interview with Coleman Dowell." *Contemporary Literature* 22, no. 3 (Summer 1981): 272–91.

———. "Miss Ethel and Mr. Dowell." *Review of Contemporary Fiction* 2, no. 3 (Fall 1982): 129–34.

Lacan, Jacques. *Écrits*. Trans. Alan Sheridan. New York: Norton, 1977.

Langbaum, Robert. "New Modes of Characterization in *The Waste Land*." In *Eliot in His Time: Essays on the Occasion of the Fiftieth Anniversary of "The Waste Land."* Ed. A. Walton Litz. Princeton: Princeton Univ. Press, 1973.

LeClair, Thomas. "Missing Writers." *Horizon* 24 (October 1981): 48–52.

———. "William Gaddis, *JR*, & the Art of Excess." *Modern Fiction Studies* 27, no. 4 (Winter 1981–1982): 587–600.

LeClair, Tom and Larry McCaffery. *Interview with Contemporary American Novelists*. Urbana: Univ. of Illinois Press, 1983.

Leverence, John. "Gaddis Anagnorisis." In *In Recognition of William Gaddis*. Ed. John Kuehl and Steven Moore, 32–45. Syracuse, N.Y.: Syracuse Univ. Press, 1984.

Lewicki, Zbigniew. *The Bang and the Whimper: Apocalypse and Entropy in American Literature.* Westport, Conn.: Greenwood, 1984.

Lewis, R. W. B. *Trials of the Word.* New Haven: Yale Univ. Press, 1965.

Lodge, David. *The Modes of Modern Writing.* London: Arnold, 1977.

Mailer, Norman. *Armies of the Night.* New York: NAL, 1968.

Mangel, Anne. "Maxwell's Demon, Entropy, Information: *The Crying of Lot 49.*" *TriQuarterly* no. 20 (Winter 1971): 194–208.

Martin, Jay. *Harvests of Change: American Literature, 1865–1914.* Englewood Cliffs, N.J.: Prentice, 1967.

Martin, Stephen. "A Comparative Study of Androgyny in Twentieth-Century Experimental Literature." Diss. New York Univ., 1984.

Martin, Stephen Paul. "Exorcism and Grace: A Study of Androgyny in *Island People. Review of Contemporary Fiction* 2, no. 3 (Fall 1982): 124–28.

———. "Vulnerability and Aggression: Characters and Objects in *The Recognitions.*" *Review of Contemporary Fiction* 2, no. 2 (Summer 1982): 45–49.

Mason, Bobbie Ann. *Nabokov's Garden: A Guide to ADA.* Ann Arbor, Mich: Ardis, 1971.

Matanle, Stephen. "Love and Strife in William Gaddis' *J R.*" In *In Recognition of William Gaddis.* Ed. John Kuehl and Steven Moore, 106–18. Syracuse, N.Y.: Syracuse Univ. Press, 1984.

McCarthy, Mary. "A Bolt from the Blue." *New Republic* 146 (June 4, 1962): 21–27.

McDonald, James L. "Barth's Syllabus: The Frame of *Giles Goat-Boy.*" *Critique* 13, no. 3 (1972): 5–10.

McElroy, Joseph. *Hind's Kidnap: A Pastoral on Familiar Airs.* New York: Harper, 1969.

McKeon, Michael. *The Origins of the English Novel, 1600–1740.* Baltimore: Hopkins, 1987.

Melville, Herman. *The Confidence Man: His Masquerade.* 1857. Ed. Hershel Parker. New York: Norton, 1971.

———. *Moby-Dick; or the Whale.* 1851. Ed. Charles Feidelson, Jr. Indianapolis: Bobbs, 1964.

———. "Preface." 1849. In *Mardi and a Voyage Thither.* Ed. Harrison Hayford, Hershel Parker, and G. Thomas Tanselle. Evanston, Ill.: Northwestern Univ. Press, 1970.

Mendelson, Edward, ed. *Pynchon: A Collection of Critical Essays.* Englewood Cliffs, N.J.: Prentice, 1978.

Mikriammos, Philippe. "The Last European Interview." *Review of Contemporary Fiction* 4, no. 1 (Spring 1984): 12–18.

Moholy-Nagy, L. "Literature." *The Avant-Garde Tradition in Literature.* Ed. Richard Kostelanetz, 78–141. Buffalo, N.Y.: Prometheus, 1982.

Moore, L. Hugh. "The Undersea World of Robert Stone." *Critique* 11, no. 3 (1969): 43–56.

Moore, Steven. "Additional Sources for William Gaddis's 'The Recognitions.' "
American Notes & Queries 22, no. 7/8 (March/April 1984): 111–15.
———. "Alexander Theroux's *Darconville's Cat* and the Tradition of Learned
Wit." *Contemporary Literature* 27, no. 2 (Summer 1986): 233–45.
———. "Parallel, Not Series: Thomas Pynchon and William Gaddis." *Pynchon
Notes* 11 (February 1983): 6–26.
———. *A Reader's Guide to William Gaddis's "The Recognitions."* Lincoln: Univ.
of Nebraska Press, 1984.
Mottram, Eric. *William Burroughs: The Algebra of Need.* London: Boyars, 1977.
Muller, Gilbert H. *Nightmares and Visions: Flannery O'Connor and the Catholic
Grotesque.* Athens, Ga.: Univ. of Georgia Press, 1972.
Nabokov, Vladimir. *Ada or Ardor: A Family Chronicle.* New York: McGraw,
1969.
———. *Lolita.* 1955. New York: McGraw, 1970.
———. *Pale Fire.* New York: Putnam's, 1962.
———. *Speak, Memory: An Autobiography Revisited.* New York: Capricorn-
Putnam's, 1966.
Nordhoff, Charles. *The Communist Societies of the United States.* New York:
Harper, 1875.
O'Brien, Flann. *At Swim-Two-Birds.* 1939. Harmondsworth, England: Pen-
Harper, 1875.
O'Brien, Flann. *At Swim-Two-Birds* 1939. Harmondsworth, England: Pen-
guin, 1967.
O'Brien, John. "Every Man His Voice." *Review of Contemporary Fiction* (Spring
1981): 62–80.
O'Brien, John. "Interview with Coleman Dowell." *Review of Contemporary
Fiction* 2, no. 3 (Fall 1982): 85–99.
———. "An Interview with Gilbert Sorrentino." *Review of Contemporary Fiction*
(Spring 1981): 5–27.
———. ed. *Interviews with Black Writers.* New York: Liveright, 1973.
O'Connor, Flannery. *The Complete Stories.* New York: Farrar, 1971.
———. *Mystery and Manners.* Ed. Sally and Robert Fitzgerald. New York:
Farrar, 1970.
O'Connor, William Van. *The Grotesque: An American Genre and Other Essays.*
Carbondale: Southern Illinois Univ. Press, 1962.
Olderman, Raymond. *Beyond the Waste Land: The American Novel in the Nine-
teen-Sixties.* New Haven: Yale Univ. Press, 1972.
Orth, Ralph and Alfred E. Ferguson. *The Journals and Miscellaneous Notebooks
of Ralph Waldo Emerson.* Cambridge: Harvard Univ. Press, 1971.
Ostrom, John Ward, ed. *The Letters of Edgar Allan Poe.* New York: Gordian,
1966.
Paine, Albert Bigelow, ed. *Mark Twain's Notebook.* New York: Harper, 1935.
Poe, Edgar Allan. *The Complete Works of Edgar Allan Poe.* Ed. J. A. Harrison.
17 volumes. New York: de Fau, 1902.

Pynchon, Thomas. *The Crying of Lot 49.* New York: Bantam, 1967.
———. "Entropy." *Slow Learner.* Boston: Little, 1984.
———. *Gravity's Rainbow.* New York: Viking, 1973.
———. *V.* Philadelphia: Lippincott, 1963.
Rank, Otto. *The Myth of the Birth of the Hero.* Trans. Dr. F. Robbins and Dr. Smith Ely Jelliffe. 1910. New York: Brunner, 1952.
Reed, Ishmael. *The Free-Lance Pallbearers.* 1967. New York: Avon, 1977.
Reilly, Charlie. "An Interview with John Barth." *Contemporary Literature* 22, no. 1 (Winter 1981): 1–23.
Robinson, Douglas, *American Apocalypses: The Image of the End of the Road in American Literature.* Baltimore: Hopkins, 1985.
Roth, Philip. "Writing American Fiction." *Commentary* 31 (March 1961): 223–33.
Rowson, Susanna Haswell. *Charlotte, A Tale of Truth.* Philadelphia,1793.
———. *The Inquisitor.* Philadelphia, 1793.
Safer, Elaine B. "The Allusive Mode, the Absurd and Black Humor in William Gaddis's *The Recognitions.*" *Studies in American Humor* n.s. 1 (October 1982): 103–18.
Saltzman, Arthur M. *The Fiction of William Gass.* Carbondale: Southern Illinois Univ. Press, 1986.
Sanders, Scott. "Pynchon's Paranoid History." *Twentieth Century Literature* 21, no. 2 (May 1975): 177–92.
Scholes, Robert. *The Fabulators.* New York: Oxford Univ. Press, 1967.
Shattuck, Roger. *The Banquet Years.* New York: Knopf, 1968.
Siegel, Mark Richard. *Pynchon: Creative Paranoia in "Gravity's Rainbow."* Port Washington, N.Y.: Kennikat, 1978.
Silverman, Kenneth. *The Life and Times of Cotton Mather.* New York: Harper & Row, 1984.
Šklovskij, Victor. *Russian Formalist Criticism: Four Essays.* Ed. Lee T. Lemon and Marion J. Reis. Lincoln: Univ. Nebraska Press, 1965.
Smith, Henry Nash. *Mark Twain's Fable of Progress: Political and Economic Ideas in A Connecticut Yankee.* New Brunswick, N.J.: Rutgers Univ. Press, 1964.
Sontag, Susan. *Death Kit.* New York: Delta-Dell, 1967.
Sorrentino, Gilbert. *Blue Pastoral.* San Francisco: North Point, 1983.
———. *Mulligan Stew.* New York: Grove, 1979.
———. *Something Said.* San Francisco: North Point, 1984.
———. *Splendide-Hôtel.* Elmwood Park, Ill.: Dalkey,1984.
Southworth, E. D. E. N. Mrs. *Cruel as the Grave.* Philadelphia: Peterson, 1871.
———. *The Family Doom.* New York: Lupton, 1897.
Stark, John O. *The Literature of Exhaustion: Borges, Nabokov & Barth.* Durham, N.C.: Duke Univ. Press, 1974.
Stephenson, Gregory. "The Gnostic Vision of William S. Burroughs." *Review of Contemporary Fiction* 4, no. 1 (Spring 1984): 40–49.
Stevens, Wallace. "Esthetique du Mal." In *Poems by Wallace Stevens.* New York: Vintage, 1982.

———. *The Necessary Angel: Essays on Reality and the Imagination*. New York: Vintage, 1951.

Stone, Robert. *A Hall of Mirrors*. Boston: Houghton, 1967.

Stubbs, John C. "John Hawkes and the Dream Work of *The Lime Twig* and *Second Skin*." *Literature and Psychology* 21, no. 3 (1971): 149–60.

Sukenick, Ronald. *Long Talking Bad Conditions Blues*. New York: Fiction Collective, 1979.

Tanner, Tony. "V. and V-2." In *Pynchon: A Collection of Critical Essays*. Ed. Edward Mendelson, 16–55. Englewood Cliffs, N.J.: Prentice, 1978.

Tate, Allen. "The Angelic Imagination." In *The Recognition of Edgar Allan Poe: Selected Criticism Since 1829*. Ed. Eric W. Carlson, pp. 236–254. Ann Arbor, Mich.: Univ. of Michigan Press, 1966.

———. *The Forlorn Demon*. Chicago: Regnery, 1953.

———. "Our Cousin, Mr. Poe." in *The Man of Letters in the Modern World*. New York: Meridian, 1955.

Theroux, Alexander. *Darconville's Cat*. Garden City, N.Y.: Doubleday, 1981.

———. "Theroux Metaphrastes: An Essay on Literature." *Three Wogs*. Boston: Godine, 1975.

Thomas, Dwight and David K. Jackson. *The Poe Log: A Documentary Life of Edgar Allan Poe, 1809–1849*. Boston: Hall, 1987.

Tilford, John E. "James the Old Intruder." *Modern Fiction Studies* 4 (1958): 157–64.

Turner, Arlin. *Nathaniel Hawthorne: An Introduction and an Interpretation*. New York: Holt, 1961.

Twain, Mark. *Adventures of Huckleberry Finn*. Ed. Henry Nash Smith. Boston: Houghton, 1958.

———. *A Connecticut Yankee in King Arthur's Court*. New York: Washington Square, 1948.

———. *Letters from the Earth*. Ed. Bernard De Voto. New York: Harper, 1974.

———. "The Mysterious Stranger." *The Portable Mark Twain*. Ed. Bernard De Voto. New York: Viking, 1951.

———. *Puddn'head Wilson*. New York: Collier, 1922.

Vonnegut, Kurt, Jr. *Slaughter-House Five*. 1969. New York: Dell, 1971.

Waugh, Patricia. *Metafiction: The Theory and Practice of Self-Conscious Fiction*. London: Methuen, 1984.

West, Nathanael. *A Cool Million or The Dismantling of Lemuel Pitkin*. 1934. In *The Complete Works of Nathanael West*. New York: Farrar, 1957.

———. *Miss Lonelyhearts*. 1933. New York: New Directions, 1962.

Wiener, Norbert. *The Human Use of Human Beings: Cybernetics and Society*. 1950. Garden City, N.Y.: Anchor-Doubleday, 1954.

Wilson, Edmund, ed. *The Crack-Up*. New York: New Directions, 1956.

Wolfe, Tom. "Author's Note." *The Electric Kool-Aid Acid Test*. 1968. New York: Bantam, 1969.

Young, Marguerite. *Miss MacIntosh, My Darling*. New York: Harvest-Harcourt, 1979.

Zavarzadeh, Mas'ud. *The Mythopoeic Reality: The Postwar American Nonfiction Novel.* Urbana: Univ. of Illinois Press, 1976.

Zurbrugg, Nicholas, trans. "Burroughs, Grauerholz, and *Cities of the Red Night:* An Interview with James Grauerholz." *Review of Contemporary Fiction* 4, no. 1 (Spring 1984): 19–32.

Index

a (Warhol), 335
Abish, Walter, 62, 93
  and alphabetical play, 86–87
  and fictitious history, 336–37
  and game playing, 289
  and language, 322
  and ludic impulse, 59, 85–87
  and reflexivity, 289
Absalom, Absalom! (Faulkner), 21, 46,
  133, 153
Account of the Arctic Regions, An
  (Scoresby), 42
Ada (Nabokov), x, 66, 85, 108, 120, 164,
  169–72, 179, 263, 269, 295, 300
Adam Bede (Eliot), 26–27
Adamov, Arthur, 288
Adams, Henry, 54, 56, 109, 251, 254,
  307
Adler, Renata, 113
Adventures in the Alaskan Skin Trade
  (Hawkes), 173
Adventures of Augie March (Bellow), 7, 41
Adventures of Huckleberry Finn (Twain), 8,
  12, 14, 29, 35, 41, 45, 61, 234, 296
*Adventures of Jonathan Corncob, Loyal
  American Refugee* (anon.), 34
Adventures of Tom Sawyer, The (Twain), 8,
  29
Aeneid, 42
Aesop, 104
Age of Innocence, The (Wharton), 6
Algerine Captive, The (Tyler), 6
Alienation effect, 173–74
Allegories of Reading (de Man), 3
Alone (Harland), 7
Alonzo and Melissa (Mitchell), 6, 47
Alphabetical Africa (Abish), 59, 85–87,
  159, 289, 332
Alphabetical play, 79–80, 85–87, 289
Alter, Robert, 284

Amar sin saber a guíen (Vega), 110
Amateur, The (Barth), 320
Amateurs (Barthelme), 85
Ambassadors, The (James), 7, 69
American Apocalypses (Robinson), 341
American Fictions 1940/1980 (Karl), 112
American Novel and Its Tradition, The
  (Chase), 4
Anarchiad (Trumbull), 41
Anatomy of Criticism (Frye), 289
Anatomy of Melancholy (Burton), 43, 108
Ancient Regime, The (Taine), 45
Anderson, Sherwood, 14, 144
  and fragmentation, 14
  and landscape, 46–47
Androgyny. See *specific writers*
"Angelic Imagination, The" (Tate), 24
Angel's Island (Gillmore), 49
Annotated "Lolita," The (Appel), 96
Antirealism, ix
  and Cambridge writers, xii
  defined, x
  and plot, 8–9
  and romance tradition, 2–3, 4, 5
  vs. realism, xii, 2–3
  roots of, 2
  themes and techniques of, 1
Apocalypse/Armageddon, 272–84, 303
  defined, 272–73
  and earlier American writing, 52–56,
  273
  see also *specific writers*
Apocalypse Now, 272
Apollinaire, Guillaume, 87
Appel, Alfred, Jr., 66
"Après le Déluge" (Rimbaud), 86
Aristophanes, 263
Aristotle, 113
Armageddon. *See* Apocalypse/Armageddon

Armies of the Night, The (Mailer), 44, 62,
  205, 217–24, 230, 336
Arnold, Matthew, 308
Arthur Bonnicastle (Holland), 7
Arthur Mervyn (Brown), 47
"Art of Fiction, The" (James), 8
"Ash Wednesday" (Eliot), 96
As I Lay Dying (Faulkner), 46, 105, 113,
  133, 180
Asylum, The (Mitchell), 47
At Swim-Two-Birds (O'Brien), 70
Auchincloss, Louis, 5
Aurifodina (Bigly), 48
Awkward Age, The (James), 21

Babbitt, Irving, 305
Babbitt (Lewis), 7
"Babysitter, The" (Coover), 63
Bacon, Francis, 32
Bad Man, A (Elkins), 144, 232
Balch, Anthony, 131
Bald Soprano, The (Ionesco), 105
Baldwin, James, 309
Ballad of the Sad Café, The (McCullers),
  144
"Balloon-Hoax, The" (Poe), 36
Balzac, Honoré de, 46
Barnes, Djuna, xii, 144, 269, 277, 307,
  309
Barth, John, ix, x, 1, 2, 11, 31, 57, 62,
  64, 83, 84, 87, 93, 116, 193, 252,
  264, 288, 294, 309, 310, 313, 327,
  336, 341
  and alphabetical play, 79–80
  and apocalypse, 275
  and character, 8
  and crucifixion, 275
  and deconstruction, 290
  and defamiliarization, 193
  and entropy, 301
  and epigraphs, 72
  and Eros, 187
  and fact and fancy, 205, 210, 211, 216
  and family life, 296–97
  and fictitious history, 208–16, 293,
    300–301, 337
  and frames, 58, 71–73, 74–76, 77–79,
    80, 184, 290–91
  and heterocosms, 76

  and Hudibrastic verse, 210
  and intertextuality, 78, 79, 80–81,
    211, 214–15, 335
  and juxtaposition, 210
  and landscape, 158
  and language, 290
  and maximalism versus minimalism,
    104
  and metamorphosis, 185
  and minimalism, 326
  and myth, 73, 77, 81, 120, 183–84,
    187, 293, 300
  and the Old Testament, 184
  and parody, 185, 188, 192–93, 293,
    324
  and plagiarism, 80–81
  and quests, 120, 183–88, 193, 293
  and reflexivity, 59, 71–81, 184, 285
  and *regressus in infinitum*, 73, 77
  and satire, 185, 188, 300
  and tale-within-a-tale, 72–73
  and transcendence, 214–15
Barthelme, Donald, ix, 1, 8, 9, 49, 57,
  62, 93, 107, 167, 179, 252, 326, 327
  and blending of genres, 97, 117
  and collage, 329
  and defamiliarization, 97
  and dystopia, 163
  and entropy, 105
  and Eros, 116
  and excrement, 263
  and fairy tale, 59, 97–100
  and fictitious history, 337
  and fragmentation, 328–29
  and frames, 97, 114
  and heterocosms, 164
  and juxtaposition, 164
  and lists, 97, 113
  and landscape, 162–64, 294
  and language, 60, 106
  and ludic impulse, 59, 85, 97–100
  and minimalism, 60, 104–6, 112–16,
    287, 288
  and montage, 329
  and myth, 113
  and parody, 59, 97–100, 113, 117
  and quest, 113
  and reflexivity, 97
  and tale-within-a-tale, 114

and typographical play, 97
Baumbach, Jonathan, 278
Beagle, John S., 327
Beard, Dan, 31, 34
Beattie, Ann, 326
Beaumont and Fletcher, 42
Beckett, Samuel, xii, 1, 62, 112
   and minimalism, 288
Beetle Leg, The (Hawkes), 59, 101–2, 151,
   173, 174, 177, 193, 252, 294, 300,
   310, 327
Bellamy, Edward, 11
Bellamy, Joe David, 188, 288
Bellerophoniad (Barth), 73
Bellis, Peter J., 13
Bellow, Saul, ix, 5, 13
Bendixen, Alfred, 22
"Berenice" (Poe), 14, 32–33
Bergson, Henri, 339
Bierce, Ambrose, 144
Big Money, The (Dos Passos), 133
Bill and Tony, 131
Billy Budd (Melville), 43, 45, 61, 216
"Black Cat, The" (Poe), 9
Blair, Walter, 268
Blake, William, 110
Blanchot, Maurice, 288
Blithedale Romance, The (Hawthorne), 31,
   153, 217
Blood Oranges, The (Hawkes), 62, 120,
   173, 175, 177–79, 286, 296, 332
Blue Pastoral (Sorrentino), 87, 91, 93,
   120, 183, 188–92, 193, 203, 204,
   288, 289, 290
Bobbed Hair (Parker et al.), 22
Bockris, Victor, 130, 237, 238, 263
Boltzmann, Ludwig, 255
"Bone Bubbles (Barthelme), 85
Book of Breething, The (Burroughs), 91
Book of Daniel, The (Doctorow), 205,
   224–30
Book of Martyrs, The (Fox), 110
"Book of the Grotesque, The" (Ander-
   son), 14, 144
Booth, John Wilkes, 113
Borges, Jorge Luis, 1, 62, 72, 76–77, 83,
   84, 169, 179, 193, 247
   and landscape, 164–68
Bosch, Hieronymous, 331

Bostonians, The (James), 29, 31
Brackenridge, Hugh Henry, 5
   and quest, 38–39
Brautigan, Richard, 62, 113
   and fragmentation, 328
Breakfast of Champions (Vonnegut), 91,
   328
Breasts of Tiresias, The (Apollinaire), 158–
   59, 338
Brecht, Bertolt, 131, 132, 173–74, 224
   and realism vs. antirealism, 333
Breton, André, 269
"Bride Comes to Yellow Sky, The"
   (Crane), 8
Brighton Rock (Greene), 100
Brillouin, Leon, 255
Brodsky, Joseph, 308
Bromfield, Louis, 22
Brooke-Rose, Christine, 62, 309
Brossard, Chandler, ix
Brothers Karamazov, The (Dostoyevski),
   110
Brown, Charles Brockden, 9, 144, 273
Brown, Norman O., 206
Bruke, Kenneth, 143, 310
Burroughs, William S., 1, 2, 5, 9, 18, 31,
   56, 62, 85, 100, 167, 179, 252, 263,
   264, 281, 297, 304, 309, 310, 311,
   327, 335, 336
   and apocalypse, 160, 238, 273, 275
   and character, 8
   and collaboration, 132
   and collage, 128, 130, 131, 329
   and conspiracy/paranoia, 206, 237,
   238–43, 295, 299, 303
   and cut-up method, 119, 129–30, 239,
   291
   and determinism, 302–3
   and excrement, 302, 306
   and fact and fancy, 221
   and fold-in method, 119, 130, 132
   and fragmentation, 128–32
   and frames, 239
   and the grotesque, 294
   and heterocosms, 164
   and intertextuality, 63
   and juxtaposition, 129, 130, 131, 164
   and landscapes, 159–60
   and metamorphosis, 128, 130

Burroughs, William S. (*Continued*)
   and misogyny, 128, 238
   and montage, 131
   and myth, 242
   and nightmare, 270–71, 294, 341
   and politics, 299
   and realism, 131
   and relflexivity, 63, 243
   and science fiction, 242–43, 250, 275
   and surrealism, 239
   and tape/films, 119, 130–31, 132
   and Thanatos, 238, 240
   and typographical play, 129
Burroughs File, The (Burroughs), 129–30, 329
Burton, Gabrielle, 309
Burton, Robert, 43, 106, 107, 113
Butler, Samuel, 210
Butor, Michel, 62
Byron, George Gordon, 43

Cage, John, 309
Calligrammes (Apollinaire), 89
Call of the Wild, The (London), 53
Calvino, Italo, 62, 68
Camino Real (Williams), 268
Campbell, Joseph, 188, 293
Camus, Albert, 112
Cannibal, The (Hawkes), 67, 119, 145–47, 148, 151, 173, 174, 176, 178, 263, 286, 297, 299, 310
Canterbury Tales, The (Chaucer), 26
Cantos, The (Pound), 39, 124, 311
Capote, Truman, 46
Carlyle, Thomas, 43
Carpenter's Gothic (Gaddis), 63, 206, 232, 258–62, 301–2, 306, 339
Carver, Raymond, 288, 326
"Cask of Amontillado, The" (Poe), 10, 51
Castle of Otranto, The (Walpole), 47
Catch-22 (Heller), ix, 51, 135, 144, 205–6, 232, 233–37, 242, 243, 296, 299, 310
Cather, Willa, 112
Cat's Cradle (Vonnegut), 52, 232, 275, 306
Caucasian Chalk Circle, The (Brecht), 135
Céline, Louis-Ferdinand, 308

Cervantes, Miguel de, 2, 38, 43, 104, 107, 263
Chainbearer, The (Cooper), 44
Chairs, The (Ionesco), 338
Chants de Maldoror, Les (Lautréamont), 330
"Characters" (Theophrastus), 104
Charlotte (Rowson), 23
Cherry Orchard, The (Chekov), 135
Children of Sanchez, The (Lewis), 335
Chimera (Barth), 73–74, 76, 77, 79, 89, 184, 214
Cities of the Red Night (Burroughs), 120, 132, 136, 142, 144, 159–60, 164, 179, 271, 273, 296
City Life (Barthelme), 49, 85, 91, 312
Clancy, Laurie, 172
Clausius, Rudolf, 251
Clemens, Samuel L., 29. *See also* Twain, Mark
   and fragmentation, 10
   and metamorphosis, 12
Clement of Rome, 111
Codicillus (Lully), 110
Coleridge, Samuel Taylor, 20, 106, 285
Collage. *See also specific writers*
   defined, 123
Collective novel, 135
"Colloguy of Monos and Una, The," (Poe), 55
Columbiad (Barlow), 41
"Comforts of Home, The" (O'Connor), 151
Commedia (Dante), 108
Communist Societies of the United States, The (Nordhoff), 53
Concrete poetry, 87
Confidence Man, The (Melville), 12, 20–21, 22, 27, 31, 153
Connecticut Yankee in King Arthur's Court, A (Twain), 31, 33, 45, 54–55, 268, 273
Conquest of Canaan, The (Dwight), 41
Conrad, Joseph, 131, 308
Conspiracy/paranoia, 232–50. *See also specific writers*
   and earlier American writing, 50–52
"Contemporary Novel, The" (Wells), 104

"Conversation of Eiros and Charmion, The" (Poe), 55
Cooke, Ebenezer, 209
Cool Million, A (West), 61–62, 180, 201, 204
Cooper, James Fenimore, 14, 45, 217, 234, 273
  and the grotesque, 19
  and history, 44–45
Coover, Robert, ix, 2, 5, 8, 56, 62, 93, 99, 264, 341
  and apocalypse, 206, 274, 275, 276–77
  and blending of genres, 229
  and conspiracy/paranoia, 295
  and detective fiction, 101, 324
  and epigraphs, 276
  and excrement, 228, 306
  and fact and fancy, 205, 224–25
  and fairy tale, 59, 64–65, 96–97
  and fictitious history, 7, 300, 336, 224–30
  and fragmentation, 328
  and frames, 59, 65
  and the grotesque, 229, 294
  and heterocosm, 63
  and juxtaposition, 228
  and landscape, 228–29
  and language, 229
  and lists, 229
  and ludic impulse, 59, 85
  and myth, 227–28, 300
  and nightmare, 294
  and parody, 59, 64–65, 96, 101, 324, 337
  and politics, 298
  and reflexivity, 63–65
  and satire, 205, 228, 300
  and surrealism, 227
  and tale-within-a-tale, 64–65
  and western fiction, 337
Coquette, The (Foster), 32
Cortázar, Julio, 1, 62
Cotton, John, 15, 53, 273
Court of Charles II, The (Forneron), 45
Crane, Stephen, 14, 112, 144, 287, 314
  and conspiracy/paranoia, 51
  and the grotesque, 20
  and minimalism, 43–44

Crowds and Power (Canetti), 264
Cruel as the Grave (Southworth), 30
Crying of Lot 49, The (Pynchon), 97, 206, 232, 245–49, 232, 252, 255, 256, 258, 259, 261, 306, 338
Crystal Vision (Sorrentino), 91, 93, 190, 301, 319
Cummings, E. E., 33–34
Cut-up method, 119, 129–30, 239, 291
"Cut-Ups, The," 131
Cypher in the Plays and on the Tombstone, The (Donnelly), 32

Daisy Miller (James), 29
Damnation of Theron Ware, The (Frederic), 32, 51
Darconville's Cat (Theroux), x, 59, 94–96, 107, 108, 109, 112, 117, 120, 153, 154, 159, 191, 286, 289, 305, 310
Day of Doom, The (Wigglesworth), 53, 273
Day of the Locust, The (West), 69, 273, 274, 276
Dead Father, The (Barthelme), 60, 105–6, 107, 112–16, 117, 203, 288, 310, 332
Death House Letters (Rosenberg and Rosenberg), 224
Death Kit (Sontag), 144, 206, 252, 269
Decentralization, 132–43. See also specific writers
  and earlier American writing, 21–22
Decline of the West, The (Spengler), 54
Defamiliarization. See also specific writers
  defined, 23, 320–21
Defense, The (Nabokov), 84
Degeneration (Nordau), 54
Degradation of the Democratic Dogma (Adams), 251
Dent, John, 129
De Quincey, Thomas, 43, 110
Derrida, Jacques, 3, 308
Der Ring des Nibelungen (Wagner), 326
Detective fiction, 59, 101–2, 174, 294, 324
Development of American Romance, The (Bell), 5

Devil, the, 144–57. See also *specific writers*
and earlier American writing, 15–17, 19
"Devil and Tom Walker, The" (Irving), 15
Devil's Dictionary, The (Bierce), 16, 153
Dickens, Charles, 311
Dickinson, Emily, 104, 237
Diderot, Denis, 2, 61
Divine Comedy, The (Dante), 42, 108, 159, 180, 184, 268
Doctorow, E. L.
   and epigraphs, 225
   and fact and fancy, 205, 224–25
   and fictitious history, 224–30, 337
   and landscape, 228–29
   and myth, 228
Dog Soldiers (Stone), 232
Don Quixote (Cervantes), 41, 61, 108, 184, 287
Dos Passos, John, 219–20, 283
   and collective novel, 135
   and decentralization, 119, 133–35, 138, 292
   and juxtaposition, 133
   and montage, 134, 138
Dostoyevski, Feodor, 104, 311
Double or Nothing (Federman), 59, 63, 87–89, 91, 263
Dowell, Coleman, ix, 1, 62, 68, 128, 167, 179, 287, 304
   and androgyny, 119, 124, 125, 126–27, 327, 328
   and apocalypse, 274–75, 306
   and blending of genres, 125, 127
   and collage and montage, 119, 127, 291
   and crucifixion, 274–75, 306
   and epigraphs, 126
   and family life, 297
   and fragmentation, 124–28
   and game playing, 125–26
   and heterocosms, 164
   and juxtaposition, 119, 126, 127, 128, 164
   and landscape, 160–62
   and metamorphosis, 119, 124, 125, 132, 327, 328

and reality, 125
and reflexivity, 63, 125
and tale-within-a-tale, 126, 127
Drayton, Michael, 190
Dream Life of Balso Snell, The (West), 120, 180, 188, 191, 204, 264
Dream Play, A (Strindberg), 124, 268–69
Dreiser, Theodore, 14, 287, 302, 314
Duino Elegies (Rilke), 110
Dumbwaiter, The (Pinter), 105
Dunyazadiad (Barth), 59, 73, 74
Durrell, Lawrence, 62
Dystopia/utopia, 163, 300
   in earlier American writing, 48–49

"Earth's Holocaust" (Hawthorne), 53
"Easter Wings" (Herbert), 89
Eco, Umberto, 62
Ecrits (Lacan), 3
Education of Henry Adams, The (Adams), 54, 56, 251, 254, 307
Edwards, Jonathan, 15, 341
Edwards, Thomas R., 81
Eilenberg, Max, 93, 95
Eisenstein, Sergei, 134
Electric Kool-Aid Acid Test, The (Wolfe), 217, 335
Eliade, Mircea, 102, 272
Eliot, George
   and reflexivity, 26–27
Eliot, T. S., 54, 83, 110, 128, 131, 138, 173, 183, 255, 282, 327
   and androgyny, 124
   and associational flow, 123
   and collage, 123
   and entropy, 301, 307
   and fragmentation, 122, 124, 143
   and history, 304
   and juxtaposition, 122, 123, 143
   and metamorphosis, 124, 132, 292
   and montage, 123
   and myth, 123
   and quest, 123
   and spatialization, 122
   and supernaturalism, 305
Elizabeth Appleton (O'Hara), 7
Elkin, Stanley, 327
   and maximalism, 324

Ellison, Ralph, 62, 276, 296, 309, 327, 341
  and apocalypse/Armageddon, 207, 277–81, 306–7
  and dream/nightmare, 277–81
  and the grotesque, 307
  and juxtaposition, 278
  and quest, 281
  and realism, 278
  and surealism, 278, 279
Elsie Venner (Holmes), 20
Emerson, Ralph Waldo, 16, 28, 31, 51, 56, 110, 305, 311, 341
  and the grotesque, 19
Empedocles, 326, 327
Encyclopedic novel. See specific writers
End of the Road, The (Barth), 67, 77, 80, 81, 214, 290, 296
Entropy, 251–67. See also specific writers
  defined, 251, 267
  in earlier American writing, 52–53, 54, 55
"Entropy" (Pynchon), 206, 252–55, 262
Epigraph, 42, 67, 68, 72, 86, 87, 110, 126, 139, 167, 177, 190, 262, 264–65, 276
  in earlier American writing, 34
"Epoch-Eclipse and Apocalypse" (Ketterer), 55
Erasmus, 107
Eros, 116, 178, 179, 187, 206, 236, 238, 306
Essays (Montaigne), 43
"Esthetique du Mal" (Stevens), 17
Etchings of a Whaling Cruise (Browne), 42
Eureka (Poe), 22, 52, 56
Excrement, 228, 262, 263, 264–67, 302, 306, 339–40
Executioner's Song, The (Mailer), 217
Exercises in Style (Queneau), 93
"Explanation, The" (Barthelme), 85
Exterminator! (Burroughs), 130, 271
Eyck, Hubert, 110
Eyck, Jan, 110

Fact and fancy. See also specific writers
  and earlier American writing, 37–38
"Facts Concerning a Recent Carnival of

Crime in Connecticut, The" (Clemens), 10–11
"Facts in the Case of M. Valdemar, The" (Poe), 9, 18
Fairy tale, 59, 64–65, 96–100, 182, 195, 246
"Fall of the House of Usher, The" (Poe), 9–10, 55
Family Doom, The (Southworth), 30
Farewell to Arms, A (Hemingway), 51
Faulkner, William, 8, 17, 144, 156, 167, 284, 300, 310, 311, 335, 341
  and apocalypse, 273–74, 306
  and Christian imagery, 273–74
  and decentralization, 21, 292, 133
  and the grotesque, 307
  and reflexivity, 31
Faust (Goethe), 108, 110, 111
Faust II (Goethe), 110
Federman, Raymond, ix, 1, 9, 62, 288, 294
  and epigraph, 87
  and frames, 87
  and ludic impulse, 59, 87–89
  and reflexivity, 63, 87–88
  and typographical play, 87–89
Feidelson, Charles, Jr., 42, 43
Female Quixotism (Tenny), 41
"Few Words About Minimalism, A" (Barth), 326
Fiction and the Figures of Life (Gass), 62
Fictitious history, 208–31. See also specific writers
Fiedler, Leslie, 336
Fielding, Henry, 43, 61, 263, 308
"Figure in the Carpet, The" (James), 35–36
Film/tapes, 119, 130–31, 132
Finnegans Wake (Joyce), 70, 106, 124, 132, 269, 289, 311
Fion, Emile, 68
"Fire and Ice" (Frost), 53, 273
Fitzgerald, F. Scott, 2, 104, 281, 287
  and entropy, 251
  and fairy tale, 182
  and myth, 120, 182
  and parody, 180, 181
  and quests, 181–83
Fitzgerald, Robert, 152

Flag for Sunrise, A (Stone), 232
"Flannery O'Connor's Devil" (Hawkes), 120, 149, 150
Flaubert, Gustave, 287, 302
Floating Opera, The (Barth), 11, 77, 80, 81, 214, 290, 296–97
Fold-in method, 119, 130, 132
Following the Equator (Twain), 19
Fortune's Foot-ball (Butler), 34
42nd Parallel, The (Dos Passos), 133
Four Quartets (Eliot), 110, 122, 291
Fowles, John, 62
Fragmentation, 122–32, 291, 292. See also *specific writers*
  and earlier American writing, 9–14
Frame. See *specific writers*
Free-Lance Pallbearers, The (Reed), 67, 144, 159, 203–4, 206, 252, 263, 264–67, 269, 275, 302, 337
Freeman, Mary Wilkins, 22
Fretwork (Sorrentino), 95
Friday Book, The (Barth), 59, 71–73, 76, 183, 205, 208, 209, 324
Friedman, Ellen, 309
From Ritual to Romance (Weston), 123
Frost, Robert, 52, 282
Frye, Northrop, 108
Fuchs, Miriam, 309
Future for Astyanax, A (Bersani), 3

Gaddis, William, ix, 1, 31 52, 62, 68, 93, 104, 106, 119, 125, 128, 140, 187, 252, 290, 304, 309, 310, 311, 327
  and apocalypse, 274, 306
  and Christian tradition, 274, 303
  and the Clementine *Recognitions,* 110, 111, 326
  and collage, 291
  and conspiracy/paranoia, 206, 260
  and decentralization, 119, 136–39
  and the devil, 111, 155–57
  and encyclopedic novel, 108–9, 286, 287, 325, 326
  and entropy, 116–17, 206, 256–62, 301–2, 303, 339
  and epigraph, 110
  and excrement, 262, 302, 339
  and fragmentation, 206
  and the grotesque, 155–57, 294

  and intertextuality, 63
  and language, 60
  and learned with tradition, 60, 287
  and maximalism, 60, 109–11, 288, 324–25
  and montage, 138, 291
  and nightmare, 294
  and objectification, 338, 339
  and parody, 111
  and plagiarism, 110, 325
  and reflexivity, 63, 111
  and quest, 109–11
"Gaddis' Debt to T. S. Eliot," 122
Gale, Bob, 91
Game playing, 290, 309–10. See also *specific writers*
  defined, 321
  in literature, 32, 84–87
"Games and Play in Modern American Fiction" (Detweiler), 84
Games Authors Play (Hutchinson), 84
Garden of Eden, U.S.A. (Bishop), 49
Gargantua and Pantagruel (Rabelais), 43, 108, 287
Gass, William, ix, 3, 33, 62, 68, 286
  and Eros, 89–91
  and ludic impulse, 59, 87, 89–91
  and typographical play, 33, 89–91
Genet, Jean, 131, 288
Genres, blending of, 288, 289, 290. See also *specific writers*
  and earlier American writing, 38
Gerald's Party (Coover), 101, 263, 324
Gide, André, 62
Giles Goat-Boy or, The Revised New Syllabus (Barth), 59, 74–76, 77, 79, 82, 108, 120, 183–88, 189, 190, 191, 193, 203, 204, 215, 232, 275, 285, 290, 291, 293, 297, 320, 324, 334
"Gingerbread House, The" (Coover), 59, 96, 328
Ginsberg, Allen, 239
Glass Key, The (Hammett), 70
"Glass Mountain, The" (Barthelme), 85
Goddess of Atvatabar, The (Bradshaw), 48
Goes, Hugo van der, 110
Goethe, Johann Wolfgang von, 43
Goffman, Erving, 12
Goldberg, Rube, 22

"Good Country People" (O'Connor), 151, 152–53
"Good Man Is Hard to Find, A" (O'Connor), 149, 151, 274, 310
Good Soldier, The (Ford), 69, 177, 178
Goose on the Grave, The (Hawkes), 173, 297
Gordon, Lois, 99
Graff, Gerald, 99, 311
Grandissimes, The (Cable), 41
Graves, Robert, 110
Gravity's Rainbow (Pynchon), x, 52, 108, 109, 112, 115, 119, 136, 138, 139–43, 238, 239, 243–45, 255, 258, 262, 275, 287, 302, 305–6, 306, 307, 338, 339
Great American Novel, The (Roth), 85
Great Cryptogram, The (Donnelly), 32
Great Expectations (Dickens), 292
Great Gatsby, The (Fitzgerald), 14, 70, 120, 180, 181–83, 204, 220, 236, 251, 293, 300
Great God Brown, The (O'Neill), 156
Greco, El, 110
Greenberg, Clement, 61, 82
Green Hills of Africa (Hemingway), 61, 217
"Greenleaf" (O'Connor), 274
Griffith, D. W., 134
Grotesque, the, 144–57, 302. See also specific writers
  defined, 144–45
  and earlier American writing, 14–21
"Grotesque, The" (O'Connor), 144
Grotesque in American Negro Fiction, The (Gysin), 144
Grotesque in Art and Literature, The (Kayser), 147–48
Gruppe 63, 62
Guardian Angel, The (Holmes), 13
Guerard, Albert, ix
Gulliver's Travels (Swift), 159, 295
Gysin, Brion, 129, 131
Gysin, Fritz, 278

Habit of Being, The (O'Connor), 150, 152, 153
Habitations of the Word (Gaes), 33, 93
Hale, Edward Everett, 22

Haliburton, Thomas C., 12, 228
Hall of Mirrors, A (Stone), 135, 138, 144, 206, 232, 269, 275–76, 277, 282, 292, 298, 306
Hamill, Pete, 217
Hamlet, The (Faulkner), 153
Hard Times (Dickens), 216
Hardy, Thomas, 311
Harrowing of Hell, The (Adams), 110
Hawkes, John, ix, x, 1, 8, 9, 49, 56, 57, 62, 153, 154, 157, 252, 272, 277, 281, 309, 310, 327, 329–30
  and animal imagery, 145–46
  and apocalypse, 270, 273
  and Christian tradition, 303
  and crucifixion, 273
  and death imagery, 146
  and defamilarization, 179
  and detective fiction, 59, 101–2, 174, 294
  and the devil, 148, 149, 150–52, 303
  and entropy, 252
  and epigraphs, 177
  and Eros, 178, 179, 306
  and family life, 296–97
  and fictional history, 300
  and the grotesque, 119, 145–47, 294, 307
  and the insane asylum, 299
  and juxtaposition, 174, 178, 296
  and landscape, 173–79, 294
  and ludic impulse, 59, 100–102
  and metamorphosis, 270
  and myth, 59, 101–2, 174, 175, 176, 300
  and nightmare, 269–70, 294
  and parody, 59, 100–102, 174, 179, 294
  and quest, 101–2
  and reflexivity, 285–86
  and satire, 300
  and surrealism, 270, 286, 340
  and Thanatos, 178, 179
  and western fiction, 59, 101–2, 174, 294
Hawthorne, Nathaniel, 3, 4, 5, 11, 17, 31, 42, 140, 144, 153, 156, 269, 273, 277, 304, 311, 341
  and Armageddon, 53–54

Hawthorne, Nathaniel (*Continued*)
and the demonic, 15
and the grotesque, 19
and landscape, 47–48
and reflexivity, 27–29
Haydn, Franz Joseph, 113
Hazard of New Fortunes, A (Howells), 8, 15
Heartbreak Hotel (Burton), 323
Heart of Darkness (Conrad), 182
Heidegger, Martin, 339
Heller, Joseph, 327
and conspiracy/paranoia, 205–6, 233–37, 238, 243, 296
and Eros, 206, 235
and insane asylum, 299
and juxtaposition, 233
and misogyny, 234
and nightmare, 271
and Thanatos, 206, 235
Hemingway, Ernest, 62, 112, 234, 287, 311
and minimalism, 44
and reflexivity, 30–31
Heptameron (Margaret of Navarre), 43
Herland (Gilman), 49
Hero, The (Raglan), 183
Herodotus, 104
Hero with a Thousand Faces, The (Campbell), 180, 181, 182, 183, 186, 187, 188
Heterocosm. See *specific writers*
High Noon, 337
Hindoo Holiday (Ackerley), 110
Hind's Kidnap (McElroy), 97, 120–21, 193–99, 203, 204
History, fictitious, 208–31. See also *specific writers*
in earlier American writing, 44–46
History of European Morals, A (Lecky), 45
History of New York, A (Irving), 37, 44, 107–8
History of the Kingdom of Basaruah, The (Morgan), 53, 273
Hoffman, Daniel, 10, 18, 24, 56, 296
Holder, Alan, 209
"Hollow Men, The" (Eliot), 273, 304
Holmes, Oliver Wendell, 13

and the grotesque, 19–20
Home as Found (Cooper), 7
Homer, 42
Homeward Bound (Cooper), 7
Homology
dream/nightmare/apocalypse/Armageddon, 270, 277, 281, 282
excrement/sex/death, 206, 263, 265, 282
Hooper, J. J., 12
Hope Leslie (Sedgwick), 7
House of Mirth, The (Wharton), 7
House of the Seven Gables, The (Hawthorne), 244, 299
Howells, William Dean, 2, 5, 6, 22, 27
and landscape, 49
and reflexivity, 29
"How to Write a Blackwood Article" (Poe), 24–25
Human Use of Human Beings, The (Wiener), 252, 254, 256, 260, 338
Huss, John, 110
Huxley, Aldous, 62

Ibsen, Henrik, 285
Iceman Cometh, The (O'Neill), 135
Ideology and Utopia (Mannheim), 48
If on a winter's night a traveler (Calvino), 68
Illuminations (Rimbaud), 86
Imaginative Qualities of Actual Things (Sorrentino), 69, 91, 93, 95, 319
Imlay, Gilbert, 5
"Imp of the Perverse, The" (Poe), 51
In Cold Blood (Capote), 217
Indian Summer (Howells), 29
Inferno, The (Dante), 110
Information theory, 301, 302
Innocence in Extremis (Hawkes), 173
"Innocent Party, The," 176–77
Inquisitor, The (Rowson), 23
Insane asylum, 233–34, 299. See also *specific writers*
and earlier American writing, 49–50
Integration of the Personality (Jung), 110
Intertextuality. See *specific writers*
In the Clearing (Frost), 52

Invisible Cities (Calvino), 158
Invisible Man (Ellison), ix, 12, 62, 144,
    203, 206–7, 232, 270, 277–81, 282,
    306, 310
In Watermelon Sugar (Brautigan), 328
Ionesco, Eugene, 288
Irving, John, 62
Irving, Washington, 15, 144
    and blending of genres, 44
    and fictitious history, 44
    and landscape, 48, 332–33
    and ludic play, 37–38
    and parody, 44
Island People (Dowell), 119, 124–28, 132,
    142, 310, 327
"Istanbul Papers, The" (Abish), 336–37

James, Henry, 2, 6, 17, 22, 27, 31, 33,
    46, 144, 158, 159, 311
    and decentralization, 21
    and fragmentation, 10
    ludic play, 35–36
    and minimalism, 43
    and reflexivity, 29
James, William, 54, 56
"James the Old Intruder" (Tilford), 29
Jargon, 100
Jodorowsky, Alexandro, 131
Johnson, B. S., 62
"Jolly Corner, The" (James), 10
Jones, Ernest, 279
Jonson, Ben, 42
Journal of Julius Rodman, The (Poe), 36
Journal of the Plague Year, A (Defoe), 216
Journal to Mars (Pope), 48
Journal to Philadelphia, A (Adelio), 34
Joyce, James, 1, 2, 62, 68, 83, 93, 117,
    131, 173, 191, 255, 263, 288, 310,
    311
J R (Gaddis), x, 39, 63, 108, 109, 116–
    17, 206, 256–58, 261, 262, 286,
    287, 301, 326, 327
Julian the Apostate, 110
Jung, C. G., 110, 183
Junger, Ernst, xii
Juxtaposition, 290, 291. See also *specific
    writers*

Kafka, Franz, xii, 1, 2, 131
Kaplan, Justin, 12
Karl, Frederick R., 140, 143, 200, 272
Katz, Steve, 62
Kayser, Wolfgang, 153, 154
Keats, John, 20, 104
Kenner, Hugh, 93
Kermode, Frank, 3
Kerouac, Jack, 131
Kesey, Ken, 49, 327
    and conspiracy/paranoia, 205–6, 233–
        37, 238, 243
    and Eros, 206, 236
    and the insane asylum, 233–34, 299
    and misogyny, 234, 235
    and the pastoral, 234–35
    and setting, 233
    and Thanatos, 206
King Ubu (Jarry), 158
Klinkowitz, Jerome, 86, 87, 322
Koenig, David, 136, 137
Kosinski, Jerzy, 327
Kostelanetz, Richard, 88
Kuhlmann, Susan, 12

Lacan, Jacques, 3
La Disparition (Perec), 86
L'Age d'Or (Luis Buñuel film), 131
Laing, R. D., 299
Lamb, Charles, 311
"Lame Shall Enter First, The" (O'Con-
    nor), 150, 151
Lamplighter, The (Cummins), 7
Landscape, imaginary, 158–79. See also
    specific writers
    and earlier American writing, 46–49
Langbaum, Robert, 124
Language, 60, 117, 308. See also *specific
    writers*
    games with, 32, 85–87
Laplace, Pierre, 52, 56
Last of the Mohicans, The (Cooper), 44–45
Last Tycoon, The (Fitzgerald), 220
Last Words of Dutch Schultz, The (Bur-
    roughs), 131
Late George Apley, The (Marquand), 7
Late Great Planet Earth, The (film), 272

Lautréamont, le comte de, xii, 308
La Vida (Lewis), 335
Law of Civilization and Decay, The
　(Adams), 54
Learned wit tradition, 42–43, 107–8.
　See also *specific writers*
Leatherstocking Tales, The (Cooper), 7,
　44–45, 46
Leaver-outers. *See* Minimalism
Leavis, F. R., x
LeClair, Thomas, 238, 286
Lectures on Literature (Nabokov), 96
Lemaire, Gérard-Georges, 132
Lenin, Vladimir, 113
Le Sage (Alain René), 38
Lessing, Doris, 62
Letters (Barth), x, 28, 59, 73, 77, 78, 79–
　81, 82, 92, 108, 205, 208, 211, 214–
　16, 224, 230, 232, 290, 297, 300,
　320
Letters from the Earth (Twain), 16, 17
Letters to Allen Ginsberg, 1953–1957 (Bur-
　roughs), 132
"Letter to American Teachers of His-
　tory, A" (Adams), 251
Lewicki, Zbigniew, 255, 279
Lewis, R. W. B., 272
Life Against Death (Brown), 263–64
*Life and Times of Father Quipes, otherwise
　Dominick O'Blarney, The* (Fidaddy),
　34
Life on the Mississippi (Twain), 216
"Life You Save May Be Your Own, The"
　(O'Connor), 149, 151
"Ligeia" (Poe), 10, 34
Light in August (Faulkner), 273–74, 306
Lime Twig, The (Hawkes), 59, 100–101,
　151, 173, 174, 193, 232, 269–70,
　273, 274, 281, 294, 297, 310
Lindberg, Gary, 12
Linwoods, The (Sedgwick), 7
Lipogram, 86, 87, 289
Lists. *See specific writers*
Lolita (Nabokov), ix, 10, 35, 59, 65–66,
　82, 84, 96, 203, 290–91
Lonelyhearts, Miss (West), 153
Long Talking Bad Conditions Blues (Suken-
　ick), 85

Look Homeward, Angel (Wolfe), 8
Looking Backward (Bellamy), 11, 268
Lookout Cartridge (McElroy), 232, 252
Lost in the Funhouse (Barth), 18, 23, 25,
　59, 73, 77–79, 144, 184, 215, 336
Love and Death in the American Novel
　(Fiedler), 234
"Love and Strife in William Gaddis' *J R*"
　(Matanle), 257–58
Love in the Ruins (Percy), 275
Lower Depths, The (Gorky), 135
Lucian, 107
Ludic impulse, 83–103, 289, 290. See
　also *specific writers*
　and earlier American writing, 31–38
Luther, Martin, 113
Lyrical Ballads (Wordsworth and Coler-
　idge), 288

McCarthy, Mary, 84
McDonald, James L., 75
McElroy, Joseph, ix, 62, 100
　and conspiracy/paranoia, 121, 195
　and entropy, 252
　and fairy tale, 195
　and juxtaposition, 193
　and the pastoral, 193, 194–95
　and quest, 120–21, 193–99
McGuane, Thomas, 113
MacLeish, Archibald, 304
McTeague (Norris), 11, 53
Madness. *See* Insane asylum
Maggie (Crane), 14
"Magic Poker, The" (Coover), 59, 64–
　65, 82, 96
Magnalia Christi Americana (Mather), 41
Mailer, Norman, ix, 46, 62, 263
　and decentralization, 135
　and fact and fancy, 205, 220–21
　and fictitious history, 217–24
　and language, 336
　and realism, 220, 224
Making of the New, The (Symons), 311
Manatitlans, The (Smile), 49
Manfred (Byron), 83
Manhattan Transfer (Dos Passos), 133–35,
　138, 139, 143, 292
Man in the Iron Mask (Dumas), 45

Mannheim, Karl, 48
"Man That Was Used Up, The" (Poe),
    17–18
Marble Faun, The (Hawthorne), 48, 51
Mardi (Melville), 46, 47
Marlowe, Christopher, 32, 42
Márquez, Gabriel García, 1, 62, 68
Martin, Jay, 53, 54
Martin, Stephen-Paul, 126
Mason, Bobbie Ann, 288, 326
Mather, Cotton, 15, 50
Mather, Richard, 15
Maximalism, 4, 104–17, 286–88. See
    also specific writers
    and earlier American writing, 41–43
Maxwell, James Clerk, 255, 338
Maxwell's demon, 252, 255, 338
"Maxwell's demon, entropy, information"
    (Mangel), 255–56
"May Day" (Fitzgerald), 300
Melville, Herman, 3, 4, 5, 17, 23, 28,
    109, 144, 156, 234, 273, 281, 304,
    311, 341
    and apocalypse, 54
    and blending of genres, 42
    and conspiracy/paranoia, 51–52
    and epigraphs, 42
    and fragmentation, 12–13
    and the grotesque, 20–21
    and landscapes, 47
    and learned wit tradition, 43
    and maximalism, 41–43
    and Menippean satire, 43
    and metamorphosis, 13, 132
    and quest, 40–41
    and reflexivity, 27
Mendelson, Edward, 108
Menippean satire, 116, 286
    defined, 108
Menippus, 108
Metafiction, x, 59
    and apocalypse/Armageddon, 303,
        306–7
    and blending of genres, 288, 289, 290
    and collage and montage, 291
    and conspiracy/paranoia, 295–96
    and crime fiction, 294
    and crucifixion, 306

    and cut-up method, 291
    and decentralization, 292
    and deconstruction, 290, 308
    and defamiliarization, 288–89
    defined, 62
    and determinism, 302–3
    and the devil, 303, 304
    and the encyclopedic novel, 286–87
    and entropy, 301–2, 307
    and Eros vs. Thanatos, 306
    and excrement, 302, 306
    and family life, 296–97
    and fragmentation, 291, 292
    and frames, 290–91
    and game-playing, 289, 290, 309–10
    and the grotesque, 294, 302, 307–8
    hallmarks of, 283–84
    and history, 293, 300–301, 304
    and the insane asylum, 299
    and juxtaposition, 290, 291, 296
    and landscape, 294–95
    and language, 290, 308
    and learned wit tradition, 287
    and ludic impulse, 289, 290
    and maximalism, 286–88
    and Menippean satire, 286
    and metamorphosis, 292
    and minimalism, 287–88
    and misanthropy, 302
    and misogyny, 302, 305
    and myth, 293
    and nightmare, 294, 304
    and parody, 288, 293, 294, 308
    and politics, 298–99
    and quest, 293
    and realism, 307
    and reflexivity, 285–86
    and satire, 288, 302
    and science fiction, 300
    and surrealism, 290
    traits of, 62–63, 82
    and utopia/dystopia, 300
    and western fiction, 294
Metamorphosis. See specific writers
Miami and the Siege of Chicago (Mailer),
    217
Michaels, Leonard, 328
Michener, James, 41

Miller, Henry, 239, 262, 302
"Minds Meet" (Abish), 86, 144
Minimalism, 4, 104–7, 287–88. See also
    specific writers
    and earlier American writing, 43–44
Minutes to Go (Burroughs and Gysin),
    87, 129, 131
Misanthropy, 302
Misogyny, 94, 128, 154, 234, 235, 238,
    302, 305
Miss Lonelyhearts (West), 120, 149, 155,
    251, 306, 327
Miss MacIntosh, My Darling (Young), x,
    108, 120, 153, 310
Miss Ravenel's Conversion (De Forest), 7,
    41
Mithras, 110
Moby-Dick (Melville), 4, 27, 40–43, 52,
    54, 108, 110, 132, 153, 182, 273,
    287
Modern Chivalry (Brackenridge), 38–39,
    41, 107
Modern Instance, A (Howells), 14
Moholy-Nagy, L., 87
Moll Flanders (Defoe), 34
"Monster, The" (Crane), 20
Montage. See also *specific writers*
    defined, 123, 138
Montaigne, 32, 106
Moore, Steven, 139
Morris, Wright, 91
Mosquitoes (Faulkner), 31
Mother Courage (Brecht), 174, 189
Mottram, Eric, 130, 131
Mozart, Wolfgang, 110
Mrs. October Was Here (Dowell), 120, 124,
    125, 160–62, 164, 232, 263, 274–
    75, 306
Mulligan Stew (Sorrentino), x, 38, 59,
    68–71, 75, 82, 91–94, 95, 96, 108,
    188, 190, 191, 232, 289, 291, 310,
    319, 323
"Murders in the Rue Morgue, The"
    (Poe), 35
Murdock, Iris, 62
My Ántonia (Cather), 7
My Life as a Man (Roth), 62
Mysterious Stranger, The (Twain), 16, 17,
    22, 153, 269

Mystery and Manners (O'Connor), 145
"Mystery and Tragedy" (Barth), 183
Myth. See *specific writers*
"Myth and Modernism" (Barth), 183
Myth of the Birth of the Hero, The (Rank),
    180

Nabokov, Vladimir, 1, 9, 16, 57, 62, 71,
    83, 173, 294, 304, 305, 310, 319,
    335
    and encyclopedic novel, 169
    and epigraphs, 67, 167
    and fabricated language, 167
    and frames, 59, 65–68, 290–91, 319
    and heterocosm, 167
    and juxtaposition, 169
    and landscape, 164, 166–72, 295
    and ludic spirit, 84–85
    and madness, 67–68, 299–300
    and parody, 10, 96
    and reflexivity, 59, 65–68
    and science fiction, 149
    and tale-within-a-tale, 170
Nachtwachen (Bonaventura), 147, 148
Naked and the Dead, The (Mailer), 135
Naked Lunch (Burroughs), ix, 63, 66,
    129, 206, 232, 239–43, 245, 263,
    302, 336
*Narrative of Arthur Gordon Pym of Nan-
    tucket, The* (Poe), 34, 83–84
*Narrative of a Whaling Voyage Round the
    Globe* (Bennett), 42
Narrative . . . of the Whaleship Essex, The
    (Chase), 42
National tales, 108–9
Natural, The (Malamud), 85
Natural History of the Sperm Whale
    (Beale), 42
Naturalists, 314
Nature (Emerson), 19
Necessary Angel, The (Stevens), 9
Necessity of Reformation, The (Mather),
    273
Neil, Malcolm, 91
"Never Bet the Devil Your Head" (Poe),
    16
*New Home . . . ; or, Glimpses of Western
    Life, A* (Kirkland), 7

New Journalism, The (Wolfe and Johnson), 217
"New Novel, The" (James), 104
Nietzsche, Friedrich, 308
Night Games, 264
Nightmare, 268–84, 304. See also *specific writers*
Nightwood (Barnes), 306, 327
Nin, Anaïs, 269, 270, 309
1919 (Dos Passos), 133
Nonfiction novel, 205, 217, 221, 222
Norris, Frank, 144, 287, 314
and fragmentation, 11
"Notes on the Apocalypse" (Edwards), 273
Nouveau nouveau roman, 87
Nouveau romanciers, 62
Nova Express (Burroughs), 63, 128, 129, 130, 131, 239, 242, 243
"Novel-Writing and Novel-Reading" (Howells), 5–6

Oates, Joyce Carol, 62, 309
O'Brien, Flann, 68
and intertextuality, 319
and plagiarism, 319
O'Brien, John, 192
Ocean of Story, The (Somadeva), 293
O'Connor, Flannery, ix, 154, 173
and animal imagery, 145–46
and apocalypse, 274
and Christian tradition, 274, 303
and death imagery, 146
and the devil, 120, 148–53, 303
and the grotesque, 119–20, 145–47, 307, 330, 331
and supernaturalism; 305
Octopus, The (Norris), 31
"Ode to a Nightingale" (Keats), 277
Odyssey, The (Homer), 180
Oedipus Rex (Sophocles), 184, 185
Of a Fire on the Moon (Mailer), 217
Of Time and the River (Wolfe), 8, 104
Olderman, Raymond M., 186, 232, 235
Old Man and the Sea, The (Hemingway), 44
Old New York (Wharton), 43
Omoo (Melville), 47

One Flew Over the Cuckoo's Nest (Kesey), ix, 67, 205–6, 232, 233–37, 242, 243, 279, 299
One Hundred Years of Solitude (Márquez), 104
One of the Children Is Crying (Dowell), 124, 135–36
On Nature (Empedocles), 122, 257
On the Equilibrium of Heterogeneous Substances (Gibbs), 251
On the Nightmare (Jones), 270
On the Road (Kerouac), 239
"Open Boat, The" (Crane), 45–46, 216
Origin of the Brunists, The (Coover), 65, 85, 135, 144, 206, 275, 276–77, 282
Origin of the Species, The (Darwin), 110
Orlando (Woolf), 327
Ortega y Gasset, José, 61
Our Gang (Roth), 230
"Our Work and Why We Do It" (Barthelme), 85
Ovid, 124
Owl, The (Hawkes), 151, 173, 174–75

Paine, Thomas, 51
Pale Fire (Nabokov), 59, 65, 66–68, 82, 84, 85, 96, 120, 164, 166–69, 232, 295, 299–300, 319
Paradise Lost (Milton), 42
Paradise on Earth (Hayes), 48
"Paraguay" (Barthelme), 49, 120, 162–64, 294
Paranoia/conspiracy, 232–50. See also *specific writers*
and earlier American writing, 50–52
Paranoid Style in American Politics and Other Essays, The (Hofstadter), 232
Parker, Dorothy, 22
Parody, 103, 308. See also *specific writers*
defined, 16, 96
"Partridge Festival, The" (O'Connor), 149, 151
Pascal, 113
Passion Artist, The (Hawkes), 173, 174, 176, 297
Pastoral, the. See *specific writers*
"Pastorals bold upon a new straine" (Drayton), 191

Peer Gynt (Ibsen), 110
Percy, Walker
  and apocalypse, 275
  and science fiction, 275
Perseid (Barth), 73
Petronius, 104, 107
Picasso, Pablo, 34
Pilgrim's Progress (Bunyan), 180, 268
"Pillar of Fame, The" (Herrick), 89
Pinguet, Robert, 62, 87
Pinter, Harold, 288
Pioneers, The (Cooper), 7
Pirandello, Luigi, 1, 62
Place. See landscape, imaginary
Plagiarism. See *specific writers*
Pnin (Nabokov), 67
Poe, Edgar Allan, 3, 10, 57, 144, 269,
    272, 273, 277, 294, 296, 300, 304,
    341
  and androgyny, 36
  and apocalypse, 55–56
  and conspiracy/paranoia, 51
  and the demonic, 16
  and entropy, 52–53, 55–56
  and epigraphs, 34
  and fragmentation, 9–10, 14
  and the grotesque, 14, 17, 18
  and the insane asylum, 49–50
  and landscape, 47, 48
  and the ludic spirit, 32–33, 35, 36–37
  and parody, 16, 26
  and reflexivity, 23–26, 36
  and quest, 39–40
  and satire, 25
"Poet, The" (Emerson), 19
Poetics (Aristotle), 285
"Politics of Antirealism, The" (Graff), 3,
    311
Portable Faulkner, The (Faulkner), 162
Portrait of a Lady, The (James), 7, 29
Postmodern fiction
  defined, x
Pound, Ezra, 302
Power of Blackness, The (Levin), 304
"Power of Words, The" (Poe), 52, 55, 56
"Predicament, A" (Poe), 24, 25–26
Pricksongs & Descants (Coover), 64, 96
Prince and the Pauper, The (Twain), 6, 45
Princess Casamassima, The (James), 7

Proust, Marcel, 62
Public Burning, The (Coover), 12, 65,
    108, 203, 205, 224–30, 232, 252,
    263, 274, 298, 300, 310
Pudd'nhead Wilson (Twain), 18, 30
Purdy, James, 62
Putnam, G. P., 22
Putter-inners. *See* Maximalism
Pym (Poe), 36–37, 39–40, 48
Pynchon, Thomas, ix, 1, 2, 9, 43, 100,
    104, 128, 187, 260, 264, 291, 294,
    296, 309, 310, 311, 327, 335, 341
  and apocalypse/Armageddon, 121,
    201, 238, 275, 306
  and Christian tradition, 303
  and conspiracy/paranoia, 121, 142,
    201, 206, 238, 243–49, 295, 303
  and decentralization, 119, 139–43
  and determinism, 302–3
  and encyclopedic novel, 108, 109, 287
  and entropy, 121, 202, 206, 245, 252–
    56, 301
  and epigraphs, 139, 262
  and Eros, 238
  and excrement, 306, 339–40
  and fairy tale, 246
  and frames, 246
  and the grotesque, 290
  and intertextuality, 63, 243
  and juxtaposition, 143, 244, 246
  and learned wit tradition, 287
  and Maxwell's demon, 252, 338
  and metaphor, 245
  and misogyny, 238
  and montage, 143
  and objectification, 255
  and parody, 97
  and politics, 299
  and quest, 120–21, 193, 199–203, 245
  and science fiction, 250
  and surrealism, 245, 290
  and Thanatos, 238
"Pynchon's Paranoid History" (Sanders),
    244, 245

Queneau, Raymond, 62, 68
Quest, 180–204. See also *specific writers*
  and earlier American writing, 38–41
Quintillian, 95

Rabbit, Run (Updike), 7
Rabelais, 38, 106, 107, 263, 308
Raglan, Lord, 113, 183, 188, 293
Ragtime (Doctorow), 337
Rank, Otto, 183, 188
"Rappaccini's Daughter" (Hawthorne),
    28
Rayon Violet (Sorrentino), 95
*Reader's Guide to William Gaddis's "The
    Recognitions," A* (Moore), 109
Realism, ix, 131, 224, 307
    and character, 6–8
    and common experience, 8
    evolution of, 5
    and plot, 8
    and postmodern antirealists, 285, 286
    and verisimilitude, 5–6
Recognitions (Clement), 110, 111, 326
Recognitions, The (Gaddis), x, 17, 60, 63,
    108, 109–11, 112, 113, 114, 115,
    119, 120, 122, 136–39, 140, 142,
    143, 153, 155–57, 203, 206, 256,
    257, 258, 261, 262, 274, 287, 297,
    305–6, 307, 327, 338, 339
Red Badge of Courage, The (Crane), 4,
    43–44, 51
Redskins, The (Cooper), 44
Reed, Ishmael, ix, 62, 309
    and apocalypse/Armageddon, 206,
        265, 266–67, 275
    and entropy, 264–67
    and epigraphs, 264–65
    and excrement, 264–67
    and fictitious history, 337
    and homology of feces/sex/death, 206
    and satire, 264
    and science fiction, 275
    and surrealism, 265
Reflexivity, 61–82. See also *specific writers*
    and earlier American writing, 22–31
Regressus in infinitum, 38, 73, 77, 82
Reilly, Charlie, 214
Religio Medici (Browne), 43
Remembrance Rock (Sandburg), 41
Ricardou, Jean, 61, 82
Richardson, Dorothy, 309
Rimbaud, Arthur, 86, 110, 132
Rise of Silas Lapham, The (Howells), 7, 29
"River, The" (O'Connor), 151

Robbe-Grillet, Alain, 159
"Robert Kennedy Saved from Drowning"
    (Barthelme), 337
Robison, James, 326
Robison, Mary, 326
Roche, Maurice, 87
Rockwell, John, 116
Roderick Hudson (James), 6, 7
Roman à clef, 31–32, 217
Romance in America, The (Porte), 4
Romance tradition
    and antirealism, 2–3, 4, 5
    and the poetic, 4–5
Romantic Agony, The (Praz), 200
Rosenberg File, The (Radosh and Milton),
    224
Roth, Phillip, ix, 62, 263, 308, 335
Roussel, Raymond, xii
"Rush for Second Place, The" (Gaddis),
    256

Sabbatical (Barth), 77, 83–84, 232, 297
Sade, Marquis de, 308
"St. Louis Return" (Burroughs), 128
Sarraute, Nathalie, 62
Satanstoe (Cooper), 44
Satire, 302. See also *specific writers*
    defined, 16, 96
Scarlet Letter, The (Hawthorne), 6, 14,
    27–28, 45, 47–48, 61, 153
Scarlet Plague, The (London), 48
Scholes, Robert, 184
Schweitzer, Albert, 113
Science fiction, 300. See also *specific writ-
    ers*
Scott, Sir Walter, 45
"Second Coming, The" (Yeats), 273,
    277
Second law of thermodynamics, 52, 54,
    251, 252, 301, 302
Second Skin (Hawkes), 62, 120, 151, 173,
    175–76, 177, 203, 286, 296, 297,
    300, 310
Seeker, The (Barth), 320
Seize the Day (Bellow), 43
"Self-Reliance" (Emerson), 295
"Sentence" (Barthelme), 85
Setting. *See* Landscape, imaginary
Seven Deadly Sins, The (Bosch), 110

Shakespeare, William, 32, 42, 104, 132, 311
Shannon, Claude, 255
Shattuck, Roger, 61, 123
Shelley, Percy Bysshe, 104, 192
Shklovsky, Viktor, 23, 320
Short Novels of Thomas Wolfe, The (Holman), 43
Sinclair, Upton, 302
"Sinners in the Hands of an Angry God" (Edwards), 53
Sirens of Titan, The (Vonnegut), 48
Six of One by Half a Dozen of the Other (Stowe et al.), 22
Sketch Book, The (Irving), 37–38
Sky Changes, The (Sorrentino), 95, 189
Slaughter-House Five (Vonnegut), 48, 63, 66, 159, 205, 221–24, 230, 263
Slow Learner (Pynchon), 254, 301
Snow White (Barthelme), 59, 97–100, 104, 116, 288, 326
Soft Machine, The (Burroughs), 63, 130, 239, 240, 242, 243, 275
"Some Aspects of the Grotesque in Southern Fiction" (O'Connor), 145
Something Said (Sorrentino), 68
Song of Myself (Whitman), 61, 93
Sontag, Susan, ix, 93, 113, 309
    and apocalypse, 206, 272
    and minimalism, 272
    and nightmare, 271–72
Sorrentino, Gilbert, ix–x, 2, 62, 64, 95, 294, 310, 327, 335
    and alphabetical play, 86
    and blending of genres, 59, 91–94, 288
    and collaboration, 70
    and collage, 91–94
    and deconstruction, 192, 290
    and defamiliarization, 69, 93, 120, 193, 288, 323
    and the encyclopedic novel, 286
    and epigraphs, 68, 86, 190
    and frames, 59, 68–69
    and game playing, 322
    and heterocosm, 68
    and intertextuality, 69–70, 191–92, 319
    and language, 290
    and lists, 93–94, 286, 323
    and ludic impulse, 59, 85–86, 91–94, 191
    and myth, 188
    and parody, 59, 95, 120, 188, 190, 191, 192–93, 288–89, 323
    and the pastoral, 120, 190–91, 192, 193, 288
    and plagiarism, 70, 298
    and quest, 120, 188–92
    and reflexivity, 59, 68–71, 188, 191–92
    and satire, 189, 288
    and tale-within-a-tale, 69
Sot-Weed Factor, The (Barth), 44, 77, 80, 108, 183, 205, 208–14, 215, 224, 230, 232, 263, 297, 300, 324, 334, 337
Sot-weed Factor: Or, a Voyage to Maryland, The (Cooke), 209
Sound and the Fury, The (Faulkner), 133, 239, 292
Southworth, Mrs. E. D. E. N., 30, 34
Spanish Tragedy, The (Kyd), 110
Spark, Muriel, 62
Speak, Memory (Nabokov), 67, 166
Spenser, Edmund, 192
Spicer, Jack, 93
Splendide-Hôtel (Sorrentino), 59, 70, 85–86, 87, 91, 93, 319
Sport and the Spirit of Play in American Fiction (Messenger), 84
Spy, The (Cooper), 6, 51
Steelwork (Sorrentino), 93, 95, 323
Stein, Gertrude, 309
Stephenson, Gregory, 263
Steps (Kosinski), 326
Sterne, Laurence, 2, 106, 308
Stevens, Wallace, 56, 310
Stone, Robert
    and apocalypse, 206, 275–76, 277, 306, 341
    and decentralization, 138, 292
    and politics, 298
Stowe, Harriet Beecher, 22
Strange Manuscript Found in a Copper Cylinder, A (DeMille), 48
Strindberg, August
    and dreams, 268–69

Sturdy Oak, The (Elizabeth Jordan, ed.), 22

Styron, William, ix

Sukenick, Ronald, x, xii, 1, 9, 57, 62, 294, 318, 336
 and fragmentation, 328

Sun Also Rises, The (Hemingway), 217, 236

Surrealism, 158–59, 269, 290. See also *specific writers*

Swift, Jonathan, 38, 302
 and psychosexual infantilism, 263

Sybil (Auchincloss), 7

Symzonia (Symmes), 48

"System of Dr. Tarr and Prof. Fether, The" (Poe), 49–50

Szilard, Leo, 255

Tales of the Grotesque and Arabesque (Poe), 14, 144

Tale-within-a-tale. See *specific writers*

Tapes/film, 119, 130–31, 132

Tate, Allen, 9, 17, 24, 55

Tatham, Campbell, 183

"Tell-Tell Heart, The" (Poe), 10, 14

Tel Quel group, 62

Tempest, The (Shakespeare), 159, 176, 177

"Texts for Nothing" (Beckett), 104

Thanatos, 178, 179, 206, 235, 238, 240, 306

Their Wedding Journey (Howells), 8

Theroux, Alexander, x, 84, 91, 106, 294
 and blending of genres, 59, 94–96
 and Christian tradition, 303, 318
 and defamiliarization, 95–96
 and the devil, 153, 154
 and the encyclopedic novel, 286
 and learned wit tradition, 107–8
 and lists, 94, 286
 and ludic impulse, 59, 94–96
 and maximalism, 106–7
 and misogyny, 94, 154
 and parody, 323
 on realism, 2
 and satire, 59, 95
 and supernaturalism, 305

"Theroux Metaphrastes" (Theroux), 106, 318

"They Do Not Always Remember" (Burroughs), 271

Third Mind, The (Burroughs and Gysin), 129, 130, 131, 329

Thomas, D. M., 62

Thomas, Dylan, xii

Thoreau, Henry David, 110

Those Extraordinary Twins (Twain), 18, 30

Thousand and One Nights, The, 2, 72, 73, 74, 293

"Thousand-and-Second Tale of Scheherazade, The" (Poe), 313

Three Deuces (Sorrentino), 95

Three Soldiers (Dos Passos), 133

"Three Thousand Years Among the Microbes" (Twain), 19

Through the Eye of the Needle (Howells), 49

Thucydides, 104

Thyra (Bennet), 48

Ticket That Exploded, The (Burroughs), 63, 130, 239, 242

Tidewater Tales, The (Barth), 104

Tilford, John E., Jr., 29

Titian, 110

"Tlön, Uqbar, Orbis Tertius" (Borges), 120, 164–66, 167

To Damascus (Strindberg), 268

Todorov, Tzvetan, 289

Tolstoy, Leo, 311, 312

To Mars via the Moon (Ticks), 48

Tom Jones (Fielding), 38, 292

Tom Sawyer, Detective, and Other Stories (Twain), 8

Tom Sawyer Abroad (Twain), 8

Toomer, Jean, 144

Too Much Flesh and Jabez (Dowell), 124, 125

Torrents of Spring, The (Hemingway), 30–31

Towers of Open Fire, 131

Traveller from Altruria (Howells), 49

Travesty (Hawkes), 173, 330

Treatise on Electricity and Magnetism (Maxwell), 338

Tristram Shandy (Sterne), 38, 61, 68, 108, 189, 287

Trollope, Anthony, 8, 27

Trout Fishing in America (Brautigan), 326

Trucs et truqueurs (Eudel), 110
Turn of the Screw, The (James), 43, 153
Tuten, Frederic, 113
Twain, Mark, 17, 144, 156, 263, 269, 273, 286, 335, 341. See also Clemens, Samuel L.
  and apocalypse, 54–55
  and conspiracy and paranoia, 52
  and the demonic, 16–17
  and fictitious history, 45
  and the grotesque, 18–19
  and ludic play, 33
  and parody, 45
  and reflexivity, 29–30
Twelfth Night (Shakespeare), 177
Tyler, Royall, 5
Typee (Melville), 47
Typographical play, 32–34, 87–91, 97, 129
Tzara, Tristan, 129

Ulysses (Joyce), 91, 93, 96, 108, 269, 289
Unamumo, Miguel de, 62
Uncle Tom's Cabin (Stowe), 41
"Unparalleled Adventures of One Hans Pfaall, The" (Poe), 36
Unspeakable Mr. Hart, The (Burroughs), 91
Updike, John, ix, 169
U.S.A. (Dos Passos), 133, 135, 292
Utopia/dystopia, 163, 300
  in earlier American writing, 48–49

V. (Pynchon), 57, 109, 120–21, 193, 199–203, 204, 243, 245, 255, 256, 258, 280
Valéry, Paul, 57
Vein of Iron (Glasgow), 7
Vidal, Gore, ix, 83
"Views of My Father Weeping" (Barthelme), 63
Violent Bear It Away, The (O'Connor), 149–50, 151
Virginie (Hawkes), 173, 174
Vogel, Philip, 68
Vonnegut, Kurt, Jr., ix, 62, 214, 327, 335

and apocalypse, 275, 306
and fact and fancy, 205
and fictitious history, 221–24
and fragmentation, 328
and frames, 221
and juxtaposition, 222
and realism, 224
and reflexivity, 63
and science fiction, 221, 222–24, 275
Voyages and Discoveries of the Companions of Columbus (Irving), 332
Voyage to the Moon, A (Tucker), 48
"Voyelles" (Rimbaud), 86

Wadlington, Warwick, 12
Waiting for Godot (Beckett), 105
"Wakefield" (Hawthorne), 28
Walpole, Horace, 2
Waste Land, The (Eliot), 33, 99, 110, 119, 122–24, 126, 127, 128, 129, 132, 139, 142, 143, 180, 251, 267, 269, 283, 291, 292, 302, 304, 306, 327
Waugh, Patricia, 62, 63
Weavers, The (Hauptmann), 135
Web and the Rock, The (Wolfe), 8
Welty, Eudora
  on landscape, 158
West, Nathanael, 52, 62, 144, 156, 173, 269, 341
  and apocalypse, 273, 274
  and the devil, 148, 149, 155
  and entropy, 251, 301
  and excrement, 264
  and the grotesque, 155, 307
  and reflexivity, 286
Western fiction, 59, 101–2, 174, 294, 337
Weston, Jessie L., 102
Weyden, Roger van der, 110
Wharton, Edith, 2
Whatever Happened to Gloomy Gus of the Chicago Bears (Coover), 336
What Is Man? (Twain), 16
What Maisie Knew (James), 15
Whilomville Stories (Crane), 46
White Goddess, The (Graves), 110
White on Black on White (Dowell), 63
Whitman, Walt, 104

Whole Family, The (Howells et al.), 21–22

Why Are We in Vietnam? (Mailer), 62, 203, 219, 336

Wieland: or The Transformation (Brown), 9, 51

Wiener, Norbert, 301

Wild Boys, The (Burroughs), 128, 130

Williams, William Carlos, 86, 93

Willie Masters' Lonesome Wife (Gass), 59, 89

Winesburg, Ohio (Anderson), 14, 46

Wise Blood (O'Connor), 119, 145–47, 148, 149, 151

Witches of Eastwick, The (Updike), 17

Wolfe, Thomas, 43, 46, 104, 239, 287–88

Wolff, Tobias, 326

Women and Men (McElroy), x, 108

Wonder-Working Providence (Johnson), 53, 273

Woolcott, Alexander, 22

Woolf, Virginia, 309

Wordsworth, William, 192

Wright, Richard, 144, 309

Wurlitzer, Rudolph, 113

"X-ing a Paragrab" (Poe), 33

Yeats, W. B., 255, 283

Yemassee, The (Simms), 4, 45

You Can't Go Home Again (Wolfe), 8

Young, Marguerite, x, 309
  and the grotesque, 153–54

"Young Goodman Brown" (Hawthorne), 15–16, 47

Zavarzadeh, Mas'ud, 220

Zola, Emile, 302

In *Alternate Worlds: A Study of Postmodern Antirealistic American Fiction*
John Kuehl offers eleven chapters on the themes and techniques of recent
antirealistic fiction: "Reflexivity," "The Ludic Impulse," "Maximalism
versus Minimalism," "Fragmentation/Decentralization," "The Grotesque
and the Devil," "Imaginary Landscapes," "Absurd Quests," "Fictitious
History," "Conspiracy and Paranoia," "Entropy," "Nightmare and Apocalypse." Several books have addressed some of these subjects, but no
single work has presented a comprehensive view of what American
antirealism was and is. A wide variety of authors and works are discussed
Walter Abish, John Barth, Donald Barthelme, William Burroughs, Robert
Coover, Coleman Dowell, Ralph Ellison, Raymond Federman, William
Gaddis, William Gass, John Hawkes, Joseph Heller, Ken Kesey, Joseph
McElroy, Vladimir Nabokov, Flannery O'Connor, Thomas Pynchon, Ishm-
ael Reed, Susan Sontag, Gilbert Sorrentino, Ronald Sukenick, Alexander
Theroux, Kurt Vonnegut, Jr., Marguerite Young, and many others.

Alternate Worlds contends that while foreign sources, past and present,
have influenced contemporary American antirealism, our tradition, as
represented by Poe, Melville, Hawthorne, Twain, and Faulkner, has
already found the fabulous congenial. Earlier native novelists and especially their descendants often see God as a cosmic joker, and substitute
"the story of writing" for "the writing of story." An interview between
James W. Tuttleton and the author, John Kuehl, concludes the book and
evaluates the material that has been explicated in the text.

The Gotham Library

JOHN KUEHL is Professor of English at New York University, where he
specializes in American literature and modern drama. He has written
and/or edited eleven books, including *Write and Rewrite: A Study of the
Creative Process; John Hawkes and the Craft of Conflict;* with Steven
Moore, *In Recognition of William Gaddis;* and *F. Scott Fitzgerald: A Study
of the Short Fiction.*

JAMES W. TUTTLETON is Professor of English at New York University. He is
the author of *The Novel of Manners in America.* He is also editor, with
Agostino Lombardo, of *The Sweetest Impression of Life: The James Family
and Italy,* published by New York University Press.

NEW YORK UNIVERSITY PRESS
Washington Square
New York, NY 10003

ISBN 0-8147-4614-4